D1545819

The Tsarist Secret Police Abroad

Also by Fredric S. Zuckerman

THE TSARIST SECRET POLICE IN RUSSIAN SOCIETY, 1880–1917

The Tsarist Secret Police Abroad

Policing Europe in a Modernising World

Fredric S. Zuckerman
Senior Lecturer in History
University of Adelaide
Australia

First published 2003 by
PALGRAVE MACMILLAN
Houndmills, Basingstoke, Hampshire RG21 6XS and
175 Fifth Avenue, New York, N.Y. 10010
Companies and representatives throughout the world

PALGRAVE MACMILLAN is the global academic imprint of the Palgrave Macmillan division of St. Martin's Press, LLC and of Palgrave Macmillan Ltd. Macmillan® is a registered trademark in the United States, United Kingdom and other countries. Palgrave is a registered trademark in the European Union and other countries.

ISBN 1–4039–0438–3

This book is printed on paper suitable for recycling and made from fully managed and sustained forest sources.

A catalogue record for this book is available from the British Library.

Library of Congress Cataloging-in-Publication Data
Zuckerman, Fredric Scott, 1944–
The Tsarist Secret Police abroad : policing Europe in a modernising world / by Fredric S. Zuckerman.
p. cm.
Includes bibliographical references and index.
ISBN 1–4039–0438–3 (cloth)
1. Russia. Departament poliëìåi. Zagranichnaëì agentura (Paris) 2. Intelligence service—Russia. 3. Intelligence service—France—Paris. 4. Secret service—Russia. 5. Espionage, Russian—Europe. 6. Russians—Europe. I. Title.

HV8225.7.O54 Z82 2003
363.28′3′094709034—dc21

2002068340

10 9 8 7 6 5 4 3 2 1
12 11 10 09 08 07 06 05 04 03

Printed and bound in Great Britain by
Antony Rowe Ltd, Chippenham and Eastbourne

For Lorre, Michael and Nicola

Contents

List of Tables

Acknowledgements

I am indebted to many libraries and archives. The Hoover Institution on War, Revolution and Peace which was my home away from home for many years is certainly one of the most congenial libraries in the United States. Its librarians, archivists and staffers made my stay there both rewarding and pleasant. In the Hoover Archives where I spent over two years digging through the wealth of primary documentation necessary for this work I made good friends who went out of their way to locate hard-to-find material for me. Some of the people are no longer at the Hoover, others are still there: Dr Franz Lassner, the former Director of Archives; Mr Charles Palm, the current Director of Archives; Mr Ronald Bulatoff, Archivist; Mrs Krone Kernke, former Archivist. At Columbia University's Boris Bakhmeteff Archive I intially received considerable help from Mr Lev Magorevsky and subsequently from Ms Ellen Scaruffi and her staff.

The Barr-Smith Library of the University of Adelaide purchased many obscure books and manuscripts for me after they were located with skill and patience by Subject Librarian Margaret Hosking and Inter-Library Loan Librarian Maria Albanese. I owe special thanks to Mr Ray Choate, the University Librarian who always seemed to locate sufficient funds for the purchase of the material I requested.

I would also like to thank the staffs of the New York Public Library and the Sterling Memorial Library of Yale University which were my hosts at various times while I researched this book.

The Australia Research Council funded a vital summer's research in the United States and the Faculty of the Humanities and Social Sciences supported my work with several University Research Grants.

I especially wish to thank my wife, Lorre, for her eternal patience, her steadying good humour, and skills as a grammarian; all of which have made this a better book than it otherwise would have been.

I would like to thank Sage Publications Ltd for granting me permission to reprint, in large part, my article 'Vladimir Burtsev and the Tsarist Political Police Conflict, 1907–1914', © Sage Publications Ltd, 1977, which first appeared in the *Journal of Contemporary History*, 12 (1977) 193–219.

A Note on Transliteration and Dates

I have used a modified version of the Library of Congress transliteration system. The Julian Calender used by Tsarist Russia was behind the western or Gregorian Calender by twelve days in the nineteenth century and thirteen days in the twentieth century. For domestic Russian history this is of no consequence. Tsarist police documents originating in western Europe contain both dates.

A Note on Police Terminology

The common terms used by contemporaries as well as subsequent historians to identify the Tsarist political police are *Okhrana* or *Okhranka.* Though imposing in both sound and appearance they are really meaningless and only further obscure an already confused and complexly intertwined group of organisations and bureaus. A somewhat finer distinction must be drawn to the reader's attention. This is the usage of the terms 'Special Section', 'Department of Police' and its nickname, 'Fontanka' in the text. The Special Section, as we shall see, sat atop the political police organisational pyramid and was located in the Department of Police Headquarters in St Petersburg. When I use the term 'Special Section' it refers to orders, intelligence data, circulars and so on which emanated specifically from this bureau. When I refer to an opinion, circular, order and the like as having originated in the 'Department of Police' or 'Fontanka' it signifies information appearing under the general imprimatur of the Department of Police, though it was in fact issued by any one of the nine secretariats and in the case of the Weekly Intelligence Surveys, the Special Section. The reason for this awkward explanation should, I hope, become manifestly clear as the reader moves through the book.

Another point worth noting. The word *agentura* as in *Zagranichnaia agentura* has as its English equivalent 'secret service'. I found the translation of the above term, literally Foreign Secret Service, too cumbersome and not entirely accurate. I decided, therefore, to resort to some literary licence by adopting the word *agentura* into the English language, making the Russian political police abroad the 'Foreign Agentura'.

Abbreviations and Glossary

AHR	*American Historical Review*
AJS	*American Journal of Sociology*
ASEER	*American Slavic and East European Review*
BO	*Boevaia Organizatsiia* (Battle Organisation), the agency of Central terror for the Socialist-Revolutionary Party
CEH	*Contemporary European History*
Cheka	*Chrezychainaia Komissiia* (Extraordinary Commission)
chinovnik	civil servant
CJH	*Criminal Justice History*
Extraordinary Commission	Depositions by former tsarist officials before the Extraordinary Commission investigating the illegal activities of former ministers and others (MSS Nikolaevsky Collection)
FAAr	The Archive of the Foreign Agentura, located at the Hoover Institution on War, Revolution and Peace
filer	detective
Fontanka	The nickname for the Department of Police which was located at 16 Fontanka Quai in St Petersburg
GM	*Golos Minuvshago* (*Voice of the Past*)
gradonachal'nik	mayor (closest but inexact equivalent)
HJ	*Historical Journal*
IR	*Istoriko-Revoliutsionnyi Sbornik* (*Historical-Revolutionary Collection*)
IV	*Istoricheskii Vestnik* (*Historical Herald*)
IZ	*Istoricheskie Zapiski* (*Historical Notes*)
JCH	*Journal of Contemporary History*
JG	*Jährbucher für Geschichte Osteuropas*
KA	*Krasnyi Arkhiv* (*Red Archive*)
KaS	*Katorga i ssylka* (*Penal Servitude and Exile*)
KL	*Krasnaia Letopis'* (*Red Chronicle*)
klichka	code name
MVD	*Ministerstvo Vnutrennikh Del* (Ministry of Internal Affairs)
OI	*Otechestvennaia Istoriia*

OO	*Okhrannoe Otdelenie* (Security Division), these political police bureaus were located in major cities and centres of revolutionary activity
ordena	decoration
Osobyi Otdel	The Special Section, the headquarters of the political police system, controlling all operations at home and abroad
PTsR	*Padenie Tsarskogo Rezhima* (*The Collapse of the Tsarist Regime*)
Protokol no. 8, 22 January 1909 *Protokol* no. 21, 7 February 1909 *Protokol* no. 22, 18 January 1909 *Protokol* no. 34, 2 March 1909	Procurator's pre-trial statements, the A. A. Lopukhin treason case, in Russian (MSS Nikolaevsky Collection)
RH	*Russian History*
RR	*Russian Review*
RSDWP	Russian Social Democratic Workers' Party
sanovnik	A very senior official
SDs	social democrats
sekretnyi sotrudnik	undercover agent
Sl R	*Slavic Review*
SR	*Sotsial-revoliutsioner'* (*Social-revolutionary*)
SRs	socialist-revolutionaries
VI	*Voprosy Istorii* (*Issues of History*)
Zagranichnaia agentura	Foreign Agentura, also known as the Paris Office, it was the headquarters of Tsardom's political police abroad

Preface

This book is about the operations of the Russian secret police in Europe throughout the almost four decades that preceded Tsardom's collapse in February 1917. The narrative itself encompasses two major themes. The first of these is concerned with the increasingly bitter struggle between the Russian revolutionary emigration and the tsarist police system during the reigns of Alexander III and Nicholas II. Interwoven with this straightfoward but heretofore largely missing element in Russian revolutionary history is another theme, long debated amongst the Russians themselves and those who study their culture: Russia's place in Europe.

This question is dealt with at three levels: firstly, the evolution of political policing in industrial Europe and how both in societal and administrative terms it resembled the development of policing in Russia during the same time frame; secondly, the role of international police co-operation in an informal alliance against political dissent in Europe in which the tsarist police, and the Russian government itself, played a central role; thirdly, the struggle by the Russians to develop a united European and American front against terrorism that ultimately laid the groundwork for Interpol and established many of the criteria for such co-operation.

In 1883, as we shall see in the chapters that follow, the recently formed Department of Police created a special branch of its secret police with its headquarters in Paris. The primary purpose of this agency known as the Foreign Agentura (*Zagranichnaia agentura*) was to forewarn the Russian government of terrorist plots and if possible defuse planned acts of terrorism against High Personages. As the years passed and the emigration grew in size and its political composition became more complex the Foreign Agentura steadily expanded its collection of intelligence to penetrate every nook and crany of revolutionary émigré life, placing under surveillance any émigré group or individual who raised the Agentura's slightest suspicion. In order to undertake this task the Foreign Agentura spread its tentacles across Europe, England and, to a lesser degree, into Russian neighbourhoods in the United States.

The Foreign Agentura kept all such people under close surveillance. The bureau employed detectives (*filery*) to place individual suspects under observation. More importantly, the Agentura engaged undercover agents (known as *sekretnye sotrudniki* or just *sotrudniki* for short) in order to infiltrate their circles and report on their ideological debates as well as on their every day conversations and, above all, to sniff out plans for acts of terrorism. As we shall see, the staff of the Paris Office collated the raw data supplied by the various agents in the field and condensed the material into dispatches and reports which they sent to St Petersburg. The director of the Foreign Agentura would often forward his own summary analysis of intelligence to Headquarters as well. His analysis and the dispatches and reports from the Foreign Agentura's chancery would again be reviewed by expert analysts within the political police, and the portions thought useful would be incorporated in Intelligence Surveys distributed throughout the political police system and at times to the tsar himself.[1]

The Paris Office became expert in harrassing the émigrés, using provocateurs to subvert their purpose and to embarass them before European public opinion. It also undertook special tasks as necessity required including both espionage and counter-espionage and a significant anti-gun running campaign during the 1905 Revolution. All of this is elaborated upon in the following chapters.

The Foreign Agentura operated mostly in states where the social and political transformation of industrial societies was placing mounting pressure on elites to share power, wealth, and even social standing with new classes arising as an integral part of a modern industrial society. This phenomenon, as we shall see in the first chapter of this book, led to an explosion in the development of political policing across the industrial world in the years approximately between 1880 and the First World War.

For the past twenty years or so the growth and spread of police throughout Europe has become the subject of a growing scholarly literature some of which is cited, especially in the first part of this book, and more broadly noted in the appended bibliography. A portion of this literature is comparative in nature discussing the development and performance of police, including the political police, across the Continent and in Great Britain. In their discussions about the evolution of the European policing system these studies, at best, include Russia in only the most peripheral manner.[2] It seems that as far as European historians of the police are concerned the Russian police system appears to be beyond the pale. Why? The Foreign Agentura itself, operated in non-Russian Europe as a critical, even indispensable element of the maturing European political police network This bureau of the Russian secret police functioned in Europe for about 34 years. Its presence there was never a secret.

Part of the explanation for this lacunae is to be found in the recent exciting writings of Norman Davies and Larry Wolff. In his book, *Inventing Eastern Europe: The Map of Civilization on the Mind of the Enlightenment,* Wolff convincingly argues that the idea of Eastern Europe was the creation of the eighteenth century Enlightenment. To the Enlightenment mind and to subsequent generations thereafter 'eastern' Europe became both a philosophical and geographical construct designed to serve as a measuring stick for those who invented it. This measure is what characterised western Europe as 'civilization'. Eastern Europe, according to Wolff, was 'located not at the antipode of civilization, not down in the depths of barbarism, but rather on the developmental scale that measured the distance between civilization and barbarism'. As for Russia, 'the Enlightenment would rediscover Russia as an eastern region of the continent, and would align its reputation, philosophically and geographically, with the other lands of Eastern Europe'.[3] In order for 'Western Europe' – a phrase which became synonomous with 'civilized Europe' – to come into being, therefore, eastern Europe needed to exist 'as a paradox of simultaneous inclusion and exclusion, Europe but not Europe'.[4] As the nineteenth century progressed this view of there being two Europes, 'ours' and the 'other' became entrenched in western thought and writing, especially European historiography. This intellectual aberration created a divide which has left Russia's integral role in European history as a whole out in the cold. This has been the fate of the Russian political police abroad.

Norman Davies with both clarity and courage in his innovative study, *Europe: A History*, proposes that it is time that this great historiographic divide that prevents eastern European history from being integrated into a global 'Eurohistory' be brought to an end. He is not optimistic about this happening soon. Davies, does hope, however, that 'the reformulating of European history must inch forward alongside the gradual construction of a wider European community'.[5]

Davies' viewpoint brings me back to the Foreign Agentura. The history of this single bureau will allow us to take up the process of 'inching forward' that Davies describes in the quotation just above. It allows us to inch forward in the movement toward that 'Eurohistory' which will allow historians (and others) to perceive the development of the modern world from a fresh, more inclusive, perspective.

So while this work is a history of the Foreign Agentura *per se* it is also an integrated study of the development of police in industrialising Europe – including Russia – whose nations confronted common problems presented by the movement toward modernity. By 'integrated' I do not just mean 'comparative'. I mean that the leadership and employees of the Foreign Agentura and the police in the West shared a common ethos, and struggled to achieve common goals on behalf of their governments.[6]

The forces of order formed a united front against those whom they and/or their superiors believed challenged the stability of their governnments. The Foreign Agentura was accepted in the West by police and governments alike and for most of its tenure it felt at home there.

Originally, when I conceived the structure of this book the European campaign against 'anarchist terror' or 'propaganda by deed' as the Anarchists labelled these tactics led by the Russians was meant to serve as an example of Russian influence on the European strategy for policing the Continent. But the tsarist campaign against terrorism which forms a sub-theme in this book has taken on new significance since the tragedy of 11 September. The foundations constructed at the Rome Conference in 1898, the St Petersburg Conference in 1904 and through the bilateral anti-anarchist agreements negotiated by the Russians with the Germans and Americans, for example, remain largely intact to this day. The problems confronted by Russia, too, in struggling to move this process forward also, sadly, are as persistent today as they were more than a century ago. For these reasons in an Epilogue I have addressed the historic and contemporary issues confronting the effort to develop a European (and American)-wide anti-terrorist police network.

There are two other matters which need to be addressed in this Preface. What is a political police and how secret is it? In this book a political police is one that searches for evidence of subversion, the criteria for which are established by law, through decree, or parliamentary undertaking. In carrying out its brief the political police pries into the everyday lives of its suspects to determine their political opinions and to uncover any behaviour considered by the police to be inimical to the well-being of the state. The role of the political police, then, is not merely to hunt those guilty of disturbing the tranquility of the state but to pursue and harrass those merely suspected of being capable of such behaviour in the future. At its best a political police is an agency of prevention. Failure to uncover a scheme before it is implemented or the inability to disrupt an action already underway (whether it be organising a political strike, printing radical anti-government brochures, or blowing up a minister on his way to the office) is considered to be a mark of failure by its superiors for which the policemen involved may themselves suffer unpleasant consequences.

As for the adjective 'secret', political police are viewed with distaste in open societies and with outright fear in repressive ones. This is why you are more likely to have a truly secret police in a democratic society such as Great Britain where the operations of the Special Branch are still shrouded in mystery, than in an oppressive society where the openly aggressive behaviour of the political police, such as the KGB in its heyday, contributes the essential intimidatory element to the authoritarian regime's power structure. After all, if in a repressive society only very few people are aware of the predatory and arbitrary nature of their political police its impact is considerably reduced. Remember, prevention of dissent is its strong suit. But, of course, at certain levels all political police are secret. Specific operations, certain targets and, it goes without saying, undercover agents remain 'secret'. So for the sake of diversity the terms 'political police' and 'secret police' are used interchangeably in the following pages.

FREDRIC S. ZUCKERMAN
Adelaide

Part I

Turmoil, Émigrés and the Development of Political Policing in Western Europe

1

Europe in Turmoil: Protest, Violence and Maintaining Order in a Changing World

All is changed in civilization. It has made fortunate progress but has brought new vices. There is no longer the same stability any more. A new sort of trouble has arisen through the previously unknown pressure of public opinion. While the security of the state and public repose are exposed to more dangers, repression has lost its speed and even strength as a result of the guarantee of individual liberty.... The most a government may achieve is to influence its people, and now its means are completely changed. Religion and morality are now only weak supports for the law.

Joseph Fouché to the Duke of Wellington, 1816

We are moving to a general revolution. If the transformation under way follows its course and meets no obstacle, if popular understanding [*raison populaire*] continues to develop progressively, if the education of the lower classes [*classes intermédiares*] suffers no interruption, nations will be levelled to an equality in liberty. If that transformation is halted, nations will be levelled to equality in despotism.

Excerpt from a pamphlet written by François-René de Chateaubriand, after the July Days, 1830[1]

Tsardom's political émigrés and the political police who pursued them inhabited a European world deep in political and social turmoil. This world endured growing, although at times exaggerated, social, economic and political tensions as the established orders believed themselves threatened by new and often only vaguely identifiable forces. One thing is certain: these forces appeared in common to demand alterations in the *status quo*. Arno Mayer argues that the elites overreacted to the threats against their preeminent positions in the order of things. They feared the pace of change, the radicalism of the new mass politics, the weaknesses of their own state apparatus and grossly exaggerated the renegade nature of the industrial worker and the professional bourgeoisie. But it is the perception of disorder, not necessarily the reality, that motivates governments to turn to their forces of order.

This is not to say that the foreboding sensed by the traditional order did not have a basis in fact.[2] Anxiety, hostility, hope and fantasy: emotions unleashed amongst the lower orders by the jerky, uneven march towards modernity, began to crystallise into a broad spectrum of political movements – peaceful and violent, reformist and revolutionary of both the Right and the Left – which challenged the *status quo*.

The beginnings of mass politics caught the governments of Europe unaware. The spread of Anarchist terror unnerved Europeans as terrorism still does to victimised populations today. Add to this the growing dread of the working class – the domestic outsider – which became endemic amongst the traditional elites and their allies and you have a recipe for repression and the expansion of the forces of order.[3] As the second half of the century unfolded these elites and their allies amongst the *haute bourgeoisie* and the capitalist class came to the conclusion that in order to preserve their positions of authority and power they required the protection of sophisticated political police forces that possessed the skill to disarm, subvert and scatter the harbingers of modernity.

Terrorism – propaganda by deed – became the most frightening expression of the growing discontent they confronted. The birth of 'Anarchist' terror coincided with the discovery of dynamite invented by Alfred Nobel in 1866. Easily manufactured, composed of readily available materials, dynamite eliminated the problem of accuracy and proximity that plagued other previous forms of explosives. Far more stable than nitroglycerine and less bulky than gunpowder, dynamite could be easily transported and even smuggled across borders beneath women's skirts, as we shall see in Chapter 9. Advances in chemistry led to a steady improvement in dynamite and to other chemical concoctions such as the bomb that killed Alexander II: a metal cylinder containing a sophisticated mixture based on nitroglycerine and fulminate of mercury arranged within small tubes in such away that the bomb would explode on contact.[4]

Indeed, although groups detonated explosives as a means of political assassination or more indiscriminately as a method of squeezing socio-political concessions out of the traditional orders before 1881, it was the assassination of Tsar Alexander II in March of that year which initiated a European-wide panic amongst the national establishments. During the last decades of the nineteenth century and the first decade of the next the wave of terrorism spread and intensified throughout Europe. Important personages rarely made public appearances without bodyguards, but such protection did not prevent an attempt on the life of Gladstone in England, nor against Tsar Alexander III. It did not prevent the following tragedies: the murder of President Carnot of France in 1894, the murder of the mayor of Chicago in his own house; the murder of Empress Elisabeth of Austria by an Italian Anarchist in 1898, the murder of of King Umberto of Italy in 1900 by an Anarchist who plotted the assassination in distant New Jersey, the shooting of the governor of Barcelona; or the assassination of the American President McKinley in 1901. In Russia, of course, assassinations continued as well. Even though the killers were not Anarchists, the tsarist government did its best to blur these distinctions as we shall see in Chapter 3. In 1901 Peter Karpovich mortally wounded N. P. Bogolepov, the reactionary minister of education; in 1902 the SRs killed Minister of Internal Affairts S. N. Sipiagin; in July 1904 they blew up his successor V. K. Plehve; and in August 1906 the Maximalists blew up Prime Minister P. A. Stolypin's summer home, missing him but maiming one of his children and killing at least 27 innocent bystanders.[5]

The general public itself, never knew when an innocent trip to a café or restaurant would end in tragedy as bombers became more daring and less discriminating. Between 1892 and 1894 eleven dynamite explosions rocked Paris and killed nine people. The ignition of a bomb in the French Chamber of Deputies and the subsequent terrorist explosions in Prague and Pilsen were outdone by bombs hurled at a Corpus Christi procession and at a theatre audience in Barcelona which resulted in a substanial loss of life.[6] Bloodthirsty 'Anarchists' appeared to be everywhere.[7]

The number of 'militant anarchists' roaming across Europe and the United States numbered about 5,000 and the authorities found it exceptionally difficult to combat them. Yet while the partial list of terrorist actions enumerated above gives the reader, let alone contemporary witnesses, the sense that terrorism was all-pervasive, it was not. In fact the impact of terrorism on society often served the interests of the very elements of society that the terrorists strove to undermine. Despite the fear, anger and frustration these attacks engendered, they very probably enhanced the authority of the ruling classes in the eyes of the vast number of people who looked towards their governments and rulers for protection. Ironically, the actions of Anarchists and other assorted terrorists succeeded only in eroding the tolerance of European governments toward 'political offenders'.

This meant that the rise of Anarchism and Socialism were accompanied simultaneously by the development of the forces designated to contain these movements. At first, Europe's forces of order responded to disorders with crude forms of repression, often through use of the army which itself played a major role in inciting the collective violence that dotted the political landscape of the latter decades of the nineteenth and first decade of the twentieth centuries. The Bismarck government in Germany, the Crispi and Ruddini governments in Italy and the Plehve government in Russia all discovered this unfortunate dynamic for themselves.[8]

The underlying anger and fear which generated the desire for expanded political police power went much deeper than the motivation to exterminate the Anarchist 'plague' or mass street protests. The powers-that-be wanted nothing less than to destroy every perceived challenge to their privileged position. The real fear was not Anarchism or Socialism, or the trade union movement *per se* but the rise of the lower orders to political influence.

In the final decades of the nineteenth century the forces of law and order came to understand what such a defence entailed. After the assassination of Empress Elisabeth of Austria in 1898 the Italian minister of police sent a letter to his minister of justice marked 'most reserved and personal'. Its contents and tone reflected the political environment that was beginning to nurture the growth of professional political policing in Europe:

> The defence of a Society seriously menaced cannot halt before abstract theories of respect for liberty when this degenerates into unrestrained license or in the tyranny of the rabble. Information reaching the Government from our informers abroad, and from several of the great powers, point to a vast conspiracy against the lives of all heads of State....
>
> From now on it is urgent to think about preparing measures now necessary for restricting the subversive press, for striking more energetically at associations contrary to the order of the State when these associations show signs of *becoming criminal* [my italics], even if it is necessary to modify the penal code in order to obtain an efficacious result. I reserve the right to discuss this with our colleagues at the next [meeing of the] Council of Ministers.[9]

The key phrase here is 'becoming criminal'. What does it mean? A general definition of 'criminality' is not difficult. Barton Ingraham proposed the following:

> Crime is any act or omission or course of behavior deemed to be wrongful or injurious to the society as a whole or to its political leaders which they, acting through their law makers, interpreters, and enforcers seek to punish or permanently prevent from recurring.[10]

Ingraham argues that societal behaviour determines what conduct is regarded as criminal and what criminal behaviour is regarded as political. These criteria vary from culture to culture and are even likely to change within the same culture over time. According to Ingraham, therefore, an analytical definition of 'crime' within a culture must include the effects and symbolism of actions which produce repressive behaviour. Equally, the 'political' nature of crime 'depends on the kind of legal response the act evokes from those in authority'.[11]

So in Tsarist Russia for example, the Criminal Code of 1845 did not distinguish deed from intent in describing state criminal activity, giving Russian authorities the gross latitude to harass, arrest and punish their subjects at will. No other country promulgated statutes that defined 'political' crimes so broadly and with such vagueness of language.[12] At the other legal extreme is Great Britain. British jurisprudence did not contain provisions for a category of crime identified as 'State Crime' and it maintained a rather holier-than-thou approach to the entire business of repressing political opposition.[13]

One thing is certain, no matter the formal (official) attitude towards the suppression of dissent, whether Russian or British or somewhere in between, the informal reaction amongst the European forces of order was remarkably similar. Although there is some dispute over the complexion of the socio-political dynamics that causes the growth and the development of modern political policing institutions, the evidence shows that collective violence within political systems enduring the processes of modernisation mightily contributes to the creation or expansion and the professionalisation of political police systems as a means of preserving or restoring equilibrium to the national polity.

But how to proceed? Politicians and police officials alike realised, as expressed by Chateaubriand in one of the quotations that introduce this chapter, that while too little repression will make a government appear feeble and disorganised too much could lead to an equally unpleasant outcome. No one wanted a police system which imitated the Russian one (or so they claimed). The men charged with maintaining order at the turn of the century strongly preferred to employ strategies of prevention rather than the tactics of crude repression.[14] This strategy involved surveillance, harassment, infiltration of suspect groups, and often preventive arrest. By the early twentieth century even the most liberal of governments looked the other way as their forces of order employed these tactics to maintain internal order.

How industrial Europe contained dissent and controlled the lower orders is a huge subject beyond the scope of this book. The following discussion, then, is meant principally to offer a cursory comparative discussion of the evolution of political policing within the turbulent environment that characterised European life in the thirty or so years prior to the First World War. This approach will allow us to place the Foreign Agentura of the Tsarist Department of Police within the policing milieu in which it operated and with which it had to come to terms.

This review will focus on France, Italy, Germany and Great Britain, each of which became a home in exile for hundreds of Russian émigrés and for the agents of the tsarist political police who observed and harassed them and infiltrated their groups.

Switzerland, which for more than forty years also served as a refuge for Russian students and political émigrés is not included in this discussion, for it developed neither significant cantonal or federal political policing institutions. This is not to say that it did not employ political police. Federal offices responsible for police matters only came into existence in the late nineteenth century mainly in response to diplomatic pressure placed upon the Helvetic Republic by the Great Powers. Each canton maintained its own forces of order. The French-speaking cantons maintained a *genndarmerie* and a *sûreté* and worked regularly with their French equivalents on political cases. The German-speaking cantons worked at a lower level with German authorities, particularly at frontier regions.[15] These police forces co-operated only sporadically and their relationships were only lukewarm and at times chaotic.[16] Political policing was never more than a collateral activity for the Swiss, one really forced upon them by others. Switzerland's stubbornness over these matters in the face of increasing pressure from much of industrial Europe frustrated Europe's police forces virtually until the First World War as we shall in the following chapter.

France

Throughout the nineteenth and early twentieth century to the outbreak of the First World War succeeding French governments monitored the actions and thoughts of their population more closely and consistently than any other European political police system, including Tsardom's up until 1880.

Barton Ingraham remarks that the French political police from the time of the First Empire onwards employed its police powers as largely preventive measures against subversion. Censorship of the press, preventive detention and arrests were temporarily imposed during emergencies,[17] but, in general, especially after the rise of the Third Republic, arbitrariness and abuse of the law were contained by the judiciary system under the sway of liberalism.[18]

By the time of the Second Republic the government employed a major police system strongly supported by spies, informers and secret agents. The police maintained widespread and arbitrary surveillance networks which included observation of most foreign visitors. The Government treated its opponents harshly. So when the Republic came to be replaced by the regime of Louis Napoleon, the police system basically carried on as before; only the politics of its victims had changed.[19] Louis Napoleon, however, considerably expanded both its reach and the depth of its intrusion into the private lives of his subjects, even extending the work of his political police to foreign shores. By the end of the regime the French maintained 62 secret agents many of whom operated in England, Italy and Germany. At home, the *Sûreté Generale* regularly perlustrated the mail of its suspects by bribing postmen and *concierges* to supply it with letters written by or to people held under suspicion.[20] Ominously, the threat of administrative justice came to the French countryside as well. In each *département* representatives of the Ministries of Justice, War and the Interior convened 'departmental commissions' or tribunals to to deal with opponents of the regime through administrative rather than judicial procedures. The verdicts they could render included: dismissal from one's position; formal surveillance or internment within France; indefinite expulsion from French territory; transportation to penal colonies; and transfer to trials before either a courts martial or a tribunal of police.[21] Still, during this era the term 'political' police did not signify any specific specialised unit devoted to rooting out subversion. The responsibility for political policing fell to a large number of officials: ministers, prefects, public prosecutors as well as their subordinates. This lack of professionalism created an odd situation. The men who directed political police operations for Louis Napoleon were members of the administrative elite with traditions of state service. They were generalists, without police training, capable of collecting, collating and analysing information and, at times, condemning opponents of the regime to severe punishments.[22] How would they cope with the post-1870 world which presented France with all sorts of new policing problems, especially in the more than two decades preceding the First World War?

The humiliating defeat in the Franco-Prussian War, the collapse of the Second Empire and the horror of Frenchman killing Frenchman during the suppression of the Paris Commune made an indelible impression upon the Third Republic as it strove to bring political renewal and stability to France. Despite the trauma these events brought to French life, surprisingly, much appeared to remain unchanged within the social and economic fabric of French society, even within the police system. The Third Republic inherited a complex political policing machine from the Second Empire. Political policing remained virtually tied to Paris – where most political dissent arose – firmly ensconced in the hand of the Prefect. In theory, provincial France (that is France beyond the *départment* of the Seine) remained the bailiwick of the *Sûreté Generale*, an institution that proved little more than useless. Throughout France the Ministry of the Interior presided over a meagre network of officials who barely resembled a modern internal security force. What to do?

The Republicans still suffering the bitter aftertaste of the Napoleonic regime had reduced the funds dedicated to political police work, but political culture is a persistent bugbear to which politicians usually succumb. The policing aspect of that culture remained deeply ingrained within the politicians of the new Republic who in traditional French fashion wished to provide information on indiviudals and groups suspected of posing a threat to the regime.[23] This activity could not successfully be undertaken without the participation of a political policing system.

Nevertheless, during the first 20 years or so of the Third Republic's life, the political police, and, in fact the police in general, stagnated. And why not? The future of the Republic appeared secure. The ripples of change that would determine the weave of France's social and economic fabric at the end of the century were hardly apparent.[24]

The hostility to the incumbent regime bubbled to the surface in the 1890s and the early 1900s catching the government and the forces of order completely by surprise. The outburst of discontent manifested itself in both old and new ways. The Anarchist practice of 'propaganda by deed' with assassination attempts against prominent people reappeared after an absence of several years – Kropotkin first remarked upon them in France in 1882.[25] By the 1890s the terrorists reached directly into the Chamber of Deputies and the murder of President Sadi Carnot, as noted above. Nonetheless, cool heads understood the limits of terror. Kropotkin himself warned the terrorists that acts of this sort could, to be sure, cause panic amongst the populace at large but that 'an edifice [the French state] based on centuries of history . . . cannot be destroyed with a few pounds of explosive.'[26] For the police, too, individual acts of terror worried them far less than the fear that the anarchist ideology was infiltrating the nascent union movement where it represented a much greater danger to the stability of the regime. Anarchists penetrating the workers' associations depicted unionism to its followers as an opportunity to engage in economic experimentation while avoiding the despised electoral politics. They decreed that trade unions will overthrow their authoritarian oppressors and prevent any attempts at counter-revolution. The Anarchists pronounced that their principal weapon in this revolutionary war would be the general strike. This world view appealed to the semi-industrialised worker who populated France's small factories and workshops. These skilled and relatively sophisticated workers were attracted to the Anarchists' slogans dealing with education and management by self-producers. Although the number of trade unionists in 1895 remained small the founding of the *Confédération Générale du Travail* (CGT) in 1895 alarmed the French government who in the early years of the following century became obsessed with its activities.[27]

While the CGT itself remained weak and divided for years to come the strike movement grew relentlessly if somewhat sporadically. In 1895 600,000 labour days were lost to strikes. What must have been particularly worrying to the Ministry of the Interior, however, was the changing complexion of the strike movement. The usual summer respite from strikes disappeared and strikes that began with one union were quickly acquiring the support of additional unions in different industries who would join the walkout. In 1906 438,500 workers struck and, to the chagrin of the government, these strikers (as in the previous year) were not just industrial workers. Many of those on strike in 1905 and 1906, in particular, were civil servants. For the first time policemen in Lyon, some postal workers, primary school teachers and the like walked off their jobs. Even France's agricultural workers began to show signs of stirring, much to the annoyance of the land-owners.[28]

The demands being made by these strikers became the battle cry of workers across France (the eight hour day and designated days of leisure – that is, the concept of the weekend) and challenged the very core of the industrial culture of the day. The radical syndicalists of the CGT, now rapidly growing in strength, repeated these demands over and over again in their propaganda during the wave of strikes in 1906.[29]

The involvement of civil servants in the strike movement, the length of the strikes (in 1906 they averaged 19 days but some strikes went for months with workers refusing to return to work even though they were starving) combined with the aims of the strikes deeply disturbed the Republic's leadership. The French workers who struck in the years between 1905 and 1910 wished to fundamentally alter the fabric of French culture. All of this superimposed upon the background of the 1905 Revolution in Russia led the French Government under the premiership of Georges Clemenceau to believe that the Republic was in danger. Clemenceau's government dealt with the strikers accordingly. The traditional French practice of offering the carrot after employing the stick was at least temporarily abandoned.[30]

Yet in reality did radical syndicalism pose a serious threat to the Republic? The answer is no more so than anarchist terror did – hardly any at all. In 1906 nearly half of France's workers remained employed in firms of less than five employees and even though big firms began to appear with increasing regularity French industry remained dominated by small and medium sized businesses down to the First World War. In 1914 the standard of living in France remained higher than in Germany and closer to that of Great Britain than ever before. So while the crises caused by radical labour and extreme politics contributed to the shaping of the Third Republic, they did not threaten the regime's survival. Scanning the political stability of Europe in the early summer of 1914, one could argue that few countries appeared as solid as France.[31]

But at the time, particularly between 1892 and 1910, the combination of terrorism, labour and peasant unrest, the rise of both right-wing (and especially) left-wing extremism, the revolving cabinets – which really affected little, but, nevertheless, contributed to a sense political fragility – combined with a steadily increasing sense that a major European war was just around the corner, to create a milieu particulary suited to the expansion of the forces of order. Clearly, Clemenceau's and his government's perception of danger to the regime was an overreaction, which like the anarchist outrages substantially benefited the French police system as will be made clear below.

In France, the maintenance of order was the responsibility of the Ministry of the Interior which delegated this assignment to three of its subordinate branches: the Paris Prefecture of Police; the *Sûreté Générale* which bore responsibity for law and order in provincial France; and the nation's corps of prefects who managed the essentially autonomous local police forces. The forces of order in pre-war France performed three principle tasks: they collected intelligence on individuals and groups that the Ministry of the Interior believed threatened the stability of the Republic; served as technical advisors to the Ministry, offering strategies and tactics devised to anticipate and neutralise confrontations before they arose; and ultimately, if worst came to worst, fulfilling the Ministry's orders in the field.[32]

In 1892, the renewal of terrorism led the Republic to place its forces of order in the forefront of its two-decade-long struggle to subdue its enemies. The Minister of the Interior turned over the reigns of the Paris Prefecture to Louis Lépine, one of France's brightest prefects. Lépine became renowned as an innovative police reformer.

The failure of the Ministry of the Interior to draw a clear demarcation line between civil and political policing led most Frenchmen to tar the former with the latter's brush. Over the years to come Lépine developed a strategy to win over this hostile public opinion. Like so many of his European colleagues (as we shall see) Lépine admired the English police for its ability to foster the image of the police as the protector of the public good, and he endeavoured to duplicate this image *vis-à-vis* the Paris Prefecture reconciling Parisians and the defenders of order. To the Prefect a popular police is an effective police and an effective police offers security to a grateful and accepting population. Indeed, more than any other policemen of his age he recognised that ultimately the police can only be effective if it is respected by the population.[33]

At the same time Lépine understood that the role of a police in a democracy is to protect liberty against its own excesses and to disarm manifestations of subversion before they led to violence. Prevention, not repression became his motto. Control the streets and conduct intense surveillance on any individual or group considered a potential source of disorder. With Paris under siege from a crime wave and Anarchist terrorism Lépine declared that 'order, security, these things are the missions of the police'.[34] Perhaps this is why that in 1894 the Ministry of the Interior chose to partner the Prefect with the talented but sinister A. C. Puibaraud. Puibaraud, a long serving official in the Ministry, was to supervise the Prefecture's political police operations.

Puibaraud served as *Directeur-Général des Recherches* between 1894 and 1903 with the specific brief to wipe out Anarchist terrorism. The *Directeur* employed dozens of informers and secret agents to undertake this task. In fact, in the zealous pursuit of their task Puibaraud's agents intruded into the lives of the innocent as well as the suspicious and rumour has it that he was not above creating acts of provocation himself. Quite often his office collected more information on French political life than did other agencies such as the *Sûreté* – still understaffed – and the departmental prefects combined.[35] Several of Puibaraud's colleagues in the Prefecture found his methods distasteful arguing that the persecution of such groups only served to nourish subversion.[36] One person, however, who most certainly appreciated Puibaraud was P. I. Rachkovskii, the chief of the Foreign Agentura of the Russian political police headquartered in Paris who, as we shall see in Chapter 7, employed exactly the same methods against the Russian revolutionary emigration.[37]

The French government supplied Puibaraud with the legal framework for his operations against the Anarchists and other enemies of the Republic. Like other European states, France issued anti-anarchist legislation possibly at the behest of Puibaraud himself whose provocations may have contributed to the popular panic that prepared the way for its enactment. On 10 November 1893, the day after an Anarchist attack rocked the Chamber of Deputies itself, the Deputies passed the first of several anti-anarchist bills designed to curtail the Anarchist (as well as any other opposition) press. French legislation, however, although it successfully harassed perceived enemies of the state (unlike the Italian legislation discussed below) relied entirely on the due process of the law. Thus, while the anti-anarchist legislation provided for lifetime deportation to French penal colonies or to places of internal exile, these sentences depended upon conviction by the courts. Also, unlike Italian legislation which was vaguely stated, French legislation specifically detailed the nature of the crimes to be prosecuted under the statute and the type of propaganda ('Anarchist') to be outlawed.[38] Puibaraud, like so many of his contemporaries, behaved as a law unto himself and spread his net much further than the legislation permitted. He not only arrested practising terrorists, but a number of literary fellow travellers as well. The courts usually did not convict these intellectuals and journalists[39] but as we will see European governments increasingly frowned upon those who incited terrorism through the written word.

Eventually Puibaraud's excesses infuriarated Lépine, but the Prefect of Police was powerless and, in any case perhaps, unwilling to countermand his subordinate's crude tactics until the threat of Anarchist terror had passed. During the first years of the twentieth century Lépine saw his chance to be rid of Puibaraud as Anarchism in France altered its strategy by more or less abandoning terrorism and becoming increasingly involved in working class organisations. The Prefect of Paris could now safely dispense with Puibaraud's services. The government dismissed him in 1903. His successor as *Directeur Général des Recherches* brought an end to the arbitrary and excessive practices of the *Brigades des Recherches*.[40]

Lépine's stay at the Prefecture was marked by two sorts of reform destined to create a more professional and acceptable police force for the French people.

The Prefect of Paris first focused his attention on increasing the standard of policing by selective hiring and by professionally schooling his police in all of the latest techniques of policing. Lépine ensured that the administrators, too, serving within his Prefecture were well prepared for their posts. He fostered an inhouse political culture that could be labelled 'conservative republican' and although Lépine himself disliked the politics of most of the ministers he served, he loyally obeyed them all. The Prefect of Paris recognised that the performance of the police had become an electoral issue and, therefore, the subject of regular debate in the Chamber of Deputies. Lépine understood that, no matter what he or his minister thought, public opinion demanded that the Puibarauds of French policing must be consigned to the pension lists and their methods modified and employed only in the most serious emergencies.[41] Like his Russian colleague and contemporary, Sergei Zubatov, the chief of the Russian political police, Lépine argued that mass arrests and physical violence would only contribute to further discontent and resolve nothing. But this was easier said than done.

Better people, improved training and public relations did not resolve the problem of preserving order with a minimum of repression. At the dawn of the new century Lépine believed that France confronted three obvious sources of disorder: labour, revolutionary syndicalism and anti-militarism.[42] All three movements practiced their politics on the streets. Inevitably this meant the involvement of the army, violence and bloodshed. The Prefect told the American police expert Raymond Fosdick that police constituted the principal constitutional force for the 'preservation of order, the security of the person and the safety of property'.[43] How to achieve these ends without the army and a modicum of force became Lépine's goals.

The diminutive Prefect rose to the occasion by devising the dual strategy of surveillance and the selective arrest of ringleaders. Zubatov also practiced the same tactics briefly, in Russia in 1902–03, as did one of his disciples A. V. Gerasimov between 1907 and 1909. But unlike his Russian colleagues, Lépine would only order the arrest of ringleaders immediately before an expected eruption of protest such as May Day or during the first stages of a major strike. By employing this tactic the Prefecture decapitated the leadership of any protest movement just before an action, thus throwing it into confusion and defusing the danger to the city of Paris.

At the same time he trained the police in crowd control and the use of concentrated force as a show of strength to intimidate potential rioters or strikers. Lépine still kept mounted troops available just in case a situation got out of hand but he held them back, out of sight, so that their presence did not inflame the very people he was trying to discourage from making trouble. The classic example of the success of Lépine's approach to maintaining order is reflected in the manner in which he handled the demonstrations of 1 May 1906.[44]

As effective as the Prefect of Police was, he did not control the French countryside. Labour unrest, and in particular, the activities of the CGT were often beyond his grasp. In the twentieth century, as before, the countryside remained the province of the *Sûreté Générale*. The *Sûreté*, despite attempts to reform it, remained the poor cousin of the Prefecture of Paris down to the First World War. Because it did not carry the Paris Prefecture's prestige or working conditions, it drew less talented recruits, was badly organised and virtually useless as a force for the preservation of internal order.[45]

Historians of the French police system are universal in their praise of its relative even-handedness in dealing with the regime's opponents.[46] The general view is that French policemen considered themselves professionals who served the Third Republic loyally as member of a Republican consensus. This consensus decreed that firm action should be taken against those who threatened the Republic but stopped short of sanctioning drastic measures of repression. To these scholars the forces of order in France appeared the picture of tolerance as the government strove to incorporate new and expanding socio-economic and political elements within the body politic.[47]

Calhoun and Berlière tell us that the French police believed in strong action against any group that threatened the regime, but they were constrained by the political dynamics of a democracy. Public opinion, expressed in the Chamber of Deputies and the press – especially in the left-wing press – constrained them and an independent judiciary protected their victims. As Calhoun argued 'a Republican Premier could not operate like Napoleon III nor even like Bismarck'.

As we shall see in the following chapters of this book, the French political police were not nearly so pristine nor the government so honest when it came to co-operating with the Foreign Agentura of the Russian political police over the surveillance and harassment of the Russian political émigrés living in France. Political policing systems maintain an extraordinary degree of independence from the formal political culture of their state no matter the complexion of the government they serve. Professional comradeship and the fortress mentality that all political policemen share often bind them closely to their foreign comrades, whose bidding they often undertake, no matter the political principles of their own government. As we shall see, the Tsarist political police could especially count on this support.

Italy

In the second half of the nineteenth century the new Italian state, a constitutional monarchy, appeared to be heading toward chaos. To its political and economic elite the Italian Republic appeared to be teetering on the edge of chaos. Massive, widespread criminality combined with the growing strength of revolutionary Anarchism seemed about to overwhelm the Republic. In the 1880s Italians committed sixteen times as many murders as Englishmen, even though one expert wrote that 40 per cent of all crime went undetected. Italy's prison population was twenty times greater than that of Britain's with a prisoner population large enough to populate a city. This combined with the ongoing agrarian crisis and growing unrest in the cities to paint a bleak picture of Italy's future indeed.[48] The Anarchist uprising in the late 1870s collapsed, but by the 1880s they had infiltrated the peasant and worker leagues which they planned to lead towards revolution. The challenges to the regime of Anarchism and crime intensified as the industrial boom of the 1880s dried up throwing the Italian economy into a depression that extended into the next decade.[49]

Italy responded to the law and order crisis caused by these circumstances with time-tried methods of repression: martial law and administrative authority. The governments of the Italian states prior to unification employed martial law as a regular means of repression, and this policy carried over into the Republican era time and time again as the regime employed the army as a substitute for civil policing, which meant that it could keep expenditure on developing a civil policing establishment to a minimum. The institution of administrative justice or 'forced internal exile' (*domicilio coatto*) permitted the forces of order to exile alleged criminals to one of several small islands off the coast of the peninsula as well as to remote villages in the interior of Italy or worse, to Italy's African colonies, all without trial. The victims of *domicilio coatto* – a mixture of 'anarchists' and common criminals – were completely at the mercy of commissions composed of government bureaucrats and police officials. This system persisted to the end of the regime. Its heyday spanned the decades of the 1860s and 1890s. By the 1880s internal exile led to the creation of a system of penal settlements which had no legal status in Italian law.

Thousand of suspects were placed under *ammonizione*, a special status which restricted a suspicious person's movements and could place them under especially intense police supervision.[50] In 1876 the minister of justice revised these procedures making them more liberal while simultaneously retaining the provisions for those 'who set themselves up in the systematic and calculated defiance of society'. At the same time the government decreed a new offence of 'insult or outrage directed against any representative of the public authorities'.[51]

These vague descriptions of political crimes under *domocilio coatto*, reminiscent of portions of the Russian Criminal Code of 1845, were made even less clear by the unwillingness of the Italian government to recognise the legitimacy of the burgeoning labour movement or the plight of the peasantry in Central and Southern Italy. This view combined with a not unwarranted obsession with 'revolutionary anarchism' caused it to place all left-wing political movements beyond the pale of legitimate political action, thoroughly blurring the distinction of what is legal and what is illegal in Italian society. The rigid stance taken by the regime towards dissent of any sort only exacerbated hostility to the government.[52]

As prosperity evaporated under the economic constrictions resulting from the onset of a depression, popular unrest increased. Ordinary strikes rose sharply after 1887 and growing militance led to increasing violence on the picket lines. The mounting crises in the town and countryside – 96,200 agricultural and industrial workers were on strike in 1896[53] – combined with the anarchist outrages discussed above, especially the assassination of French President Sadi Carnot, created widespread panic in Rome. Prime Minister Crispi, who was already implementing emergency legislation and martial law in Sicily and other parts of Italy, told the President of the Italian Senate that the Anarchist danger 'menaces everything and everybody'.[54] The Crispi government convinced Parliament to pass several decrees designed to repress the smallest measure of dissent. Repression resolved nothing. During the winter of 1898 the strikes and protests, which had never entirely ceased, erupted again. This time the Anarchists fought truly in the vanguard of the uprisings. By May 1898 the government believed the *Risorgimento* to be under serious threat from both Anarchists and Socialists with the forces of law and order incapable of distinguishing between them. *Haute société* blamed the social and political crises on the Left, clerical counter-revolutionaries and foreign subversive intervention. This developing political paranoia fuelled an offensive by the traditional elites to increase the monarchy's powers at the expense of representative government. The forces of order appeared to be in control of the state.

In 1898 the new Prime Minister, the Marquis di Rudini embodied these anti-democratic sentiments by proclaiming a state of siege, severely restricting both civil liberties and constitutional rights and ordering the army to restore calm. Rudini's campaign left hundreds of people dead, thousands arrested and scores of newspapers, labour unions and political associations suppressed. Still the disorders continued. King Umberto removed Rudini replacing him with a military man, Luigi Pelloux, who found himself hamstrung by the Italian Chamber of Deputies which refused to pass his repressive legislation. He sought the support of the King, attempting to get his legislation passed by royal decree, but the courts declared this process invalid. In 1900 the impotent Pelloux's resignation was shortly followed by the King's assassination. The brutal, largely ineffective repression came to an end.[55]

The politics of repression fostered so strongly by the Prime Ministers of the 1890s failed dismally. It embarrassed Italy before European opinion and instead of repressing dissent served only to temper the will of those it assaulted. The near-decade of repression only served to unite the opposition and strengthen socialism giving mass politics electoral influence which it had not held before.[56] In the end, the forces of order succumbed to the liberal democratic outlook of both the majority in the Chamber of Deputies and within the Ministry of Justice which had prevented General Pelloux, in particular, from implementing draconian laws and royal decrees that, had they been successful, would have seriously eroded the future of democracy in Italy.

The crisis of the 1890s overwhelmed the Italian police system. The Italian police force was too small – much smaller than the police forces of the other European powers – and too disorganised to handle its assignments.[57] Technical backwardness made record keeping and identification of suspects a nightmare. The constant change in the leadership of the forces of order did not help matters either. During the 1890s six ministers of the interior and five director generals of public security followed one after the other. Prime Minister Crispi battled to increase police spending especially on informers in order to obtain political intelligence. But Crispi, hamstrung by financial constraints, never managed to rationalise the police system. He even reduced the number of policemen in an already seriously undermanned force. It is not surprising then, that Crispi, like his predecessors, turned to the army to fulfil tasks for which it was unsuited. Rudini, Crispi's successor, continued the struggle to reform and enlarge Italy's police administration and strove to develop a modern nationwide detective service. He managed to increase the number of police somewhat and hoped to enlarge the force still more. More significantly he created three brigades of detectives charged with 'services of investigation, research and of surveillance'. The government also employed 'trustworthy' citizens in effect to serve as informers.

During the 1890s the Italian police finally entered the new 'technological' era of policing by establishing an anthropomorphic bureau to identify criminals. This department adopted the Bertillon method of identification already widely used across Europe. The system identified suspects through physical description supplemented by photographs (see Chapter 2). The previous method of identifying people used by the Italians was so inexact as to be useless and prevented Italian law and order agencies from successfully co-operating with their European and American colleagues. Some of Rudini's reforms built upon established foundations. The police already possessed a biographical file service containing information on persons associated with parties whose activities the government considered inimical to its survival.[58]

The policies of repression convinced the Italian people, including the elites, that following the proper due process of the law, and movement to a more inclusive constitutional democratic form of government, would be more likely to bring stability than the violent and arbitrary measures practiced by Crispi, Rudini and Pelloux. In the elections of 1900 the Socialist Party – although then only eight years old and under constant pressure from the forces of order for its entire existence – attracted nearly a quarter of a million votes.[59]

The ground was now prepared for possibly the most prosperous and stable decade in Italy's entire history, the Giolittian age, named after the prime minister of these years Giovanni Giolitti, and lasting from 1901 to 1914. Giolitti was a new sort of leader for Italy. Politically courageous, he embarked upon social and political policies inconceivable only a few years before. He collaborated with the far left, enshrined the right to strike and protected other civil liberties. Indeed, the Giolitti era is known as the 'Golden Age' of Italian Labour and the policy of this government fostered the rapid development of trade unions.[60] In a sense Giolitti's policies provided a government of national unification and renewal.

Nonetheless, Giolitti's overblown fear of Anarchist terrorism combined with strands of common sense caused him to recognise that Italy, like all other modernising states, required a sophisticated, national police force as a means of prevention, as both Lépine and Zubatov believed, not as an agent of suppression.

Despite Rudini's efforts, the police inherited by Giolitti remained the most backward in industrial Europe. The Italians still lacked a professionalised detective force, made little use of forensic photography, the telephone or the telegraph in fighting crime. Giolitti tackled the police's shortcomings as soon as he took office. Under Giolitti the police academy in Rome, established in 1902–03, soon acquired an international reputation. It taught the latest techniques of scientific identification including fingerprinting, modern psychology and anthropology. In 1908 the government installed photographic equipment and laboratories in major police bureaus throughout the country, soon giving Italy one of the most advanced police systems in Europe.[61]

Giolitti made a sincere but fruitless attempt to vitiate the hated and feared administrative procedures of *ammonizione* and *domiciilio coatto*. Even so, invoking these procedures became a rarity against political offenders[62] as better police with more sophisticated methods of collecting and evaluating evidence made administrative justice increasingly superfluous.

The Giolitti regime, like the French, used its reformed and modernised police to pursue and harass the radicals within its midst. In France, as we have seen, Lépine and his government targeted the syndicalists. Giolitti and his police chiefs also, especially between 1906 and 1909, dedicated considerable time to the Anarchist movement. Giolitti employed a worldwide network of secret agents who kept him informed about Anarchist intentions.

The new-found tranquility did not serve police interests. Increased steady growth and increasing power depended upon reports of continuing turmoil in the future. So, as the Anarchist era of 'propaganda by deed' drew to a close and revolutionary plots diminished, police invented conspiracies where none existed. Giolitti, with the reports dealing with the assassination of King Umberto and the 1905 Revolution in Russia at the forefront of his mind remained in a constant panic about the possibility of Anarchist violence.[63]

Paradoxically, as we shall see in the following chapter, Russian émigrés, many of them terrorists, residing in Italy were hardly bothered by Giolitti's police.

Germany

Of the four systems of internal order being discussed in these pages the following two, that of Germany and Great Britain, are the most difficult to unravel. In the British case, very little is known about the day-to-day operations of the Special Branch, as Bernard Porter, its historian confirms. So our knowledge of its internal workings and policies remain largely based on secondary sources, glimpses of documentation here and there, and hearsay. As for the German case, even after unification the various German states still passed their own laws on the maintenance of internal order and operated their own police forces. As we shall see the number of political forces with which the *Okhrana* had to deal and the various attitudes of these police toward the Russian emigration living in their midst reflects the difficulty of reviewing the German political police system as a whole. The Second *Reich*, so concerned with good order, did not establish a national ministry of police.

The history of policing in teutonic cultures can be summed up in a single term: *polizeistaat*. Under such a regime every aspect of society was regulated by minutely detailed ordinances, breaches of which were often severely punished administratively on the spot by the local forces of order.[64] Over time, especially during the eighteenth century, Germans came to consider this oppressive milieu as the norm. For the security police, then, the control of public opinion and the 'pursuit of demagogues' was not a difficult chore since most rebellious groups were small and the 'demagogues' were generally well-known academic or literary figures. Although the security police could be arbitrary, even brutal, their actions were never directed against an entire class or estate.[65]

In general, policing within the German states during the first half of the nineteenth century prior to the Revolutions of 1848 suffered from benign neglect. Let us review the condition of the forces of order in Prussia, the soon-to-be-home of a large number of Russian revolutionary émigrés. In Prussia, rural areas, which contained about 75 per cent of the country's population, were policed by about 1,600 *Landgendarmen*. Even though urban centres were better staffed, like Italian cities, they remained thoroughly underpoliced. In Berlin the ratio was one policeman to 2,000 inhabitants. Most other Prussian cities were worse off than this. In the absence of a sophisticated well-manned policing system Prussia employed its army to maintain order.[66]

The impact of the 1848 Revolution stunned the Prussian forces of order and reinforced their hostility towards those who survived through wage earning and those associated with stirring them up. The embattled forces of order saw themselves more than ever confronted by 'the enemies within'. As one enforcer of internal order subsequently wrote 'the dream of a general levelling between the rich and poor has taken firm hold amongst the working people'.[67] Steps to tighten up the security police began.

Prussia replaced incompetent and over-age policemen, appointed energetic and unyielding police chiefs, and strove to develop improved state co-ordination and supervision all within a highly militarised and visible police establishment. Its government decreed that the forces of order must monitor all suspicious activities that could lead to renewed dissent and disorder. Berlin allowed Prussia's police forces the widest latitude in dealing with its citizens when combating perceived threats to Germany's stability. Responsibilty for this duty fell upon the provincial police as well, who were expected to detect the first appearance of trouble at grass roots level. In line with this policy, the government promulgated legislation to buttress police action. On 11 March 1850 legislation appeared limiting Prussians' right of association directly contravening the provisions of the constitution. In 1851, the press law of 12 May bullied journalists and editors into political silence, controlled the issuing of permits for the distribution of handbills and pamphlets and controlled the book trade. The police also kept a suspicious eye on the movement of individuals, recorded all the residents within their purview and especially noted those whom they considered political suspects. Innkeepers supplied the police with lists of overnight guests. Persons had to report the names of any non-residents who spent the night in their homes and so on.[68]

Unlike the French and Italian forces of order who spoke of emulating the English 'Bobby', the culture of the friendly policeman on the beat placed there to protect citizens did not penetrate Prussia. The German police treated the average citizen with distain. They displayed the arrogance, arbitrariness and rigidity bred into them in their previous careers as soldiers. Even efforts by the Ministry of the Interior to lessen the negative impact caused by police harassment of its citizens had surprisingly little impact upon them.[69] They perceived themselves, as they indeed were, as agents of imperial government responsible only to their immediate superiors rather than as servants of the people. These characteristics, combined with their right to fine and imprison without judicial process[70] continued unabated into the twentieth century. Relations between the police and the lower orders were so bad that Raymond Fosdick, in the immediate pre-First World War era, witnessed the open animosity toward the police by the 'poorer' classes.[71] A more counter-productive approach to the maintenance of order would be difficult to fathom.

In the history of the German police national unification had little impact on police reform. Law enforcement remained the responsibility of the individual states.[72] Overall, the complexion of German law and order culture served the interests of Otto von Bismarck, the Second *Reich*'s first Chancellor. By the first decade of the twentieth century, however, the German forces of order, despite Bismarck's best efforts to contain political opposition found themselves constrained, at least in their formal public behaviour, by growing centre and left opinion within the *Reichstag* and the popular press as did their colleagues in France and Italy.

By the late 1880s attitudes toward confrontation with the opposition and the nature of subversion in Germany were changing. The growing influence of the *Reichstag* as the voice of the people and the power of electoral politics began to influence those responsible for internal order. However, the struggle between those who persisted in the traditional approach to maintaining order and those who understood the nature of the political milieu would not be easily resolved, this at the very time that Bismarck's Anti-Socialist Laws were to run their course.[73] The recently crowned Kaiser Wilhelm II allowed the Anti-Socialist Laws to lapse as a sign of his government's newfound post-Bismarckian flexibility and conciliatory nature. But the assassination of French President Carnot unsettled the young Kaiser who believed that the crown and his own family were in danger. In June 1894 Wilhelm ordered Chancellor Caprivi to prepare legislation which would emulate the repressive anti-Anarchist legislation promulgated by the French and Italians. Caprivi expressed his reservations about presenting such legislation to the *Reichstag*. To pass such a bill it might be necessary to dissolve the *Reichstag* and rewrite the electoral law. Caprivi thought any attempt to take such measures would only benefit the Social Democrats. He persuaded the Kaiser to abandon any draconian measures and, instead, to submit an innocuous bill that would not offend anyone. Caprivi's moderate stance, very different from that of Bismarck's sixteen years before, reflected a public opinion increasingly opposed to the policy of repression. Armed with a growing political sophistication Germans could see through the hysteria generated by the pro-government press as nothing more than a partisan game and in no way representing a genuine concern over a perceived threat of oncoming revolution.[74]

The demise of the Anti-Socialist Laws and the *Reichstag*'s rejection of subsequent pieces of repressive legislation proposed by the government were the only successful skirmishes in society's intensifying struggle with the forces of order. The government remained adamantly opposed to the spread of social democracy and encouraged its police to be as petty as ever in enforcing the Ministry of the Interior's orders.

In 1889 a bitter miners' strike suppressed by the military with a large number of casualties convinced the authorities that Germany required a police capable of 'effectively countering public disorder at the outset' and especially the activism of 'the working masses, who were inclined to such disorders' which the police must strangle 'at birth'.[75] As early as 1883 the Berlin police had already begun to compile a register of political suspects and the Berlin Police Presidium intensifed this data collection process after the repeal of the Anti-Socialist Laws by employing undercover agents who infiltrated political associations to report on their activities. These political policing activities were not limited to Prussia. In Hamburg the police sent undercover agents into working class bars and hangouts to discover their political attitudes. Political policing as a systematised task, however, was something rather new to Germany. Outside of Berlin, regional political police bureaus were poorly developed. This was largely the case because ordinary civil police had long assumed political duties especially from the 1890s onwards.

At the same time, however, those who managed the forces of order had come to understand that Germany's political world had grown considerably more complex since Bismarck's chancellorship. The German policemen's notorious behaviour needed to be modified through both police education and a restructuring of the rules by which they operated. The *Reich* established police schools during the last pre-war years which strove to ensure that policemen understood the law and followed it. Not only was the *Reichstag* watching, but perhaps more significantly local officials – mayors and councilmen – of the socialist, centrist and liberal stripe expected the police within their jurisdiction to abide by the law. Courts, too, influenced by popular opinion protected the accused from any remaining arbitrariness of the police.[76]

In the years leading up to the war the policies of close surveillance and repression achieved little, for the forces energising the changing complexion of German society were beyond the control of the police. The adoption of universal manhood suffrage by the newly formed *Reich* in 1871 began a momentous process of social and political transformation. By 1914 the Social Democratic Party boasted one million members and perhaps more significantly over 2,500,000 workers belonged to trade unions, and all of this manifested itself in regular strikes reaching a peak in 1914.[77] In political terms the moderate Catholic Centre Party often allied itself with the liberals in the *Reichstag* to protect Germany's fundamental liberties. Indeed, *Reichstag* debates over determining exactly what constituted a political crime and the treatment of alleged political criminals even when they were Russian émigrés, as we shall see in Chapter 8, have a quality and sincerity that cannot be found in either the French or Italian parliaments.[78]

Great Britain

The image of British policing, one the Home Office and British policemen themselves purposefully cultivated, is of a rather benign and friendly force whose purpose was to protect the safety of the individual and the sanctity of property. As Alexander Herzen, one of the first and certainly the most illustrious Russian émigré to settle in England wrote 'in England a policeman at your door merely adds to your sense of security'.[79] The police itself could not have summed up their desired public image more succinctly. Three-quarters of a century later Raymond Fosdick, another foreigner with great experience in the varieties of policing, wrote when comparing British and German law in regard to policing:

> The German laws.... confer upon the police forces extraordinary powers with which the English police are totally unacquainted.... [I]n short, the bulwarks which English tradition and the common law have erected against offical tyranny and abuse are unknown to the German people.[80]

The Metropolitan Police Force, founded in 1829, contained no plain clothes officers. The Met's detective bureau, established in 1842, could boast only 15 members a quarter of a century later. This is not to say that the mid-Victorians did not possess a political police. Informers and undercover agents in pre-Victorian England regularly maintained surveillance over and within radical and working class movements. They were, however, of the most unreliable type, submitting false, or distorted reports which misled the government.[81] The Metropolitan Police in particular developed excellent crowd control technique.[82]

None of this, of course, applies to the Irish Question. During the winter of 1867, in response to the first Fenian bombings, the cabinet set up a Secret Service Department independent of the Metropolitan Police to protect London from expected outrages which, luckily, never eventuated. As a result, the cabinet disbanded this 'Special Service' four months later. In Ireland itself, though, the British Government maintained covert political police agencies which were highly skilled in counter-subversive techniques. Unfortunately, in mainland Britain the Home Office did not maintain sophisticated surveillance over native radicals. The inexperience and amateurishness of the Metropolitan Police in these matters came to light when European governments asked the British authorities to keep former Communards from the French Commune under observation. The naive, rather comical approach adopted by the Met could only have caused laughter amongst the French émigrés and consternation at Scotland Yard.[83]

The aura of security, of political stability, of the bright future promised to Britain by Victorian Liberalism and the increasing wealth of the Empire convinced British elites that the nation only required minimal internal security and that this security, no matter how limited, must not be obtained at the expense of the culture of toleration and the rule of law. Even Fenian violence and the wildfire of Anarchist terror on the Continent, including the shock caused by the assassination of Tsar Alexander II in early March 1881, did not drive English lawmakers into following Italian, French and German examples of incorporating political crime within their body of domestic law. In Britain, with one minor exception, the law never developed special principles, special procedures or special punishments for dealing with political criminals.[84]

But times were changing. The renewal of the Fenian bombing campaign which ran from about 1881 to 1886 confronted the government with both practical and philosophical issues *vis-à-vis* the role of its forces of internal order. The Fenian assaults like many of the outrages committed by Anarchists on the Continent were indiscriminate. Any orderly person, minding his own business, walking peacefully past a government building or a public lavatory could be blown to pieces by one of their bombs. The Home Office bore full responsibility for these deaths which could have damaged the government's chances at the next election. Foreign pressure, too, played a role in undermining Britain's traditional *sang froid* in these matters. A third source of concern was the small size and general incompetence of the Metropolitan Police itself in dealing with political cases. The Met never developed a French or Russian-like detective or spy service to counter subversion, and strong opinion against initiating such a service remained deeply imbedded in England's police culture. Fourth, as we shall see in the following chapter, the arrival of Russian political émigrés in England coincided with a flood of mostly Jewish immigrants fleeing the repressive rule of Tsar Alexander III. Most immigrants simply wanted a better life for themselves and their families. They intended nothing more than either to become good Englishman, or to earn enough money to move on to the United States, but many of these people were infected by Socialism and Anarchism absorbed in their homeland and they made receptive audiences for the variety of political émigrés who lived and often worked among them. These people, both political émigrés who used Britain as a temporary refuge, and immigrants who envisioned Britian as chance to begin a new life, needed to be watched.[85]

The whiff of insecurity stirred by the infiltration of Socialism, Marxism and Anarchism into the body politic was whipped up by the shock of the Franco-Russian alliance. This alliance, consummated in 1892, allied Britain's two traditional enemies and appeared to threaten both the future well-being of liberal capitalism and British security. This sense of insecurity was heightened still further by the increasingly bellicose Germans, who in the post-Bismarckian era were less concerned with the *status quo* in Europe than with Germany's 'rightful' place in the sun. British confidence in Albion's unassailably bright future turned to doubt, and doubt to fear of conspiracy. Who knew what group, or what set of ideas could influence people to disrupt the road towards gentle and inevitable progress decreed by liberal capitalism? Who knew what subversive outsider in another nation's interest would strive to influence disgruntled elements of British society to take action against the established order?[86]

By the mid-1880s the Fenian bombing campaign came to an end, thanks to the work of the men in Dublin Castle and their agents abroad, but terrorism of one sort or another was here to stay.[87] In 1887 the cabinet established the Special Branch to deal with it. The establishment of a political police created considerable *angst* within the forces of order for it ran contrary to the very essence of British political culture. For the first time domestic policing in Britain (excluding Ireland) would involve spying on one's own people, invading their privacy. This meant of course, that the activities of the Special Branch were to be kept a closely guarded secret and largely remain so to this day. We do know that the Branch reported directly to the Home Office and to the Metropolitan Police and that its relative independence allowed it to exceed its legal powers from time to time.

During the 1890s it employed only 25 men even though its basic duties such as port control and maintaining surveillance on the growing revolutionary émigré population, in particular the terrorists amongst them, combined with its detectives' special duties as bodyguards to important personages, both domestic and foreign, required greater manpower.[88] The small pool of detectives qualified for close surveillance is probably the reason for this lack of personnel. Apparently the Special Branch did not have a professional school for its men – all of whom initially had come either out of the Irish Special Branch or from the port police – to teach the necessary additional recruits the required skills.[89] As the Special Branch was forced to employ more detectives they stuck out like sore thumbs.[90]

At the outbreak of war in 1914 the Special Branch still employed only 70 people. Its still small size, however, did not reflect the Branch's widening concerns. Labour unrest, as one policeman wrote 'broke into open strife', between 1910 and 1912 and with it came a fear of syndicalism and of the Independent Labour Party. The suffragette movement, too, becoming more aggressive in their demands for the vote, required closer attention. The Special Branch expanded its net to include these groups. Perhaps most of all, the threat of war and fear of German espionage gave the Special Branch a task worthy of a secret police and promoted the value of the Branch in governing circles. In any case, by the outbreak of the First World War British liberalism had retreated before the international political situation. As Bernard Porter sees it, liberals may still have objected to the use of *agent provocateurs* but they were less anxious to know about these things or any other nefarious activity undertaken by the Special Branch than they were before.[91] By November 1918, at the end of the war, the Special Branch possessed 700 policemen supported by a staff of 1,453 men and women, mostly postal employees who intercepted and censored the mail.[92]

The historian of the Paris Prefecture Jean-Marc Berlière wrote that the model of 'community policing' employed by the British policing establishment was not designed for use as the Special Branch intended and that the system of Joseph Fouché, emulated by the political police on the Continent, was much more suitable for spying on the whole of society.[93] In the immediate pre-war years the Special Branch was moving in Fouché's direction, but it had not got there yet.

In the decades prior to the First World War, European society began to undergo a fundamental transformation: a process of modernisation. Modernity did not appear suddenly from any single cause. The process is to be found in a complex formula of socio-economic, political, technological and scientific evolution that began to reshape European life in combination with the industrial and philosophical revolutions of the eighteenth century. In the decades prior to the First World War modernity moved forward at something more than a glacial pace although not nearly so joltingly fast as the traditional elites imagined. As Europe moved towards the twentieth century the traditional elites and their allies found challenges to their preeminent position arising from all sides: the *haute bourgeoisie*; the new professional classes; the changing nature of the economy that generally made land less valuable if not less prestigious, than money; the rise in number and militance of the industrial workers who were coalescing in trade unions, some of them being seduced by either Marxism or Syndicalism; the success of parliamentary socialism especially in Germany and Italy; and, finally, the deteriorating international situation. In retrospect, then, it is difficult to blame them for the sense of ill-ease they felt about their future, especially when their already blossoming fears were exacerbated by acts of terrorism. Both targeted assassinations and indiscriminate bombings caused panic amongst them and the governments who serviced their needs.

To make matters worse, by 1904–05 the smug European order suffered further blows to its way of life. The victory of a non-white nation over a European power in the Russo-Japanese War and the rise of the lower orders in a frenzied assault against Tsardom in the 1905 Revolution shook the European establishment to its roots and signalled the destabilising of the European international order as well as the domestic one. In response to the socio-economic and political turbulence arising from the birth of the modern age Europeans became not only fearful and insecure, they also became suspicious at times to the point of paranoia.

These phenomena ushered in the age of political policing. As Louis Lépine asserted, one 'cannot possibly conceive of a relatively well-organised society' without the existence of a political police department.[94] By organised Lépine meant stable and safe. Although scholars such as Barton Ingraham and Otto Kirchheimer contend that during the half century or more before the outbreak of the world war the maintenance of order was dominated by 'the restricted system of hesitant and conscious-stricken state protection' this is less so then they would like us to believe. The burgeoning reliance on the police by *haute société* to contain the suspicious and openly threatening miasma before them had long term and continuing effects on the growth in power and influence of those organisations who police European politics to this very day.[95]

This is the world into which both the Russian political émigrés and the members of the Russian political police who pursued them came to live.

2
Émigré Lives: the Russian Revolutionary Abroad

> It was very painful for me to emigrate and I do not advise anybody to do this without the utmost necessity. Only when all possibilities of useful activity in the homeland are cut off, only then emigration is pardonable or obliged. For me the possibilities were cut off.
>
> Peter Lavrov[1]

> Isolation from culture, estrangement from familiar social relations, means solitude, and solitude may destroy or elate the human being; in it he may find or lose himself; from it he may return wiser or broken.
>
> Hans Speier[2]

Who were the émigrés and how many of them were there? These are questions the responses to which depended upon whose stereotype one accepted and who did the counting – contemporaries, the police who kept them under surveillance, the historians who studied them. The label 'Russian revolutionary émigré' is a generic description encompassing a diverse group of people manifesting a kaleidoscope of political views. Despite the revolutionary emigration's central place in both revolutionary and Soviet history the composite portrait drawn of the émigré world and those who peopled it is blurred by historical selectivity and the myth-making brew of memory, passing time and intentional distortion. The historian's gaze often, although not exclusively, fell on the most fascinating and significant personalities amongst them: a spectrum of personalities that included at its top the tribunes of the revolutionary movements – winners and losers – people of sparkling intellect, the marvellous propagandists amongst them – and who could forget the terrorists. But most revolutionary émigrés – at first a handful, then dozens and ultimately thousands of people – whose talents did not match their dreams, or who simply suffered from a lack of luck including being born too soon, have not left much of a trace. Some like Aron Liberman, who shot himself in a cheap boarding house on a cold November day in Syracuse New York in 1880, succumbed to bad luck compounded by the isolation and bitterness of exile.[3]

Others, better known than Liberman, played important but largely forgotten roles in the emigration, or worse, suffered the indignity of having those roles claimed by others. E. D. Kuskova, S. N. Prokopovich and V. V. Grishin, for example, led the Association of Social Democrats Abroad, an organisation known for its moderate socialist stance and its initiation of the mass smuggling of revolutionary propaganda and the publications of the émigré intelligentsia into the Russian Empire. The Association disappeared in 1903 under a factional onslaught of people more gifted and ruthless than themselves – the *Iskra* group – led at this time by G. V. Plekhanov and V. I. Lenin. With the Association defeated and dispersed the *Iskra* group began to take credit for the incredible smuggling achievements of its less renowned and now defeated rivals even though *Iskra*'s smuggling operation was not nearly as successful.[4] The Association and its members, like Aron Liberman, became little more than a curioisity of émigré history. Most members of the emigration did not achieve more than this.

Contemporaries, too, fell into confusion over the composition and number of revolutionary émigrés in their midst. The massive westward migration of Russian immigrants and sundry others, especially students, during the final quarter or more of the nineteenth century created an homogenous image that confused both the officials and ordinary citizens of their host countries.

The differences between émigrés and immigrants to the well-informed few who could manage to observe the influx of humanity across their borders with equanimity would, of course, be straightforward. The immigrant is escaping his homeland to begin life anew. Migrants are usually driven abroad by one or a combination of three conditions: religious persecution, economic deprivation, and/or dissatisfaction with the political and social conditions within the homeland. The immigrant intends to take up residence in a new country, establish a permanent life in this alien environment with no intention (at least initially) of returning home. Integration into the new majority culture became the migrants' *raison d'être* driven by their dream to achieve secure and comfortable lives for their children if not for themselves.

While they struggled to achieve what was for most of them an insuperable goal, they remained in neighbourhoods populated by their fellow countrymen comforted by similar customs, the intelligibility of their common language, and often a common religion all of which buffered them against the hostility and suspicion of the native population.

Émigrés resided abroad for quite different reasons. Foreign lands served as sanctuaries not new homes. Often they were driven from their homelands by a hostile government. Whether forced to flee abroad with the police in pursuit or choosing to leave of their own volition, émigrés understood that for most of them to return home would mean imprisonment, exile or worse.

Yet, the revolutionary émigrés lived in hope. They spent their time abroad plotting the destruction of the oppressive regime causing so much misery in the homeland. By the 1880s they dreamed of a new order shaped by the ideology to which they fanatically adhered, all the while living in intellectual and social isolation and personal insecurity exacerbated by their status as stateless people.[5]

Of course, the ability to discriminate between immigrants and émigrés was not so clear cut to the majority of Europeans and their forces of order in those countries whose borders were being overrun by the thousands of Russian migrants settling in the West. The sense of social and political instability raised by the flow of migrants westward exacerbated the nascent xenophobia already spreading throughout Europe. To Europeans this flood of strange looking, unintelligibly speaking, seemingly bizarre behaving humankind appeared a most unappealing undifferentiated multitude with which both political émigrés and visiting students became confused.

Amongst this flow of Russian subjects westward it was the students who proved especially difficult for the forces of order – both in Russia and Europe – and the citizenry of the host countries in general to differentiate from the political émigré population. Hundreds of Russian students, many of them women and Jews, travelled abroad legally in order to obtain a tertiary education. Many of these enthusiastic and altruistic young people, once abroad, participated in anti-tsarist demonstrations especially in Switzerland and Germany. Émigré groups made a concerted effort to recruit as many of these teenagers as they could to their particular world view. The tsarist Department of Police understood the importance of the student population to the emigration's well-being and did not hesitate to identify any student who participated in an anti-tsarist demonstration as a 'revolutionary'.[6] For this reason the political life of Russian students abroad forms an integral part of the following discussion.

As a result, extracting an accurate composite picture of the revolutionary émigré population abroad at any given time between the 1880s and the outbreak of the First World War is not a clear cut process. With this caveat in mind one can estimate that over this more than thirty-year period the Russian revolutionary population abroad grew from about 200 to between 4,000 and 5,000 in the post-1905 Revolution years.[7]

Anyone reviewing the history of the Russian revolutionary emigration is immediately struck by its remarkable persistence and steady growth over time in the face of intensifying harassment by the tsarist political police abroad supported by the forces of order in western Europe. Dating the beginnings of the emigration is somewhat of a dicey business, although the late 1860s seems a reasonable date to begin. Until then the personality of the few Russian émigrés dotted across Europe reflected the strong individualism and intellectual independence that drove them abroad in the first place. Most of these men possessed the option of applying to return to Russia, as we shall see in Chapter 7, and some driven by hunger for things Russian, and despair not dissimilar to that of Aron Liberman's did so.[8] These early émigrés did not form strong coherent groups bound together in colonies determined by ideological unity. As Martin Miller in his insightful analysis of the Russian emigration up to about 1870 notes, these were people of strong social conscience who took themselves abroad for their own particular reasons. Once abroad they bickered incessantly with one another over matters of no serious consequence. None of these émigrés possessed a clear sense of what they wished to do in the West. As Miller writes, they saw their time abroad as a respite from the stifling intellectual atmosphere that permeated Russian life under Nicholas I (1825–55) and even under his supposedly more tolerant successor Alexander II (1856–81): a breathing space that would permit them freedom to think and to write. These people remained throughout their stay abroad incapable of sustained co-operation amongst themselves.

By the 1860s Miller contends that the evolution of revolutionary ideology in Russia stimulated in part by the whiff of openness introduced by the Great Reforms and the involvement of young radicals in revolutionary events created a different sort of émigré arising from an *intelligentsiia*, drawn not so much from the aristocracy or the gentry as from the *raznochintsy* (the sons and daughters of priests, merchants and tradespeople, for example) – bound together in exile by a communality of belief and a desire to work together within an organisational framework. But this unity faltered in the 1870s as the growing number of exiles fell into groups led by charismatic personalities such as Lavrov and Bakunin who, although driven by new and powerful ideas which attracted supporters, ironically were not temperamentally suited to the task of leadership. It is true that Lavrov, although aloof and aristocratic and philosophically inconsistent, continued to draw people to him. In Paris, where he lived out the majority of his exile, he remained a magnet for young émigrés who admired his writings and benefited from his vast library, but he never truly served as a leader of a community or a sustainable organisation.[9]

By the late 1870s a new generation of revolutionary émigrés – the men and women with whom the tsarist political police would soon become deeply concerned – began to arrive in Europe. These men and women would build revolutionary communities around them. P. B. Akselrod, Lev Deich, Georgii Plekhanov and Vera Zasulich, for example, established a continuity with the émigrés of earlier times while at the same time laying the ideological and political foundations for the next generation of revolutionaries abroad by drawing younger admirers to them. These tribunes of the revolutionary movement became the focal points for early émigré colonies. In their turn these colonies, mostly in Switzerland and England, offered succour and an ideological home to the young radicals escaping abroad in the late 1880s and 1890s whose skills as organisers, ideologues and polemicists laid the groundwork for the Russian Revolution. By the first years of the twentieth century Russia's revolutionary émigrés had formed political parties – although for some of them at least their political platforms could best be described as vague – and had organised themselves into discrete colonies.

Some of these colonies as we will see, such as those in Italy, fell into internal dispute, dissolved and then reformed with stunning regularity. Others such as the SDs in Berlin persisted through thick and thin until finally being driven by police harassment to outlying provincial cities. Many of the colonies boasted rigid membership rights basing themselves on the ideological and factional purity of the membership; the membership of others such as the colony in Milan, Italy, came from assorted ideological backgrounds, having in common only the desire to participate in the vibrant Milanese socialist movement – but more of them later.[10]

While the social and political dynamics generated by émigré colonies could ameliorate the isolation of emigration, paradoxically the milieu they helped to create exacerbated the internecine tensions that made life practically unendurable for many of them. Virtually every author who writes about émigré life, Russian or otherwise, refers to the émigrés' sudden sense of isolation from their historic mission and the boredom and depression brought on in exile by forced inaction. Frustrated and angry, these people could only sustain themselves with utopian and millenarian dreams of the future that in their collective *mentalité* gave them the fanatical dedication necessary to endure years, often decades, in exile. Of course, not everyone shared the same image of Utopia. The seemingly endless disputes over whose vision represented the true path generated an ideological rigidity and political exclusivity within the various revolutionary factions for which they became infamous. Maintaining the purity of one's millenarian vision required a stubborn self-righteousness coated in often convoluted but sometimes magnificent rhetoric which ignored the problems the making of revolution confronted, and instead focused entirely upon some perfect solution. This drive for absolute outcomes structured around ideological constructs, without much regard for reality, led the emigration into a bitter divisiveness that was not often understood by 'practical' party workers at home. Political moderation and compromise with the existing order in Europe under these psychological conditions was considered nothing less than treason to the revolutionary cause.

This climate of constant tension caused by bitter, seemingly unrelenting ideological warfare between émigré colonies, played into the hands of the

Russian political police abroad, who did not find it difficult to convince the raw-nerved and twitchy emigration that no place on earth was truly beyond its grasp. The émigrés' fear of unrecognisable police spies within their circles terrified them as they watched the tsarist police arrest their comrades, one after the other, as soon as they returned to Russia on a revolutionary assignment.[11]

Vladimir Bonch-Bruevich summed up these feelings and their impact when he remembered:

> Here in a foreign country [Switzerland] we could observe the very fresh beginning of a free Social Democratic life for students. Yet at the same time we all knew that among them ... had to be agents .... The knowledge that there were traitors among the crowd streaming to lectures poisoned the lives of the young people ....[12]

With all of this said, let us look at émigré lives over time and distance.

Switzerland

Political émigrés principally employed five criteria to determine where they would settle: the attitude of the host nation toward political criminals; the host nation's geographic proximity to Russia; familiarity with and attitude towards a particular culture – a comfort zone – that would create as little dislocation as possible; the quality and intensity of émigré life within the possible choices of refuge; and the cost of living within a particular city.

In the early 1880s most émigrés congregated in Geneva, London and Paris. Geneva was the closest to Russia and Paris the least expensive. But the emigration was a movable feast. By the first years of the new century a very large colony existed in Berlin, and from 1905 onwards Paris drew the largest number of Russian political exiles, followed, especially in the summer, by the Ligurian coastline of Italy, whose mild climate attracted large numbers of Russian revolutionaries, especially SRs.

The West first encountered Russians *en masse* when young men and women travelled abroad as students. The Russian students served as the essential fertile environment for the still small number of political émigrés who made their way to western Europe in the 1870s. Without the student colonies it is difficult to imagine how the growing number of Russian revolutionaries abroad would have been able to establish themselves so quickly.

As for the students themselves, they sought out Swiss and German universities first of all. Swiss civil liberties and political neutrality, even offering residence permits to Russian students with shady political records, and their generous asylum legislation, proved particularly atttractive to young people seeking an education abroad. So did Switzerland's relatively inexpensive cost of living, its proximity to Russia, the multi-lingual nature of the society, its broad university curricula and, after 1867, admission of women to tertiary education.[13]

Russian women, especially those intending to study medicine, something they could not do within the Russian Empire, travelled to enrol in the University of Zürich which accepted its first Russian women students in 1867. By 1873 more than 300 women were studying at Zürich along with 150 of their male colleagues.[14]

Russians in Switzerland kept to themselves. While many of the émigrés and students admired Swiss industriousness and expressed admiration for some Swiss institutions, on the whole they found Swiss society stultifying and boring. The well-known Oberstrass district in Zürich near the Polytechnic became a microcosm of Russian life, a tranformation of a neighbourhood to be duplicated in the future across Europe and England. The students' staple diet could be said to be that of the less fortunate political émigrés themselves: tea, bread, milk and, every so often, perhaps a little meat. Students and émigrés alike searched for work in order to survive. Some émigrés operated small businesses while others, less fortunate, worked in watch factories. A group of students even trained to become masseurs thereby managing to support themselves.

The exiles, still few in number, developed small cultural centres to which Russian students came to seek good conversation and to discuss and argue about the deteriorating political conditions at home and how to remedy them. Some of these young people chose to immerse themselves in political activism and merged with the small node of political exiles that had grown up around Peter Lavrov, whose library and seminars attracted them. Lavrov, however, was not the only émigré who settled in Switzerland in the first half of the 1870s and the colony became a hothouse for a variety of political movements.

The potentially volatile combination of student idealism and sophisticated political agitation worried the tsarist authorities who undertook two tactics to defuse this combination. In June 1873 Tsardom decreed that Russian women enrolled either at the University of Zürich or the local polytechnical school who continued to attend lectures in these institutions after 1 January 1874 would be denied entry to any Russian institution of higher learning and refused admission to any profession which depended upon government examination.[15] The Third Section then flooded Zürich with its agents who maintained close surveillance of both student and revolutionary émigré life. The first tactic appeared to work. The colony slowly evaporated. Some students returned home while others took advantage of a loophole in the June 1873 decree – it only mentioned Zürich – to continue their studies elsewhere in Switzerland. Others made their way to universities outside of Switzerland, especially in Germany. The disappearance of the students appeared to dishearten the political émigrés. It was not long before the most famous and important member of the Zürich colony, Peter Lavrov, left Switzerland for England and the remaining student/émigré organisations collapsed.[16]

Unfortunately for Tsardom, the destruction of the Zürich colony became little more than a pyrrhic victory. The Swiss Federation allowed its cantons substantial juridical and diplomatic independence. The surveillance of foreigners was a cantonal obligation. Indeed, the federal police did not command a single policeman nor did it possess a single agent in the cantons.[17] Each canton developed its own attitudes towards foreign intrusions in this matter as well. The Genevan authorities in particular displayed a strong distaste for the Third Section's operatives, going so far as to ask the Director of Central Police for permission not to pass on the names of those engaged in the manufacture of anti-tsarist propaganda to the Russian authorities.[18] This is not to say that the Third Section's presence in Switzerland did not have an impact on Russian revolutionaries and others in residence there. Vera Zasulich, whose courage is beyond question, believed herself besieged by 'spies' and as we have seen, she was not alone in her feeling. This sense of constantly being under Tsardom's microscope drove most émigrés to distraction[19] but without the co-operation of Europe's governments the Third Section could do little more than observe and report on Russian life abroad (see Chapter 3). It would not be until the mid-1880s that the first important chief of the Foreign Agentura, P. I. Rachkovskii, would bring the fight directly to the émigrés in Switzerland and elsewhere, as we shall see in Chapter 7.

It is no wonder, then, that by the late 1870s and for decades afterwards, despite the number of *mouchards* in residence there, Geneva became at one time or another the home of a who's-who of the revolutionary emigration. G. V. Plekhanov, Vera Figner, Paul Axelrod, S. M. Stepniak-Kravchinskii, Mikhail Gots and Lev Tikhomirov are just a few of the revolutionaries plaguing tsarism who spent time in this most hospitable environment. Geneva witnessed the birth of the Russian social democratic movement itself, served as the base for a substantial *Narodnaia Volia* (the People's Will)[20] publishing effort and as the home of terrorist plotters as well.[21]

To make matters worse for Tsardom, Switzerland remained a centre of tertiary education for Russian students. The Russian government tried in vain to convince Swiss university authorities to accept only those students who came with official recommendations, but the Swiss steadfastly resisted pressure not only from Russia but from all the great powers to implement much more stringent residence criteria. In particular, Swiss medical schools increasingly became a haven for Russian women denied access to a medical education at home.

By 1900, 805 Russian students attended Swiss universities and these numbers began to trouble the Swiss themselves. By 1906–07 more than half the students at Swiss universities were Russian and they found themselves immersed in a general Russian population, spread throughout the cantons that had reached about 8,500 by 1910, with the largest settlements in Zürich and Geneva. This number did not even include the over 2,000 Polish-speaking residents amongst them.[22]

Prior to the 1905 Revolution, despite the large numbers of Russians living in their midst, the Swiss police paid little attention to these people, considering them to be harmless. This was a mistake. The Socialist-Revolutionaries Battle Organisation under the guidance of Mikhail Gots had in fact established its headquarters in Switzerland where it was planning the assassination of the new Russian Minister of Internal Affairs, V. K. Plehve.[23] The Geneva police seemed more concerned with arresting and expelling tsarist political police agents than it did in prosecuting the Russian political émigrés and student activists who were living amongst them.[24] This created considerable frustration for the Foreign Agentura which viewed Switzerland as the hotbed of Russian student and émigré activism to the great embarassment of the tsarist government.[25]

During the 1905 Revolution and afterwards the Swiss, finally responding to Russian pressure (see Chapter 3), began to deal more aggressively with suspect Russians residing in the cantons by searching their dwellings with greater vigour and expressing a willingness to undertake administrative expulsions. Ironically, A. M. Harting, the chief of the Foreign Agentura between 1905 and 1909, did not wish to pursue this course with the Swiss or anyone else. He believed that the expelled émigrés would simply move to France, already becoming the new centre for the revolutionary emigration, stretching his detective force nearly beyond its capacity.[26]

Although the Russian population in Switzerland reached its peak in 1910, émigré and student activism had long since begun to decline. The Foreign Agentura still kept a close eye on their doings, of course, but considered revolutionary life rather moribund.[27] Émigré existence in Geneva still had some life in it compared to Zürich, but Switzerland, while not a backwater of the Russian revolutionary emigration, had ceased to be the focal point of important revolutonary activism to which the major Russian revolutionary exiles were drawn.

Germany

The pattern of Russian student-revolutionary émigré mutual sustenance extended into Germany as well, where it developed into a much more vibrant and politically active movement. Russians had been travelling to the German states for an education since the times of Tsaritsa Anna Ivanovna in the 1730s. To the Russian elite Germany meant the 'West'.[28] The bubbling cultural and intellectual life of Germany's university towns such as Heidelberg, Karlsruhe, Munich, Leipzig and most of all Berlin attracted Russian students. German thought permeated Russian intellectual consciousness from Kant to Fichte, from Hegel to Marx and beyond. Also, unlike Switzerland, German culture and heritage belonged to the Germanised Romanov dynasty and to hundreds of Russian families who boasted German ancestry as well.

The vibrant Russian student life received support from the growing number of radical intelligentsia who sought respite in the German states from Alexander II's Russia during the late 1860s. The two groups combined to create Russian reading rooms in university towns. Soon illegal publications emanated from clandestine presses in Leipzig and students and revolutionaries alike matched wits with Russian agents (see Chapter 4) assigned to keep them under surveillance.

This promising beginning to a vibrant émigré community stumbled over national and international events inimical to émigré life in the German states. The unification of Germany in 1870, the promulgation of the Anti-Socialist Laws in the late 1870s and finally Bismarck's Three Emperors' League and the Reinsurance Treaty – which kept tsarist Russia in the German diplomatic camp – meant that Russian émigrés, at least temporarily, would have to abandon their activities in Germany and move to London, Paris or Zürich. It was not until the latter part of the 1880s with the deterioration of Russo-German relations, the subsequent lapsing of the Anti-Socialist Laws and the consequent rapid growth of the German social democratic movement that Germany again became a relatively attractive home for Russian émigrés.[29]

After 1900, Robert William's tells us that although outstanding intellects from upper class Russian society still studied in Germany to imbibe German *Kultur*, most Russian students were now of a different sort: of lower middle class background, many Jewish, who came to Germany to study medicine and engineering – as they did in Switzerland – as well as law and chemistry. The number of Russians in German technical high schools and universities almost tripled between 1900 and 1914. In 1912–13 alone nearly 5,000 Russians registered during the summer and winter semesters. Berlin, Leipzing and Munich contained the majority of these students although Königsberg, Heidelberg and Halle also serviced several hundred each.[30]

While it is clear, then, that Russian émigré and student colonies grew up across Germany, here we will discuss only the most important ones, those located in Berlin and Munich. In both of these cities the students and émigrés fed off each other's enthusiasm as the students eagerly sought a vision for Russia's future that they could passionately embrace.

By 1902 Berlin housed a substantial Russian émigré community. The capital of the *Reich* offered considerable advantages to Russians interested in political life: it served as the centre of the German social democratic movement; it was the traffic and communication hub for Europe providing several routes to Russia; Berlin's large and sympathetic working class presented a strong market for the sale of Russian political literature thereby bolstering the income of the usually financially strapped émigré community; it contained many socialist meeting halls and reading rooms that could be used for the training of agitators and propagandists; and finally, the political and transportation conditions appeared to ensure successful conspiratorial work, especially the smuggling of illegal literature and subsequently, during the 1905 Revolution, of arms into the Empire (see Chapter 9).[31]

The vibrant political life of Russia's students and revolutionary exiles in Berlin troubled the Foreign Agentura so much that its chief sought and received permission from St Petersburg for the establishment of a separate tsarist political police bureau in Berlin[32] (see Chapters 4 and 8). Life for Russian students and the political emigration in the *Reich*'s capital involved an intimate political and social relationship with the German Social Democrats, who permitted Russians to join their Party, stored Russian literature, hiding it from the police until it could smuggled into the Russian Empire, and defended Russians' civil rights in the *Reichstag* (see Chapter 8).[33]

By 1904 Russian émigré life in Berlin was in full swing. Despite the split of the RSDWP into Bolsheviks and Mensheviks, the Russian SDs in Berlin who leaned toward Bolshevism remained largely unaffected by Party disputes in most practical matters. As the colony became more professional, it began to pay closer attention to surveillance and possible infiltration by tsarist and German police agents. The SDs began to practice fiscal responsibility, keeping accounts and controlling unnecessary disbursements of their limited funds and most important of all, the colony intensified its political activity, becoming more clandestine by employing legal institutions as fronts for their revolutionary work.[34]

As early as 1899, director of the Foreign Agentura P. I. Rachkovskii in Paris wrote the Department of Police that Munich was fast becoming an émigré and student centre with 'masses of young social democrats participating in the general activities of the local [German] social democrats'. Only five or six Russians were enrolled in the University of Munich, but there were about 80 Russian students enrolled in the Polytechnic Institute about 90 per cent of whom were Jewish. Many of these students, according to Rachkovskii, regularly attended lectures delivered by social democrats. Some of them, the Foreign Agentura chief told his superiors, develop close relationships with German social democrats even lodging in their homes and imbibing the world view of their hosts and of the radical working class environment which surrounded them.[35]

On 6 September 1900 Lenin arrived in Munich where he was quickly joined by Plekhanovite colleagues Vera Zasulich, Alexander Potresov and Iu. Martov. From the end of 1900 into the spring of 1902 Munich served as

Lenin's home and the centre of operations for the Plekhanovites' new publication *Iskra* (*The Spark*). Why choose Munich for this new colony? The revolutionaries liked Munich's central location: by train Zürich could be reached in eight hours, Vienna in eleven hours, Berlin in twelve hours and Paris in fourteen hours.[36] The combination of Munich as a centre of radical Russian students and a colony of some of Russia's most brilliant émigrés proved a volatile mixture.[37]

By 1909 the political, academic and cultural atmosphere in the Bavarian capital attracted between 700 and 800 Russian students who attended school or university in Munich with an indeterminate number involved in political life of one sort or another. As for Russian political activism, the students could choose between the Social Democrats, the Socialist-Revolutionaries and the Jewish *Bund* all of which manifested a presence there. Indeed, by this time Munich had become a hotbed of Russian political – although not necessarily illegal – life.[38] All of the political parties undertook the same tasks including everything from forging passports for their couriers to spreading propaganda amongst the general public.[39] Acquiring recruits for the cause from amongst the Russian student population appeared to be their principal goal. The Russian police compared the energy of the colony in Munich to that of Berlin in the tumultuous and exciting first year of the 1905 Revolution. Important revolutionaries such as Trotskii and Chernov spoke to large audiences in student halls which had become venues for revolutionary agitation. All of this, wrote the Foreign Agentura, occurred right out in the open in front of the local authorities who remained indifferent to it all. 'In Berlin and generally in Prussia', the Foreign Agentura noted, 'similar performances would be inconceivable'.[40]

This is probably true, but the comment did not reflect the complexity of Russo-Prussian police relations. Prior to the 1905 Revolution, German and especially Prussian police reaction to the Russian radicals in Berlin was mixed. The Prussian police understood the difference between social democrats and 'anarchists' and resisted Russian attempts to portray the entire spectrum of Russian revolutionary émigrés and students as bloodthirsty cutthroats.[41] As a result, the Berlin Police Presidium viewed the persecution of Russia's student and émigré populations as a political obligation rather than a matter of national security. The Prussian forces of internal order, then, co-operated with their Russian colleagues, although never as much as the Russians desired. Still, with the full support not only of the German Government but of Kaiser Wilhelm II himself the police in Berlin undertook a harassment campaign that was duplicated, to one degree or another by other police agencies throughout Germany. In December 1903 Karl Liebnickht issued a questionnaire to Russians living throughout Germany which reveals the nature of these infringements on the émigrés' civil rights. The questionnaire itself must be considered against a background of a police culture where the forces of order took the view that it possessed the ultimate administrative authority to deal with those foreign nationals who allegedly threatened the stability of the state. So, for example, a foreign resident could be deported merely for political agitation against his or her own government even though this was not an offence under German law. It is with this circumstance in mind that we consider Liebnicht's questionnaire:

> In Germany have you experienced any harassment from Russian or German police especially through:
> a. body searches
> b. searches of your home
> c. examination of your papers
> d. arrests in the home, train stations or the streets or elsewhere
> e. repeated detentions at police stations
> f. through confiscation and examination of passports
> g. through deportation
> h. through the perlustration of your mail
> i. questioning of your landlords or co-tenants, possibly with payment or offer of payment to the interviewee
> j. through being placed under surveillance.[42]

Liebnicht also requested information from the respondents about any repression of university students they might have heard about knowing that most of them would have heard plenty. After the assassination of Russian Minister of Education Bogolepov in February 1901 the police throughout Prussia, again with the strong encouragement of the Kaiser, began a crackdown on Russian students in Prussian educational institutions that would intensify steadily down to the First World War.[43]

Three circumstances affected German attitudes toward the Russians living amongst them after 1905: the 1905 Revolution and its impact on German Social Democracy; the wave of immigration into Germany during the first decade of the twentieth century and the consequent spread of anti-Semitism; and the state of Russo-German relations (see Chapter 3).

The 1905 Revolution first awakened the German populace at large to the number of Russians living in its midst and what some of them were capable of. By 1910 138,000 Russians resided in the *Reich*, an increase of 91,000 over 1901.[44] The Jews amongst this mass stood out. These impoverished Jewish migrants spoke a gaggle of East European languages, although they were bound together by Yiddish and a form of Judaism which even fellow German Jews found archaic and embarassing. As the unfamiliar and often strangely costumed shapes moved from one soup kitchen and compulsory delousing bath to another their alien appearance frightened the ordinary German and this fear aroused suspicion and, at worst anti-Semitism, which flowed out onto resident Russian revolutonaries and students. The number of Jews attending German universities was never more than 1,000 at any given time but their number soon became exaggerated as their ability to move comfortably between Russian and German social democratic circles magnified their importance and lent credence to tsarist propaganda that Jews formed the core of the Russian revolutionary movement. These two stereotypes – of Jew and revolutionary – blended together and contributed to the growing hostility towards all Russian émigrés during and especially after the 1905 Revolution.[45] The enthusiasm of the German social democrats for the events in Russia led the German aristocratic estate and middle class establishments, already feeling uncomfortable with the stereotype of the Russian revolutionary placed before them by the Russian police (see Chapter 3) and fleshed out by the downtrodden and frightening 'other' coming in droves to live amongst them, acquiesced in the breaches of civil rights inflicted upon Russian students and émigrés by the German police, particularly in Prussia and Saxony in the post-1905 years. Arrests of Russian revolutionaries grew apace in 1906 as the government passed ever more restrictive legislation.[46]

As the 1905 Revolution collapsed in Russia the number of Russian revolutionaries escaping retribution by fleeing to Germany (and elsewhere) grew markedly.[47] Berlin, again, became the homing point particularly for the SDs who quickly re-established a lively colony of both young and experienced revolutionaries. Overall, both the SDs and SRs successfully re-established themselves in their old haunts throughout Germany.[48] They soon discovered that life, especially in Prussia, had become less secure. The police of Prussia and Saxony pursued Russian's targeted by the Foreign Agentura[49] with increasing intensity, expelled them and at times put them on trial.[50]

Repression and harassment took their toll as the émigrés fled Berlin. Feeling the pressure of German police repression, most important political émigrés shifted their residency to Paris, where the French police, bound by the Republican ethos discussed in the previous chapter, were, as we shall see, more of a nuisance than a serious threat to the emigration's security. By 1912 those émigrés who remained in Germany found themselves on the periphery of the revolutionary movement.[51]

France and Great Britain

As both Switzerland[52] and Germany became less welcoming, most of the leading revolutionaries made their way to France where they were soon surrounded by colonies populated with true believers. In 1908 the Bolsheviks formally moved the centre of their organisation to Paris, joining the Mensheviks who were already there.[53] The Socialist-Revolutionaries, in particular its terrorist branch, had always found and still found Paris congenial[54] although after 1906 more and more of their leadership chose to enjoy the climate of Italy's Ligurian coast, as we will see below. Still as one émigré remembered, 'in the years between the two revolutions there is no doubt that Paris was the capital of the Russian political émigrés'.[55]

At first glance Paris seems a strange choice. The Franco-Russian Alliance and the subsequent military and financial commitments France made to Russia meant that the French Ministry of the Interior would be inclined to support the operations of the Russian police within its borders and look the other way as both the Prefecture of Paris and the *Sûreté* deepened their co-operation with the Russian police abroad. Worst of all, from the revolutionaries' point of view, the headquarters of the Foreign Agentura operated out of the Russian embassy in Paris itself at 79 Rue de Grenelle as we will see in the second part of this work. Was there no place else for them to go? England and Italy remained options, and as just noted many SRs did eventually resettle, for at least part of the year, in Italy. A few émigrés, however, such as the future Soviet diplomat Ivan Maiskii, made their way to England.

On the face of it England appeared the most attractive destination for Russia's post-1905 political emigration. Britain boasted a long history of political toleration, treating political criminals searching for refuge with mid-Victorian liberal generosity. The Extradition Act of 1870 directed that 'fugitives residing in Britain should never be surrendered for extradition if their crimes were of a political character'. Certainly, in the years before the establishment of the Special Branch in 1887 the Home Office looked the other way as Europe's political émigrés launched large-scale propaganda campaigns from London designed to embarrass their governments with foreign audiences.[56] Indeed, to the vexation of first the Third Section and then of its successor, England, especially London, seemed to attract the literati of the Russian revolutionary movement. The most prominent members of this generation of revolutionaries abroad, men such as Peter Kropotkin, S. M. Stepniak-Kravchinskii, Peter Lavrov and M. A. Bakunin, considered themselves part of the international movement of anarchists and socialists, and along with Alexander Herzen before them acquired broad reputations as writers and thinkers. Still, they wrote often and eloquently about the plight of the Russian people living under tsarist repression, driving the Third Section to distraction. It was not long before London seemed to be swarming with its agents who reported to St. Petersburg on their every move.[57]

It was easy for the Home Office and the English public to welcome such men. Although they seemed bigger than life both to their admirers and enemies alike they were, in fact, loners unwilling or incapable of serving as the magnet for other less esteemed political exiles, as Aron Liberman discovered in his rather unpleasant relationship with Lavrov. These men came from the 'right' background, as scions of the noble estate. Well-educated, they could handle themselves in polite society and they all spoke intelligible English.[58]

By the early 1880s this was about to change. Between April 1881 and June 1882 225,000 Jewish families fled from Russia. While the majority of this first Jewish exodus from Eastern Europe ended up in the United States – the *goldene medina* – others not willing to travel so far settled in East London. By 1891 30,000 of these poverty stricken, bedraggled immigrants resided in England.[59] Their living conditions were horrific and remained so for more than a generation as the slums of Whitechapel could barely cope with the steadily increasing numbers.[60] Along with these migrants came a new generation of émigrés who settled in Whitechapel as well. More than any other Russian émigré cohort, many of those based in London, as opposed to exiles such as Lenin who were just passing through, developed a relationship with the immigrants themselves on the one hand and British radical socialism on the other.[61] England was welcoming and open. Stepniak-Kravinchinskii in a letter to Peter Lavrov wrote excitedly about the oratory he heard in Hyde Park, a venue he attended regularly. Kropotkin and Stepniak-Kravchinskii flourished in the exciting political environment that appeared to be seizing Britain in the late 1880s. Kravchinskii threw himself into all sorts of activities, meeting with English social activists and writers as well as with political émigrés drawn to England from all over Europe, including Italian anarchists (old friends), aging French socialists, and refugees from the Paris Commune. He gave lecture after lecture to students and academics, to workers in sheds and to members of high society in refined salons and, of course, his articles dotted the columns of the British press. In the East End he spoke to the immigrants and declared that Russian workers – he meant those living in London – must band together with their British comrades for a shorter working day.[62]

For his part, Kropotkin's involvement with the British working class grew swiftly. In the fall of 1886 he began a speaking tour that took him through the industrial towns of England and Scotland. He wrote in his memoirs that 'the socialist movement in England was in full swing',[63] telling Peter Lavrov 'of the enormous successes, without exaggeration, of socialism in England'.[64]

The vigorous political life about which Kropotkin wrote continued throughout the 1890s. The complexion of this scene differed markedly from that of the émigré settlements in Switzerland, Germany and France, mostly because of its dedication to international issues expressed partly in the émigrés' concern over local, British, affairs and immigrant politics, and primarily through their literary or journalistic propaganda intended for English-speaking audiences around the world. The absence of the important post-1878 Russian émigrés amongst them did not diminish Tsardom's respect for their literary talent. The high public profiles of Kropotkin and Kravchinskii – Kravchinskii's book *Underground Russia* had created a sensation in the English-speaking world – combined with the even more audacious journalistic achievements and publishing skills of the younger Vladimir Burtsev and Feliks Volkhovskii and their colleagues on the journal *Free Russia*, infuriated the Russian political police abroad which did its best to neutralise their impact (see Chapter 7).

The London emigration had nothing to fear, however, as long as the British government continued to pursue its policy of offering Britain as a safe haven for political émigrés. It is difficult to tell how and when this attitude began to erode, since Scotland Yard and the Special Branch have been anything but forthcoming over their activities from the 1890s onwards. Still, the changes came. In 1890 Rachkovskii wrote to the Director of the Department of Police that he would travel to England in order to develop contacts with the local police which he hoped would be similar to the connections he had already established with the Paris Prefecture. In the winter of 1891 Rachkovskii arrived in London and met with a variety of officials where he encountered a sympathetic hearing.[65]

Rachkovskii developed close relations with several important English police officials[66] whose attitudes toward the foreign political criminals residing on their patch hardened steadily over time.[67] Scotland Yard and the Special Branch had long been used to working with foreign police on the Continent, sending their own detectives to Belgium and France to keep an eye out for well-known political troublemakers who were about to embark for England. While it was not difficult for political refugees to gain entry into England[68] they were closely shadowed by Special Branch detectives from the moment they stepped off the boat.[69] All the major centres of revolutionary life and the homes of significant revolutionary figures, as well, came under surveillance from the late 1880s onward.[70]

As we saw in the previous chapter the British police found themselves in a milieu where no matter what its attitude toward these foreigners, it needed to remain, at least on the surface, honourable and even pristine in the manner with which its agents dealt with them. The Special Branch kept its collusion with foreign police forces secret even from the Home Office although, when the ministry did get a whiff of 'improper' behaviour on the part of its political police, the Home Secretary turned a blind eye in any case. By fostering the stereotype of a benign police system the Home Office encouraged its people to believe themselves free of the invidious political police systems that polluted the Continental political atmosphere.[71] As Bernard Porter has argued, Britain's rulers masked police indiscretions because the entrenched image of toleration for all made easier their efforts at social control. If people contentedly thought themselves free of government surveillance there was less likelihood of serious dissent.

Little did the English public know that the Special Branch employed paid informers to report on émigré political life. And this is only one step away from encouraging political provocation by using these informers to manufacture political conspiracies designed to discredit the refugees in the eyes of the British public. Indeed, it is extremely likely that provocation, possibly without the knowledge of the Home Office or even the senior officers in the Special Branch, became part of the standard operating procedures within the ranks.[72] The Special Branch certainly behaved improperly by co-operating with Rachkovskii's hounding of Vladimir Burtsev.[73]

Burtsev's arrest and subsequent incarceration for the preaching and glorifying of terrorism and regicide in his own rabidly inflammmatory journal *Narodovolets* (*The People's Will*) in 1898[74] served as a warning shot across the emigration's bow that the winds of British politics had begun to shift as the British government began to seek improved relations with Tsardom.[75] Still, the emigration flourished, Kropotkin continued to speak frequently at Jewish meetings in the East End and after Lenin arrived he too offered a series of lectures in London so successful that Kropotkin believed they threatened the place of Anarchism within the London emigration's political spectrum.[76]

But these events, even the establishment of the famous anarchist workers' club on Jubilee Street which hosted a cross-section of Europe's political fugitives (including Lenin on his 1908 visit to London) during its lifetime, and offered local émigrés and their sympathisers, particularly amongst the Jewish immigration, a haven from the stresses of their everyday lives, could not conceal that the heyday of England as a centre for Russian revolutionary life had come to an end.[77] Kropotkin, who lived in England for sixteen years, witnessed this decline. The failure of radical socialism in Britian by the early new century combined with the hardship of living so far from the new revolutionary centres in Switzerland and Germany drove him into a depression. To a comrade in Paris he wrote: 'Such gloom. This London: I passionately detest this English exile.'[78]

Following the success of Stolypin's counterrevolution in 1906 and 1907 émigrés made their way to England again. It remained a relatively easy place to live. Although the Special Branch was becoming more professional it did not yet compare with French intrusiveness or German brutal arbitrariness in police matters. British liberalism had worn thin but it still existed and political criminals remained, at least down to the war, an acceptable category of resident. Ivan Maiskii portrays a life far more tranquil and happier than émigré existence in France:

> And then the phlegmatic character of the English, their tolerant and homely way of life and their traditional moderation in politics produced an atmosphere very different from that which prevailed in France. All this made things very much easier for the émigré colony. Of course there were feuds and private quarrels here too, but they never reached

> the heroic proportions which were common on the other side of the Channel.[79]

At first glance it is hard to believe that more Russian revolutionaries did not settle in this welcoming environment. Maiskii, himself, offers two reasons for this. First the size of London itself. London is such a large city in population and area, Maiskii remembered, that the Russians felt lost there and that distance alone prevented frequent meetings. A second factor he considered important was the widespread opinion of England as an ideological backwater, where socialism stagnated in these pre-First World War years. The lack of radical political activity of the kind upon which émigré intellect thrived meant that none of the leaders of the revolutionary movements chose to reside in London and no newspapers or journals were published there in the post-1905 era. As Maiskii remarks, the revolutionary leadership 'showed marked reluctance to include London in those rounds of visits which were customary in those days'.[80] Lenin made his last visit in 1908 and other giants of the Russian emigration rarely made an appearance. The emigration felt isolated and cut off from the ideological battles being fought in France and, in terms of geographical distance, cut off from Russia itself. The colony fell into inertia, offering virtually no help to the cause of revolution.

The isolation of the Russian revolutionary émigré colony in England at the turn of the century had almost nothing to do with the machinations of either Russian or British police, or even the parlous state of radical socialism in Great Britian; rather it reflected a sea change in the strategic focus of the revolutionary emigration, of the revolution itself.

By the first years of the twentieth century two political parties – both with rapidly growing domestic Russian memberships – dominated the revolutionary emigration. The Russian Social Democratic Workers Party and the Socialist-Revolutionary Party were surrounded by satellite political parties based most often on nationality. The Russian émigrés in London of the 1880s and 1890s had become political dinosaurs whose literary and journalistic efforts had been directed outward towards European and American audiences. The founders of the new parties, men such as G. V. Plekhanov, A. N. Potresov, P. B. Akselrod, V. I. Lenin and IU. Martov, F. I. Dan, V. I. Zasulich, V. M. Chernov, M. Natanson and the terrorists such as Boris Savinkov and Mikhail Gots, amongst dozens of their fellows, did not look westward at all but back to Russia. Even in the terrible days durng the Stolypin era between 1906 and 1911 when internicine warfare within the political emigration became particularly vicious, the revolutionaries' focus remained on Russia. England was simply too far away, too self-satisfyingly bourgeois in its politics to become a base for launching the Russian Revolution. The 'filth of [British] imperialism and reaction' which so infuriated the frustrated Kropotkin repelled the leaders of the revolutionary movements in exile and their most dedicated followers as well.[81]

Life in England, then, remained safe, but it was not stimulating. It was Paris that became the post-1905 emigration's staging ground for the next assault on Tsardom. Paris, bathed in the romantic revolutionary aura that permeated the city's political history, became the acknowledged centre of émigré life in the post-1905 years. The dynamic of left-wing life that newly arrived Russian revolutionaries encountered[82] led them to think, as the writer Ilya Ehrenberg remembered, that everything in Paris 'seemed unexpected and everything was possible'.[83]

There were other more practical reasons for settling in France too, as the Paris Prefecture noted: Paris is a difficult city for the maintenance of surveillance. In addition, the Russians maintained several libraries where they had access to a full list of Russian newspapers, books and other reading material which sustained their connection with the homeland. If they could afford it, Russian restaurants catered to their familiar tastes and offered meeting places for conversation, which as the Prefecture noted was always in Russian which, of course, made eavesdropping extremely difficult. Public meetings dealing with Russian revolutionary politics also conducted solely in Russian were commonplace as well. And lastly, the foreign radical press in German, Russian and Yiddish, along with Paris-based Russian newspapers of all political stripes blanketed the Parisian scene, immersing the revolutionary emigration within a familiar milieu.[84]

As for the French police, they had taken the Russian émigrés seriously since the days of *Narodnaia Volia* and the assassination of Tsar Alexander II.[85] Nevertheless, although noisy and willing to harass and arrest émigrés they caught in the act of preparing for terrorist campaigns in Russia, they always remained reluctant to co-operate openly with the tsarist government.[86] After the signing of the Franco-Russian Alliance in 1894 the *Sûreté* and the Paris Prefecture certainly maintained close surveillance over the Russian revolutionaries living in France, and looked the other way as French agents of the Russian police harassed members of the emigration, even allowing them to body search émigrés in public.[87] At more senior levels the French government still feared the influence of its own left-wing press and politicians and this concern limited how far it would go in support of its Russian allies in matters of arresting and deporting even the most hated and feared revolutionaries.[88]

In any case, French police intelligence never attained any great heights. The reports of both the *Sûreté* and the Paris Prefecture are often innaccurate, prone to hysteria and at times extraordinarily simplistic.[89] It is difficult to see how they could have added much to the intelligence gathered by the Foreign Agentura (see Part II of this work).

Whatever the political and strategic benefits of life in Paris, the harshness of everyday life in the City of Lights comes through both French and Russian police reports and the memoirs of revolutionary émigrés.[90] Members of the political emigration in Paris were shunned by the majoirty of the 35,000 Russians who made France their home by 1911.[91] Isolation was not the only discomfort. Émigrés lived five and six to a room. In the Gobelin district of Paris every home housed three or four Slavic tenants crammed together. They pooled their resources, struggling to survive on a few *centimes* worth of bread and some tea per day while doing their best to avoid the census takers and the agents of the Prefecture's *Brigade des Garnis* which maintained surveillance over Parisian hotels and rooming houses.[92]

Daily political life was no less stressful.[93] The émigrés met informally each day across a particular set of restaurants and cafés where they circulated news and shared gossip.[94] The conversation at these times reflected their subdued mood. Unlike the pre-1905 emigration, this group, of veterans and newcomers alike, believed that their failure to take advantage of the revolutionary situation in 1905 meant that the opportunity to overthrow Tsardom had been lost, perhaps forever. The prime ministership of Peter Stolypin, with its agrarian reforms and restructuring of the electoral law that led to the election of a conservative Third Duma combined with the exhaustion of both the working class and the peasantry to create a bleak picture of Russia's revolutionary future. Vladimir Burtsev's exposure of dozens of undercover agents within the revolutionary movements between 1907 and 1914 increased the emigration's sense of hopelessness. Several of these *agent provocateurs* were up to the time of their disgrace prominent members of the revolutionary movements (see Chapter 11 for Burtsev's campaign and its impact both on the émigrés and the Russian political police).

The appalling pyschological state of the emigration in France caught the eye of the Foreign Agentura which reported it to Headquarters in St Petersburg. The Special Section, the bureau managing the political police throughout the Empire and abroad (see Chapter 4), duly included the Paris Office's analysis in one of its memoranda:

> The Department of Police has received information from the field concerning émigré circles in Paris whose existence at the present time is severely disorganised. [The reasons for this state of affairs] are [mutual] distrust and the decline in the level of morale [of the emigration]. As a result, the majority of émigrés wish to return to Russia and live here, even though they are fearful of painful punishment for current or past political crimes in Russia.

The report concluded that for every illegal escaping into emigration, there was one desiring to return to Russia.[95]

The Special Section may have been exaggerating the extent of the demoralisation to which the emigration in France had succumbed. After all, by 1913 the strike movement reborn in response to the Lena goldfield massacre in the spring of 1912 probably drew dozens of émigrés back to Russia who desired nothing more than to participate directly in the struggle against Tsardom. Still, none of this alters the bleak portrait of life in Parisian emigration. Constant ideological battles amongst the various parties and fractions, hunger, and miserable winter and summer climates often endured in stiflingly crowded shelters, led to both nervous and physical disorders. For many who suffered from the seemingly endemic chest complaints from bronchitis to tuberculosis a warmer, drier, cleaner climate was essential. Others just wished to escape the stifling heat of a Parisian summer by spending July through August at the sea coast. For all of these reasons Italy's Ligurian coast appeared an attractive alternative to Paris for at least part of the year.

Italy

Residence on the Mediteranean coastline offered ill, exhausted and psychologically fragile émigrés welcoming surroundings where those who wished to shun factional disputes could do so. Italy appeared attractive for other reasons as well and these involved the revolutionary myth surrounding Italy's formation on the one hand and the nature of the Italian state on the other.

The Garibaldi myth strongly influenced the Russian émigré intelligentsia in the post-1905 era. The emigration chased out of Russia by the counter-revolution found Garibaldi's trials and tribulations in exile and his ultimate victory over the old order heartening and something to be emulated. The centenary of Garibaldi's birth celebrated in Italy by Russian émigrés of every political stripe and by Russian students studying at Italian universities reflected this special bond between Russian and Italian radical traditions that so attracted the Russians to the peninsula.

To the Russians Italy under Giolitti seemed not merely a free country with a strong constitution but one which embraced both socialism and the working class. The Giolitti government, emulating the protection that England and Switzerland offered Italian revolutionaries years earlier, declared that it would deny tsarist requests for extradition. Even the Socialist-Revolutionaries who came to live in the Ligurian arc believed that despite Giolitti's hatred of terrorists they would be able to live in freedom. The Ligurian coast also offered excellent communications between the various émigré colonies and other centres of the revolutionary emigration outside of Italy. Also, ships from the Black Sea regularly commuted beween the Ligurian port towns and

Odessa allowing communication and smuggling networks to be established between Liguria and Russia itself.[96] Finally, Italian socialists themselves buoyed their Russian comrades' outlook by pronouncing that the revolutionary movement in Russia required the unqualified support of socialists everywhere and particularly of Italian socialism.

The number of colonies in the arc did not change much in the post-1905 era. Each colony manifested a particular ideological, cultural or political perspective and the dynamic of life within them followed a consistent pattern. They grew slowly and then suddenly some ideological schism caused them to disintegrate in the blink of an eye, only so that they could reform anew around a resident family, old friends or sympathisers. Unfortunately it only took someone from 'cursed Paris' to re-introduce questions of principle, intrigues and futile arguments to disrupt a colony's equilibruim and cause it to collapse again.[97]

The major Russian émigré centre was Nervi, a medium sized town with a population of between 8,000 and 10,000 people. Its climate made it a perfect place for people suffering from tuberculosis. About 2,000 people ill with a variety of pulmonary diseases made Nervi their summer home. Nervi became so populated with Russians that hotels catering completely to a Russian clientele did a thriving business and the Russian community even established its own hospital.[98] The numbers of émigrés in Nervi changed constantly from season to season. Although the emigration enjoyed the climatic and pyschological relief Nervi and towns like it offered, their living conditions remained much as they were in Paris. For the most part they endured poverty stricken lives. The Prefect of Genoa writing about the conditions of Russian life in Nervi reported, 'there are around 300 refugees nearly all of them members of the Russian terrorist group.... They crowd together in furnished rooms where they live in the most squalid misery in inconceivable filth.'[99]

San Remo, so close to France, became the base for the SR terrorist Battle Organisation and a popular retreat for such feared revolutionaries as Boris Savinkov, Peter Karpovich, Vladimir Burtsev and the grand old man of Populism, Mark Natanson, as well as other prominent SRs who also vacationed there. The Italian police maintained a close watch over this colony enlisting the aid of the French authorities to help them keep track of the comings and going of the most infamous residence of San Remo.[100]

Throughout the years of the emigration's residence on the peninsula between 1905 and 1917, the Italian government's attitude toward the emigration remained ambivalent, swaying between its democratic principles and Giolitti's obsession with terrorism. By 1910 the Giolitti government's obsession with anarchism and terror spilled over into the Russian emigration. Part of the reason for this was the growing number of SRs who were taking up residence on the Ligurian coast combined with the successful impact of tsarist propaganda that labelled virtually all revolutionary émigrés as terrorists (see Chapter 3). Poorly qualified Italian prefects often unable to distinguish between SRs and SDs resorted to painting the entire emigration with the twin labels of 'terrorist' and/or 'revolutionary party-man'. At the highest administrative level within the institutions of internal order, however, the attitude *vis-à-vis* the Russians was different. The surveillance of foreigners within Italy was under the direction of the *Delegato di Siccureza*, a humane man who thought of the Russians only as an economic problem. As for Giolitti himself, he faced a dilemma. Although deeply worried about any scent of terrorism and anxious to accomodate the Russian government, he could not deal with the Russians harshly without tarnishing the liberal and democratic political image he so carefully fostered over the years. This meant that his government would only take action against those very few émigrés who commited crimes under Italian law. As for the SRs, they may have plotted against Tsardom in endless discussions, but on the whole they lived retiring lives often in grinding poverty, so outside of the normal supervision of foreigners that the Italian police largely left them alone.[101]

Unfortunately for the emigration, none of this prevented the Italian government from clandestinely supporting Russian police operations on their soil. In 1911 with the knowledge of the Italians, St Petersburg dispatched Russian undercover agents to infiltrate the Ligurian colonies, while at the same time the Foreign Agentura in Paris sent Italian-speaking detectives to initiate surveillance over the movements of important émigrés.[102]

Detectives in the Foreign Agentura's employ swarmed over the Russian communities, and sometimes accompanied by a local police official had the audiacity to search their quarry's flats and question them.[103] Much of the most intense surveillance took place in and around Cavi di Lavagna which the Prefect of Genoa called 'a nest of terrorists'.[104]

In 1910 the Foreign Agentura in Paris established a resident agent in Cavi named Eugene Invernizzi. Invernizzi operated out of a room above the town's Trattoria where he could observe all the local goings on. Perlustration of émigré mail became his first task and he enlisted the support of the local postal officials to supply him with all the outgoing and incoming correspondence addressed to members of the Russian colony. It proved to be rather easy for an Italian agent to enlist the aid of the ordinarily suspicious local population who instinctively distrusted these unusual foreigners in their midst. The local Italian communities viewed men such as Invernizzi, whom they respected and envied, as protectors against the Russian 'cutthroats' living amongst them.

Every morning with the help of one of the postmasters, Invernizzi perused the mail looking for any suspicious markings on envelopes that would indicate the nature of their contents, since the revolutionaries often exchanged correspondence through false postal drops. He opened any suspicious letter. The agent could not read a word of Russian so he copied the letters by placing a piece of wax paper over them and then carefully outlining the

Cyrillic. He then sent the wax paper copies to the Foreign Agentura in Paris for analysis.

Invernizzi kept a detailed diary of each émigré's movements. The task was not as daunting as it may seem. The Russian revolutionaries living in Cavi, as elsewhere on the Ligurian coast, remained isolated from the Italian population, coming into contact with only their landlords and those Italians who worked for them. Many of these people, of course, were on Invernizzi's payroll.

Across the Italian Riviera other agents duplicated Invernizzi's activities. The Russians suspected what was going on and complained but the Italian authorities did nothing.[105] Prominent émigrés such as Viktor Chernov attempted to give their shadows the slip by moving from town to town especially to Spezia, an Italian naval base where Russian policemen could not follow. The Italian authorities worried about the presence of so many Russian radicals living amongst naval personnel and arsenal workers with whom they might wish to share their 'advanced' ideas and clearly considered expelling them from the town, but it was a radical measure that the cautious government decided not to take. Instead it chose merely to keep them under surveillance and issue regulations which restricted their movements.[106] At least the émigrés who resided in Spezia had shed the Russian police surveillance. Whether they had left the undercover agents behind is another matter.

The focus of the Giolitti government fell upon other Russian revolutionaries, less interested in the charms of the Ligurian coast, who formed other sorts of colonies on Italian soil. One such colony of non-affiliated social democrats established itself in Milan hoping to take advantage of Giolitti's industrial boom in order to find work. These revolutionaries came from assorted backgrounds. They rejected organised factions considering themselves 'practicals' who wished to work with the energetic Italian socialist movement in Milan on behalf of the Italian proletariat. Eventually, 300 of these émigrés made a conscious decision not to remain on the periphery of Italian society and formed an association of Russian workers. Milanese authorities, although socialist, became suspicious of the association and the Prefect of Police in Milan undertook to keep them under surveillance. A concerned Prime Minister wrote his Prefect, 'you need to oversee particularly these émigrés in Milan. It is essential to keep special watch over them.'[107]

The Russian revolutionaries in Milan were an example of the urge by revolutionary émigrés to do something besides argue and condemn. They wanted to participate in Milanese life; give their lives meaning; do something useful. They believed that by throwing themselves into this work they would be able to throw off 'the blind alley of senseless party feuds'.[108]

Maxim Gorky, the internationally acclaimed author, offered an alternative émigré experience on the Isle of Capri. The story of Gorky's famous Capri school is too well-known to repeat here in its entirety. There are, however, some aspects of the pyschology underlying the school's creation which vividly reflect the impact of emigration on its participants. An article in *Russkaia Mysl* (*Russian Thought*) in 1908 portrayed the exiles as tired of wandering from country to country, always fleeing the police, being forced to hide their identity and suffering from ever-present poverty. Many wished to abandon this life, buy a piece of land on the Isle of Capri, build a house there and participate in the idealised intellectual life that supposedly characterised the Capri community. The reality of life on Capri for its Russian residence was, of course, something else entirely. Nevertheless, a Russian colony grew up around Gorky in Capri. Gorky conceived of the colony after he arrived in Naples from the United States in late 1906. The writer made his way to Capri where he established a small community – a little bit of Russia 'thousands of miles' from home. Gorky surrounded himself with those who shared his hatred for Tsardom and, like the storyteller himself, were suffering from the pain of exile.[109]

In July 1909 the tsarist Department of Police issued a memorandum informing its political police bureaus that Gorky had begun a school for propagandists to prepare young social democratic cadres for 'practical work' amongst ordinary Russians within the Empire.[110] It attracted both veteran revolutionaries who would teach there and 'green youths' from Russia who wished to be taught by them.[111] All of the school's students – committed social democrats of no particular faction – attended classes given by some of the most interesting and creative social democrats residing in Europe.[112] The school, boasting only a small enrollment and quickly isolated from both the Bolshevik and Menshevik factions of the RSDWP,[113] created a stir out of all proportion to its possible impact.

The Giolitti government, never quite sure exactly what forces within Russian socialism presented a danger to Italy, did its best to contain the impact of Gorky's presence on the Italian political scene, and turned a blind eye to the Russian undercover agents who descended on the island colony. The presence of Russian agents on Capri became an open secret, but the colonists' protests fell on deaf ears. As for the Capri school's graduates, the Russian Border Gendarmes, notified of their movements by the Foreign Agentura, arrested them at the frontier as they attempted to infiltrate back into the Empire to carry out their work.[114]

Despite the trials and tribulations confronted by the Russian emigration in Italy, overall the revolutionaries thought this their most secure and welcoming refuge. Plekhanov who spent considerable time in Italy – his wife established a sanitarium in San Remo[115] – wrote an open letter of gratitude to the Italian people. In *Il Popolo d'Italia* (*The People of Italy*) in 1918 he expressed his and most other émigrés' feelings, perhaps with some hyperbole, about their Italian sojourn:

> The time of banishment has finished for us, but that time was very long. Most banished Russians came to Italy seeking refuge. And they always found the widest hospitality and the most noble sympathy. The Italians have been brothers to those who were oppressed and who fought for liberty. We thank the Italian people for their hospitality and for their noble sentiments. We will never forget how much we owe your beautiful country.[116]

In retrospect Plekhanov could afford to be generous in expressing his gratitude for Italian refuge. The dreamed-of revolution had finally come. For a brief moment in Russian revolutionary history all of those agonising years of exile, laden with ideological warfare, internecine battles for power amongst the factions within each movement, material deprivation, overwhelming loneliness and homesickness, psychological depression and most of all the immense burden of self-doubt that plagued even the most single-minded and dedicated revolutionaries, appeared worthwhile. For a few amongst the Bolsheviks it certainly was.

3

Brothers in Arms? The Beginnings of International Police Co-operation and the Russian Revolutionary Emigration

Tsardom understood that an effective campaign against Russian revolutionaries abroad required the support of those countries in which the émigrés resided. The minister of foreign affairs believed that such co-operation would not be difficult to obtain as long as he and his fellow minister from internal affairs could somehow connect the Russian revolutionary emigration to the Anarchist terror that so coloured European politics in the last quarter of the nineteenth century, spreading panic wherever it appeared.

Ironically, the terrorists who plotted against tsarist royalty and officialdom during the reigns of the last three tsars were in the main not Anarchists. Most were members of the populist *Narodnaia Volia* (People's Will) group and its descendent, the *Boevaia Organizatsii* (Battle Organisation or BO) of the Socialist-Revolutionary Party. Later, the most daring terrorists belonged to the Maximalists. As the Russian revolutionary movement grew in both size and complexity Tsardom understood that the evolving complexion of the Russian revolutionary movement was simply too difficult and too confusing to explain intelligibly to outsiders. Indeed, even if they had managed to do so, the image of Russia under siege from a variety of political groups would have irreparably damaged Tsardom's reputation amongst the Europeans. Instead, as we shall see in subsequent chapters, the tsarist authorities did their best to create a stereotypical Russian terrorist designed to match the profile of their western anarchist brethren – a group that Europe's forces of order recognised with crystal clarity.

At first the word 'Nihilist' – originally a literary creation of the great novelist Ivan Turgenev in his book *Fathers and Sons* – and the scary image of a humourless fanatic it conjured up served this purpose. Afterwards, as we saw in the previous chapter and will again see below, the Russian police tried largely without success to expand the already fuzzy stereotype still further by including most of the revolutionary emigration within it. The purpose of such obfuscation was to encourage Europe to join Tsardom in a united anti-'anarchist' campaign which would, of course, as part of its brief unsettle if not destroy the Russian revolutionary emigration as a political force.

The Russian desire for a united European effort to stem the tide of terrorism infesting Europe in the last quarter of the nineteenth century, like so much of the story contained in this book, places Tsardom at the centre of European domestic and international affairs. Nonetheless, Russia's overriding concern was with its own terrorists whose ability to evade Tsardom's grasp by absconding abroad where they could operate in virtually complete freedom drove Tsardom to distraction. So, when tsarist Minister of Internal Affairs A. T. Loris-Melikov, long worried about the potential of the revolutionary émigré terrorists to wreak havoc at home, strove to create an international agreement against 'anarchists' he was acting in Russia's interests alone and never realised or probably never cared about the future implications for law and order in Europe that his campaign set in motion. Not quite half a century later Russia's initial efforts to create a unified front against the Russian revolutionary emigration would lead to the establishment of Interpol: an international police organisation designed to pursue criminals across the world's borders.

At first, Loris-Melikov focused on much less ambitious goals *vis-à-vis* Russian terrorism, including the deployment of only Russian institutions in the war against the emigration. He soon discovered that being part of the European community of nations complicated life considerably.

Shortly after the explosion in the Winter Palace of 5 February 1880, a young terrorist named Lev Nikolaevich Gartman who had participated in the affair fled to Paris with the agents of the Third Section in pursuit. After a street brawl with the Russian agents who were tracking him Gartman was arrested, apparently on the orders of Prefect of Paris Andrieux without any consultation with his own Ministry.[1] On 16 February the Tsarist government formally requested Gartman's extradition[2] on political grounds and clearly expected a rapid positive response.

As the word spread of Gartman's plight, left-wing Parisian public opinion mobilised in his defence. The pressure brought to bear on the French government on Gartman's behalf seemed to come from every quarter of left-wing European society. Even the threat made by the Russian Ministry of Foreign Affairs that the failure to extradite the terrorist would be considered an unfriendly act and could lead to closer ties with Germany could not overcome the Third Republic's reticence as it confronted this groundswell of opinion. In the end the French refused the Russian request.[3]

The decision did not sit well with Loris-Melikov, who now came to believe that only an enforceable international convention could prevent a repetition of the Gartman case. In a report to the tsar he identified Europe as a safe haven for Russia's terrorists where they could plan regicide and other terrorist acts virtually under the protection of friendly governments. As we shall see in subsequent chapters Loris-Melikov and his director of the Department of Police wished to expand Russian police operations designed to harass and undermine the revolutionary emigration. He believed that such action should form part of what the Russian government considered a three-pronged campaign. The soon-to-be established Foreign Agentura of the Department of Police would maintain continuous and intimate informal contacts with European political police forces and carry out the harassment of the emigration by both legitimate and nefarious means; the Department of Police itself would oversee the Foreign Agentura's operations, serve as an intelligence hub and manager of communications for operations abroad; and the Ministry of Foreign Affairs would arrange for as much co-operation as it could through official diplomatic channels, and represent the interests of the Russian political police abroad when formal agreement or acquiescence in its activities proved necessary, and when matters of extradition were to be negotiated.[4]

Melikov made it clear, however, that a successful campaign against Russian revolutionary terror depended most upon the conclusion of an anti-anarchist agreement with other European states as an effective means of dealing with political crime. A European-wide anti-anarchist pact would *inter alia* sanction the open co-operation amongst Europe's political police in a united war against terrorism.

The assassination of Tsar Alexander II on 1 March 1881 by *Narodnaia Volia* increased the urgency of these negotiations. The Ministry of Foreign Affairs and the Minstry of Internal Affairs (through the newly formed Department of State Police) undertook secret diplomatic negotiations with most European states in an effort to establish the extradition treaty arrangements Tsardom so desired. The Ministry of Foreign Affairs managed to wheedle agreements of a sort out of Austria-Hungary, Rumania and subsequently Germany. Director of the Department of State Police Plehve, undoubtedly grateful for whatever co-operation he could acquire, boasted about the agreement negotiated with the Germans even though these very limited agreements only dealt with control over the comings and goings of suspicious persons at border checkpoints in areas contiguous to the Russian Empire.[5]

France, Switzerland and Great Britain, where most émigrés resided, would not consider joining Russia in any agreement that even hinted at inconveniencing the enemies of Tsardom living in their midst.[6]

France, not wishing to exacerbate the tension between itself and Russia raised by the Gartman affair, chose to play a diplomatic game which protected the Russian revolutionary émigrés sheltering in France, while, at the same time, appearing to satisfy at least some of Russia's requests *vis-à-vis* the revolutionary emigration. In November 1882 the President of France allowed the Vice Director of the Department of State Police to visit the offices of the Paris Prefecture, and from 10a.m. to 7p.m. for the period of one week to peruse the Prefecture's files on Russian revolutionaries living in Paris. The Vice Director, a man named Zhukov, was not a political policemen and did not know much about the revolutionary emigration. As a result, he returned to St Petersburg with virtually no useful information.[7]

This does not mean that the French chose to do nothing. Part of the game was to do something but not much. In December of 1882 the Prefecture of Paris arrested Peter Kropotkin along with other members of the International for propagandising amongst French workers in the city of Lyon. In this case Kropotkin had made the terrible mistake of breaking French law. Despite the intercession of Europe's intellectual elite he received a five-year prison sentence. The Russians were overjoyed, awarding the French minister of justice, the procurator and senior police officials on the case with orders and rewards.[8]

Switzerland, a small and powerless nation, could not afford to ignore Russian demands for access to information on their revolutionaries or to demands for their extradition. Russian pressure on Switzerland was unrelenting.[9] In 1873 the Swiss signed an extradition treaty with the Russians. Nonetheless, the Swiss resisted extraditing anyone charged with the commission of a political crime and its dilatory behaviour discomforted the tsarist regime no end.[10]

The British government proved to be the most recalcitrant of all. As we have seen, Britain prided itself as a haven for political refugees and formally did very little in response to Russia's call for police co-operation in maintaining surveillance over the growing number of Russian political émigrés in England during the 1870s and 1880s. Even though the British government began to co-operate more with the Russian authorities as Anglo-Russian relations warmed toward the end of the nineteenth century (see Chapter 7) the policy of asylum remained until the early twentieth century. Britain rigorously adhered to the principles on extradition defined by the so-called Oxford Resolutions which were adopted by the Institute of International Law at its Oxford Meeting in 1880 (Articles 13 and 14 were remodelled at the Geneva meeting in 1892). As Professor of International Law John Westlake wrote in 1904, Articles 11 and 12 decreed 'that extradition ought only to be granted for acts which are also criminal by the law of the state on which the demand is made and which are of some gravity'. Article 13 of the Oxford Resolutions proved even more vexing to the Russians. It stated in part:

> Extradition is inadmissible for purely political crimes or offences: Nor can it be admitted for unlawful acts of a mixed character or connected with political crimes or offences, also called relative political offences...
>
> [T]hey cannot give occasion to extradition unless they are acts of odious barbarism or vandalism forbidden by the laws of war.... [11]

In the face of such obstinacy, the Russian Ministry of Foreign Affairs chose to pursue the Loris-Melikov idea of an anti-anarchist pact which it hoped would override democratic Europe's legal and customary practices with respect to the protection of political criminals.

Such an agreement would be eagerly welcomed at the informal level of international policing where by the 1880s Europe's police could point to – at least amongst themselves – a rather long history of police co-operation especially in political matters, except, of course, for the stubborn British.[12]

The technological advances in recordkeeping and suspect identification steadily improved throughout the nineteenth and early twentieth centuries further facilitating such co-operation. Although a completely uniform system of suspect identification could not be agreed upon before the First World War the process of discussing this issue itself contributed to the sense of a developing international police culture. A common language of identificiation came into being that allowed policemen no matter what their native language to communicate with each other over the tracking of suspects.[13]

The evolution of a common police culture amongst the forces of European order received a considerable stimulus from the Rome Conference convened in response to the wave of anarchist terror that appeared to be sweeping across Europe in the 1890s. The assassination of Tsar Alexander II in 1881 stunned Europe to be sure, but it did not drive the Europeans to support Count Loris-Melikov's call for an international agreement directed against Anarchism. No doubt most European states saw in Melikov's call his desire to conflate the anarchist issue with the growing domestic crisis in Russia, which went far beyond the assassination of a tsar. Europe displayed little sympathy for Tsardom's plight.

By the late 1890s things had changed. The shoe was on the other foot. The assassination of their own politicians and finally in 1898 the murder of the Empress of Austria in Geneva drove Europe – even the reticent French, British and Swiss – into declaring war on anarchism. For the first time the diplomats and their police appeared united.

The Rome Conference opened on 24 November 1898 before 54 delegates representing the whole of Europe. In attendance beside the bevy of senior and lesser diplomats and the necessary bureaucrats could be found the directors of the Russian, French and Belgian police systems and several important municipal police chiefs. Russia and Germany led the discussions which focused on three issues: the creation of a single, straightforward definition of Anarchism which would serve as the basis for marking this doctrine as a criminal offence acceptable to all of Europe; the promulgation of an international agreement on the handling of Anarchism by Europe's forces of law and order; and the organisation of the technical arrangements amongst the appropriate authorities to facilitate the war against Anarchism.[14]

The Conference lasted for a month, breaking up on 21 December after it appeared to accomplish its aims. First of all, the conferees arrived at a definition of 'Anarchism' which even the most politically unsophisticated of Europe's citizens could understand. It characterised Anarchism not through its ideology but rather by its behaviour, decreeing an anarchist act to be one 'having as its aim the destruction through violent means of all social organisation'. An Anarchist was any person who committed such an act.[15] Not surprisingly the definition had been proposed by Ambassador Nelidov, the Russian delegate to the Conference, for it was so vague that it could be applied to Russian terrorists who were not Anarchists. As the final protocol declares 'anarchism has no relation to politcs'.[16] Terrorists killed for killing's sake. If this was the case, the assassination of Alexander II and attempts on the life of his successor did not have political meaning but were simply the acts of lunatics who, like their western counterparts, were beyond the pale of civilisation. Therefore, implicitly Russia's political condition was no more or less unstable than those of other European states equally plagued by terror.

The French signed the protocol with the proviso that establishment of direct contact amongst the police chiefs of Europe must be strictly veiled from public view. Both the British and the Swiss delegates to the Conference found the definition of an anarchist act to be so broad as to be meaningless and refused to sign the protocol, although they expressed their support for its purpose. The Swiss declared that they would informally support it on a case-by-case basis.[17] As for the British, Albion's delegate to the Conference, Sir Philippe Curie, declared that Great Britain supported the goals of the Conference and acknowledged that Britain, too, shouldered an international responsibility 'as far as possible and by legitimate means' to protect other countries from 'the violent acts of anarchists'.

The Russians must have returned to St Petersburg believing they had won a great victory. Finally, it seemed, the tsarist government had achieved Loris-Melikov's dream of a united front against terror which through adroit use of propaganda and calculated measures of provocation could be effectively employed in Tsardom's deepening struggle with the revolutionary emigration as a whole.

Russian euphoria did not last long. While it is true that the improvement in international police co-operation added considerable pressure to revolutionary émigré life,[18] serious formal co-operation proved illusory. The issue of the uniqueness and at least partial incompatibility of each nation's legal culture and its justice system that plagues international police co-operation to this day prevented the type of intimate relationship among the forces of law dreamed of by tsarist officials. In a secret memorandum sent to Berlin, the Russians complained to German colleagues that the Rome Conference had not fulfilled their high hopes. The memo admitted that since 1898 the police departments of Europe exchanged intelligence on the better known Anarchists more freely than had previously been the case 'clearly facilitating the surveillance of dangerous elements'. Unfortunately, the Russians noted, the system failed to prevent further assassinations.[19] The author of the memorandum could not know that Tsardom's struggle with terror and revolution had not even begun.

On 14 February 1901 Peter Karpovich mortally wounded N. P. Bogolepov, Russia's reactionary minister of education. Four days later an attempt was made on the life of K. P. Pobedonostsev, the man most closely identified with Tsar Nicholas II's reactionary policies, forcing the Department of Police to redouble its protection of Russia's most senior officials. Fontanka's intensified security failed to save the life of Minister of Internal Affairs D. S. Sipiagin gunned down in his own reception room by a young member of the Socialist-Revolutionary's Battle Organisation on 15 April 1902. The terrorists, as we shall see in subsequent chapters, planned their murderous assaults against Russian officialdom in the relative security of foreign exile to where they returned after their deeds were done. The outcomes of the Rome Conference did not secure the safety of Tsardom's *sanovniki* (high ranking officials).

In response to Sipiagin's assassination the Russians increased and systematised the seeding of the European press with a wave of anti-émigré and pro-tsarist propaganda.[20] This disinformation made little impact on European public opinion. In late 1903 the Russians then resorted to a request that the signees of the Rome protocol acquiesce in the implementation of a provision that had been slotted into its conclusion at Russia's insistence. This provision declared that the states of Europe make a sincere effort to arrive at an understanding over the critical issue of taking joint administrative, that is, extra legal, action *vis-à-vis* anarchist terror, and it reminded the participants in the Rome Conference, whether they were signatories to the protocol or not, of their good intentions expressed six years before to frame a more specific agreement to counteract terrorism.

In response to Russian pressure Europe convened another conference in 1904 with St Petersburg as its venue. Without great enthusiasm this Anti-Anarchist Conference produced a document entitled a 'Secret Protocol for the International War on Anarchism' signed on 14 March according to the Russian documents by nine[21] states: Austria-Hungary, Bulgaria, Denmark, Germany, Norway, Roumania, Russia, Serbia and Turkey. Switzerland refused to sign despite Russian willingness to accept Swiss amendments to the protocol dealing with articles on expulsion. In 1907, however, succumbing to both German and Russian pressure, Switzerland reluctantly signed the protocol in secret. Britain, France, the United States and, surprisingly, Italy – even though the Giolitti government deeply feared anarchist terror – refused to sign. The liberal and conservative split amongst the Great Powers did not bode well for the future of international relations.[22]

The signatory states declared in the first paragraph of the Protocol that they 'are joined together in the conscious need to oppose with energetic resistance the developing anarchist movement'. Within the main section of the Protocol itself its authors gave substance to the initial aim of the Rome Conference of spreading and intensifying police co-operation across Europe by presenting detailed instructions for the creation of an administrative structure for international police co-operation that would ultimately serve as the schematic for the development of Interpol in 1923.[23] 'In each [signatory] state', decreed the Protocol, 'there will be established a Central Police Bureau whose purpose will be to gather information about anarchists and their activities'. The Protocol called upon each such national bureau to exchange detailed intelligence on the movements of all anarchists across international borders and on any 'criminal plots of an anarchist nature about which it has received information'. All communications between signatory nations were to be carried out in a code especially created for the purpose and constructed in the Latin alphabet.[24]

Although more impressive in appearance than its Roman predecessor, and despite its long-term impact, the Anti-Anarchist Protocol did not obligate any of the signatory powers to undertake these measures. Clearly the failure to acquire all but lip service from the French, British and Italians and only reluctant support from the Swiss undermined its aims from the start. After 1905 Russia's most dangerous revolutionary émigrés would reside in either France or Italy, both non-signatory states.

While the Anti-Anarchist Protocol did not satisfy Russia's diplomats, it did present Fontanka with some positive outcomes by increasing the levels of communiciation and data exchange amongst the highest echelons of Europe's police bureaucracies. For the Foreign Agentura's men, however, the provisions of the Anti-Anarchist Protocol made little difference to either its mode of operations or its already strong informal relationships with their western colleagues. The simple fact is that irrespective of the modest outcomes of the 1898 and 1904 agreements the Foreign Agentura, especially from the 1890s to the outbreak of the First World War in 1914, never confronted the total refusal of political police collaboration from any European state.[25]

Of course, at the same time, the Foreign Agentura almost never encountered unfettered or unqualified support for any of its campaigns against the revolutionary emigration either. For one thing, the persistent failure of Europe's policemen and diplomats to construct a sophisticated definition of what exactly constitutes Anarchism, and Tsardom's inability to take the discussion of definition one step further by focusing on terrorist groups in general, no matter their political complexion, remained serious sticking points. For instance, after a lethal explosion in Rue Blanche in Geneva that city's police chief asked the chief of the Foreign Agentura about one of the Russian suspects. 'Is he an anarchist, a terrorist, or simply a socialist-revolutionary?'[26] This query forced the chief of the Paris Office into a rather convoluted reply. 'He became a member of the Socialist-Revolutionary Party', and 'I am obliged to tell you that the Socialist-Revolutionary Party *is* [italics in the original] the Russian terrorist party'.[27] The Anti-Anarchist Protocol had not clarified anything. The Swiss remained unsure of exactly who fitted the vague definition offered by either the Rome or St Petersburg protocols.

Whatever difficulties the Foreign Agentura encountered at the inter-police level in this matter paled into insignificance when compared to the interference and embarrassment it faced from the behaviour of its own government, which strove to convince and then cajole Britain and France, the two major non-signatory powers, into some form of compliance. To make matters worse, Fontanka, anxious to convince the forces of order in Europe that all Russian politicals living amongst them were dangerous, began to communicate with Europe's police forces directly in a formal manner. Fontanka conducted these discussions in a code, probably the one devised as part of the St Petersburg agreement, without informing the Paris Office of the cipher. As a result, decisions were taken without the Foreign Agentura's knowledge. These actions worried the Foreign Agentura which feared that such contacts only served to undermine its informal and often secret relationships with Europe's police systems. The Paris Office complained bitterly to Fontanka about its interference in matters which the Foreign Agentura clearly believed did not concern it.[28]

Nonetheless, the Ministry of Foreign Affairs persisted in pressuring Britain and France over the matters it believed were contained within the provisions of both the Rome and St Petersburg agreements. The level of tension between Russia and France intensified in 1909 when one of the principal suspects in the Tiflis bank robbery affair, the Bolshevik Maxim Litvinov, was arrested in Paris. The French ignored the tsarist government's repeated requests for his extradition. The Russians were more than upset. Prime Minister Stolypin instructed the Russian ambassador in Paris to reprimand the French for behaving like anything but an ally. He noted that émigré circles well knew that revolutionaries were 'guaranteed against the danger of arrest only in France'. And he wrote in frustration that as a result of the Republic's attitude many terrorists lived in Paris, and he angrily noted that the SR Central Committee plotted acts of mass terror against Tsardom in the French capital unabated.[29] Stolypin's cajoling came to naught.

The Russians dealt with equal energy with British stubbornness over their lack of formal co-operation. The tsarist Ministry of Foreign Affairs ordered its embassy in London to convince the Home Office that Russia's terrorists presented a serious danger to British society. Tsarist diplomats let the Home Office know that Russian revolutionaries, who had carried out bank robberies on behalf of the revolutionary movement in Russia, currently were robbing banks in Switzerland and were employing strong arm tactics to squeeze 'protection money from Lausanne's merchants' (or so the Tsar's representatives claimed). Tsardom claimed that these one-time 'respectable' revolutionaries had broken with their parties and were little more than gangsters for whom robbery and terrorism – the murder of police and children – were now a way of life. The Russian's pointed to the attack on the Sherman Rubber Factory by Russian 'Anarchists' which resulted in the deaths of a policeman and a child and the wounding of 'more or less' 17 persons as an example of the violence that could overwhelm Britain unless the British government undertook to join the Anti-Anarchist Protocol and make a stand against the Russian émigrés sheltering in England. The Russians went further, questioning the legitimacy of British civilisation if the Home Office chose not to join the international fight against 'anarchy'.[30] Foreign Minister Izvolskii hoped that this approach would induce Britain to sign the protocol.[31] Unfortunately, as Izvolskii himself understood, the international situation made British compliance unlikely. As he wrote the assistant minister of internal affairs, Izvolskii believed that one of the major obstacles to Britain's signing the Anti-Anarchist Protocol was the fact that the Germans had already signed it. He told Assistant Minister of Internal Affairs Kurlov that the British government probably did not want to become involved in any international agreement previously signed by the Germans.[32] Ironically, after Russia entered into alliance with Great Britain in 1907 the Germans and Austrians cooled considerably in their willingness to co-operate over political police matters. Collaboration took place halfheartedly at best.[33]

Indeed, as early as 1907 chief of the Foreign Agentura Harting noticed a serious deterioration in his relationship with the President of the Berlin Police Presidium. Harting wrote to Fontanka that while his relationship with the police within Germany's secondary states remained strong, this was not the case with 'the Prussian King and His Berlin'. Harting noted that the President of the Berlin Police Presidium always approached their discussions in the most polite manner, speaking of the Russian government with the utmost respect. This, Harting, told the director of Fontanka, was only a façade. While promising help, he basically used their conversations to draw information out of Harting for his own purposes while often acting counter to Russia's interests.[34]

Possibly as a direct result of this communication, Director of the Department of Police A. I. Trusevich travelled to Berlin in July 1907 where he met with senior German officials to discuss unified action against the Russian revolutionary émigrés residing in Germany in accordance with the provisions of the Anti-Anarchist Protocol. It is clear from these discussions that

Trusevich strove to expand the net thrown by the provisions of the Protocol to include all émigrés belonging to 'secret societies' and 'all persons propagating' the idea that terror is the highest form of anti-tsarist action. Trusevich requested that the German authorities expel all such émigrés from the *Reich*. In addition, he called for the development of communications networks between lower police organisations of the German police and tsarist political police units located in Riga, Vilna, Warsaw and Kiev as a means of keeping track of émigré movements across the Russo-German border. He elaborated on this point by requesting that any intelligence derived from Prussian police investigations into the affairs of the revolutionary emigration be turned over to these local agencies. And almost before the Germans had a chance to absorb Trusevich's suggestions, the director of Fontanka went further, suggesting a joint central police establishment designed to facilitate exchanges of information and, at the same time, joint action against common revolutionary targets.

Most of the German officials listened in amazement. President of the Berlin Police Presidium Eckhardt listened to Trusveich, too, in cold, unresponsive silence. When Trusevich took a breath Eckhardt spoke up to remind him of the scandal caused by the exposure of the tsarist political police's Berlin Agentura's operations in Germany which deeply embarrassed his government (see Chapter 8) and asked Trusevich point blank if his department of police was currently operating a bureau in Berlin. The director of Fontanka assured Eckhardt that the Russian government would not permit the establishment of a political police office in Germany again without the knowledge, and one assumes the permission, of the *Reich*'s government (Trusevich lied, the Berlin Agentura was still active).

One of the German foreign ministry officials demonstrated enthusiasm for at least a part of Trusevich's proposals, expressing the need for a thorough exchange of information between Fontanka and the Berlin Police Presidium. He thought the creation of a telegraphic code especially adopted for the purpose should be developed. Trusevich expressed his support for the proposal. Eckhardt remained silent. Trusevich wrote that the Berlin police chief appeared worried about possible breaches in German law that acquiescing in some of Trusevich's suggestions might entail and he made excuses for not being able to turn intelligence over to the Russians.

The director of Fontanka noted that Eckhardt's lack of flexibility made him short-tempered. He asked Eckhardt could it really be that his police recently conducted nearly 30 searches involving members of the Russian colony in Berlin, collecting a significant amount of correspondence and incriminating notes the contents of which he chose not to communicate to the Russian government? Eckhardt, maintaining his *sang-froid*, told the incredulous Trusevich that the material is in Russian and his police could not read it! Trusevich wryly suggested that the confiscated evidence be photographed with the copies being handed over to him.

Fontanka's director told Eckhardt and his fellow Germans that he understood this seemed like a one-way street with all the benefits of such an agreement apparently going to the Russians while the Germans bore all the risks. So he offered Eckhardt a carrot; the Russian police would be pleased to help their German colleagues with the Polish problem, meaning Rosa Luxemburg and her ilk, whom Trusevich noted were not 'loyal Germans'.

In the end the two-day meeting came to nothing with Trusevich asking the Russian Ambassador to Berlin, Count Osten-Sacken, to make representations to his German colleagues in the *Reich*'s Foreign Ministry about the critical necessity of maintaining a Russian police presence in Berlin. And as an aside, the director of Fontanka told Osten-Sacken to offer supplying the Berlin Police Presidium with a person who could translate any confiscated Russian language material into German! Trusevich must have thought Eckhardt was an idiot.[35]

Trusevich's disappointment reflected a conundrum that still plagues international policing today. Modern criminologists such as Frances Heidensohn emphasise that the major hindrance to international police co-operation is culture, which so deeply colours the interpretation of language, political and social attitudes and the nature of the legal and justice systems.[36] To this we should add perhaps the most deeply imbedded obstacle of all: self-interest.

The Foreign Agentura, as we shall see, established in France in 1883, operating behind a façade of convenient government ignorance, and with the equally unacknowledged support of most European police systems, overcame two of the roadblocks to international police co-operation noted by Heidensohn: the problem of legality and the problem of political and social attitudes. Legality, as we shall see throughout the remainder of this work, could with rare exception be sloughed off with a minimum of fuss. Although most European governments at least suspected that the Russian political police operated within their borders, when the issue came up as it did in the legislative chambers of Germany, France and Italy, the government of the day, even when confronted with supporting evidence, simply denied it. Russian–European political police mutual assistance did not lose a beat because of its illegality. Most of Europe, while giving lip service to the law, valued domestic security above any legal inhibitions to maintaining it.

As for political and social attitudes, by the end of the nineteenth century, as we discussed in the previous chapter, these were at least partly overcome by a policing sub-culture that had begun to develop throughout much of Europe, led by the French (who possessed a tradition to build upon), and even followed closely by the British who may have owned the most sophisticated political police force in western Europe by the outbreak of the

First World War. In France and Italy especially, but in Great Britain and Switzerland also, the evolving police sub-culture began to challenge the restraints imposed on the policing systems by mechanisms of control employed by the political culture of each of these states.

The Russian government understood the importance of furthering the sense of a single, unified police culture that was spreading across Europe and it strove to bond the tsarist political police to their western brethren by means of a plethora of emoluments and awards it made to foreign police officials.[37] These rewards became an important status symbol and enhanced the prestige of those receiving them. They served as a strong inducement to continued collaboration while, at the same time, strengthening the sense of community amongst European political policing circles. The Orders of St Anne II and III class and St Stanislav I, II, and III class appeared to be the most frequently awarded prestigious symbols of gratitude.[38] Recipients of such orders included the President of the Berlin Police Presidium (despite Fontanka's dislike for the man) and somewhat surprisingly Sir Edward Henry, the Chief of Scotland Yard. Henry probably received his medal in recognition for the informal exchange of information that regularly took place between the Yard and the Foreign Agentura.[39] The Foreign Agentura considered this practice to be an essential element in the dynamics of European police culture. So when the Ministry of Internal Affairs refused to reward European policemen accordingly, because it deemed their acts of insufficient merit, the Foreign Agentura chastised its own ministry for its niggardliness.[40]

Smaller gifts and monetary awards also abounded as a regular part of culture-building. The Russian government routinely paid members of European police forces for protecting High Personages travelling abroad. In one case, Superintendent Patrick Quinn of the Special Branch thanked the Russian government for the cigarette case it had presented to him and for the 'presents for my four officers who have been engaged in the protection of Her Imperial Majesty the Dowager Empress of Russia during her Imperial Majesty's visit to this country'.[41]

By the first decade of the twentieth century emoluments and rewards, bestowed by grateful nations to foreign policemen – as we shall see Russian police operating abroad received orders from most western governments as well – played an integral role in the evolution of an international police culture. The Foreign Agentura, however, tightened its connections with European police forces still further by employing a large number of detectsives who previously served the police of their own countries (see Appendix A.1). The Paris Office usually relied on the recommendations of the applicant's former employer and sometimes asked a police chief to suggest a likely candidate for a position. In one case, the chief of the Paris Office asked Patrick Quinn the Superintendent of the Special Branch to recommend a man capable of directing the Foreign Agentura's operations in Great Britain. Quinn enthusiastically suggested the Chief Inspector for Criminal

Investigations for the Metropolitan Police Francis Powell for the post, and according to the Foreign Agentura's employment records, Powell accepted the subsequent job offer (see Appendix A.1). This did not stop Powell, while in the employ of the Russian political police, from sitting at the table of honour at the 1914 Dinner of the Criminal Investigation Department put on by the Metropolitan Police.[42]

The attempt by Imperial Russia to create a formal alliance against terrorism based on common principals of law and international police co-operation did not succeed. The project fell victim to too many variables including the deteriorating international situation, which the concerned states proved unable to overcome.

This failure should not detract, however, from the growing power of political police throughout Europe in the years prior to the First World War. Towards the end of the nineteenth century there began the evolution of a new police sub-culture brought about by the political and social elites' fear of modernity, and of the growing political and economic influence of groups its processes stimulated. This outlook, full of foreboding for the established order, made an excellent growth medium for police in general but most especially for the development and extension of political police institutions across Europe. Over time, the power and role of the political police in different states evolved in a variety of ways. Some would became states within states, and in at least in two cases – Nazi Germany after 1939 and the Soviet Union of the Great Purge era – they would rule over the political machinery that had created them in the first place; others would more or less remain subordinate to the institutions of their governments although their power and influence would vary from society to society.[43]

Between 1880 and 1914 early political police evolution passed through, if you will, its own geological time frame, and in moving forward it left evidence behind, as those studying political police systems know too well – mostly sporadically, often unintentionally, difficult to discover and, surprisingly, as in the case of the records of the Foreign Agentura, sometimes in unexpected clusters.

The first part of this book, now concluded, has been, to continue the analogy, a sifting of the geological background sediment as a means of establishing a context for the main body of the work: the study of the fossil evidence of a single institution operating in this milieu. Studying the life of the Foreign Agentura leads to the uncovering of a still largely unknown world that helps us determine how the foundations were laid for subsequent post-war forms of this type of institution. It is as if a palaeontologist discovered a whole mass of fossil-laden sediment revealing before his educated eye the life of a world he hardly knew existed.

Of course, as any palaeontologist will tell you, one intact fossil no matter how beautifully preserved rarely tells you the whole story for which you are searching. The same is true of the life of the Foreign Agentura that unfolds in the following pages. The Paris Office is, after all, a Russian institution administered by tsarist officials of varying talents and differing prospects. St Petersburg considered the Foreign Agentura as one its weapons against the emigration, a cog in a more or less steadily expanding political police machine at home and abroad. The Foreign Agentura's enemies were Russian, and its campaigns were directed against them, the members of the revolutionary emigration.

Europe became one of the principal battlefields upon which the Russian revolutionaries and the tsarist political police conducted their struggle for Russia's future, and this circumstance makes the fossil evidence doubly valuable for it fills in a heretofore too little known piece of Russian revolutionary history. The complexion of the Foreign Agentura's more than thirty-year campaign against the emigration adds substance to the history of the men and women on both sides of the struggle most of whom, such as Aaron Liberman, sadly have come down to us only as disjointed pieces of sediment.

So, this is a story as much about Russia in Europe and the history of the Russian revolutionary movement as it is about the development of a political policing institution from its inception in 1883 to its demise in 1917.

Part II

The Foreign Agentura: the Russian Secret Police Abroad

4
The Russian Secret Police Abroad: the Early Years

The Russian political police first became active abroad during the reign of Nicholas I. The growth and institutional development of the tsarist political policing system, as I have noted elsewhere, began slowly and rather haphazardly during the reign of Alexander I (1801–25). Thereafter it evolved quickly under Nicholas I (1825–56), faltered during the first, reforming decade, of Alexander II's reign (1856–66) and then began to grow in size and institutional sophistication, eventually spreading untrammelled throughout the Empire and abroad during Tsardom's remaining years.[1]

The creation of the Third Section of His Imperial Majesty's Chancery by Nicholas I in response to the traumatic experience of the Decembrist Revolt signals the beginning of the modern Imperial Russian political police system. The *Ukaz* (Decree) establishing the Third Section appeared on 3 July 1926. The Third Section together with the soon-to-be established (28 April 1827) Separate Corps of Gendarmes (*Otdel'nyi korpus zhandarmov*) formed the tsar's political police force.[2] The Third Section occupied itself with the opinions and behaviour of Russia's educated classes: bureaucrats, officers, gentry, courtiers, and later intellectuals. It also became active abroad.

In 1832 the Third Section dispatched agents to Europe initially in order to keep Nicholas I infomed about the activities of Polish émigrés[3] who escaped tsarist retribution for the Polish Revolt of 1830, and to acquaint themselves with both the internal politics of the European states and the activities of various western political parties *vis-à-vis* Russia. As a subsidiary duty Count Benckendorf commissioned two men to serve as the Third Section's 'literary agents' abroad whose principal duties, at first, required them to contain and defuse the anti-Russian sentiment of the liberal press in western Europe. The best known of these agents, Iakov Tolstoi, worked in Paris for 30 years (1837–66). In addition to writing dozens of reports on the state of European affairs, Tolstoi also began to describe the literary activities of the still very small but growing number of dissidents living abroad. Those who wrote pieces neither insulting to the monarchy nor preaching sedition could – if Tolstoi wrote well of their family life and the circumstances which caused them to resort to journalistic criticisms of the Motherland – be forgiven and permitted to return home if they so requested. Others whose writings Tolstoi considered detrimental to the reputation of the monarchy itself might be summoned home. To refuse the summons meant permanent exile in the West, to accept it could mean a term of Siberian exile. All of this made Tolstoi a powerful figure, dreaded by the dissidents residing in Europe.[4]

The quality of Tolstoi's reports, often intimate and revealing, could not be sustained as the demands placed on him and his agents multiplied and stretched them beyond their rather limited capacity.[5] Russian political police operations in Europe exposed the ineptitude of the Third Section on a grand scale. The function of keeping émigrés under surveillance devolved into confusion with both the Third Section and the Ministry of Foreign Affairs failing to establish definite precedence of authority. Even the repugnant *Sviashchenaia druzhina* (The Holy Brotherhood) paralleled Tsarist government agencies in harassing Russian émigrés between 1881 and 1883 much to the disgust and anger of the political police.[6]

It was the Ministry of Foreign Affairs, however, that dominated the management of surveillance operations abroad at first. The Ministry of Foreign Affairs through its Consulates operated in a more or less open fashion with surveillance matters being discussed at the highest levels.[7] In addition, the Third Section itself possessed no political influence abroad, so as a matter of expediency its agents were attached to the Consulates in Berlin, Vienna and Paris. This led to an awkward situation for the tsarist government. The Third Section's agents, poorly trained and unfamiliar with European life, contributed to Russia's already sullied image abroad with their embarrassing bumbling.[8]

This situation apparently did not unduly disturb the Ministry of Internal Affairs. The Third Section operations abroad were both understaffed and seriously underfunded. It maintained about fifteen agents spread out across Europe with the largest number of agents (three) resident in Paris.[9] These men would soon be confronted with a different sort of émigré than Tolstoi had encountered. The few émigrés who Tolstoi kept under surveillance, believed that their journalistc and literary critiques of Tsardom would encourage further reform largely through the pressure of unfavourable European public opinion. As we have seen, the men and women who journeyed into exile beginning in the 1870s were of a different, more dangerous, sort.

During the 1870s the complexion of political opposition in Russia and Tsardom's response to it underwent a fundamental and tragic transformation. Alexander II's Great Reforms, perhaps unintentionally, encouraged the growth of civil society in Russia with rights and privileges guaranteed under the law. This civil society confronted ruling and governing elites who believed that the law served only one purpose: the preservation of the monarchy and through it their privileged and powerful positions. As these elites began to feel themselves threatened they strove to erode the political impact of the Great Reforms through a series of unpublished statutes dealing with political crime and enacted by the government throughout the 1870s. The essence of these secret decrees focused upon the imposition of administrative authority.[10]

On 1 January 1875 the number of people under police surveillance for 'political causes' (excluding Siberia, the Caucasus, and the Transcaucasus regions) was 15,829. In May that same year it had already increased to 18,945 people – an almost 20 per cent increase in only four months![11] These statistics reflect the capricious and high-handed behaviour of the political police, which mirrored the general approach to law and order taken by its superiors in the provinces, who freely punished those whom the political police accused, even on the flimsiest of evidence, by applying administrative justice. The abuses of administrative justice were legion.[12]

Clearly by the mid-1870s the euphoria of the reform era had truly worn off. Between 1875 and 1879 Russia's provinces endured 152 rural disturbances, 16 of which could only be subdued with the help of the army. In 1878 and 1879 the economic consequences of the Russo-Turkish War hit the villages particularly hard. So much so that peasant riots seized 14 provinces in 1878, 29 in 1879 and 34 in 1880. The new working class, too, began to express its still rather muted discontent through factory floor disturbances and a nascent strike movement that grew steadily throughout the second half of the 1870s. Nevertheless, it was the actions of the few, not the growing discontent of the peasant masses and workers that rattled the regime.

The appearance of the terrorist movement under both the anarchist and populist political banners confirmed what had long been suspected, the ineptitude of the Third Section and the Separate Corps of Gendarmes as bulwarks against the spreading political opposition. By the late 1870s tsarist *sanovniki* (high officials) had every reason to believe that their lives were under threat and that very little was being done about it. In a famous incident Vera Zasulich, a daughter of the minor nobility and a member of *Zemlia i Volia* (Land and Liberty) who had already served a two-year sentence for revolutionary activity, now acting independently, shot and wounded General F. F. Trepov, the Governor (*gradonachal'nik*) of St Petersburg as a reprisal for his order to have a young student prisoner flogged. Zasulich's trial became a *cause célèbre*, an indictment of the regime's withdrawal from the promise of the Great Reforms. The jury's not guilty verdict set off a pattern of increased repression noted above and which incited further violence. Some of the better known cases emphasised the Third Section's ineptitude, including the assassination attempts – one successful, one not – against two of Russia's most senior police officials: in August 1878 S. M. Stepniak-Kravchinskii stabbed to death Chief of Gendarmes N. V. Mezentsov followed by another assassin's failed attempt against his successor

A. P. Drentel'n. Perhaps what worried law and order officials the most, however, was that young revolutionaries had begun to shoot back at Gendarmes in pursuit of their duties. In one incident a shootout in Odessa left several gendarmes wounded in a battle over a clandestine printing press.[13]

The growing pattern of intimidation and violence drove many of the terrorists, along with their less violent and more thoughtful colleagues, into exile abroad largely throughout Europe. The names of these people which included Zasulich and Kravchinskii are too numerous to cite but, as we argued in Chapter 2, by the late 1870s the foundation of the Russian revolutionary movement for the next two generations abroad had been laid. Ideologically motivated, these men and women, although still relatively few in number, were committed to the destruction of the Romanov dynasty. By the late 1870s at least some Russian officials began to take note of the potential danger of these émigrés to Tsardom's future.

N. A. Orlov, the Russian Ambassador in Paris and the son of the former head of the Third Section A. F. Orlov, wrote General N. D. Seliverstov, the Deputy Chief of Gendarmes, that he was extremely unhappy with the performance of the Third Section's agents under his supervision and condemned the 'primitive' nature of the Russian police establishment abroad. He recommended that the Third Section enter into a relationship with the Prefect of Paris, duplicating its already close relationship with the Berlin police. 'Then', Orlov told his minister in disgust, 'we will not be dependent on the powerful and foolish and it will be possible to investigate [things] ourselves.' Orlov did not specify who the 'powerful and foolish' were but given what we saw in the previous chapter one could assume he was describing the French officials from the Ministries of the Interior and Foreign Affairs with whom he dealt. Orlov went on to inform Seliverstov that 'in general we have here pitiful information and the French police could render us a certain significant service'.[14] Orlov's concerns did not impress his superiors who considered the revolutionary émigrés to be only an insignificant offshoot of the main revolutionary movement located within the Empire.[15]

In 1880 Orlov's complaints found a sympathetic ear with the appointment of M. T. Loris-Melikov as minister of internal affairs. Melikov took immediate measures to increase political police operations abroad for in his opinion there existed strong ties between the revolutionary emigration and the activities of 'evil doers' residing within Russia. He found the reports produced by the Third Section on this growing group of people virtually worthless. In April 1880, to remedy this situation he established what he called 'external political agenturas' (*vneshnei politicheskoi agentury*) designed for surveillance only in Roumania, Switzerland, France and Germany and placed them under two MVD officials. However, in addition to the task of collecting information on the emigration, these 'agenturas' verified the work of the Third Section's agents who still carried on their duties as before.

Loris-Melikov ordered the more important of the two MVD men he despatched abroad, Colonel M. N. Baranov, to develop a plan to reorganise the Third Section's activities abroad and, at the same time, to make himself familiar with the operations of the Parisian police. Once Baranov had familiarised himself with the Paris Prefecture's operations he wrote that the Prefecture's police work outstripped that of the Third Section. His observations *vis-à-vis* the Paris Prefecture's *modus operandi* convinced him more than ever of the 'wretchedness', 'primitiveness' and the 'ineffectiveness' of Russian political policing abroad. Baranov considered the structure of both the Prefecture's civil and secret police well advanced and believed that many of their procedures could be applied to the organisation and operations of the tsarist forces of order.

The Colonel conceded that the operation in Roumania, where he claimed the best agents worked, went rather well, and in Switzerland he recommended that 'agentura' activity be increased. However, in a report to Loris-Melikov written in June 1880 Baranov observed that Paris had become the 'centre of revolution' (which was in reality not the case) and therefore should be the focus of the Russian political police. At the present time, the Colonel noted sadly, that Russian police work in Paris could only be described as shoddy. Like most Third Section operations elsewhere in Europe, assignments were carried out by a few poorly supervised small-time agents, who operating without the support of the local police, floundered hopelessly about .[16]

Baranov almost at once developed a working relationship with the Paris Prefect of Police Louis Andrieux. Andrieux suggested he establish a bureau with the special purpose of keeping Russian émigrés under surveillance which would report through the Prefect to Baranov. The Prefect requested that the co-operation between himself and Baranov be kept secret known only to his His Imperial Majesty Alexander II and Minister of Internal Affairs Loris-Melikov. In return, Andrieux wanted a guarantee from Baranov that there would be no Third Section agents operating in Paris.[17]

A developing if *sub rosa* relationship between the Prefect of Paris and Baranov made perfect sense, especially since Loris-Melikov paid generously for the service.[18] Nonetheless, the intelligence reports that the French supplied, although numerous, proved of little value. As a result Baranov discontinued the operation.

Finally, Baranov suggested that Loris-Melikov undertake the establishment abroad of 'a centre in which all data and reports from the foreign bureaus [of the Russian police] could be centralised and, equally, would be able to guide and direct their affairs'.[19] It is this idea that the MVD would eventually bring to life in 1883.

After the assassination of Alexander II on 1 March 1881 and the consequent severe repression, the size of the emigration swelled. Loris-Melikov came to believe like Ambassador Orlov that the heart of the terrorist campaign – indeed of the revolutionary movement itself – flourished in Europe where the revolutionaries could avoid justice and punishment. However, Loris-Melikov also believed as we have seen, that only international agreements concerning the arrest and extradition of revolutionary émigrés charged with allegedly committing terrorist acts could resolve the problem. But, as we saw in Chapter 3, these conventions signed by a handful of countries proved to be worthless as far as Russia was concerned, although they planted the seeds of later attempts at international police co-operation.

As for the establishment of a 'Foreign Agentura' as suggested by Baranov to guide Russian political police operations abroad, that would have to await the arrival of police reform and the efforts of the newly arrived director of the Department of Police, V. K. Plehve.

The government's awakening interest in police reform[20] arose from three circumstances: the assassination attempt made against Alexander II by D. V. Karakozov which caused the government to become acutely aware of the potential for disaster caused by the gendarmes' failings; the failure of the legal reform at least in the government's eyes; and notably, the economic, social and political dislocations wrought by the Great Reforms as a whole and Russia's steady movement into the industrial age.

After the Karakozov attempt on the tsar's life on 4 April 1866, the government fell under the influence of Count P. A. Shuvalov, the chief of Gendarmes. Shuvalov recognised the failings of both the Third Section and the Separate Corps of Gendarmes as forces of internal order and he endeavoured to compensate for them by establishing a new type of police bureau in St Petersburg and giving it the impressive name: The Division for the Preservation of Order and Public Safety (*Otdelenie po okhrane poriadka i obshchestvennoi bezopasnosti*). This bureau would become the prototype of the new-fashioned political police bureaus established in the 1880s in Moscow and Warsaw and between 1902 and 1914 throughout the Russian Empire. As a weapon against sedition, however, it remained inert until major political police reform in the 1880s brought it to life. For more than another decade Tsardom took no further steps to create a force capable of counteracting dissent.

On 5 February 1880 an explosion at the Winter Palace just missed killing the tsar. A week later Alexander II decreed the convocation of a Supreme Commission for the Preservation of State Order and Social Tranquility (*Verkhovnaia komissiia po okhrane gosudarstvennago poriadka i obshchestvennago spokoistviia*). The chairman, the very same General Loris-Melikov, did not favour repression for its own sake and set about to modify some of the administrative measures of the 1870s while, at the same time, developing constructive proposals for the preservation of the autocracy.

In late February 1880 Loris-Melikov presented a report to Alexander II which recommended the unification of the various branches of the police within a single department in order to better co-ordinate the campaign against sedition. In line with this recommendation Loris-Melikov subordinated the Third Section and the Separate Corps of Gendarmes to the Supreme Commission, placing them under his direct authority.

On 6 August 1880 Loris-Melikov finally took the long overdue step of abolishing the Third Section altogether and establishing the new Department of State Police. At the same time, considering its usefulness to be at an end, he abolished the Supreme Commission, following this action on 10 November with a report to the tsar which suggested 'the combining of the entire higher management of the police in one establishment – the Ministry of Internal Affairs'. Alexander II agreed and in an Imperial Decree of 15 November 1880 the Department of Executive Police (*Departament Ispol'nitel'noi Politsii*), the unit supervising the civil and general police throughout the Empire, was amalgamated with the Department of State Police This reorganisation of the police in Russia appears to have been suggested by the structure of the Paris Prefecture.[21]

Originally, the Department of State Police consisted of three secretariats (*deloproizvodstva*). The Third Secretariat or Secret Bureau fulfilled the duties of a political police, that is, it implemented the struggle with subversion. By 1883 the Department had grown to five secretariats. Eventually, by 1914, the Department of Police (the MVD shortened the name in 1883) had expanded to nine secretariats. In 1898 the MVD created a new bureau, the Special Section, designed to oversee political police affairs throughout Russia and abroad.

The Special Section became the apex of Fontanka's political intelligence-gathering pyramid. On the isolated and heavily guarded fifth floor at 16 Fontanka Quai it mapped the master plan of assault against subversion. Shrouded in myth evoking secrecy its operations remained virtually unknown to other Department of Police employees. Entry except for its own staff and senior Fontanka officials was forbidden. The Special Section's archive quickly accumulated a card file on 50,000 suspects, a total that expanded steadily over the ensuing years.

A crucial link in the development of the tsarist police network was the creation of the *Okhrannye Otdeleniia* or Security Divisions. The administration for these OOs, as they became known – particularly after their proliferation between 1902 and 1904 – traced its origins to the Divisions for the Preservation of Order and Public Safety. The first of these, established in St Petersburg in 1866 as already noted, served as a model for two additional OOs set up in Moscow and Warsaw in 1880. It was not until 1882, however, that they acquired any real authority when the minister of internal affairs raised the OOs status to full-fledged political police bureaus. During the 1880s the OOs remained small, managed by high-ranking and highly reliable gendarme officers with the support of a few loyal and hardworking *chinovniki* (bureaucrats). These few civil servants, however, controlled large networks of detectives and undercover agents, their authority spreading beyond the city and even the *guberniia* (province) in which they were located.[22] In 1902 another burst of political police reform initiated by the newly appointed Minister of Internal Affairs V. K. Plehve led to the untrammeled expansion of the OOs and the creation of lesser political police bureaus throughout the Empire from 1902 onwards.

The creation of the Foreign Agentura in Paris in 1883 under the guidance of a much younger V. K. Plehve, then serving as the director of the Department of Police, served as a forerunner for all the provincial OOs Plehve and his successors would spread throughout the Empire in the early twentieth century.

In the midst of domestic police reform in the early 1880s, V. K. Plehve continued to press his case with Loris-Melikov's successor as minister of internal affairs, P. N. Ignat'ev. He argued that the émigrés of the 1880s, unlike their earlier compatriots, did not devote themselves exclusively to literary protests and anti-tsarist propaganda (as if this was not bad enough). He repeated Count Orlov's fears that in the security of western Europe members of the emigration freely planned innumerable terrorist actions against Tsardom's highest personages. Plehve argued that the government could only foil these plots if it discovered them in preparation well beforehand, something which could be accomplished only through intensive observation of émigré circles by well-trained agents of the Russian Government. In order to effectively fulfil this function the correct placement of agents would be of paramount importance. Fontanka's director suggested that agents be placed in Berlin, Bucharest, Geneva, Paris and London where in addition to their intelligence-gathering role they would liaise with local police officials, exchanging information on local socialist movements as well as on the Russian revolutionary emigration. Plehve viewed the building of successful relationships with foreign police forces as one of the principal functions of the Russian police abroad. Fontanka's agents would develop these relationships on the lower levels of police work while the local Russian Consuls would carry out this work on a higher level.

Indeed, in this initial proposal to Ignat'ev, Plehve made certain that the powerful Ministry of Foreign Affairs, which worried about the diplomatic problems ensuing from embarrassing incidents caused by Fontanka's bumbling policemen as they traipsed all over Europe, was offered a critical supervisory role over Fontanka's operations. The consuls were to bring Fontanka's men to various functions and introduce them into official circles. More formally, Plehve expected that Russia's consulates would house the headquarters of any such operation and that the police agents themselves would assume the role of diplomatic attachés and maintain offices or even live within the consulates themselves! Plehve hoped that these precautions would guarantee his police the anonymity they required when operating in a foreign milieu.[23]

What impact would all of this have on Russia's European diplomacy if it all went wrong? Ignat'ev attempted to assuage Foreign Minister N. K. Giers' misgivings, by offering him assurances of various sorts, especially promising Giers that the Ministry of Internal Affairs in no way expected the Consul General in Paris to personally supervise the revolutionary emigration himself.[24]

Ignat'ev could only convince Giers to agree to a hopelessly truncated plan. Plehve's original concept of placing his agents in several major consulates throughout Europe had been reduced by his superiors to the Paris Consulate alone. Worse, Ignat'ev gave in to Giers' demand that the Ministry of Foreign Affairs, not the MVD, would be completely responsible for the operation. Undoubtedly, and not without justification, Plehve's ambitious concept of a European-wide network of Russian undercover police operations frightened both Ignat'ev and his Foreign Ministry colleague. However, the two ministers' plan, although it considerably circumscribed Plehve's more ambitious proposal, certainly did not eliminate the possibility of scandal. Chance slip-ups were actually enhanced when an already busy Consul General now burdened with this new responsibility and totally untrained in the ways of policemen could easily make a mistake by paying too little attention to security.

The Consul General in Paris began his work by openly requesting the aid of the French government in probing the Russian revolutionary emigration. In the name of his government he asked the French to take the following administrative measures against members of the revolutionary emigration:

a. Increase supervision on émigré activities and movements within France.
b. Arrest, search and question those who were planning or discussing criminal action.
c. Deport émigrés from France on Russian instructions.

The Consul General in Paris always requested copies of the protocols of investigations concerning Russian émigrés as well as the physical evidence found by the French police while searching émigré quarters at the time of arrest. As Vice Director of the Police Zhukov discovered, the French could be almost sadistically niggardly in their information sharing, but all the information the French Ministry of the Interior did supply underwent verification by Russian agents.

His colleagues in Vienna and Berlin (operating without Plehve's police agents) had an easier time. After all, thanks to Bismarck, Austria-Hungary,

Germany and Russia formed The Three Emperors League and allies often helped each other in these matters. France viewed Russia as a potential enemy; thus whatever the Paris Prefect felt about helping his Russian colleagues, the French ministers of foreign affairs and interior were bound to be more reticent.

So, the Russian Consul in Berlin, especially, proved to be far more effective than his counterpart in Paris. He developed liaisons with the President of the Berlin Police Presidium and other high-ranking police officials outside of Prussia. Of course, the German police themselves operated an extended network of agents beyond the borders of the *Reich*. Indeed, the German Federal Police maintained agents in London, Paris, Geneva, Berne, Zürich, Florence, Genoa and Rome – the same cities where their Russian colleagues would soon flock – in order to keep an eye on German socialists and other possible troublemakers, including members of the Russian emigration. The tsarist government particularly valued any information the Germans acquired about these centres of dissident activity relevant to Russia. In Vienna, too, the consul after a poor start managed to satisfy St Petersburg's requirements for information.

The Russian Ministry of Foreign Affairs ordered its consuls in Berlin and Vienna to stay in touch with the Consul General in Paris, but the latter was to direct the entire operation.[25] The consul in Paris, therefore, had the unenviable task of reading, sorting, verifying and synthesising the reports received from sources in Paris, Vienna and Berlin, and forwarding them through his ministry to the Department of State Police.

This system produced limited results, which dissatisfied Plehve, who wished to devote a large part of his energy as director of the Department of Police to the exiles. He firmly believed this business was not a job for diplomats. By 1883 two of Russia's most powerful men concurred in the police chief's views of the matter. Both D. A. Tolstoi, Ignat'ev's successor as minister of internal affairs, and, of greater significance, K. P. Pobedonostsev, tutor of the tsar and now Procurator of the Holy Synod and Alexander III's most influential advisor, strongly believed in the formation of a bureau of the Russian political police abroad with its headquarters in Paris.[26]

With the support of these *sanovniki* Plehve established the Foreign Agentura (*Zagranichnaia agentura*) of the Department of Police in 1883. The government designated its Paris Embassy at 79 Rue de Grenelle as the location of the Paris Office's headquarters. Initially the Agentura looked very much like an amateur operation. The original Paris Office included only four operatives of nebulous backgrounds. On 29 May 1883 the Department of Police assigned five more agents to service abroad. Fontanka realised that it could not allow these agents to roam around Europe unsupervised so it created an administrative and supervising bureau in June. The first director of the Foreign Agentura was *Nadvornaia Sovetnik* (Aulic Councillor) Korvin-Krukovskii. The man, an adventurer at heart with no administrative experience and a somewhat unreliable background, appeared a poor choice as the official to get this new bureau off the ground and he was. It is possible that his experience as a police agent and in military intelligence along with his extensive residence in various western countries (he spoke French fluently) impressed Plehve.[27]

It seems strange that as important as Plehve considered the development of the Foreign Agentura to be, he never appointed a man as its director whom he respected. As we shall see, he considered appointment to the directorship of the Foreign Agentura as the equivalent of exile for incompetent, misbehaved, or in the case of Korvin-Krukovskii, inconsequential officials. This may have reflected his attitude towards Europe and the knowledge that careers in the bureaucracy are made in St Petersburg not Paris. Nevertheless, Plehve surrounded the directors with men of both experience and ability. Plehve ordered Korvin-Krukovskii to employ Alexander Barle, a former French police official, to supervise the agents (both detectives and undercover agents) of the Paris Office and he hired three other experienced former French police operatives who were placed under Barle's supervision. Promotions came slowly in Europe's police forces[28] and frustrated detectives and supervisory personnel would retire at a still relatively young age and earn extra income above their meagre pensions by working for the Foreign Agentura.

Korvin-Krukovskii only survived in office for one year. He could not resist using Department of Police funds for his own pleasures. The Paris Office received 4,000 roubles per month for operating expenses. Out of that sum he greedily kept 1,500 roubles for himself. Unfortunately for the director his assistant Alexander Barle possessed sufficient integrity to inform the Department of Police about his chief's behaviour, implying that it bordered on embezzlement. Fontanka's decision to replace Korvin-Krukovskii was not long in coming and the Department of Police used this opportunity to place the Paris Office on a more professional basis. Fontanka decided to establish a formal detective agency within the Paris Office, populated by French operatives who would carry out local surveillance. These detectives worked under the direction of the honest and able Barle. Vice Director of Police Semiakin who directed these changes also created a small chancery staffed by three *chinovniki* he selected from the Department of Police's Third Secretariat (charged with managing the political police) to manage and rationalise the burgeoning paper flow. He placed these minor officials in charge of collating all reports from the Foreign Agentura's own detectives, those of the Border Gendarmerie (*Pogranichnye Zhandermerii*), the Warsaw Gendarme *okrug* (region) and consular reports concerning émigré activity. Semiakin ordered his Paris chancery to compile complete listings of Russian political émigrés living in Paris with adjoining physical descriptions, addresses, hangouts and daily routine.

These administrative functions, however, were of secondary importance. Fontanka informed the Foreign Agentura that its most valuable and secret function involved collecting intelligence on subversive activities directed at the persons and institutions of the tsarist government. In order to carry out this most vital duty, Semiakin instructed the Foreign Agentura to place under surveillance any person who had committed a State Crime[29] within Russia and then subsequently travelled abroad to escape prosecution. He ordered the Paris Office to peruse the Russian language revolutionary press, and any other press having contact with Russia or Russians, gleaning information relevant to the security of Tsardom. These straightforward instructions remained the guiding principles for the Foreign Agentura's duties throughout its lifespan.

Although the Foreign Agentura continued to give lip service to the role of the consuls in acquiring intelligence on the emigration, in practice, the consular staff in Berlin, Vienna and Paris allowed their police type duties to atrophy until, without objection from the minister of foreign affairs, Fontanka excluded them entirely from police work.[30]

The appointment of Korvin-Krukovskii's successor, Peter Ivanovich Rachkovskii, was hailed by Vice Director of Police Semiakin when he called Rachkovskii, 'a capable man holding many attitudes in accordance with his position'.[31] Director of the Department of Police Plehve may have appreciated Rachkovskii's cunning, his lack of scruples and his capacity to do anything to enhance his shaky career within Fontanka, but his overall opinion differed considerably from that expressed by Semiakin and, as we shall see, it is the latter man's opinions that got Rachkovskii sent to France.

Even before Rachkovskii arrived at his new post the Foreign Agentura began to take on a new, active, more menacing form. Fontanka further enhanced Barle's position. He not only controlled six French detectives of his own, but now also served as paymaster for co-operative members of the Paris Prefecture who supplied information to the Paris Office. The Foreign Agentura also rented two apartments which they turned into Black Cabinets for the perlustration of émigré mail 'borrowed' from the constantly bribable *concierges*. The Foreign Agentura hoped that by invading the privacy of the mail it would discover close associations, terrorist plots and the comings and goings of the correspondents and their friends. More often than not, however, the letters discussed the émigré correspondents' hopes for the future, rumours on the periphery of their parties or organisations or sometimes about party leaders and, therefore, were of little importance, especially given the risk of exposure and scandal that perlustrating the mails created.[32]

Still, *concierges* became an indispensable part of the Foreign Agentura's intelligence network and the Paris Office paid them well for their services. A typical émigré view of their ever-present *concierges* appeared in Lev

Tikhomirov's diary where he sarcastically noted that he and his friends paid only 13 francs rent for their *concierge* wished to keep them in residence. If her Russian tenants moved elsewhere she would no longer receive the money given her as a reward for keeping Tikhomirov and his associates under surveillance.[33] Detective Farce in England, where the position of *concierge* or porter did not exist, lamented their absence. 'There are no porters here', he complained, 'as in Paris for example, where with a hundred *sous* you can buy their souls'.[34]

At almost the same time a directive from Fontanka extended the Foreign Agentura's domain beyond the borders of France. A dispatch from St Petersburg stated that the Paris Office was authorised to establish contacts with the German and Austrian police, the Cracow Police Commissioner and to correspond with the police of Bucharest, Vienna and Geneva in order to facilitate the development of this network of international police co-operation out of sight of European public opinion.[35] Over a 20-year period Tsardom established four subsidiary agenturas, beginning with the one in Bucharest which opened almost simultaneously with the Paris Office, led a life independent of the Paris Office, and will not be discussed here. In 1904 the Department of Police found its Balkan Agentura to be redundant and dismantled it. The agenturas in London and Geneva, whose activities are discussed throughout the book, contained only a few operatives each and really did not deserve the title. The Paris Office controlled their operations, as we shall see. The Berlin Agentura came late, in 1900, with the approval of the German government, and it served as an important arm of the Paris Office. After 1908 its value diminshed as fewer and fewer émigrés settled in Germany.[36]

The creation of a Berlin Agentura, however, took place long after Rachkovskii's arrival in Paris. Upon taking up his duties he found that his entire staff consisted only of three clerks, six French detectives under the direction of Barle and seven Russian operatives. With this small staff Rachkovskii undertook the daunting task of guiding the surveillance of the entire Russian revolutionary emigration in western Europe, Great Britian and the United States, a virtually impossible task. Overcoming his bureau's inadequate staffing problems became Rachkovskii's priority.

Under the new director's energetic, if unorthodox and erratic leadership the Foreign Agentura expanded its detective service and developed a network of undercover agents which infiltrated every major émigré site. Rachkovskii, a man of urbane charm, cultivated the leadership of Europe's and Britain's police forces until the Paris Office maintained professional contact with the police of every major city in Europe. On his own initiative he entered into direct discussion with foreign police officials about joint operations involving searches, seizures and arrests, and in special cases extraditions.

Judging from relevant correspondence within the Ministry of Internal Affairs as we shall see, it appears that although the Department of Police created general guidelines for the Paris Office in 1886, it allowed Rachkovskii to mould the Foreign Agentura as he saw fit. Rachkovskii, the most ambitious director in the Paris Office's history, took full advantage of this leeway. Although his approach to police work did not equal the most efficient or the more 'regular' methods employed by his successors, it is unlikely that the Foreign Agentura of the Russian political police would have been as prominent and so troublesome to the émigrés without his adventurous, independent and unorthodox leadership (as we shall see in Chapter 7).

His three successors continued to enlarge and shape the Foreign Agentura during the pre-First World War years to cope with a revolutionary emigration that grew (as we noted in Chapter 2) from several hundred in the 1880s to a steady population of between 4,000 to 5,000 from 1905 to 1917.[37] There were dozens of Russian colonies in cities and town spread throughout the western world including: Berlin, Stuttgart, Münich, Frankfurt, Heidelberg, Geneva, Zürich, London, Paris, Nice, New York, Rome, Genoa, Nervi and San Remo.

Observing and infiltrating such a large number of groups spread out over such great distances required a dedicated body of professional detectives and a corps of undercover agents who to one degree or another immersed themselves in émigré circles as observers and in some cases as provocateurs. These men and women required skilled supervision themselves and the intelligence they collected required collation and analysis before the Foreign Agentura sent it on to St Petersburg.

Without the talents of these people – detectives, undercover agents, case officers and quality administrators – the Foreign Agentura could not have fulfilled its prodigious brief: discovering and undermining any terrorist campaigns against the Royal Family and Russia's *sanovniki*, while, at the same time, harassing, subverting and demoralising the revolutionary emigration as well as counteracting the emigration's portrayal of Tsardom as a barbarous kingdom not worthy of belonging to the European community of nations.

It is to the lives and careers of these indispensable cogs in the Foreign Agentura's machinery to which we now turn our attention.

5
Bureaucrats and Case Officers: the Sinews of the Paris Office

The directors of the Foreign Agentura were the most noticeable protagonists in the various episodes of Russian police activity abroad, but they could not have functioned without the support of dozens of unknown people in their employ. Chancery personnel and case officers, detectives and undercover agents supplied, evaluated, and processed the thousands of bits of indispensable information upon which the chiefs of the Paris Office built their reputations. This chapter and the one that follows expose the members of the Russian police abroad to the light of historical scrutiny for the first time.

The chancery held a central place in every political police bureau, with the political police chief depending on his *chinovniki* for the swift and accurate processing of intelligence data. It was the chancery staff with whom the bureau chief most closely interacted. On the one hand it was the chancery staff's common feelings of loyalty and obligation that formed the basis of their chief's authority while, on the other hand, the friendly confidence the boss placed in his chancery gave its employees subterranean power to carry out their duties.[1] At the highest level within the chancery such power permitted the chancery supervisor to take on himself the responsibility of determining what should or should not be forwarded to Fontanka in reports and dispatches.

The number of *chinovniki* serving within the Paris Office varied but there were never more than five at any one time. They worked in an office located within the Russian Embassy at 79 Rue de Grenelle. There is no extant description of the office as it originally appeared. The chancery was remodelled in 1915 and the Provisional Government's Investigation Commission described the rooms as they appeared in the spring of 1917. The Foreign Agentura occupied the lower floor of the Russian Embassy in only two medium sized rooms. The first of these received some sunlight from two grated windows which looked out upon the courtyard of the Embassy.

A large ceiling-high cupboard holding the Foreign Agentura's archives dominated this room. Two large card catalogues were also found in the office. The first of these two filing systems contained between 15,000 and 20,000 cards with the names and short personal resumés of persons arrested for participation in the revolutionary movement within Russia. These cards described the subjects' physical characteristics and noted their level of involvement in the revolutionary movement. The second held the Foreign Agentura's cross reference file. It held between 2,000 and 3,000 cards containing in alphabetical order the names and code names of each person referred to in the Agentura's reports. Each card noted the year and dispatch number of every report mentioning the subject's name. Resting neatly on desks topped with typewriters, one could find albums displaying the photographs of revolutionaries.

The second room, the director's study, was furnished with an exceptionally large redwood desk adorned with luxurious bronze candelabras resting among other unnamed knick-knacks. The remaining furniture in the room consisted of a sofa, armchair, a chair of red morocco leather and two large portraits of the tsar and his family. The clerks kept dispatches and memorandums in two files one for 'Incoming' dispatches and the other for copies of 'Outgoing' dispatches. The director placed urgent ongoing matters in separate files containing information on dangerous revolutionaries, such as the terrorist Boris Savinkov, and other documents including letters, Agentura leaflets, various *spravki* and photographs deemed important at the moment.[2]

This plush and well-ordered office reveals an organised and systematised chancery in 1917, but this had not always been the case. Initially, P. I. Rachkovskii, director of the Paris Office from 1884 to 1902, had only one administrative assistant, Nikolai Nikolaev Chashnikov, born into the hereditary nobility and a professional civil servant. In 1880 Fontanka invited him to work for the Russian police abroad because of his excellent command of French. Almost until Chashnikov's retirement in 1906 he and his clerk-typist Aleksandr Konstantinovich Il'in were the only full-time Russian *chinovniki* assigned to the Paris Office.[3] Il'in came to Paris with four years experience in the Department of Police behind him and with the reputation of being a 'thoroughly devoted *chinovnik* deserving encouragement'. Chashnikov, however, must have served alone for most of his years abroad since Il'in came to Paris only on 1 January 1905.

In the early years of the chancery's operation Chashnikov worked alone transcribing Rachkovskii's reports by hand, for typewriters did not come into regular use until the mid-1890s. Chashnikov found the entire process of transcription too time-consuming to make duplicates for the Foreign Agentura's own records. It is only with the introduction of the typewriter and carbon paper that a systematic method of documentation and record keeping appears within the Foreign Agentura's chancery. Considering the growing size and importance of the revolutionary emigration it is truly unbelievable that the tsarist government allowed the Paris Office to be so understaffed. The appalling conditions under which both Rachkovskii and his successor L. A. Rataev worked remove some of the stigma attached to their lack of qualifications as bureaucrats. But it is to neither man's credit that the chancery remained understaffed and neglected throughout their administrations.

Fontanka expanded the size of the Foreign Agentura's chancery when it appointed A. M. Harting as director in 1905 and began to recognise the danger to Tsardom presented by the revolutionary emigration, in particular its arms smuggling operations. In 1906 Chashnikov more or less retired, remaining on the payroll only as a translator.[4] The Foreign Agentura replaced him with a bureaucrat named Gol'shman about whom no information is available.[5] Fontanka made additional chancery appointments in rapid succession: *Kollezhskii assessor* (Collegiate Assessor) Ivan Mol'chanov and *Kollezhskii sekretar'* (Collegiate Secretary) Ivan Mel'nikov. Their respective ranks indicate that Mol'chanov, a middle-ranking bureaucrat, formulated and edited reports and corresponded with Fontanka. In addition, he probably helped to direct the chancery's operations while Mel'nikov functioned as a clerk-typist. Harting's staff, then, was composed of four members two of whom, Gol'shman and Mol'chanov, carried out the major tasks of the chancery while Mel'nikov and Il'in served as the chancery clerks.

On 1 March 1908, *Statskii sovetnik* (State Councillor) Boris Sushkov replaced Gol'shman. Sushkov's appointment reflected the substantially increased workload incurred by the Paris chancery as a result of the Foreign Agentura's anti-smuggling campaign (see Chapter 9). Sushkov held a very high rank (V *chin* on the Table of Ranks) and earned a salary of 500 francs per month, a sum denoting his importance; he produced many of the Foreign Agentura's reports on police matters. Since Harting wrote the dispatches concerning the Foreign Agentura's anti-smuggling campaign himself, Sushkov held responsibility for the dispatches dealing with the day-to-day activity of the emigration. He became so skilled in the production of reports that in 1911 alone A. A. Krasil'nikov, the current director of the Paris Office, permitted him to produce 500 of them although, of course, his signature did not appear on a single one.[6]

Krasil'nikov, as Harting before him, had every reason to be confident in Sushkov's ability since the *Statskii sovetnik* possessed outstanding professional credentials. After the young Sushkov had completed a course of study at the Imperial School of Jurisprudence he entered government service with the rank of *Titularnyi sovetnik* (Titular Councillor) in the Ministry of Justice. A year later, in 1892, he transferred to the Ministry of Internal Affairs as an *Pomoshchnik stolonachal'nika* (Assistant to the Head of a Department). In a little more than a year another promotion conferred upon Sushkov the position of *Mladshii stolonachal'nik* (Junior Department Chief) and by 1897 he had attained the rank of *Nadvornyi sovetnik* (Aulic Councillor). In August 1906 Sushkov unexpectedly petitioned Fontanka to release him from service and Headquarters reluctantly acquiesced. The Department of Police, however, knew that men of Sushkov's ability were hard to find and on 1 March 1908, Fontanka invited him to take an important post in the chancery of the Foreign Agentura. He agreed to re-enter the civil service and was soon rewarded by promotion to the prestigious rank of State Councillor.[7] The appointment of the well-respected Sushkov to Paris affirmed the high value Fontanka placed on the Foreign Agentura's dispatches, as the embittered and hardened revolutionaries returned to their familiar European haunts following the defeat of the 1905 Revolution. The activities of the revolutionary emigration again became a principal concern of the Special Section.

Subsequently, there were further changes in the composition of the chancery as *chinovniki* came and went.[8] Even the talented Sushkov was eventually and reluctantly replaced by a much less capable man as we shall see below.[9] Generally, though, in the post-1908 era, the Paris chancery contained between four and five civil servants.

Chinovniki serving abroad were handpicked for their posts by Fontanka in consultation with the chief of the Foreign Agentura. In the one known case when Fontanka disagreed with the choice of the director of the Paris Office it still sent someone of equal ability.[10] All of them came well recommended with the standard phrases, 'of high moral standard', 'unimpeachable conduct', and 'an honest devotion to service'.[11] If anything, the conduct of these people during their tenure with the Foreign Agentura became more exemplary and their devotion to duty intensified under the Paris Office's working conditions. The interchangeability of their new jobs, the physical proximity to their chief who worked in the next room and conferred with them regularly, combined with the feeling of isolation engendered by service in a foreign atmosphere where no one, not even their fellow bureaucrats working upstairs in the Embassy could be told of the nature of their duties, contributed to binding clerks, administrators, and directors closely together.

The service records of the chancery personnel reveal that the tightly knit relationship among the Foreign Agentura staff was further enhanced by the deep concern of the Paris Office chiefs with the personal and private lives of their chancery employees, the generous rewards the staff received for work well done and the grand retirement benefits bestowed upon them. All of these circumstances bred an *esprit de corps* of considerable magnitude within the Paris Office. Working for the Foreign Agentura was a recognised hardship for which the *chinovniki* were amply rewarded.[12]

Sometimes, however, a new appointee to the Foreign Agentura's chancery did not receive his promised salary. When Nikolai Volkhovskii complained to A. A. Krasil'nikov – director of the Foreign Agentura from 1909 to the collapse of the regime (see Chapter 10) – that his pay amounted to 100 francs less per month than promised,[13] Krasil'nikov responded to his subordinates' plight by personally writing to Fontanka protesting Headquarter's breach of its word. He argued that the 300 francs a month allotted by Fontanka for Volkhovskii's salary did not permit the man to live adequately in Paris, this despite his residence in an apartment rented for him by the Foreign Agentura up the street from the Embassy, nor could he send any money to his wife in St Petersburg. The chief of the Paris Office suggested that his subordinate be given a raise to 450 francs per month, 50 francs more than he was originally promised.[14] The Department of Police retreated in the face of Krasil'nikov's persuasive argument and granted the 150 franc monthly increase in Volkhovskii's wages.[15] Volkhovskii's was not an isolated case. The directors of the Foreign Agentura regularly argued that the chancery staff were underpaid and that their salaries should be raised. After all, the work load especially during Krasil'nikov's administration grew more burdensome and the cost of living in Paris also grew over the years.

Paris Office chiefs went even further than this by entering into the private lives of their chancery employees. The file of Ivan Mol'chanov reflects every one of the personal crises of his life while in the employment of the Foreign Agentura. Mol'chanov battled a severe case of tuberculosis which absorbed his entire salary leaving him destitute. The director of the Foreign Agentura issued an exceptionally sensitive plea to Fontanka on Mol'chanov's behalf. Harting wrote St Petersburg that his budget permitted him only to advance Mol'chanov 100 rubles, not enough to do his employee much good, therefore could the MVD help to relieve this loyal civil servant's plight.[16] The director's pleas fell on deaf ears. Mol'chanov was forced to struggle along as well as he could and A. M. Harting, his chief (see Chapters 8 and 9), treated him gently and with concern. When Mol'chanov requested a six week leave of absence in April 1909, the director of the Foreign Agentura immediately approved it. Soon after Fontanka confirmed Harting's decision which meant that Mol'chanov at least would be paid his regular salary during his leave.[17] Unfortunately over the next several months serious personal problems, the demands of his job, and the Parisian weather undermined Mol'chanov's health still further.[18] By the autumn of 1909 the Provincial Secretary was in a terrible physical state. Captain Andreev, Harting's immediate successor, wrote Fontanka that:

> The heavy work load of the past winter and the constant tension has caused the extraordinary [physical] condition in which those who serve in the Foreign Agentura find themselves in the spring. This condition, an inflammation of the lungs shatters his [Mol'chanov's] strength and treatment for Mol'chanov is now a question of [saving] his life.[19]

Andreev requested that Mol'chanov be given a leave of absence, a single sum of 500 rubles and an additional advance of 100 rubles to hold him over during his illness. The last sum would have to be returned to Fontanka.

In an about turn Fontanka granted Andreev's request and Mol'chanov received the money.[20] Some time later a partially recovered Mol'chanov attempted to return to work, but he soon again had to apply for a short leave of absence.[21] Fontanka and the Foreign Agentura ultimately came to the conclusion that this much plagued *chinovnik* could no longer carry out the duties of his office. On 21 June 1910, Mol'chanov retired on the substantial pension of 1,200 rubles per year.[22] A strange conclusion to a bizzare episode. The Mol'chanov case shows that the Foreign Agentura treated its employees in the Paris Office with deep, if somewhat erratic, concern.[23]

The directors of the Foreign Agentura, especially Harting and Krasil'nikov, expressed a patriarchal concern for their chancery personnel not only for the above-mentioned reasons, but also because they were hardworking and exceptionally loyal, not the most common of traits among tsarist bureaucrats. Krasil'nikov, suggesting that these employees be given an across the board raise in salary, told Fontanka that:

> This small group fulfils all the significant duties incumbent upon the chancery of the Agentura. [This job] constantly demands entire days and not only week days, but quite often holidays when newly received information of an urgent character demands the ciphering of very long telegrams which drags work into the late hours of the night.[24]

Krasil'nikov did not exaggerate. In 1908 Sushkov supervised the production of 500 reports synthesised from data supplied by agents in the field.[25] By 1911 the number of reports had tripled when Sushkov with the help of Provincial Secretary Mikhail Bobrov and Collegiate Secretary Ivan Mel'nikov who were exclusively occupied with typing, produced 1,500 dispatches (a reflection of the increasing attention that the Foreign Agentura devoted to the revolutionary emigration).[26]

These bureaucrats, however, received special and unique compensations beyond the respect and firm support of their director to assuage the frenetic pace of their everyday duties. Chancery personnel received a variety of awards from European governments for particular jobs well-done, an accomplishment that added much prestige to the recipient and undoubtedly refuelled his desire to zealously carry out his obligations. The director of the Foreign Agentura usually solicited medallions, medals and orders for his employees knowing the value they placed upon them. Sushkov was the most frequently rewarded Foreign Agentura bureaucrat. The orders of which he could be proudest were the Victoria Cross V Class and the Italian Crown of the Cavalier with Crest.[27] Their Russian employers, however, parted with tsarist honours less readily. For preserving the emperor's safety while he travelled abroad, Sushkov and Mel'nikov, the only two members of the chancery staff to participate in this effort received gold watches and fobs. Sushkov's was engraved with the Imperial Coat of Arms and Mel'nikov's was just a plain gold watch.[28] The Russian government preferred to issue rewards of a more mundane nature. On Christmas Day in 1912, for example, Sushkov, Mel'nikov and Bobrov received cash presents.[29] The Foreign Agentura also issued small gratuities as incentives to its diligent workers. In one case Sushkov and Mel'nikov received 100 francs and Mikhail Bobrov 90 francs as tokens of appreciation. Promotions were also available to the capable bureaucrat. Both Sushkov and Mel'nikov were promoted, the former to State Councillor and the latter to Titular Councillor. Four years later, in 1916, Mel'nikov became a candidate for the post of *Mladshii Pomoshchnik Deloproizvoditelia* (Junior Assistant Manager) in the Department of Police, a step necessary before he could attain the rank of Collegiate Assessor.[30]

It must be said, however, that not all of the *chinovniki* chosen for posts within the Foreign Agentura's chancery turned out as well as Sushkov and Mel'nikov. Sushkov returned home in January 1914, and Krasil'nikov hand-picked his replacement, Titular Councillor Iusefovich. Iusefovich appeared perfectly suited for the job as chief of the Foreign Agentura's chancery. His qualifications included command of several languages and duty abroad at an earlier date and his unusually large salary reflected Headquarter's appreciation of his skills. Nonetheless, Iusefovich turned out to be a major disappointment. In exasperation, the chief of the Paris Office noted, 'he is incapable of any kind of independent work... and it is not possible to hope that he might be able to learn'. Krasil'nikov did not feel, however, that he could request Iusefovich's recall since he had asked for him in the first place. So, instead he beseeched Fontanka for permission to send Iusefovich on special assignment outside of Paris; at least this would get him out of the chancery. St Petersburg granted the request and it must have been a very long trip since his name does not appear again amongst the chancery's salaried personnel.[31]

Ultimately, Iusefovich may have requested and received a transfer back to St Petersburg, since transfers home were, of course, possible for members of the chancery who, despite the rewards, found the work too arduous and the life unbearably lonely. One such person was typist Maria Fedorovna who in 1914 expressed her wish to be transferred to Fontanka. St Petersburg granted her request and offered her a position within the Eighth Secretariat of the Department of Police which she accepted.[32] The Foreign Agentura supplied her with 300 francs travelling expenses and she went on her way. The only drawback to her new job was a considerable reduction in salary, a penalty Fedorovna willingly paid for the opportunity to return to the Motherland.[33]

While the collection of intelligence became the job of the case officers, the chief of the detective agency, and the director of the Foreign Agentura, the job of supplying that information to St Petersburg in a coherent form belonged to the *chinovniki* within the Paris chancery. This closely bound group worked in a manner similar to the chanceries of the provincial OOs (Okhrannoe Otdelenie or Security Division) within the Empire. The chancery most commonly used dispatches to communicate with St Petersburg, although coded telegrams could be sent if urgency so required. Periodically, the chancery also produced long reports on those groups it deemed important. The clerks kept a record and copies of all correspondence, particularly after 1895 with the introduction of the typewriter. Chancery personnel maintained a separate journal for incoming registered letters received from agents in the field in western Europe, the United States and Russia and like other correspondence these were cross referenced. In this case, however, the reference key referred to both the addressor and the addressee.[34] If Fontanka expected dispatches to retain long-term interest St. Petersburg ordered the Paris Office to store them in the Foreign Agentura's archive, otherwise they were to be destroyed.[35] Luckily for the historian the chancery disobeyed this command and kept every piece of paper it produced or received except for those financial records which the directors conveniently ordered destroyed.

One last important task remained to the Paris chancery – to acquire and maintain a thorough collection of revolutionary publications. The Special Section and other branches of Fontanka regularly requested copies of the whole spectrum of revolutionary publications.[36] A related function of the chancery involved the checking out of stories about interesting events abroad appearing in liberal Russian newspapers such as *Russkiia Vedemosti* (*The Russian Herald*) and *Russkoe Bogatstvo* (*Russian Wealth*).[37]

The Special Section studied the Foreign Agentura's reports with great care. Surprisingly, despite the outstanding quality of the Paris chancery staff, Fontanka regularly (especially during Krasil'nikov's tenure in office between 1909 and 1917) chastised them for producing what it considered obscure, verbose, and at times confusing reports and dispatches. How can we reconcile the clearly superior quality of the Paris chancery staff with Fontanka's grumbling about its work? A close look at the situation in Paris and the content of Fontanka's complaints reveal that the Special Section's analysts and the clerks of Fontanka's Sixth Secretariat were complaining about insoluble problems that could not be justly blamed upon the Foreign Agentura's chancery staff.

The shortage of human resources and the universal inadequacies of information retrieval and processing technology at that time seriously and unavoidably hampered the collection and collation of the innumerable bits of incoming intelligence. There is no doubt that the Paris chancery was undermanned and that the laborious procedure of intelligence processing – the sifting, filtering and collating of information – that took place within the Foreign Agentura's chancery, given the immensity of its workload, was accomplished only in a cursory and superficial manner. Krasil'nikov undoubtedly exacerbated this situation by his failure to find an adequate replacement for Sushkov as head of chancery in 1914. A cumbersome but safe method, therefore, of ensuring that the Special Section had all the data it required for its purposes was, in fact, to send to St Petersburg every piece of information that was thought to possess intelligence value, allowing the Special Section's analysts to evaluate its significance for themselves. And this is what Krasil'nikov along with his equally overworked colleagues within the empire's provincial OOs did.[38] This procedure had much to recommend it. It certainly was more appropriate to allow experts dealing with specific subversive groups to judge the importance of the data collected for themselves than to have field staffs who did not see the overall picture do it for them. Unfortunately, this practice caused Fontanka's Special Section and Sixth Secretariat to be inundated with paperwork, so much so that E. K. Klimovich, the director of the Department of Police for much of 1916, remembered that, 'our ideal is this: the less you write, the better! There is nothing worse than unnecessary chatter!'[39] Despite Klimovich's motto, however, Fontanka was hoisted on the Special Section's petard. Ironically, the Special Section's desire to acquire *all* the *relevant* data it required for the subjects and groups that interested it, sabotaged its equally valued aim of obtaining this intelligence in a compact, easily digestible form, with every piece of extraneous detail stripped away by the local political police bureau.[40] For a long time, neither the Special Section nor Fontanka itself recognised that the absence of sophisticated data processing technology, the limited supply of clerical labour, and in many OOs the poor quality of the analytical skill of the staff made this an impossible goal.

The complaint made by Klimovich concerning the Foreign Agentura's reports was that they were bulky and 'terribly perplexing' so that at times analysis of their contents was not possible. As a result the Special Section was forced to request that the Paris Office clarify and elaborate on them, even at times suggesting changes in the style of the Paris chancery's reporting.[41] These requests substantially increased the workload on the already over-extended Paris bureau without improving the quality of the picture of subversive activities that the intelligence was producing. For example, when Fontanka found reports vague or incomplete the Foreign Agentura received a critique of the inadequate piece of correspondence from St Petersburg:

> In [reference] to your report of 24 June/7 July No. 817 . . . the Department of Police requests [that you] designate in your reports . . . names, patronymic and surname, and in parenthesis party code name . . . .[42]

One can sympathise with Fontanka's demand that the full name of a suspect including his or her *klichka* (code name) be presented in reports to

St Petersburg, for its clerks had to cross reference those names to one card among 2,500,000 on file. In those pre-computer days establishing the identity of a suspect by only mentioning one of his or her possible names in a dispatch was practically impossible. Names, especially code names, were bound to be duplicated by the dozen in a name index that large. Of course in many cases it was not possible to give the full name and *klichka* of a suspect. In these cases the Foreign Agentura had to supply even more obscure information including the individual's place of birth, height, occupation, or anything that would give Fontanka 'some sort of thread for the pursuit of the Department's tasks'. For this reason the Department wanted the Foreign Agentura to construct its dispatches with as few people as possible mentioned in each one. The Paris chancery, however, in trying to minimise its own tasks ignored Fontanka's instructions. In one report they listed 13 surnames without mentioning any other distinctive features. One of the surnames listed in this dispatch was Abramov. There were 2,000 cards in Fontanka's file labelled with the surname Abramov. In fact, the Department of Police could not match any of the 13 surnames mentioned in the report to the appropriate cards.[43] Frustrated by the immensity of its task, Fontanka literally begged the Foreign Agentura for more specific information. The Department of Police was the helpless victim of its own exhaustive methodology.

Fontanka did not recognise the magnitude of the problem. For the year 1913 the last dated Foreign Agentura dispatch possessed the Registry Number 1738. In other words, five people in the Paris chancery turned out almost 2,000 reports in one year, an amazing feat in itself. It was just not realistic to expect them to break down these dispatches into several hundred more in order to comply with Fontanka's request for the most detailed data on suspects' physical and biographical characteristics.

The exchanged correspondence[44] added up into the thousands every year and the Foreign Agentura kept a careful record of each one.[45] At times dispatches were lost in transit and Fontanka made inquiries concerning them. Any dispatch not received by St Petersburg was traced as a matter of course.[46] A task of this proportion when multiplied hundreds of times, as Fontanka's directive would have required, could not have been accomplished even by a much enlarged staff. Not even so outstanding a chancery as the one in Paris could meet the maddening demands placed upon it by Fontanka. Headquarter's desperate, even laudable, but ultimately quixotic effort to completely decipher and correlate the mass of incoming intelligence it received from its vast political police network exhausted the best of its chanceries. It is a wonder the political police could keep track of anyone, especially young newcomers to the revolutionary movement who left virtually no paper trail at all.

Finally, the Foreign Agentura refused to comply with Fontanka's demands – it could not do otherwise and still maintain its chancery operation – and continued to submit reports in its customary manner much to the vexation of St Petersburg.[47]

From 1909 until the Foreign Agentura closed its doors in March 1917 the Paris Office's chancery staff increasingly found itself subordinated to the ever more numerous case officers who came to occupy an important place within the Foreign Agentura's administration.

Case officers, men who usually held the rank of Captain in the Separate Corps of Gendarmes, were generally specialists in controlling and debriefing undercover agents within particular parties or groups. Within Russia itself conferences between undercover agents (*sotrudniki*) and their controls were supposed to take place within 'conspiratorial apartments' (*konspirativnye kvartiry*). The Special Section instituted rules for the use of conspiratorial apartments and demanded that undercover agents and case officers strictly obey them for their mutual safety: to protect the undercover agent's identity and thereby his life and to safeguard the case officer from the his undercover agents. For the case officer a failure to follow appropriate procedure or become too relaxed in dealing with undercover agents could be fatal.[48]

The *sotrudniki* were exceptional people. It took an unusually strong personality to maintain equilibrium in a profession where severe psychological stress was often the most demanding part of the service. Viktor Russiian, a prominent political police official of the day, remembered that undercover agents were extremely secretive and would withhold information they held at hand if they believed their security to be threatened.[49] Unfortunately, these attributes were often the *bête noire* of the case officers. Faced with such devious and strong willed people, case officers often had to throw the rule book for dealing with *sotrudniki* aside, as dangerous as this could be, in order to cultivate the flexible, relaxed, trusting relationship with their undercover agents necessary to draw critical information out of them without lowering their own guard. To do so could lead to catastrophic results. The way Evno Azev, the terrorist, whose group murdered Minister of Internal Affairs Plehve in July 1904, toyed with L. A. Rataev, his amateurish case officer is a good example of this.[50]

Until 1903 *sotrudniki* following suspects abroad reported to St Petersburg[51] and undercover agents reported either directly to the chief of the Foreign Agentura or to the case officer attached to the regional OO within the Empire to which they were assigned. During Krasil'nikov's tenure in office the number of case officers abroad grew steadily. The case officers sent to Paris displayed outstanding records as gendarme officers, although at least one of them did not have any experience in this delicate specialty. This was Captain Rek, who transferred from the Railway Gendarmerie. Another was a civilian, certainly an anomaly in this job. Still, like the members of the Paris chancery, they were on the whole an exceptionally able lot. Originally two case officers were assigned to the Foreign Agentura: Captains Dolgov and Erghardt. In 1910 Dolgov left Paris to become an assistant to the chief of the Special Section. The appointment of Dolgov's successor abroad was the prerogative of St Petersburg.[52] The director of the Foreign Agentura did not have a say in the selection process of case officers. These were Fontanka's men, not the Foreign Agentura's.

Fontanka informed Krasil'nikov that the new case officer, Captain Rek, would assist Captain Erghardt in the conduct of political investigations and undertake duties within the Paris chancery, relieving Sushkov of the responsibility of liaison between the Foreign Agentura's External (Detective) Agency and Krasil'nikov. Rek would collect detective surveillance reports, instruct the supervisor of detectives about whom to keep under surveillance, 'and report about all this' to Krasil'nikov.[53] Rek's appointment to these chancery functions brought the Foreign Agentura's operating procedures more closely into line with those of the OOs within the Empire and it gave Sushkov more time to spend on his principle role as chief of the chancery. Nevertheless, it was a risky decision. Captain Rek was not an experienced political policeman. In assuming this portion of Sushkov's duties, he replaced a man thoroughly familiar with the emigration and the detective service, who had an excellent working relationship with the supervisor of detectives.

Upon his arrival in Paris Rek met with his immediate superior Captain Erghardt who briefed him on local conditions and the demands of his office.[54] Rek also learned that he was to receive a substantial salary and generous perquisites to compensate for the loneliness and frayed nerves that, ironically, went hand-in-hand with a tour of duty in Paris.[55] Rek lived in Paris under a fictitious name and his personal acquaintances were restricted to members of the Russian political police. Captain Rek's isolated existence protected him from exposure, but after serving abroad for more than a year a small notice appeared in Vladimir Burtsev's newspaper *Budushchee* (*The Future*) only noting Rek's address and nothing else. The Foreign Agentura could not afford to have its case officers known to the revolutionary emigration. The discovery of a case officer if left unremedied would eventually lead to the exposure of vitally important *sotrudniki*. Burtsev's little notice in *Budushchee*, therefore, caused the recall of Captain Rek from Paris in December 1911.[56]

A gendarme officer collected considerable prestige from successful service abroad. One gendarme spent the best years of his career abroad and he truly served above the normal expectations of duty. Captain Erghardt served loyally and by 1915 he held the rank of Lt. Colonel. Just at this time Erghardt became ill with severe stomach pain and his doctor recommended that he enter the hospital at once. But Erghardt refused to leave his post during the week claiming that at any rate he felt better and would hold out until Saturday. On 10 April, the following Saturday, Erghardt underwent an appendectomy too late to save his life.[57] The MVD hailed Lt. Colonel Erghardt as a hero and posthumously treated him as one. The assistant minister of internal affairs approved the issuance of 500 roubles for Erghardt's funeral and as a last gesture his government awarded Erghardt the Order of St Vladimir IV Class.[58]

Lt. Colonel Erghardt's replacement, Captain Lustig, had been serving the Foreign Agentura as a case officer since August 1912. In addition, St Petersburg added new case officers to the Foreign Agentura's staff: Captain Likhovskii in Switzerland and *Gubernskii sekretar* Litvin in Great Britain. Lustig's immediate previous experience had been in the Warsaw OO and he conducted his new operations in the efficient manner which had so impressed his superiors in Warsaw. Lustig supervised all the undercover agents working in Europe outside of Switzerland and Great Britain. He did, however, receive summary reports on émigré activities in Switzerland and Great Britain from Likhovskii and Litvin in the line of duty. He also managed those *sotrudniki* working in the United States.[59]

The case officers working within the Foreign Agentura seemed to be in a unique position. Although they were attached to the Paris Office they maintained a large degree of independence. They had access to substantial personal budgets, excluding salary payments, and they kept their accounts separately from those of the Paris Office, even though the money they received came from the Foreign Agentura's pocket. Lt. Colonel Erghardt and Captain Lustig spent over 19,000 francs per month supporting their networks of undercover agents. If the accounts for any month showed a surplus they kept it and applied the excess to the next month's balance instead of returning it to the Foreign Agentura.[60] Despite their independence the case officers met at regular intervals with the director of the Foreign Agentura to discuss intelligence received from their *sotrudniki* and to jointly plan the best methods of proceeding. They transferred the raw data gathered by their undercover agents to the Paris chancery which processed it in the standard manner by synthesising this new material with facts gleaned from earlier reports, detectives' observations, and from Department of Police circulars in order to form one final report (see below).

In theory case officers were not to have personal contact with anyone else employed in the Foreign Agentura.[61] In practice, however, this was not the case. Nevertheless, they always considered themselves separate from the Paris Office. Lustig's testimony before the Provisional Government's Investigation Commission reflects the contempt in which gendarmes, involved in political police work, held the civilian bureaucrats in their midst.[62] This attitude did not disturb the chancery personnel who accepted the gendarme officers' superior position within the political police as a justifiable fact of life. The chancery staff and gendarme case officers under Krasil'nikov's leadership formed a loyal and but for a few exceptions an efficient group which functioned well in difficult circumstances. This view is borne out by the Agentura's two crisis situations. The most important is Vladimir Burtsev's attack on the Foreign Agentura which is the subject of Chapter 11. The second is the Foreign Agentura's flight from Paris before the German onslaught in August 1914 and its resettlement in Bordeaux.

Despite the difficulty of the move south Krasil'nikov reported that it went smoothly. Much had to be left behind in Paris, locked away in a private apartment in 96 Rue de Grenelle. Once in Bordeaux, Krasil'nikov found rampant confusion but the Agentura managed to set up shop in the Berlitz language school. The room was located in the centre of the city near both the Prefecture of Police and the French Ministry of the Interior which, along with the remainder of the French government, had moved to Bordeaux. As a security measure *Gubernskii sekretar'* Bobrov and *Kollezhskii registrator* Volkhovskii took up permanent residence in the new office. Perhaps the most serious problem caused by the sudden move to Bordeaux confronting Krasil'nikov became the disruption of communications between the Foreign Agentura chief and his case officers in London, Paris, and Switzerland.[63] Yet this difficulty was overcome by the dedication of the case officers who carried on their duties as efficiently and loyally as the situation permitted, weathering the crisis until it was brought to an end by the return of the Foreign Agentura to Paris in the spring of 1915.

In December 1916 Fontanka notified Krasil'nikov that another case officer, a certain Lt. Colonel Martynov had just been assigned to the Foreign Agentura. The transfer of an obviously well-thought-of Lt. Colonel to the Foreign Agentura did not bode well for Krasil'nikov's future.[64] A Lt. Colonel in the political police did more than supervise a few undercover agents; remember Erghardt's promotion to that rank just before he died undoubtedly meant that he had a bright future in store for him. Very probably Lt. Colonel Martynov once he became acquainted with his new surroundings would have been named Krasil'nikov's successor. This action would have placed the Foreign Agentura under the guidance of a gendarme officer in similar fashion to the other political police branches within the Russian Empire. Martynov did not have the opportunity to take up his post before the February Revolution.

Indeed, the assignment of case officers abroad indicated that Fontanka wished to end, once and for all, the freewheeling days that characterised the tenures of three of the four Foreign Agentura chiefs. To be sure, Rachkovskii, Harting and Krasil'nikov displayed independent personalities, but this flexibility to be creatively non-comformist, sidestepping the rigid structure of Fontanka's chain-of-command, allowed them to develop informal relationships with their European colleagues and successfully observe and harass the revolutionary emigration as we shall see in the following chapters. Rachkovskii, Harting and Krasil'nikov came to the Foreign Agentura outside of the standard promotion procedures decreed by the Table of Ranks. Indeed, it was their independence and proactive response to their duties along with their easy integration into European society – they had this attribute in common with Rataev – that made these directors so effective and so much a part of the European policing scene. The long arm of tsarist bureaucratic culture was slowly throttling this very independence and decisiveness that characterised the success of these three men. Rataev, the only mainstream *chinovnik* amongst the four important directors of the Paris Office, proved to be by far the least successful director of the Foreign Agentura.

One further point: the size and complexity of the Foreign Agentura's chancery operations cannot be compared to those of the gigantic regional OOs located in Moscow, St Petersburg, Kiev and Warsaw. The Paris Office chancery is representative of the very much more numerous smaller provincial OO chanceries. However, unlike the provincial OOs, the Paris Office used the smallness of its chancery staff to advantage. This characteristic,[65] combined with the quality and dedication of its personnel, its location outside of Russia, and the unorthodox leadership of A. M. Harting and A. A. Krasil'nikov who directed the Paris Office between them from 1905 to 1917 (see Chapters 9 and 10), permitted the Foreign Agentura to acquire a strong sense of social cohesion. It displayed social relationships which would have been difficult to locate in the rigid, stultifying atmosphere of the domestic Russian bureaucracy. It appears that able low- and middle-ranking Russian civil servants, despite the technological and staff constrictions under which they functioned, were capable in the face of extreme pressure of operating an effective bureau under the influence of an *esprit de corps* when they were given the opportunity to do so. The Department of Police was not capable of learning this lesson.

6
Europeans and Russians in the Service of the Tsarist Secret Police: the Detectives and Undercover Agents in Exile

The work of the Paris chancery staff and the case officers assigned to the Foreign Agentura was merely routine compared to the burden of service placed upon the shoulders of the Foreign Agentura's detectives and undercover agents. The detectives (who for the most part were out of necessity West Europeans) and the undercover agents adhered to the same basic procedures as did their brethren within the Empire. Yet the lives and jobs of these men and women were made different from their colleagues within Russia – more complicated and (for the *sotrudniki* in particular) rendered far more dangerous – by their location within the unfriendly political surroundings of western Europe, far away from the security of the homeland. Those differences gave some of the Foreign Agentura's operations a unique complexion. The Paris Office's *sotrudniki* and detectives themselves, like the chancery staff discussed in the previous chapter were expected to be (though by no means were all of them) more innovative and generally more talented than the mass of their co-workers inside Russia. They carried out their duties effectively as the abundant reports within the Foreign Agentura archive overwhelmingly confirm.[1]

We begin with the story of the detectives, the 'foot soldiers' of the Paris Office, who supplied the contextual information without which the necessary panorama of subversive activity could not be constructed. The Foreign Agentura's detective service began on a very small scale. The first director, Korvin-Krukovskoi employed four French detectives, all of whom were passed on to his successor P. I. Rachkovskii. Of these four men, however, only two Henri Bint and Ernest Riant had long-term careers with the Paris Office.[2] Both of these men had previously been long-serving and respected inspectors of police for the Paris Prefecture.

In the 1890s the Foreign Agentura enlarged the size of its External Agency by increasing the number of regular long-term appointments to the detective service. Rigault was appointed in 1889, Deleamont in 1890, Bouquet in 1895, and Fernbach in 1897. The Frenchmen were joined by an English colleague, Detective Farce, in 1890.[3] No other appointments were made to the External Agency until after the turn of the century, a fact denoting the rather small size of the revolutionary emigration up to that time and the continued use of Russian detectives abroad. Rachkovskii made four additional appointments after 1900. The new men were Heinrick Neuhaus and Carl Woltz, former members of the Berlin police force, and they took up posts with the Berlin Agentura, Albert Sambian, who worked directly for Rachkovskii and Michael Thorpe, an Englishman, assigned to London. At the end of Rachkovskii's tenure in office there were nine non-Russian detectives in the Foreign Agentura's service: two in Great Britain, two in Germany, three in France and two in Switzerland.

The personnel dossiers[4] indicate that L. A. Rataev, the Foreign Agentura's third chief, continued to add to the size of the External Agency. Despite Rataev's employment of additional detectives his successor A. M. Harting found the detective service to be undermanned.[5] But the bureaucracy's wheels moved slowly; Harting received permission to hire new detectives only in 1907 with the rapid renewed expansion of the emigration swelling with battle-weary revolutionaries. In 1908, Harting made a significant appointment with Marcel Bittard-Monin. Bittard-Monin had just retired from the post of director of operations for the Paris Prefecture and upon being lured to the Foreign Agentura he assumed a similar role as head of its External Agency. By the end of Harting's administration taking into account changes brought about by hirings, firings and retirements, there were about 20 detectives in the service of the Foreign Agentura.[6] This number doubled during A. A. Krasil'nikov's directorship. The rapid increase in the number of detectives hired for the Foreign Agentura can be seen in Table 6.1.

The sudden drop in the number of appointments between 1912 and 1913 is attributable to the reorganisation of the External (Detective) Agency implemented in the autumn of 1913 which drastically reduced the number of detectives in the service and made the selection process more rigorous.

Table 6.1 Detectives hired by the Foreign Agentura 1909–1913

Year	*Number of Appointments*
End of 1909 and 1910	4
1911	10
1912	15
1913	2

Source: Appendix A.1

A final tally before the implementation of this reform shows that the External Agency contained between 41 and 50 detectives.[7] Bittard-Monin's own statistics disagree slightly with the lower number. He claimed there were 39 detectives working for the Foreign Agentura, 17 in Paris, the remainder in other areas of France and throughout continental Europe and Great Britain.[8]

Until well into 1913, Bittard-Monin directed this complex network of detectives. Money and instructions flowed from the Paris Office to Bittard-Monin who in turn passed them on to his detectives. Besides acting as liaison between the Foreign Agentura's chancery and his detectives Bittard-Monin kept a journal of reports received from his operatives on a daily basis. From these reports Bittard-Monin submitted only what he believed to be useful information to the Paris chancery, moreover, the supervisor of the External Agency often personally checked on the accuracy of the information submitted to him by his operatives. This preliminary screening of raw intelligence data by Bittard-Monin had the drawback of any filtering system, that some important bits of information might never get beyond the supervisor's desk. Overall, though, it made the job of the chancery staff much easier. The *chinovniki* also knew that they would receive information already sifted by a very experienced and talented policeman who forwarded only data deemed as accurate and important.[9]

The majority of the Foreign Agentura's detectives were men but the Paris Office employed qualified women as well. These European detectives came from a broad spectrum of professional backgrounds, although this fact should not detract from the Paris Office's highly selective approach to choosing its detectives. For example, nine of the Foreign Agentura's detectives were recommended by the *Sûreté Générale*, six by long serving Foreign Agentura detective Henri Bint, five benefited from Bittard-Monin's support, one from the recommendation of Foreign Agentura detective Maurice Voigt and fifteen from referrals by other European police agencies (see Appendix A.2).

The detectives' personnel records reflect the Foreign Agentura's preference for married operatives. Of the 54 detectives listed in Appendix A 36 were married. Because of the physical exertion involved in 'tailing' a subject a detective's age mattered to the Foreign Agentura during the selection process. Table 6.2 does not show that experience was a mitigating consideration in employment, but Table 6.3 supports the view that the Paris Office was willing to put the age factor aside in the case of well-experienced applicants. Since 42 out of the 50 detectives on whom data is available had done military service, this group also possessed the ability to take orders, or that is at least what the Paris Office hoped. Seemingly, therefore, the major concerns of the Foreign Agentura in hiring its detectives were their stamina, stability, discipline, and experience. A background in police work, though desirable, was not necessary. Also of less importance were the applicants' secondary skills such as knowledge of foreign languages. According to available information 21 detectives spoke foreign languages, 25 did not and no data

Table 6.2 Detectives' age at time of employment

Age at time of employment	*Number employed at a given age*
23–29	18
32–39	22
40–49	6
50–58	4
No data	3

Source: Appendix A.1

Table 6.3 Detective age–experience correlation

Name	*Age at the time of appointment*	*Previous occupation*
J. H. Durin	40	Chief of *Sûreté* – Versailles
G. Dusseaussois	42	Director of Police – Reims
E. Leconte	41	Inspector of *Sûreté*
E. Leveque	50	Inspector of Police
L. Otte	58	Detective
F. Powell	51	Inspector of Police – Scotland Yard
A. Kerr F. Rougeaux M. Thorpe	Data not available	

Source: Appendix A.1

exists on one detective. If Appendixes A.1 and A.2 are compared we see that the ability to speak a foreign language did not affect salaries.

In order to encourage a steady flow of applications the Foreign Agentura advertised in the proper circles that it was always interested in employing a good man or woman. When a British citizen, for instance, inquired at the British Embassy in Brussels about the possibility of joining the 'Okhrana' an embassy employee did not hesitate to tell him to write to Director of the Department of Police Lopukhin.[10] In some cases when it became difficult to recruit detectives for a particular location, other branches of the Russian government were asked to help out. In one case the Russian Consul in Berne received a request to recruit detectives, 'for here [Switzerland] and America'.[11] Probably because of the large number of applicants who came from less than reputable backgrounds[12] and because several detectives, despite the stringent acceptance requirements, defected from the ranks of the Foreign Agentura, the Paris Office decided to regularise a long customary policy of hiring only those candidates who were recommended by national police officials and who were acquainted with persons working within the Foreign Agentura.[13]

Once accepted for service the new detectives were thrown into the battle, living and working at a frenetic pace. As we can see from Table 6.4 Foreign Agentura detectives spent their summer holidays accompanying some of the more feared émigrés on their vacations; spending July and August in the villages, towns, and cities where the revolutionaries went to escape the summer heat. They could not, however, pursue their quarries back into Russia. This was a job reserved for Russian *filery* (detectives).[14]

Usually when the Paris Office assigned its detectives to keep a given person under close surveillance the subject was an SR. In comparison, surveillance

Table 6.4 Foreign Agentura detectives: Bittard-Monin's summer schedule June 1912[a]

Detectives' names	*Country of assignment*	*Place of assignment*
Frumento Sauvard Roselli	Italy	Spezzia
Pavesi	Italy	Sesfri Levante
Invernizzi	Italy	Cavi
Capusso	Italy	Lavagna
Durin Fontana Vizzardelli	Italy	Genoa (at the railway station)
Drouchet	France	To follow wife of E. Koliari
Sambian Barthes	France	Antibes
Lodie	France	Gare de Juan-les-pins
Woltz Vogt	France	Cannes
Powell Thorpe Aebersold Kerr	Great Britain	London
Laurent Neuhaus Tuppinger	Switzerland	Travel with suspect
Bonnoil Leveque Coussonnet Delangle	Switzerland	Geneva

[a] Lists all those detectives available to Bittard-Monin at that time.
Source: Service Etat des Surveillances a la date du 18 juin 1912 – Repartition des agents, FAAr, 14, IIIe, 1e.

over SDs until about 1911 was carried out in a much more leisurely manner.[15] After all, in the collective *mentalité* of every Russian political policeman, the SRs were terrorists who needed to be kept on a leash through exceptionally vigilant surveillance. Thus, when SRs such as Karpovich and Steinbeck in London, Silberberg, Somov and Prokofiev in Southern France or Sletov, Skolnik, Fabricant and Kolari in Italy were the quarry the Paris Office detectives felt almost unbearable pressure to ensure that they did not escape from surveillance. This was especially true for Boris Savinkov.

By the final days of the 1905 Revolution Savinkov was the most feared SR terrorist of all and the Foreign Agentura's most pursued revolutionary. One report details how desperately the Russian police tried to discover the significance of every one of his actions. The Paris Office learned that Savinkov and his 'gang' were using a villa in Dieppe as a base for their activities. Detectives Durin and Fontaine photographed Savinkov and two fellow terrorists Somov and Lukhanov confirming the Foreign Agentura's intelligence. Both detectives kept the villa under close surveillance, waiting for any sign of activity. On the night of 1 November 1910, the terrorists suddenly departed from the villa in three separate groups. Savinkov took the express train to Paris via Rouen at 3:15a.m., while Lukhanov boarded another train at 8:08a.m. and to the growing frustration of the detectives, the remaining group departed by rail at 12:22p.m.. Their method of departure apparently confused the detectives who would normally have followed Savinkov. Perhaps the two men thought that the ploy of travelling in three groups with Savinkov departing first was meant to entice any possible pursuers to follow him on a wild goose chase, giving Savinkov's accomplices the time and the anonymity necessary to carry out some dastardly act. As a result Durin and Fontaine hesitated, and refusing to panic, decided to collect as much information as quickly as they could (since time was of the essence) in the hope that they would be able to discover where the groups were going and whom to follow. Luckily the terrorists had given the two detectives a clue: they were carrying only hand luggage. Durin and Fontaine also knew that Savinkov employed a maid and they soon discovered the maid service he had used. From the woman in charge of the service they learned that Savinkov had rented the villa until the end of December and that if he could subsequently find an apartment after that date he would remain in Dieppe until the end of January. Now this story could simply have been planted by the terrorist to throw the Foreign Agentura off his trail, except for one thing: the hand luggage. Still the decisions the detectives had to make about whom to follow and where they were going were not easy ones and the strain on them must have been enormous. The two detectives made their decisions quickly. The combination of the information they had collected from the maid service matron and the small amount of luggage the terrorists were carrying caused Durin and Fontaine to conclude that the 'gang' was not making the long trip to Paris. 'We have made the assumption that Savinkov and his band are going to Rouen', they wrote Krasil'nikov, 'and we will go to that city to continue our surveillance'.[16] They then undoubtedly set off after Savinkov and his associates by roaming the Rouen neighbourhoods frequented by Russian émigrés until they found their quarry. There could be no second guessing of their rapid fire analysis of the situation. If they were wrong Savinkov and his band would have escaped from police surveillance. This type of pressure-filled existence was routine for the Foreign Agentura's detectives.

Always too few in number, most detectives moved from one surveillance assignment to another as the Paris Office attempted to cover as many earmarked émigrés as possible with the surveillance staff at hand. Like their Russian counterparts the operatives of the Paris Office often worked in teams. They also easily acquired the co-operation of other police forces throughout Europe either legitimately or under the guise of French *Sûreté* agents. Detectives could be responsible for more than one surveillance at a time making for a hectic schedule. Mme. Genevieve Richard, one of the few women detectives, does not appear to have taken a vacation during her tenure with the Foreign Agentura, but apparently when she tired of her assignment in Italy she received her requested transfer to Paris at once as a reward for devoted service. She generally kept the same small group of SRs under surveillance during her entire length of service.

A summary of Richard's career in her own staccato style clearly portrays the trials and tribulations of a detective in the Foreign Agentura's employ and how indispensable the support of European police services were to the Foreign Agentura's campaign against the revolutionary emigration.

> On February 15, 1911, I arrived at Cannes where I was met by M. Bittard-Monin and M. Maurice Vogt. M. Bittard-Monin introduced me to M. Fabre special commissioner at the depot of Cannes and to Giannoni his assistant. [All] this with reference to the surveillance of Savinkov and his friends .... From there I went to Nice where M. Bittard introduced me to M. Balmeyer Chief of the *Sûreté* and to M. Cottini assigned to the Special Commissioner for Nice.
>
> On March 25, 1911, I returned to Paris with Eugenie Somov Savinkov who stopped with Ksema Silberberg [they were the wives of the famous revolutionaries] at 87 Rue d'Alesia; Eugenie rents an apartment for April 1911 [at] 31 Blvd. Murat, in the 16th District on the 3rd floor. I rent one on the first floor which I leave later to my pseudo brother Jacques another operative .... Some time later Sambian (as one Sarlat) comes to live with Jacques. Once all men are in position, I back out ... he [Jacques] gets 250 francs a month serving only as a cover for all of us.
>
> April 1911 – Surveying for several days Kobeshev and Barthold ...

In May 1911, I was preoccupied with Vladimor [*sic!*] Chernov, 45 Avenue Reille, then dropped him going back to Kobeshev and Barthold.

In June 1911, arrived with Savinkov at 31 Blvd. Murat, Mme. Silberberg's mother came ahead of him. I returned then to the Blvd. Murat to shadow Savinkov who visits Dr. Feet, 5 Rue Severo, lawyers Raap and Staal, 25 de Madrid and Fundaminsky, 11 Rye St. Pierre at Neuilly. After the departure of Savinkov the Prokofievs, father and son, come to live at 31 Blvd. Murat.... The proprietress of the apartment at the Blvd. Murat having learned our identities...fires the caretaker who was our accomplice.

On July 8, I leave Paris for Cannes after receiving some recommendations from Maurice Vogt. I arrive at Theoules [resort town in Southern France] on July 10, 1911, and begin to survey the villa...replacing M. and Mme. Fontaine, an operative and his wife...who had an argument with Mme. Antide Boyer, wife of a senator. She threatened to reveal all to her husband if M. and Mme. Fontaine were not asked to leave. On July 27, 1911, Sambian (as Sarlat) arrived at Theoules to help me. He departs on Sept. 19, 1911 being of no assistance to me. I am left alone until the departure of the residents of the villa .... I leave ... for San Remo on Oct. 10, 1911.

Information [on the activities in the villa] was supplied [to me] by the maid Maria .... We had free access to the depot and to the telephone of the station master to [permit me] to communicate with my colleagues at the depot in Cannes whom I was informing of all the departures.

In San Remo, Savinkov and his friend lived in the Villa Vera on Solaro Strada. Here my colleague Maurice Vogt contacted the local [Italian] detective agency, secured free access to the depot, and received mail [delivered at the villa] from the wife of the gardener of the villa. I left San Remo for Genoa ... while my colleagues Maurice [Vogt] and Barthès proceeded with the surveillance in San Remo. In Genoa I located my colleagues Durin, Deguerre, Sauvard etc., to get information on Kobilinsky, Dr. Plekhanov and to establish free access to the depot for surveillance. Those who regularly helped us were M. Sordelli (delegate of the railroads) M. Ellia (representative of the police), and M. Mansoki (representative of the depot), who thought we were from the French *Sûreté*.

I left Genoa on December 20, 1911, for Chiavari to survey the villa at Cavi and to establish free access to the depot, receiving the co-operation of Vecchione (delegate of the police) and his assistant Notales. I left Chiavari for Spezia on May 18, 1912, to survey the [railway] station to which I had gained free access. My colleagues Arturo Frumento and Berthold go to Fezzano for correspondence service [perlustration of the mail].

M. Viktor Chernov moved from Fezzano to live in Alassio, where Arturo Frumento covers the area alone.

> I left Spezia at my request and return to Paris on May 1, 1912, where I resumed my duties on May 16, 1912 ....
>
> On July 19, 1912, I started the surveillance of Mirka Garfein .... On July 23, Rosalie Frailik (friend of Mirka), who resides at 144 Blvd. Montparnasse ... takes the train at Gare du Nord for Berlin .... I refuse to follow her ....
>
> Assigned to survey Hotel Ritz, Place Vendome. On Sept. 11 and 12, 1912 for the arrival of Grand Duke Nicholas.
>
> On January 25, 1913, M. Sushkov and M. Sambian assign me to 15 Rue Edouard Manet – the Grand Hotel Manet – to observe Kimma Zeeman ....
>
> From March 1 through the 3rd I survey at the Gare de Lyon. On March 4 I received an order to contact agent [visiting Russian detectives] Reshetnikov living in the Lux Hotel... to acquaint him with Russian anarchists residing in Paris.
>
> On March 26, 1913, at 8a.m. I see two Russian agents .... and serve as their guide through Paris for several days. After those tours I acquainted them with Russian anarchists in Paris. On April 20, 1913, these agents leave Paris for Nice and Italy.
>
> On April 20, 1913, I start observing Kurisko.... This assignment ended April 30, 1913, and I took over the surveillance at Gare de l'Est until May 3rd.
>
> On May 4, through May 25, I surveyed Gare du Nord.
>
> On May 28, 1913, I again observe Kurisko and on Sunday, July 8, Gare de Lyon for the arrival of Stefan Blikov.
>
> On June 18, I start surveying D ... at Chatillon, ending this assignment on June 24, to come back to Kurisko ....
>
> I ended surveillance of Kurisko on October 27, 1913.
>
> Dismissed from the service on October 29, 1913.[17]

Despite her devoted service Mme. Richard was not rehired by the Foreign Agentura after the reorganisation of the detective service in 1913.

Not every detective led the mobile life of Mme Richard. Some operatives were fixed in place carrying out a set routine day-after-day. The Foreign Agentura's regularised surveillance work in the small Italian mediterranean suburbs, as we saw in Chapter 2, is a good example of this type of operation.

The information supplied by the dogged determination of Richard and her colleagues filled the gaps in the material supplied by undercover agents and also verified their work. Without the hardworking detectives much information would have been unusable, seen only as isolated bits of data. The linkages between different groups and even members of the same circle would never have been made.

Despite their importance the Foreign Agentura employed too few detectives for the task at hand. Harting and his successor Krasil'nikov recognised that the External Agency was understaffed and constantly requested additional funds from Fontanka in order to enlarge the size of the detective service. The two men did this by playing on Fontanka's fears of the SRs. In 1909 at the tail end of the reign of terror that had been such a sanguine feature of the 1905 Revolution, Harting could with all sincerity write Fontanka that revolutionaries such as the extremely dangerous Boris Savinkov must be kept under surveillance day and night so that if any one of them should suddenly decide to return to Russia to carry out some sort of mischief he would be immediately detected and the government would be warned at once. Harting claimed that in order to achieve this goal he would have to hire many more detectives.[18] As time passed the Paris Office feared the SRs less; nevertheless, Krasil'nikov was quite willing to use Fontanka's ingrained fear of SR terrorism as a lever to pry additional funds out of it for his detective service. In 1911, 16 detectives worked for the Foreign Agentura throughout Europe. Krasil'nikov wrote that this did not leave him sufficient detectives to keep the SR colonies in Italy under observation.[19] He boldly requested that he be allowed to employ an additional 12 detectives. Fontanka granted this request since it would pay almost any price to prevent a recurrence of the wave of terrorism that had struck down so many of its officials a few years before. Harting's and Krasil'nikov's tactic worked and the number of detectives on the Foreign Agentura's payroll grew more or less steadily until 1913, the year detective employment policy changed.

Despite Harting's and Krasil'nikov's successful efforts to bolster the manpower of their External Agency, the Foreign Agentura's detectives remained overworked. Their salaries hardly compensated for the gruelling lifestyle imposed upon them by their employer, but incentives were available in the form of other rewards as well. Bittard-Monin's agents could be granted advances in wages and like their Russian counterparts they received the funds needed to cover their expenses in the line of duty. Unlike the expense money allotted to Russian *filery*, however, this sum was not fixed but based upon the actual expenses incurred by the detectives.[20] The most prestigious reward for loyal service was the award of an Imperial Order. The tsarist government, of course, did not award these on the spur of the moment. Imperial Orders went only to those with the most distinguished service. Of the 54 detectives on whom such data exists only 13 held such Imperial decorations. Most of the recipients of these prestigious baubles had served as Imperial bodyguards attached to members of the Royal Family travelling abroad. In 1909 Bittard-Monin received the Order of St Stanislav III Class and a brooch, while other members of the team protecting the tsar were thanked by a grateful emperor only with cufflinks or tie pins.[21] Tsardom by its niggardly approach to the distribution of its Orders and other awards caused them to be much valued. Only three detectives bore the prestigious Order of St Stanislav. It is easy to see the worth of Henri Bint who received the Order of St Stanislav III Class, the Order of St Anne with gold medallion and ribbon and the Order of St Anne III Class. Bittard-Monin, another highly prized employee, besides the Order of St Stanislav III Class bore the Order of Borodino. Henri Bint was the only detective to be honoured with more than two such emoluments. Russian honours, of course, were not the only ones adorning the chests of the Foreign Agentura's detectives. Awards received from other governments included: Chevalier de Danebrog, Petite Medaille Or du Danemark, Order of Philippe de Hesse I and II Class, Croix Argent de Hesse, Medal of the Coronation of George V, the Victoria Cross and Medaille d'or de Prusse.[22]

Generally though, the detectives valued a less obvious benefit of employment in the Foreign Agentura even more highly than the receipt of these national awards. A loyal detective knew that his employers would take care of him in times of need. This benevolence lasted until 1913, when the reorganisation of the External Agency system brought such largesse to an end. At that time, in the process of reorganising its detective service the Foreign Agentura released more than half of them with only severance pay. Before 1913, however, the Foreign Agentura dealt with its detectives in a paternal and often compassionate spirit.[23]

The Foreign Agentura viewed its detectives as an elite. Nationality, language, education, training and methodology separated them from Russian *filery* working within the empire. These differences caused friction when representatives of the two groups met. Such confrontations took place with increasing frequency as large contingents of *filery* travelled abroad on what were euphemistically labelled training exercises. Part of the problem stemmed from the Foreign Agentura's repeated complaints about being undermanned.[24] As we have seen, Fontanka usually gave in to its pleas and allowed the Paris Office to hire additional detectives, but finally these entreaties backfired. Fontanka became worried about the reported increasing SR activity in Italy and the lack of manpower at Krasil'nikov's disposal. It also wished to make its own *filery* along with those of the Court *Okhrana* (who helped protect the Imperial Family on its travels at home and abroad) more familiar with dangerous revolutionaries residing in exile. In order to relieve these concerns Fontanka decided to dispatch a number of *filery* abroad. The policy itself was not new, but never before had Fontanka sent so many detectives to Europe at one time. Several Russian detectives had served in Europe under Rachkovskii and some had been assigned to work abroad during Harting's administration, although they remained attached to the St Petersburg OO. In 1912, however, Fontanka sent 54 *filery* to Europe, 28 of them to Paris and 26 to Cavi-Lavagna and San Remo on the

Italian Mediterranean. The situation was extremely galling to the Foreign Agentura because these *filery* were responsible only to St Petersburg.[25] The Foreign Agentura's detectives held these operatives in low esteem.[26]

Finally, Krasil'nikov lost patience with the Russian *filery* in his midst and he prepared a dispatch criticising the qualities and capacities of his unwanted guests. He claimed that Russian detectives lacked knowledge of the West, did not speak foreign languages and that most of them were not intelligent. He wryly noted that such *filery* could hardly enhance his own operations. Krasil'nikov suggested that, 'tracking abroad should be mainly practiced by our Paris bureau .... ' He concluded with the strong note that detectives functioning abroad no matter what their nationality were subject to the authority of the Foreign Agentura not of St Petersburg. One could applaud Krasil'nikov's courage, if only he had sent the dispatch. He never did.[27] Nevertheless, the draft succinctly stated Krasil'nikov's and his subordinates' feelings as the number of Russian *filery* working abroad steadily increased.[28]

The additional pressure and annoyance caused by the presence of the Russian *filery* in Europe could not have come at a worse time. The prying eyes of Vladimir Burtsev's 'revolutionary police', discussed in Chapter 11, made it an absolute necessity for the Foreign Agentura to maintain a low profile. When Burtsev's operatives spotted a Russian detective being 'shown the ropes' by his European colleagues they reasonably assumed that the instructors were members of Bittard-Monin's agency. Krasil'nikov in exasperation informed Fontanka of the need for a new method of familiarising Russian *filery* with émigré revolutionary personalities. As things stood in the winter of 1914, it was the detectives who faced exposure to the ever more cynical and alert revolutionaries. And, as we shall see, some detectives did not stand up to Burtsev's tactics very well. Krasil'nikov suggested that no more than four men be sent abroad at any one time to minimise the chance of detection and Fontanka finally agreed with his reasoning and reduced the flow of *filery* to western Europe accordingly.[29]

The praise so lavished on the Paris chancery can, with some restraint, be extended to its External Agency. It is clear that some Foreign Agentura detectives were unreliable, some seeing themselves merely as freelance policemen selling their service to the highest bidder. Vladimir Burtsev took considerable advantage of this trait. But even taking these mercenaries into account, the Foreign Agentura's operatives were the best in Russian service on several counts: education, training, secondary skills (e.g. foreign languages), and familiarity with the revolutionary movements. In a single word these men and women were professionals. Fontanka's desire to train its own *filery* by exposing them to the methods and techniques of the Foreign Agentura's detectives speaks for itself. Unfortunately, the well-disciplined and able retired non-commissioned officers who populated Fontanka's political police as *filery* were far too few in number and the new recruits required by the expanding political police were not up to the class of the Foreign Agentura's long-time professionals.

Despite the talent, energy and dedication displayed by the detectives of the External Agency, it was the undercover or secret agents (*sotrudniki*) who supplied the bulk of the Foreign Agentura's insights into revolutionary life. The members of the Foreign Agentura's Internal Agency, unlike its detectives, were native Russians. The number of undercover agents who worked abroad is unknown. Rachkovskii apparently began with two *sotrudniki* and the number grew steadily.[30] Indeed, at its peak operating level there were not less than 22 undercover agents controlled by the Foreign Agentura at any one time.[31] Nevertheless, the number of *sotrudniki* attached to the Paris Office did not reach this level for quite some time. A. M. Harting at the time of his appointment complained that out of a total of 11,200 francs per month allotted to the Foreign Agentura by the Department of Police his predecessor spent only 2,500 francs on the Internal Agency.[32]

Volunteers for the Foreign Agentura's Internal Agency like those employed within the Empire came from diverse backgrounds. Since only Russian nationals could be employed as undercover agents combined with the fact that the Foreign Agentura did not hire Russian nationals for its detective service we can assume that most Russians volunteering for service in Paris wished to enter the Foreign Agentura as undercover agents, especially since several of them were hired in that capacity. If we make this reasonable assumption the archive of the Foreign Agentura contains the records of 66 persons who volunteered for service in the Foreign Agentura's Internal Agency. Of those on which data exists concerning their occupations at the time of their application we have the statistics displayed in Table 6.5.

On the whole this seems like a rather able group of volunteers. But the Foreign Agentura unlike Fontanka was quite selective in hiring *sotrudniki*. They based employment requirements solely on two criteria: the need for an undercover agent within a given group of émigrés and the ability of the applicant to attain an influential position within that group (a desirable but not necessary qualification for applicants recruited within the Empire). The usual procedure followed in the employment process can be seen in the example of a certain Abraham Fleishman who in February 1911, sent a letter to the Russian Consul General in Paris offering his services to the Foreign Agentura as an undercover agent. The Paris Office decided to speak to Fleishman. The interview began with Fleishman frankly admitting that money was his primary motivation for joining the Internal Agency. The candidate mentioned that he had friends in émigré circles and supplied several small pieces of information on émigré matters to back his claim. After verifying

Table 6.5 Professional backgrounds of persons volunteering for service in the Foreign Agentura's Internal Agency

Occupation	*Number*
People of various professions classified by the political police as revolutionaries or former revolutionaries	15
Student	5
Presently employed or former Tsarist *chinovnik*	7
Military	1
Professional man	1
Adventurer	1
Former *sotrudnik* rehired	1
Meshchanin	5
Worker	1
Peasant	2

Source: Data derived from FAAr, 37, VIa.

the data the Foreign Agentura decided that Fleishman would be a worthwhile addition and employed him under the *klichka* (code name) of 'Alma' with a salary of 200 francs per month.[33] If, however, the Paris Office showed interest in an applicant but reserved some doubt as to the applicant's motivations, it dispatched the data it obtained about him back to St Petersburg for investigation. After several days Fontanka would reply informing the Paris Office either that all was well or ordering an immediate break with the applicant in question.[34]

Undercover agents who worked for the Paris Office reported directly to the chief of the Foreign Agentura or his subordinate in Berlin until the regular system of case officers was established abroad. The relationship between *sotrudniki* and the Foreign Agentura was carefully concealed especially after Burtsev's exposure of Evno Azef. After this scandal, émigrés became more suspicious of each other's activities and the slightest deviation from the norm encountered a jaundiced eye. Preserving the identities of undercover agents became ever more difficult.[35] Breakdowns in security came from countless causes. The agents' lifestyles were one of the most consistent reasons for their undoing. *Sotrudniki* worked for and received large salaries which they liked to put to good use. An unthinking *sotrudnik* might dress a little too well, dine too extravagantly or rent a flat too grand for his apparent means. Any of these displays of unusual financial security caused grave doubts among his comrades over his integrity. In order to prevent this particular problem the Foreign Agentura did not pay out *sotrudnik* salaries in a lump sum. Instead, the Paris Office paid its undercover agents piecemeal over a period of time.[36] Such a system had to be used to defray the effects of salaries ranging from 250 to 2,500 francs per month with the average salary being 500 francs per month.[37] In 1910, the Foreign Agentura's case officers held instructions never to issue one of their agents a single payment in excess of 500 francs and in general they did not issue payments greater than 100 francs at any one time.[38]

Requests for increases in salary from undercover agents came through the Foreign Agentura's chain-of-command. When its director reviewed an appeal of this nature which he believed had merit, the request went on to Fontanka. An agent might also ask for an advance on his salary. In one such case Fontanka responded by giving an agent 2,500 francs from its *reptil'nyi fond* (a secret fund, not included as part of the Agentura's recurrrent budget) and issued the remaining amount of the undercover agent's request as an advance on his salary with repayment to take place later that year.[39] This form of action was in direct contradiction to Fontanka's own orders, but these were highly talented and valued *sotrudniki* whose financial demands just could not be refused if St Petersburg wished to maintain a steady flow of information from their lips.

Ironically, by issuing large sums of money to its best undercover agents in order to keep them happy, Fontanka at times placed them in difficult and even fatal positions. With all this money available to undercover agents, *sotrudniki* were bound to overstep the limits of propriety and safety. This meant that an extravagant *sotrudnik* had to be an ingenious liar, a skill that most of them possessed in abundance. Of course, sometimes being an adept liar was not enough and Fontanka was forced to employ a variety of ruses to mask the source of *sotrudniki* income. They were usually simple forms of deception such as dispatching money to a *sotrudnik* from fictitious persons (often non-existent relatives) living in the homeland. However, there were instances when more elaborate forms of trickery were required. For example, Dr Iakov Zhitomirskii's salary payments, even made a bit at a time, were so large that Fontanka developed a very special system to camouflage the actual source of his income. The Department of Police helped him establish a Franco-Russian publishing house specialising in the printing of medical books. The entire income from this venture belonged to Zhitomirskii as part of his salary.[40]

The political police, of course, counted on the gullibility of the émigrés who, especially before the exposure of Azef, found it difficult to suspect a comrade's duplicity. And so, they generally believed their friend's alibis,[41] but not always. Most exposed agents managed to flee, some were caught and executed. At nine o'clock in the evening of 25 May 1908, agent 'Yost' one of the Foreign Agentura's most highly prized agents was murdered in Geneva. The Foreign Agentura turned immediately to the Geneva police requesting a complete report on the incident, but they were only able to give the Foreign Agentura a vague description of the probable assassin. So ended the career of one of Russia's finest undercover agents.[42] 'Yost's' real name was Boris Chizikov. After several years of successful and well-appreciated service for Fontanka in the southern provinces of Russia

St Petersburg transferred 'Yost' to the Foreign Agentura for work among the Anarcho-communists in London and Geneva. He then returned to Russia, though still attached to the Foreign Agentura, to help round up a group of his revolutionary comrades. This proved to be one of his largest jobs and his last. 'Yost' had not wasted his time in South Russia and had close connections with the Anarcho-communist leadership. He thought of himself as a cautious and security-conscious man and therefore believed himself to be far above suspicion. On this last mission, however, he exposed 70 of his comrades to arrest yet he escaped. This in itself raised suspicion among his colleagues in Geneva. But his doom became a matter of course when a letter he wrote to the chief of the Ekaterinoslav OO upon his return to Switzerland fell into the hands of the Anarcho-communists. The Foreign Agentura searched desperately for a way to extract 'Yost' from this situation but it proved impossible.[43] Once a *sotrudnik* attached to the Paris Office found himself unmasked there was no place for him to hide or to feel safe. The Russian political police abroad could really not help him. It is this critical circumstance that separated undercover agents working abroad from their colleagues in Russia.

Agent Mass attempted to extricate himself from a similar circumstance and his story supports still further what must have been a terrifying fact of life for Foreign Agentura *sotrudniki*. Mass had to prove to his friends in the emigration that his unusually large income came from a legitimate source. Mass told his comrades that he inherited his money. His SR interrogator asked for proof; some documentary evidence that would support his claim. Mass told the following fable to Vladimir Burtsev his accuser and Mark Natanson the legendary leader of the SR Party. On a previous occasion he had invented a sister who lived in Seattle, Washington, a place far enough away to prevent verification, named Bertha Smith. He told Burtsev that his sister had just recently (January 1913) deposited in his name in a French bank, British and American securities worth 125,000 dollars with the provision that 12,000 francs from the capital be given to him annually. Bertha ordered that the money be paid at the rate of 1,000 francs per month by a notary public who in turn would draw against the securities income. Unbelievably, the members of the revolutionary tribunal interrogating him accepted the story, but just to be absolutely certain they asked for a statement from the notary handling the funds! Mass explained that the notary was absent from Paris but would return within six days. Now, having gained six days Mass asked his case officer to find a notary public willing to co-operate in this matter. He overestimated the ability of his superiors in this alien atmosphere. The Paris Office sadly informed him that it could not supply a French notary public. Always a lawyer by profession, a French notary would not commit himself to a story which could be easily disproved by simple inquiry at the alleged bank supposedly making the payment to the *sotrudnik*. Mass had no option but to flee from Paris to

Berlin where a representative of the Foreign Agentura in Berlin gave him 8,000 francs and the Agentura's official expression of sympathy. Mass soon disappeared.[44]

Both Fontanka and the Foreign Agentura understood that *sotrudniki* serving abroad were in a particularly vulnerable position and that they deserved to be well provided for in difficult times. One undercover agent who received these benefits was Lev Beitner. After serving abroad for many years Beitner returned to Russia to negotiate the size of his pension. Director of the Department of Police Lopukhin knew that Beitner maintained familiar relations with many important revolutionaries in western Europe who still regarded him as a loyal comrade. Lopukhin reasoned that as the size of the revolutionary emigration increased men such as Beitner were needed more than ever and should not be permitted to retire. In line with this view he managed to convince Beitner to return to duty in Europe with the inducement of a 2,000 franc per month salary, one of the largest salaries ever issued to an undercover agent. Assigned to the Foreign Agentura Beitner worked directly under the guidance of its director and later on became a key man in Harting's anti-smuggling campaign. He had one success after another, but the arduous work exhausted him and he contracted tuberculosis. He still carried on. In 1912, Beitner became a victim of Vladimir Burtsev's operation and the strain of exposure aggravated his already weakened physical condition. Fontanka, grateful for Beitner's devoted service, did not abandon him. He received 2,000 francs for a vacation in Egypt to recover his health and Fontanka supported him there until his health had improved sufficiently allowing him to travel to a sanitarium on the Black Sea.[45]

Fontanka's relationship with its *sotrudniki* working abroad particularly those in the employ of the Foreign Agentura, often led to friction between the Paris Office and St Petersburg at the administrative level over the proper delegation of authority. Fedor Dorozhko, for example, a tannery worker in St Petersburg had participated in a St Petersburg 'expropriation' – that is a robbery to collect funds for the revolutionary movement – but he was not immediately implicated in the event. Soon thereafter, in 1906, he travelled abroad and offered his services as an undercover agent to the Paris Office, a common enough occurrence for young frustrated would-be revolutionary-adventurers. The Foreign Agentura unsuspectingly employed him under the *klichka* of 'Moliere' and he operated successfully within the 'Maximalist Party' until 1910. Dorozhko devoted himself zealously to his tasks as a police agent and the Paris Office praised his achievements. Unfortunately, like so many of his comrades in the Internal Agency his true loyalties were uncovered through a combination of chance and the assiduous investigations of Vladimir Burtsev. In order to secure his safety, the Foreign Agentura instructed Dorozhko to move to a place in Northern France. Dorozhko objected, believing his safety depended upon his ability to return to Russia as soon as possible. By this time, however, poor Dorozhko's criminal past had been discovered by the Department of Police. Fontanka declared that if Dorozhko returned to Russia he would be arrested. The Foreign Agentura attempted to placate the Department of Police by arguing that Dorozhko's exceptional service entitled him to a pardon. Fontanka refused to listen. No matter how much Dorozhko had contributed to the security of Tsardom it was insufficient to warrant a pardon. The Foreign Agentura then decided to take matters into its own hands. It informed St Petersburg that the Paris chancery paid Dorozhko a bonus of 1,500 francs in addition to the pay he had due him so that he could emigrate to the United States where he would be free from attempts on his life.[46] How many times before had Fontanka forgiven loyal employees for youthful transgressions? The case of Sergei Zubatov comes to mind at once. Why, then, did Fontanka behave in such an obdurate fashion in the Dorozhko case? The explanation rests in the fact that Dorozhko was not one of its own but rather an employee of the Foreign Agentura. Hence Fontanka believed that it owed him nothing.

Fontanka's disdainful attitude toward the Foreign Agentura's Internal Agency manifested itself in other ways as well. The OOs had the right (with a brief interlude of a little more than a year) to send their own *sotrudniki* abroad on assignment whenever they wished without even the courtesy of notifying the Foreign Agentura that they were doing so.[47] Clearly, Fontanka did not believe that the Paris Office's *sotrudniki* were supplying sufficient intelligence of the quality the Special Section required. Nonetheless, Harting did not seem particularly perturbed by its action. He told the Department of Police that he did not mind if Fontanka dispatched undercover agents attached to OOs within the Empire abroad on a temporary basis, but he warned that their insufficient knowledge of local conditions would limit their usefulness.[48] However, the Foreign Agentura's discovery that *sotrudniki* attached to the Petersburg OO were being dispatched to Europe by Fontanka solely for the purpose of verifying the intelligence it received from the Paris Office, was too much to bear. Ironically, the conflict between the Paris Office and Headquarters over this issue was resolved when Fontanka was forced to admit that Krasil'nikov's undercover agents actually reported with a greater degree of accuracy than the *sotrudniki* dispatched to Europe to verify their work. There is strong evidence that once the Department of Police recognised that this was the case it discontinued the practice of sending *sotrudniki* abroad for this purpose, deciding instead to transfer three *sotrudniki* to Krasil'nikov in Paris in order to expand the Foreign Agentura's access to information.[49]

Sometimes, however, the Department of Police forced the Foreign Agentura to hire men for service in its Internal Agency for reasons that had little if anything to do with their qualifications, potential, or the need for them within a particular revolutionary organisation; their employment proving counter-productive to the aims of the Internal Agency and a considerable nuisance to the Paris Office. Fontanka's behaviour in this matter appears as nothing more than an attempt to bully the semi-independent Foreign Agentura into acknowledging its authority. For instance, one Il'ia Chiryev aged twenty-one and the son of a State Councillor was arrested in Moscow when the police uncovered a supply of bombs and weapons in his possession belonging to a group led by a known terrorist. Chiryev readily admitted participating in the group. After serving part of his prison sentence he requested permission to settle in Europe. Probably in deference to his father the MVD granted his request and in February 1910, he left for Paris. With Chiryev still in transit Fontanka informed the Foreign Agentura that he would arrive soon and suggested the possibility of convincing him to join its Internal Agency. The Paris Office acquiesced and in June 1910, reported that Chiryev had been hired. Despite this, the Foreign Agentura remained dubious about the man's usefulness. Krasil'nikov reported in March 1911, that Chiryev assigned for work among the Maximalists showed no interest in doing his job and did not appear well informed about revolutionary life. At the same time Chiryev possessed an avaricious interest in money. On one occasion he told his case officer that he could not 'cheapen himself' to the degree of bringing in important information for a salary of only 200 francs per month. He stated flatly that he could not prostitute himself for less than 250 francs a month. At this point the Foreign Agentura's patience evaporated and it dropped Chiryev from the service. Fontanka reacted by angrily lecturing the Paris Office on the necessity of holding on to agents, in particular those occupying important posts in revolutionary groups as they claimed Chiryev did among the Maximalists:

> We have to do everything in our power to keep at our disposal this type of agent. We must not turn them out just because we temporarily do not get any benefit from them despite having them on the payroll as happened in the case of 'Katia' [Chiryev's *klichka*] .... A whole year may pass without any tangible results, without a single bit of worthwhile information, but some day after such idleness the returns come in. Such men in the long run come forth with a single report which proves to be of greater value than the piles of daily reports from ordinary agents.[50]

In fact Fontanka's experience had taught it otherwise; agents such as 'Katia' rarely proved to be anything but trouble to the political police and Krasil'nikov himself knew this. He strongly reaffirmed his position in relation to the dismissal of agent 'Katia' and replied to Fontanka that the man 'did not merit confidence', the usual label applied to undercover agents fired by the Department of Police. He proceeded to describe Chiryev as flighty, wasting his time in various Paris dens, not trying to assert himself in any way in the revolutionary emigration and failing to maintain the necessary contacts. St Petersburg, defeated by the weight of evidence, applied no further pressure on the Paris Office for Chiryev's continued employment.[51]

In the majority of cases the Paris Office successfully rejected most candidates suggested by St Petersburg. In one instance, at least, the Foreign Agentura told Fontanka that it did not require agents among the masses, but needed only those who were capable of making their way to the inner circles of the revolutionary movements.[52] The Foreign Agentura had no desire to employ or have transferred to its service anyone who would be unable to supply quality information and in some cases influence the policy or actions of the groups to which they belonged. Nonetheless, the Paris Office did not and most probably could not reject Fontanka's suggestions for an appointment abroad when both the quality of the applicant and the need for him was apparent.[53] Of course, if Fontanka became dissatisfied with the performance of a Paris Office *sotrudnik* it would not hesitate to initiate an investigation of its own into the agent's activities. A negative report in cases such as this resulted in an order forcing the Foreign Agentura to expel the *sotrudnik* from the service.[54] What must have angered the Paris Office was the blatant hypocrisy of Fontanka's behaviour when as in the Chiryev case, it took no action against an allegedly incompetent *sotrudnik* if he was one of Headquarters' own appointments.

Krasil'nikov's battling with Fontanka over the selection of personnel for and operations of his Internal Agency consumed an inordinate amount of time and caused considerable unnecessary aggravation, especially since the Foreign Agentura employed a standard investigative procedure to ensure that its *sotrudniki* did their jobs. The Paris Office kept its *sotrudniki* under surveillance, even the most powerful such as Evno Azef.[55] It also maintained surveillance over those undercover agents abroad who were attached to OOs within the Empire.[56] And so in the spring of 1916, the Foreign Agentura wrote Fontanka that undercover agent 'Marten' rendered his services reluctantly and usually only under pressure. The information that he did supply, however, was generally of established quality. The report continued that 'Marten' who belonged to the student body of the Berne University Medical Faculty felt the pressure of his work. Although he did not refuse assignments one could tell by conversing with him that it was a burden and 'he has a weak will which demands constant surveillance over him'. The Foreign Agentura despite its criticisms of 'Marten' sympathised with the agent and concluded its analysis of his performance with the mitigating statement:

> It is necessary to add that 'Marten' was rather occupied at the University. It is necessary for him to finish his medical studies by the end of the year [for] he is subject to military service in war time [it was 1916].[57]

This gentle paternalism did not extend to those *sotrudniki* who abused their position. Undercover agents compiling large expense accounts were particularly susceptible to investigation no matter what their record of achievement.[58] The most commonly used system of checking on an undercover agent was to verify the accuracy of his reports. Case officers carried out the first phase of this procedure common to the branches of the political police.[59] The filing of false reports could have meant that the *sotrudnik* did not have any connections in émigré circles, that he was too lazy to carry out his duty, or most fear-inspiring of all, that in fact he was a double agent actively betraying the Department of Police when it suited his needs.[60] Most often, of course, cases of transgression were not nearly so dramatic. In one case a *sotrudnik* named Bartenev regularly submitted reports to the Paris Office concerning his activities in a bomb laboratory. Not convinced of his integrity, the Paris Office placed him under close surveillance. The Foreign Agentura's detectives discovered that on the days and at the time he claimed to be working in the bomb laboratory he bought and read a newspaper on a bench near the shore of Lake Geneva. He then went to a restaurant for lunch and after dining took a French lesson. He always ate at the same Russian restaurant alone and never had visitors.[61]

Some *sotrudniki* of exceptional value to the Foreign Agentura were treated with special care. One of these, the renowned Iakov Zhitomirskii, repaid this faith with absolute loyalty and first-rate information. When the Foreign Delegation of the RSDWP sent Zhitomirskii to Russia on business the Paris Office was overjoyed.

> There is no ground for doubt that 'Rostovstsev's [Zhitomirskii's *klichka*] trip will turn out well. He will [be able to] evaluate considerable interesting information dealing with the social democratic organisation within the Empire.

In this same dispatch the director of the Foreign Agentura hastened to note that Zhitomirskii because of his immeasurable value to the Foreign Agentura should be excused from military service.[62]

The eight examples just discussed reflect the four major characteristics of the Foreign Agentura's Internal Agency: the extreme danger involved for a *sotrudnik* serving abroad where after 1907 Vladimir Burtsev was always in search of his identity; the ingenuity, skill and nerve possessed by the majority of them; the general sympathy the Foreign Agentura held for these people who were in the most difficult position of any employees of the Russian political police; and the conflict between the Russian political police abroad and Fontanka over the control of undercover personnel operating in Europe and employed by the Foreign Agentura. These conditions bred a closely knit organisation of experts jealously guarding itself against incompetents and the unnecessary and even harmful meddling of St Petersburg.

The challenge to construct a political police agency located at great distance from Russia and in a completely alien environment rested in the hands of the Foreign Agentura's directors. They played a critical and as far as Fontanka was concerned not always welcome or appreciated role. It was their job to blend traditional police methods with necessary innovations in an attempt to mould the Paris bureau into a political police agency capable on the one hand of fulfilling the demands placed upon it by Fontanka and on the other hand of deftly maintaining sufficient independence and initiative to deal with the rapidly growing, steadily more cunning, and ultimately battle-hardened revolutionary emigration. They undertook these tasks in a milieu that required their soliciting the formal and, more frequently, informal and surreptitious support of Europe's forces of law and order. It is to these chiefs of the Foreign Agentura to whom we next turn our attention.

7

P. I. Rachkovskii: Adventure, Intrigue and the Foreign Agentura, 1884–1902

Peter Ivanovich Rachkovskii's name has become synonymous with the most corrupt and venal aspects of the reigns of Alexander III and Nicholas II. A man of stupendous talent and ambition, completely amoral, he rose to become Tsardom's most influential political police official during the 1905 Revolution.[1]

Rachkovskii's climb to the heights of the political police bureaucracy began in accidental, haphazard fashion, a general characteristic repeated by other police officials of eventual prominence such as the brilliant political policeman, Sergei Zubatov, who would rise to direct the Special Section between 1902 and 1904.[2]

Rachkovskii was educated by tutors at home. In 1867 he joined the civil service as a postal worker in Kiev *Guberniia* and moved slowly through the bureaucracy. In 1877 his superiors rewarded his diligence with a promotion to *sudebnym sledovatel'* (an investigator) in the Ministry of Justice and posted him to Arkhangelsk *Guberniia*.[3]

This promotion, however, did not satisfy Rachkovskii's ambition. It still left him a *mel'kii chinovnik* (a junior official) and so discouraged by his prospects he resigned from the civil service. While waiting for new opportunities to come his way Rachkovskii supported himself by working as a tutor and journalist, writing for such divergent newspapers as *Novosti* (*The News*) and *Russkii Evrei* (*The Jewish Russian*), an interesting footnote to the career of someone who would become one of Russia's leading 'professional' anti-Semites. At this time he struck up a passing acquaintance with an individual whom the Third Section would eventually charge with perpetrating an attempt on the life of Adjutant General Drentel'n. In typical fashion this casual relationship was sufficient to place Rachkovskii under political police surveillance. In the course of its investigation into Rachkovskii's life, the Third Section came across some drunken students who were overheard characterising Rachkovskii as a man prominent in revolutionary circles. In the police world of the day this most circumstantial hearsay evidence was sufficient to have the bewildered Rachkovskii arrested and accused of treason.

The charge had absolutely no basis in fact, but the Third Section used it to intimidate Rachkovskii into 'volunteering' for service as an undercover agent. In recruiting Rachkovskii the Third Section had outsmarted itself. The young man considered this an opportunity which could not be passed up.[4] Under questioning he gladly admitted to the charges made against him by the Third Section and added a few embellishments of his own. Rachkovskii falsely claimed that he maintained cordial relations with many Russian subversives including G. P. Plekhanov and N. K. Mikhailovskii. It is a sad commentary on the Third Section that it believed his tales. Thinking that it had acquired an excellent man the tsar's police only asked him 'to moderate his zeal...and obey orders'.[5] Rachkovskii would do neither throughout his amazing career.

During his brief stint as an undercover agent Rachkovskii came to relish the provocateur's role. He organised several student groups and workers' organisations, published revolutionary pamphlets and ultimately made sure that his entire group, members of *Zemlia i Volia* (Land and Liberty), were arrested. His run of good luck ended abruptly when a revolutionary spy within the Third Section exposed him to his comrades. Rachkovskii fled to Galicia in the hope of continuing his undercover work there but an announcement in the revolutionary press notifying its readers of his true character brought an end to his usefulness as an undercover agent at least in revolutionary circles.[6]

Nevertheless, the political police had not forgotten him. In 1881 the newly established Department of State Police asked Rachkovskii to return to the fold as an undercover agent for the Moscow OO and join the reactionary Holy League (briefly discussed in Chapter 4) under the name of Peter Ivanovich Leonid. Apparently St Petersburg wished to infiltrate reactionary groups that it believed threatened the tranquillity of the state as well. The League's bombast suited Rachkovskii's style and he became a member in good standing.

He proved sufficiently successful in carrying out this assignment to warrant an invitation to re-enter the civil service as a *kollezhskii registrator* (Collegiate Registrar), the lowest position on the Table of Ranks. Nevertheless, he had made considerable professional headway. Rachkovskii found himself posted as secretary to Lt. Colonel G. P. Sudeikin, Tsardom's chief of political police, from whom he would learn the intricacies of undercover work, provocation and deceit as we shall see below.[7]

Again, Rachkovskii's good fortune did not last. Sudeikin was assassinated in 1884 by Sergei Degaev, an act for which Rachkovskii bore some responsibility since he had introduced the assassin to Sudeikin in good faith as a possible recruit to Sudeikin's network of undercover agents.[8] V. K. Plehve, the director of the Department of Police, valued Sudeikin highly and he never forgave Rachkovskii for his innocent part in the murder and his shabby effort in carrying out his duties in the subsequent investigation.[9]

Plehve gave the disgraced Rachkovskii a chance to redeem himself by ordering him to track down the assassin. The trail led to Paris.

Rachkovskii was only too glad to escape the humiliation that the death of his superior had brought down on him. He arrived in Paris and the delights and the vibrancy of the French capital enchanted this young and ambitious police official at once as he saw unexpected vistas of opportunity appear almost magically before him. Rachkovskii ignored his assignment and spent his time ingratiating himself with the senior members of the Paris Embassy staff and concentrated on developing contacts with representatives of the Paris Prefecture and the *Sûreté Generale,* relationships easily established since he claimed to represent the Russian political police.[10] He did not bother to inform the people he so met that he was only a minor police functionary with his career in jeopardy.

Then, surprisingly, in March 1884, Rachkovskii found himself selected as the new director of the Foreign Agentura. How was this possible, especially given Plehve's enmity toward him? No evidence exists that will lend itself to a definitive explanation. We can surmise that Plehve made the appointment under pressure. We know that Rachkovskii had already won a powerful friend in Baron Morenheim, the Russian Ambassador to France. Other factors in his favour were that on his own initiative, he had become acquainted with representatives of the French police and, in addition, spent much time in the Latin Quarter where he came to know every nuance of émigré life.[11]

None of these circumstances could have relieved Plehve's frustration. The Foreign Agentura, a bureau he created and from which he expected great things, would now be led by a man he despised. The director of the Department of Police was not impotent, however, and Rachkovskii remained a *Kollezhskii registrator,* an anomalous rank for a post of some importance. No doubt Plehve wanted Rachkovskii to feel quite dispensable. Indeed, the Department of Police's operating orders to the new chief of the Foreign Agentura let Rachkovskii know that it expected him to be nothing more than St Petersburg's cipher.[12]

Despite attempts to keep Rachkovskii under reign the chief of the Foreign Agentura possessed more than enough intelligence and inventiveness to discover and take advantage of the loopholes in Fontanka's instructions. Of course, the greatest factor in his favour, distance from St Petersburg, effectively insulated Rachkovskii from his superiors' wrath for almost 20 years.

Rachkhovskii had not inherited much of an organisation. He maintained and expanded the number of detectives in his service to cover Switzerland, Germany, France and England (see Chapter 5). As we shall see he would come to focus his attention particularly on revolutionary émigré activities in London. He expanded the Foreign Agentura's network of *concierges* who for a not inconsiderable sum gladly tattled on the lives of their tenants. He began to employ *sotrudniki* who offered Rachkovskii details on the lives of especially targeted revolutionaries or the small groups that had begun to grow up around particular émigrés (see Chapter 2); these became the focus of Rachkovskii's provocation and harassment. Most important of all, the chief of the Paris Office employed his abundant charm enhanced by a large wad of cash to win over the co-operation of many of Europe's most influential police officials and several journalists as well.[13]

The French police service, especially the Prefecture of Paris, became the most co-operative of all of Rachkovskii's allies. Of course it did not hurt the Franco-Russian police relationship when the former head of the French political police in the immediate post-Second Empire era joined the staff of the Foreign Agentura's detective bureau upon his retirement from the French service.[14] The French harassed the émigrés, going so far as to ransack their apartments, with ever increasing vigour as Franco-Russian relations warmed in the 1890s.[15] Rachkovskii developed a special relationship with his French colleagues for another reasons as well: the belief held in common by the two governments that spying on one's own population was a *sine qua non* of maintaining the tranquillity of the state. Needless to say, the veneer of liberal political culture that served the Third Republic so well meant that police intrusion into everyday French life required a subtlety unnecessary in Russia and the outcomes of inquiries mostly followed different paths as well. Still, the Late Imperial police modelled in part on the Paris Prefecture, ironically discovered a true soul mate in the political police of Republican France.

This did not mean, however, that the French government was prepared to do Tsardom's bidding when it came to dealing with troublesome – for the Russians, not the French – émigrés residing in Paris. The French would only take action against revolutionary émigrés living within its borders if they had broken French laws.

In order to better understand the nature of Russian dissent the French Foreign Ministry in 1885 ordered its embassy in St Petersburg to prepare an *aide-mémoire* analysing the nature of the burgeoning Russian revolutionary movement. The *memoire* concluded that the Russian revolutionary movement was unrelated to European socialism and presented no danger to France.[16] As if this conclusion did not damage the Russian cause enough, the author of the *memoire* went further describing 'Nihilists' as:

> [P]eople who are witnesses of grave faults, excesses, dilapidation's, who are embittered by suffering and privation, victims of abuses of power and arbitrary measures, who know that in other countries there exist for educated men like themselves, and for the people, a happier condition, and

> therefore they rise against a regime that maintains them in a miserable condition. They demand liberties and attack this edifice of abuse, despotism, and dilapidation.... [17]

Julien des Comines de Marsilly, the author of the report, while clearly sympathetic to the revolutionaries, believed that they presented no serious danger to the Russian monarchy.[18]

Rachkovskii, therefore, ensconced in the basement of Tsardom's Paris embassy at 79 Rue de Grenelle confronted a seemingly impossible set of tasks. First of all, as we have seen, the tsarist authorities confronted sceptical European foreign ministers as it strove to convince them that the few hundred Russian political émigrés living in their midst presented a danger not only to Russia but to the stability of Europe as a whole. Even after the assassination of Alexander II which stunned the Continent, European governments remained at best lukewarm to Russia's appeals for an international anti-anarchist pact. As de Comines' report reveals, no matter how sympathetic Europe's forces of order to Russia's appeals, the tsarist police were hamstrung by the political reticence of cool, wise foreign ministry officials.

Secondly, Europe's governments may have remained unconcerned with the machinations of the Russian emigration, but this certainly was not the case in St Petersburg. Russian terrorists plotted in safety abroad; émigré propagandists from New York to Geneva blackened the reputation of the Romanov Dynasty and called for its overthrow in pamphlets and broadsheets which they had begun to smuggle into the Empire itself. Rachkovskii felt the pressure to do something against the emigration with or without the help of the Europeans.

For the sake of his own career, if nothing else, Rachkovskii needed to win over Europe to the tsarist cause while at the same time attacking the emigration, even if indirectly, with the aim of undermining its sense of well-being and security. He needed to jar the émigrés, as they lay in their European nests, to undermine their belief that although they may not have the wholehearted support of their temporary hosts they at least enjoyed their protection.

Rachkovskii approached these problems in part by employing the lessons he had learned from his mentor Lt. Colonel Sudeikin and in part by embarking upon a form of policing not unknown in Europe at that time but never used with such relentless aggression as it would be by Rachkovskii: psychological warfare.

The foundation of Rachkovskii's assault on the revolutionary emigration rested on two cornerstones: a successful propaganda campaign that painted the emigration in the darkest colours possible, as a threat to the stability of Europe, and on acts of provocation that reinforced and contributed to the Foreign Agentura's anti-émigré propaganda and undermined the emigration from within.

Rachkovskii's campaign against the emigration extended across his entire tour of duty in Paris but achieved its greatest successes within the first decade of his tenure abroad and reflected the following principles taught to him by Sudeikin:

1. With the help of specially active undercover agents stir up confusion and discord amongst the various revolutionary groups.
2. Spread false rumours depressing and terrifying the revolutionaries.
3. Recruit revolutionaries as provocateurs who could then help to discredit revolutionary proclamations and publications.[19]

In line with what Sudeikin had taught him, the director of the Foreign Agentura attempted to recruit revolutionary émigrés, at first pursuing fellow travellers or small fry. By 1888 he had recruited ten *sotrudniki* to Tsardom's cause.[20] Most undercover agents walk a very fine line between observation and significant participation in revolutionary activities. They often crossed that line in search of information that would give Fontanka an edge over its revolutionary opponents. Good *sotrudniki* betrayed colleagues who returned to Russia facilitating their arrest, supplied information that derailed smuggling operations, kept the Special Section informed about the day-to-day political battles that took place within and between different groups, and most important of all, kept the forces of order informed about the plans for acts of terrorism. Provocateurs did these things too, but they are more then mere *sotrudniki*. *Provocateurs* knowingly participated in actions which appeared to be inimical to the well-being of the state, and could indeed be so, either to enhance their reputation and position within the group to which they belonged – thereby not incidentally garnering an increase in salary – or on the specific orders of their superiors to embarrass and/or undermine the group to which they belonged. Officially, prior to the 1905 Revolution, the Department of Police warned its case officers that it did not sanction these latter forms of behaviour. In reality provocation became an integral part of political police operations.[21]

As we shall see, propaganda and provocation became intimately intertwined as Rachkovskii embarked upon his assault against the revolutionary emigration.

In 1887, as if to directly contradict de Comines' *aide-mémoire* (of which he supposedly knew nothing) of a year or so before, Rachkovskii launched his own propaganda campaign. He wrote a letter to Monsieur Fragnan, the Prefect of Police in Paris, informing Fragnan that part of his job as chief of the Foreign Agentura is to correct the image of Russia portrayed by the revolutionary press and by poorly informed and naive West European scholars.

The letter displays Rachkovskii's innate sense of what constitutes good propaganda. There is no raving here. He mixed a degree of accurate factual information and some perceptive conclusions – indeed, some of its passages seem to mirror those of de Comines exactly! – with a rather substantial amount of slander and distortion by presenting the Russian people as happy under the current regime and completely devoted to it. He gives them a political consciousness which they did not possess. This supposed 'consciousness', he argues, led them to reject the entreaties of the revolutionaries whom he portrays as foreigners – Poles, Jews and Ukrainians amongst other non-Russian peoples – who did not have the interests of the Great Russian people at heart. Rachkovskii emphasised that these enemies of Tsardom were little more than anarchists. This became a central theme of his propaganda as he strove to blur the distinctions between Anarchism, 'Nihilism' and Socialism. He argued that the exiles – all of whom were revolutionaries on the run – were both venal and dangerous. The chief of the Foreign Agentura implied throughout his letter to Fragnan that they did not display any sort of human dignity or morality.[22]

Whether Fragnan swallowed all of this is unknown for sure although the sentiment of the letter's final paragraph reveals that Rachkovskii may have been preaching to the converted.

> This memorandum M. Prefect is an expression of my gratitude for the kindness which you have always accorded me as a representative of the Russian political police abroad. It contains only facts relative to the Russian political police in Paris which the [French] press could not grasp . . .[23]

The letter may not have been intended for the Paris Prefect at all. Undoubtedly, the chief of the Paris Office hoped that Fragnan would pass the correspondence on to his more recalcitrant superiors within the French government.

Convincing Fragnan or even Fragnan's superiors did not satisfy Rachkovksii. The director of the Foreign Agentura, following Sudeikin's creed, understood that to defeat the revolutionary émigrés he would have to attack its sense of security, its self-assuredness – always a fragile emotion amongst them – thereby blunting its capacity to become a thorn in Tsardom's side. To accomplish this end he would need to strip the émigrés of their public support.

To one degree or another Russia's revolutionary émigrés felt themselves isolated, removed from their surroundings abroad. As we have seen they lived increasingly within colonies of like-minded Russians enduring the emotional pain of exile made bearable only by their common revolutionary zeal. They sustained themselves, in part, by believing that the Europeans, whom they hardly knew or understood, supported them in their endeavours and would protect the emigration from Tsardom's anti-émigré machinations. Rachkovskii needed to erase this support. The letter to Fragnan only signalled the beginning of his campaign of disinformation, forgery and deceit.

A successful anti-revolutionary propaganda campaign demanded that Rachkovskii undertake the manipulation of the European press, not a particularly difficult thing to do since most newspapers were open to at least a little bribery – they often called it a 'subsidy' – as a means of topping up their coffers. In France, Rachkovskii employed several journalists toward this end. Various journalists began to appear on the Foreign Agentura's payroll. Jules Hansen, a strongly pro-tsarist freelance journalists who supported a Franco-Russian Alliance was one of the first employed. Rachkovskii's subsequent acquisitions included the journalists Calmette of *Figaro* and Maure and some of his co-workers on the newspaper *Le Petite Parisienne*. Eventually, the Foreign Agentura would include the famous journalist Raymond Recouli of *Le Matin* and subsequently the foreign editor of *Figaro* on its payroll as well.

Unfortunately, even the most mercenary journalists would only go so far. Rachkovskii preferred, therefore, to publish forgeries resorting to the 'big lie' technique which made its greatest impact when distributed either in pamphlet or book format. The chief of the Paris Office enjoyed constructing these fabrications himself. For example, one of his booklets contained two articles 'Nihilists in General' ('*Nigilist voobshche*') and 'Recognition of Nihilists' ('*Priznaniia nigilista*'). In the first of these we begin to see Rachkovskii playing the anti-Semitic card he thought would appeal to so many Europeans, especially in the thickening nationalist and xenophobic milieu so apparent in European societies in the late 1880s. He wrote that Nihilists were, 'individuals with a strange walk and [for] the most part of the Jewish type . . . dirty ragged . . . drawing attention to themselves by sharp gestures. Their entire conduct is diffident partly [for the benefit of] the passer-by . . . ' and more specifically supposedly in the words of a *concierge*:

> Nihilists – this Russian emigrant who rarely pays for his room. Yes, and that after a thousand difficulties and the interceding of the police. [They] terribly soil the room, breaking up furniture and the walls. The neighbours of the Nihilists did not have a minute's peace as many friends and acquaintances of the Nihilists visited them at any time day or night . . . shouting and making noise with unheard of impudence.

Other supposedly respectable *petite bourgeois* citizens – the owner of a café, a baker, and a grocer – had supposedly written to the author of the pamphlet complaining that it was impossible to give Nihilists credit.[24]

Rachkovskii's slanderous pamphlets repeated the overarching theme of his propaganda: that Russian terrorists were the intellectual brethren of Europe's Anarchists separated only by the Russians' far greater use of propaganda.[25]

The Foreign Agentura often distributed pamphlets of this sort throughout Europe including Switzerland, Denmark, Germany and Austria. It also sent them to European and American newspapers in the hope that they would at least print summaries of the views expressed in them.

Sometimes Rachkvoskii developed larger projects to get his messages across. From the first, with his letter to Fragnan, Rachkovskii laid the destabilising effects of mass democracy and social and economic modernity, so despised by the Old Order, at the feet of the Jews. In a 1892 book entitled *Anarchie et Nihilisme* written over a pseudonym, but with Rachkovskii's touch visible throughout, the writer presents his readers with a thoroughly modern form of anti-Semitism. The book describes how as the result of the French Revolution, the Jew became the absolute master of European life operating as the *L'Eminence grise* behind both republican and monarchist states. Only the 'Muscovite fortress' remained free of Jewish influence. The book claimed that an international syndicate of extremely rich and powerful European Jews plotted to overthrow the Russian Empire and thereby remove the only obstacle to worldwide Jewish domination. The author concludes by calling for the formation of a league to combat the Jewish conspiracy.[26]

It was, however, Rachkovskii's attack on the émigré pysche through observation, infiltration and provocation which combined with his relentless propaganda made him one of the most despised and feared of Tsarist policemen and established his reputation at home.

Rachkovskii acted against the émigrés with impunity. He instinctively recognised that they were unprepared both in practical terms and emotionally for his strategy, as we shall see. At first, St Petersburg did not formally sanction this type of action, choosing to look the other way. And, of course, it did not object to the achievements attained through these methods.

Rachkovskii's most famous actions against the revolutionary emigration were designed, therefore, not only to be effective against the revolutionaries, but also to create sensational headlines guaranteed to attract the attention of his superiors and advance his career beyond the normal expectations of a man with his background and inadequate training. If he had merely been content to follow his instructions to the letter he might have hoped to achieve the rank of a middling civil servant. Rachkovskii's ambitions would not tolerate such mediocrity and he used the Foreign Agentura as the vehicle to satiate his cravings for fame, fortune and power. Rachkovskii moulded the Paris Office to suit these personal ambitions. Yet, as long as Fontanka was satisfied with his results, it turned its back on even the most disreputable adventures and rewarded his successes.

In accordance with his professional and personal goals, then, Rachkovskii launched a campaign against the Populist Lev Tikhomirov, one of the most famous and feared of Russia's émigré propagandists. When the Foreign Agentura's attempts to have Tikhomirov extradited from France to Russia failed, Rachkovskii undeterred ordered his agents to raid the *Narodnaia Volia* press located in Geneva and with which Tikhomirov was involved. On 24 November 1886 he dispatched a coded telegram to Fontanka worded in what would soon become recognised as his sensational style:

> On Saturday night I happily destroyed in Geneva the typography of *Narodnaia Volia* along with five notebooks of *Vestnika* and all revolutionary publications.[27]

The destruction of the *Narodnaia Volia* press was Rachkovskii's first major victory in his very personal struggle with the revolutionary movement. All totalled, the Foreign Agentura seized 6,000 copies of various revolutionary publications and destroyed six poods* of type.[28]

The dismay of the Populists turned quickly to anger, but it is a measure of their *naiveté* that they blamed the destruction of the Geneva press not on the tsarist police, but on their rivals, the Marxists. Some members of *Narodnaia Volia* accused G. V. Plekhanov and Vera Zasulich of somehow being responsible for the loss of their typography. Less hysterical comrades more sensibly blamed it upon the machinations of the tsarist Ministry of Foreign Affairs which could have pressured the Swiss Government to take actions against their press. The Russian Government denied that any such connection existed between itself and the Swiss authorities, but who in revolutionary circles would have believed the statement of denial.[29]

The destroyed printing press had been a source of hope for Tikhomirov's embattled Populists during a very bleak and repressive period at home. The *narodovol'tsy* were not about to give up. In early February 1887 they re-established their press in Paris with the aid of new type supplied by a sympathetic typesetter. Rachkovskii, informed of its location by his agents, struck again. After four hours of dedicated labour Rachkovskii's men managed to smash the typography to bits.

Tikhomirov and his followers were enraged. He rightly suspected the involvement of the Russian government in this business and decided to launch a fierce attack on the tsarist authorities in the European press hoping to engage the agents of Tsardom out in the open. This did not happen. Rachkovskii chose to do nothing that would expose his government to any form of opprobrium. Instead he approached Jules Hansen asking him to use

*One pood equals thirty-six pounds.

his influence with the French press to counteract the impact of Tikhomirov's campaign. Hansen, employing his persuasive abilities lubricated by Russian money, succeeded brilliantly. The French press, even the radical press, rebuffed Tikhomirov's complaints driving him into silence. The defeat lost him considerable prestige in émigré circles.[30]

The successful destruction of the *Narodnaia Volia* press taught Rachkovskii some vital lessons: the revolutionary émigrés, even the toughest of them, were easily demoralised and thrown into confusion when attacked directly by agents of the Russian government; that the émigrés were terribly naive and completely ill-equipped to deal with undercover agents and provocateurs within their midst, a situation that persisted into the twentieth century;[31] and that he could deal with the émigrés with impunity without being concerned about stirring up any reaction by Europe's governments that would embarrass his superiors. Most significant of all, Rachkovskii proved to St Petersburg that his strategy of harassment so distressed the members of the emigration, many of whom lived in a high state of tension in any case, that some of them finding the strain unbearable would abandon the revolutionary movement and return to the tsarist fold. One of the most famous of these was Lev Tikhomirov himself.

Rachkovskii elaborated on his use of what had been one of Sudeikin's tactics in a report of 2/14 February 1887 to Fontanka. He wrote how he enraged Tikhomirov and how the energy Tikhomirov expended this way sapped 'his mental and physical strength'. Rachkovskii told his superiors that he would continue to harass Tikhomirov making his 'existence intolerable' driving him to the brink of mental collapse. Indeed, the chief of Paris Office believed that Tikhomirov could be driven to return to Russia as a loyal citizen who 'had lost his mind abroad'. A month later Rachkovskii reported to Fontanka that Tikhomirov had fallen into a state of confusion and succumbed to a persecution complex and 'generally has the appearance of a pitiful and morbid abject coward'. Rachkovskii relentlessly continued to pressure Tikhomirov. Strange things began to happen that Tikhomirov could not explain to his comrades. Letters he wrote went missing, postal money orders mysteriously disappeared, acquaintances received telegrams over his name which Tikhomirov had not sent, his landlord suddenly threw him out of his apartment, and doctors suddenly refused to treat his children.

Once while Tikhomirov was browsing in a small bookstore a stranger handed him his visiting card. The name on the card was clearly a pseudonym and the card's bearer may have been Rachkovskii himself. Exhausted, depressed, bitter, feeling isolated and abandoned, Tikhomirov clearly struck a deal with the card's owner. He would receive payment for brochures he wrote attacking elements of the revolutionary emigration other than his own, especially the Marxists. In this way a once feared revolutionary slowly became a turncoat and one of Tsardom's most vociferous supporters.[32] Rachkovskii could rightly boast that the destruction of Lev Tikhomirov was one of his greatest accomplishments as an agent of the forces of order.

Throughout the succeeding decade Rachkovskii continued to play off the Populists versus the Marxists almost as if it was a game devised by a clever and malicious child.[33]

Playing off the Populists against the Marxists and harassing individual revolutionaries certainly generated anxiety within the emigration which no longer could lull itself into a sense of security by believing that it was beyond the reach of the tsarist police. The members of the emigration, no matter how long their exile, psychologically belonged to an age before modern political policing. Rachkovskii's 'black operations' forced them to realise that their life abroad was precariously balanced; still they did little to fight back relying on the shrinking goodwill of their hosts. It would take the battle hardening experience of the 1905 Revolution, years in the future, to instil in them the bitter cynicism and ruthlessness necessary to combat successfully the machinations of the Foreign Agentura as we shall see. Until then the Paris Office would have virtually an unhindered hand in its campaign against the emigration.

Rachkovskii should have been riding high. He had proved to Fontanka that he possessed a set of highly desirable, one could say indispensable, attributes. The chief of the Paris Office had displayed the ability and daring to deal aggressively with the émigrés in the European milieu without embarrassing the Russian government. Equally valuable was his solid grasp of Russian revolutionary history which permitted him to create believable disinformation. He understood the strain under which the emigration lived and knew how to exploit their psychological vulnerability to Tsardom's advantage. Rachkovskii, a man who would have fit better into the Bolshevik *Cheka* than Fontanka, displayed an intuitive grasp of the tactics which would be successful against these people. The government appreciated and rewarded his achievements, up to a point. Fontanka usually granted him the funds he requested for his operations even before his success in the Tikhomirov affair. After the destruction of the *Narodnaia Volia* press Fontanka increased the Foreign Agentura's budget still further even though Rachkovskii never managed to give Headquarters a proper accounting of the Foreign Agentura's expenditures. The government rewarded Rachkovskii with personal emoluments as well. St Petersburg promoted him to the rank of *Gubernskii sekretar'* (Provincial Secretary) and awarded him the order of St Anne Third Class.[34]

While the government undoubtedly believed that its largesse justly compensated Rachkovskii for his achievements, in reality, the chief of the Paris Office remained a lower echelon bureaucrat. Obviously, Fontanka appreciated his results, but his methods engendered little respect, and further promotions and rewards did not come.

If he could not advance his career through one means he would find others. Rachkovskii developed a three-pronged strategy to advance himself: he employed his considerable personal skills combined with his remarkable ability to dissemble and even less legitimate means to make a name for himself in international diplomatic circles by brokering improved Franco-Russian relations; as chief of the Paris Office he endeavoured to expand the Foreign Agentura's network of bureaus (first to London) by exaggerating the danger of the emigration to Tsardom's security and reputation; and he strove to win over important *sanovniki* whose patronage could protect him from Plehve, conveniently no longer director of the Department of Police, and, of course, advance his career.

Jules Hansen, who maintained a close relationship with both the French Ministry of Foreign Affairs and Baron Morenheim, the Russian Ambassador to France, and specialised in writing about the world of diplomacy, encouraged Rachkovksii to dabble in international affairs. Hansen, who promoted the creation of a Franco-Russian Alliance, introduced Rachkovskii into French diplomatic circles. Rachkovskii, too, believed that Russia and France should co-operate fully in the diplomatic sphere, a reality not easily accomplished between two nations at opposite ends of the political spectrum. This minor police functionary took it upon himself to further the possibility of such an alliance in the hope that it would bring him the fame and power he so desperately craved.[35] Rachkovskii surmised that he could kindle a more cordial relationship between France and Russia by inducing the French government to take strong measures against the revolutionary emigration in Paris. Unfortunately, the revolutionaries could not be counted upon to co-operate in this business with sufficient zeal or the proper timing. The director of the Foreign Agentura decided to help history along while at the same time serving the political policing aims of his bureau.

Using Abram Landezen, a trusted agent who had infiltrated Populist ranks, Rachkovskii initiated a scheme to assassinate Tsar Alexander III. The first steps of the plan dictated that Landezen recruit loyal revolutionaries who believed in the salutary effects of terror and lacked only sufficient funds to carry out a useful act. Naively they accepted Landezen's funds and direction in the creation of a bomb factory somewhere in the woods around Paris. The money for the entire venture, supposedly supplied by Landezen's rich uncle, came entirely from Rachkovksii. If Fontanka only knew how its money was being used!

The Paris Office waited until the plotters were well-advanced before informing the Russian Ambassador Baron Morenheim of the 'plot'. Morenheim, completely unaware of the true situation, immediately contacted the French Minister of the Interior and managed with considerable difficulty to convince him to take vigorous action against these most despicable enemies of Tsardom. On the morning of 28 May 1890 the Prefect of Police arrested nine so-called nihilists. These arrests involved massive sweeps into the homes of both Polish and Russian émigrés, including Peter Lavrov, the most prestigious Russian radical living in Paris, and the seizure of a large number of suspicious documents. The French police soon freed several of those arrested, while it detained others caught with incriminating documents and some infernal machines. The French eventually convicted two of the detainees sentencing the 'terrorists' to three years imprisonment. A third man, a certain Landezen, conveniently escaped from custody. Nevertheless, the court convicted him *in absentia* and as the ringleader of the group he received a five-year sentence.[36]

The effect of 'discovering' the plot on the Tsar's life planned on French soil traumatised Gallic public opinion. Jules Hansen now played his role to the hilt. The French press encouraged by the publicist produced banner headlines which decried 'Russian Terrorists in Paris' and 'Affair of the Bombers'. Most French newspapers reported the details of the plot to kill Alexander III in a light which proved beyond doubt the venality of the anti-tsarist emigration.[37] When the Prefect of Paris Monsieur Loze, discovered much to his surprise that Paris was full of Russian 'Nihilists' who occupied themselves with the manufacture of bombs, he immediately notified Rachkovskii. The two men at that point decided to launch a joint effort to keep the Paris emigration under close surveillance.[38]

The immediate impact of the Landezen Affair, as the incident became known, produced repercussions of a different sort in St Petersburg. When Alexander III learned of the arrests he reportedly exclaimed, 'Finally France has a government of significance'. Although it would be a glorious exaggeration to claim that this incident alone determined the future course of Franco-Russian relations, there is no doubt that the Russian government was extremely pleased by the action and rewarded the French participants in the Affair accordingly.[39]

The improvement in Franco-Russian relations resulting from the outcome of the Landezen Affair is only half of the story. The French police raids on émigré flats turned up a substantial pile of documents, especially correspondence between the émigrés themselves and comrades within the Empire. Rachkovskii desperately wished to be given the opportunity to study these documents. In particular he wanted to gain access to the material taken from Peter Lavrov who maintained a voluminous correspondence with revolutionaries at home. This was a ticklish matter. The French government told Rachkovskii that it would allow him to study documents related to terrorism, – a common European-wide policy – but it would not permit him to review seized documents the contents of which dealt with other matters.

Lavrov, whose papers were of paramount importance to Rachkovskii for their contents would give the political police information that would lead to arrests within the Empire, was, however, not a terrorist. In fact it was well-known that he abhorred acts of terror. The negotiations held between Rachkovskii and the French Foreign Ministry over access to these materials depict the director of the Foreign Agentura at his best. He built his case steadily line by line throughout his correspondence.

Minister of Internal Affairs Durnovo wrote Rachkovskii that he should keep the discussions on a rather low-key and informal level but, nevertheless, make it clear to the French that St Petersburg would regard a positive response to them in a favourable light while the failure of the French to co-operate in this matter might 'cause the disappearance of the magnificent impression produced here in the highest places, where one is truly moved by the benevolent conduct of the French government'.[40]

And with Durnovo's words in mind Rachkovskii at first, approached the French carefully, warning them that the danger of terrorism had not completely past. After all, there may be some terrorists on the loose in Paris with infernal machines still in their possession requiring further investigation. He implored the French government to help him prevent the possibility of any further plots against the tsar 'whose sentiments for France are a secret to no one'.[41]

The chief of the Paris Office having elliptically addressed the issue of Russia becoming the powerful good friend that France required in the world of European alliances and alignments quickly changed tack arguing that all of the seized documents particularly those seized from Lavrov would allow the Russian government to disarm the terrorists. '[In these papers] will be found the key to close the Russian frontier to the assassins of the Sovereign'.[42] According to Rachkovskii, the French government held the security of the tsar in its hands. Given the impact on both Russia and France that the assassination of Alexander III would cause Rachkovskii noted:

> That which remains to be done [turning over the documents to Rachkovskii] is, in my opinion, nothing but a trifle for the French government, but as you know, often in the world it is the smallest things that produce the greatest effects.[43]

Rachkovskii's referring to the 'smallest things that produce the greatest effects' placed the future of a Franco-Russian Alliance squarely on the table. The director of the Foreign Agentura had raised the stakes putting considerable pressure on Paris. The French understood that the act of supplying information to the tsarist government could lead to the arrests of possibly hundreds of radicals within Russia and would enrage the French Left and have domestic consequences of considerable proportions in France.

While leaving the French to ponder this oblique threat, which he was not authorised to issue, Rachkovskii appealed to them again on another level. He remarked that the documents often written in shorthand or code and laden with code names would be meaningless to the French without his expert knowledge. When the French persisted in maintaining their stance Rachkovskii dealt his last card. While he conducted discussions with the

Ministry on an informal basis, he told the French he might not be able to prevent a formal request in this matter, government to government, emanating from St Petersburg in the very near future implying that the dispute of access to the correspondence could lead to an international incident no one wanted.

The French decided on a middle course carefully reviewing the seized material before handing a selection of documents over to Rachkovksii. Ironically, what they did turn over to the Russians combined with intelligence gathered earlier by Landezen led to a substantial number of arrests within the Empire. The tsarist Ministry of Justice brought 159 suspects to trial based on the evidence supplied by Rachkovskii and the courts convicted 59 of them.[44]

Rachkovskii enjoyed a triple victory. The outcome of the Landezen Affair contributed to already improving Franco-Russian relations, it made the French sensitive to the potential danger presented by the revolutionary émigrés living in their midst and it led to the arrest of more than 150 suspected terrorists within the Empire itself.

His reputation soared at 16 Fontanka Quai. Now important people would give his opinions the respect Rachkovskii believed they deserved. How could he use this newly won status to his advantage?

The director of the Foreign Agentura realised that he could increase his influence still further by exaggerating the danger the emigration represented to Tsardom's security and thereby convincing Fontanka to expand his domain. The fiction of the Landezen provocation laid the foundation for Rachkovskii's deceptions. Nothing unnerved the police as much as the fear of assassination against the tsar, members of his family or Russia's *sanovniki*. For the ultimate blame for acts of terrorism invariably fell upon the occupants of 16 Fontanka.

As for Rachkovskii, he recognised that in 1890 the émigrés' pen was far mightier than their sword. In his desire to expand his network to England, which in truth housed the most active group of émigrés at that time, he combined the government's fear of terrorism with the journalistic output of writers such as S. M. Stepniak-Kravchinskii and Vladimir Burtsev (one a former terrorist in his youth and the other regularly labelled as such by St Petersburg) into a single argument for extending his bureau's tentacles to England and to developing a working relationship with the English police.

Rachkovskii appeared particularly irked by the activities of The Society of the Friends of Russian Freedom (SFRF) and its publication *Free Russia*. Interestingly, although Stepniak-Kravchinskii and his friend and colleague Feliks Volkhovskii[45] along with other émigrés wrote for *Free Russia* and advised the SFRF, Kravchinskii, himself, did not belong to the organisation. A General Committee of 35 people managed the SFRF. The membership of this Committee was composed of predominantly middle-class and middle-age dissenters: Englishmen. This must have worried Rachkovskii. The English SFRF published and edited *Free Russia* (with considerable help from Kravchinskii and Volkhovskii). Propaganda presented this way, that is espoused by apparently humanitarian fellow countrymen is far more effective than that produced by aliens with an axe to grind and a shady past.

Rachkovskii was not the only Russian official who expressed his concern. The Russian Embassy in London wrote to the Department of Police about the impact of *Free Russia* whose widespread circulation worried it. *Free Russia* enjoyed readerships across the United States, Germany, Australia, Java, South Africa and, of course, in Russia as well. Diplomatic protests achieved little.[46]

On 27 December/8 January 1891 Rachkovskii informed St Petersburg that he wished to establish 'special surveillance' in London over the emigration, in particular the people associated with the Society of the Friends of Russian Freedom.[47] In January 1891 Rachkovskii visited London to survey émigré life for himself and probably to strengthen ties with the British police. He met with the chargé d'affaires at Russia's London embassy where he received tacit approval for his operations in London. Developing a relationship with the English political police would be a difficult and delicate task and he knew it. The chief of the Paris Office wrote to P. N. Durnovo, the director of the Department of Police, that operating in England would be difficult since 'help from the local authorities (like in France) cannot be counted on because of the hostility of England to Russia' thanks to the literary efforts of the likes of Kropotkin and Stepniak-Kravchinskii.[48]

A relationship with the Special Branch which Rachkovskii undoubtedly cultivated during this visit to London remained a delicate and deeply held secret connection. There were several reasons for this. The British Government considered the *Okhrana* little more than an extension of tsarist tyranny. Even members of the Special Branch, largely ignorant of the Russian political system, referred to it as that 'dreaded organisation'.[49] This strong distaste for the policies of the tsarist government combined with a healthy respect for public opinion kept British politicians at arms length from anything that smacked of co-operation with the Russian political police.

Yet as we noted in Chapter 2, the Special Branch newly established in 1887 maintained a rather independent view of its role. It did not tell the Home Office everything about its activities and it closely protected the secrecy which surrounded it. Indeed, as the Special Branch slowly entered the European counter-subversive policing network it began to take on the style of a Continental political police agency.[50]

There is no doubt that Rachkovskii established contact with William Melville the chief of the Special Branch and that this contact blossomed into a close personal relationship.[51] As we shall see below Melville played an essential role in the prosecution and conviction of Vladimir Burtsev who was sentenced to 18 months in prison for advocating regicide.

Rachkovskii considered his trip to London a resounding success and he reported so to Fontanka. In a report to the minister of internal affairs dated 19/31 March 1891 he notified St Petersburg that, according to his instructions, he had established formal surveillance over the major émigrés but he wished to discuss expanding his operations in London with Director of Fontanka Durnovo in person. Rachkovskii and Durnovo met in Nice during mid-April where the director of the Foreign Agentura's use of hyperbole had its effect.

From Nice Durnovo wrote to his assistant minister in charge of the police and to the minister of internal affairs himself that Rachkovskii described to him a London emigration dominated by well-known enemies of the government such as Volkhovskii, Burtsev and Stepniak-Kravchinskii. Furthermore the group to which they belonged possessed sufficient funds to live 'without needs' while publishing the journal *Free Russia* in huge numbers as well as stirring up anti-tsarist sentiment in England, conducting meetings, and organising the collection of funds some of which were being used to support other groups such as the 'nihilists' in Paris.[52]

The director of Fontanka supported Rachkovskii's request for massively increasing the budget allotted for conducting the London surveillance and undercover operations. Durnovo told St Petersburg that Rachkovskii wished to double the number of surveillance people in London placing this operation under a particularly able operative, 'a former French agent recommended by Loze [the Prefect of Paris]'.[53] This agent was undoubtedly the ubiquitous Henri Bint who served the Foreign Agentura down to the end of the regime. Durnovo warned his superiors that these expenditures were absolutely necessary. The 'London agitation will make itself felt', he warned, 'and ... we are obliged to put ourselves in readiness'.[54]

Durnovo persuaded St Petersburg to support Rachkovskii's appeal for manpower and money and the London émigrés began to feel the impact of the Ministry of Internal Affair's attentions. They came to believe themselves surrounded by detectives and Kropotkin claimed there were more Foreign Agentura detectives in London than in any other European city. Rachkovskii's detectives kept Volkhovskii and Stepniak-Kravchinskii under constant open surveillance. The director of the Foreign Agentura wanted to make certain that these men knew they were being shadowed. This was not all. Rachkovskii also assigned two of his best *sotrudniki* to infiltrate the Russian circle around *Free Russia* whose members lacked the experience to unmask them. Rachkovskii toyed with the émigrés perpetrating all sorts of disinformation campaigns and embarrassing episodes that very well may have made an impact on English public opinion.[55] Rachkovskii boasted that the London emigration 'was under our complete control'.[56]

Nothing confirmed this statement better than the arrest in London of the radical publicist Vladimir Burtsev. Within two hours of his arrest Burtsev was brought before a magistrate and charged with planning the murder of 'persons who were not subjects of his Royal Majesty'.[57] The charge was vague enough and probably concocted by Rachkovskii with the aid of his friend William Melville, chief of the Special Branch.[58] The prosecutor's case was weak based only on the contents of three issues of Burtsev's journal *Narodovolets* (*The People's Will*). It should have appeared a bit strange to the court that representatives of the Russian government interfered in the proceedings by translating all three numbers into English in order to expedite the judicial proceedings against Burtsev.

When it became clear that the case against Burtsev could not be proved the prosecutor altered the charge from 'planning' regicide to 'advocating' terrorism as editor of an inflammatory journal. The prosecutor spent several hours the first day of the trial reading passages from the publication and, as Burtsev himself admitted, the articles appeared quite inflammatory to Englishmen not used to rhetoric of this sort. The British press launched a fierce campaign against Burtsev and terrorists in general. Even the highly respected London *Times* quoted excerpts from some of the articles declaring that their authors 'defended terror in theory and in practice'. The newspaper accounts described the *narodovoltsy* as bomb throwers who took advantage of the freedom of the press to spread their views.

Burtsev's defence counsel fought back arguing that his client was not a member of any revolutionary group and that he wrote literature, 'pure and simple'. Burtsev's barrister proclaimed that 'they arrested him in the great library in the British Museum. Is this where one finds revolutionaries!' The answer, of course, is yes. Luckily for Burtsev the court knew nothing of revolutionaries' scholarly habits and sentenced him to only 18 months imprisonment, apparently on the charge of sending his publication through the mails.[59]

Burtsev endured a difficult time in prison. Perhaps his incarceration was made less unbearable by regular visits from his friend Lev Beitner who, as Rachkovskii's principal agent in England, reported the content of each of his conversations to the Foreign Agentura.[60]

Rachkovskii appeared to be riding high even before the Burtsev trial. His annual budget had mushroomed to a stupendous 295,500 francs in 1894.[61] No Foreign Agentura budget would match this sum for another 12 years. The director of the Foreign Agentura had succeeded in establishing the foundation of his own little kingdom. His future looked bright.

Indeed, Rachkovskii's life changed markedly in the 1890s and his personality blossomed. He became ever more confident: a *bon vivant*, suave, expansive, a real operator. He maintained a luxurious villa in St Cloud where he staged lavish banquets, consulted with French deputies, ministers and police chiefs, and was always willing to place his extensive knowledge of Parisian night-life at the disposal of distinguished Russian visitors.[62]

He began to use his office and its newly won prestige as a lever into the world of big business and high finance. His penchant for dubious business and commercial ventures led him to such illegal activities as aiding a French industrialist in his attempt to acquire a concession for the construction of a locomotive factory in Siberia and carrying on negotiations with Belgian banks for the exploitation of coal and iron deposits in Russia. To make matters worse, he carried on these negotiations in the guise of an official representative of the Russian government. He gambled on the stock exchanges of Europe and his agents in England acted as his representatives in both business and police affairs. Rachkovskii's business acumen made him a very wealthy man and by the judicious use of his money he steadily increased the number of his influential friends in European and Russian society and politics.[63]

Rachkovskii's police operations came to rest on acts of provocation and the publication of scurrilous anti-émigré propaganda. He all but abandoned his primary duty to observe and report on émigré activities. As the quality of Rachkovskii's reports deteriorated he defended himself against his superior's criticisms with the weak excuse that good surveillance takes time and cannot be rushed.[64]

Rachkovskii went to fantastic lengths to enhance his image in St Petersburg. In May 1894 he composed a report addressed directly to Alexander III about the Russian emigration. The report was typical Rachkovskii, grossly exaggerating the emigration's danger to the regime, painting them as terrorists organising one plot after another. The Tsar was impressed inscribing on the face of the report 'God grant us success in apprehending all of these scoundrels'.[65] In a second long report written in late October 1894, with the nation already unsettled by the death of its relatively young and thought to be physically invincible tsar, Rachkovskii wrote Fontanka warning of revived plans for terrorist campaigns within the emigration. Then without corroboration he claimed that terrorists in London and Paris were actually planning to assassinate several High Personages and in order to add emphasis to this claim he noted that Landezen's plan which of course he had invented was 'now circulating in Paris' and may still be under consideration by terrorists. In typical fashion Rachkovskii mysteriously fails to elaborate any further.[66]

The director of the Foreign Agentura also began to establish unofficial contacts with prominent Russian newspaper editors and influential St Petersburg matrons telling them of the monstrousness of the revolutionary emigration and his successes against it.[67] Madame Bogdanovich, an influential St Petersburg matron, wrote in her diary, 'Had breakfast today with Rachkovskii. He stated that there are now 300 terrorists living Paris and he watches over them'.[68] This diary entry not only attests to the quality of Rachkovskii's imagination, but also how far he had come in so few years. His position within Fontanka might not have satiated his ambitions but his increasing stature in St Petersburg society certainly must have fed his ego and brought him immense satisfaction.

Yet Rachkovskii's professional and personal demeanour aroused doubts about his continued suitability for the post he held abroad. Despite his apparent value to the regime Alexander III simply considered Rachkovskii a 'scoundrel'.[69] As early as 1890 General N. D. Seliverstov, a prominent police official, arrived in Paris with orders from the MVD to inquire into some of Rachkovskii's more dubious commercial activities. While engaged in his investigation of the Foreign Agentura's director, Seliverstov was murdered under still mysterious circumstances, but probably on Rachkovskii's orders.[70]

Undeterred by Fontanka's suspicions the chief of the Foreign Agentura continued to collect money and influential friends at a rapid pace. The Department of Police, however, had not forgotten about him. In 1894 it dispatched another investigator to Paris. I. F. Manasevich-Manuilov, a Fontanka functionary, arrived in Paris masquerading as a journalist. Fontanka vastly underestimated Rachkovskii if it believed that he would be fooled for even one minute by such a transparent disguise. The director of the Foreign Agentura soon discovered the nature of Manuilov's assignment. He immediately dispatched a protest to the director of the Department of Police. Still Manuilov remained in Paris. Rachkovskii did not give up. He telegraphed his immediate superior G. K. Semiakin, manager of political police investigations (the Special Section had not yet been created) explaining the problem. Semiakin acted in his subordinate's behalf and Manuilov evaporated.[71]

The nature of Rachkovskii's influence became clear with Semiakin's precipitous removal of Manuilov from Paris. An order issued by the director of the Department of Police to continue the investigation into Rachkovskii's affairs was successfully countermanded by his subordinate. Obviously the source of Rachkovskii's influence did not lie in the police bureaucracy but rather through his acquired friendships in the government, at Court and to lucky circumstances out of his control including the death of Alexander III who despised him.[72]

Rachkovskii's friends and benefactors were either in or close to the Court of Alexander III's successor, the young Nicholas II. His powerful friends included Minister of Internal Affairs I. L. Goremykin, Minister of Finance S. IU. Witte and Court Commandant P. P. Hesse, the most influential of all. Rachkovskii, this barely middle-ranking official, through both instinct and observation came to recognise that the friendship of the tsar was a *sine qua non* to making a successful career within the Department of Police. This held especially true for those officials who like himself lacked the requisite background to get ahead within the political police bureaucracy. In no other way can the traditional nature of Russian authoritarianism be more accurately exposed than through the labyrinth of the patronage–clientele system with the tsar at its apex.

To win that patronage Rachkovskii took advantage of his reputation as a man-about-town to ensnare Russian dignitaries travelling in France. Witte and Goremykin were just two of the travellers entertained in Paris by Rachkovskii. Witte appeared captivated by the policeman's style and intellect and established a long-standing relationship with him and Goremykin was as effusive as Witte in his praise of Rachkovskii.[73]

The chief of the Paris Office complemented his budding friendships with these powerful men by cultivating a patron at Court. Rachkovskii knew, in fact it was common knowledge, that the court commandant enjoyed the friendship and confidence of the tsar. The appointment of a new court commandant in 1895 offered the police official an opportunity to acquire the influence at Court necessary for the satisfaction of his ambitions. Thus Rachkovskii began to make regular trips to St Petersburg specifically to report to General Hesse personally on matters concerning affairs abroad. He did this despite the fact that he was not obliged to inform the court commandant about the work of the Foreign Agentura. In fact, in doing so, Rachkovskii broke the chain-of-command within which the political police functioned and ignored the process of data analysis which strove to confirm the accuracy of the reports Fontanka received from the field before it passed them on to High Personages. Of course, Rachkovskii never worried about the accuracy of his information. As in this case, his reports often served his own rather than Tsardom's ends. Hesse succumbed to Rachkovskii's obeisance (as the policeman knew he would) and became his friend and supporter at Court.[74]

The director of the Russian political police abroad made the most of his benefactors by keeping them in the dark concerning his illicit activities and by keeping himself informed about the mood at Court. He guaranteed this arrangement by maintaining a contact at Court, sort of a 'control', who supplied him with intelligence particularly on matters concerning Hesse and Goremykin.[75] Rachkovskii felt secure in the knowledge that his views would be heard by the tsar. Yes, even Plehve sourly admitted that Nicholas II considered Rachkovskii to be 'one of the most devoted protectors of the regime and dynasty'.[76] After Nicholas II appointed Plehve to succeed the assassinated D. S. Sipiagin as Minister of Internal Affairs in 1902, Plehve blocked Rachkovskii's chances for promotion, keeping him in France where he could exert little influence on the Department of Police or the MVD as a whole.[77]

Rachkovskii's sense of security was short-lived. The chief of the Paris Office, although consumed by his own personal advancement above all else, was nobody's fool. By 1900 he recognised that the character and focus of the emigration was changing. He wrote to Fontanka of the emigration's new cohesiveness and its newly acquired toughness.[78]

The Foreign Agentura's own reports to Fontanka and those of master agents such as Evno Azef related the transformation of the emigration. The Special Section read of an emigration better organised than ever before, more focused on political platforms and systematic campaigns of terror led by hardened, exceptionally clever fanatics. Political police reports in general and those emanating from the Foreign Agentura under Rachkovskii in particular need to be read cautiously. Even so, the intelligence from the field with its warnings of widespread terrorism to come leaves the reader even today with a foreboding which must have affected the Russian political police who were completely at sea struggling to cope with the rapidly intensifying revolutionary situation within the Empire.[79] After crying wolf for so many years with his portrayal of the émigrés he kept under surveillance as rabid terrorists, Rachkovskii found himself confronting a self-fulfilling prophecy.

In a report dated 20 July/2 August 1901 Rachkovskii wrote honestly, offering his observations about the transformation of the emigration and its critical role in the spreading of a united front against the monarchy by constitutional and revolutionary groups. 'It would be a great mistake to think that the revolutionary struggle currently seizing the Empire is a struggle which can be limited by up to now customarily practised police measures.... New times – new problems.'[80]

For once Minister of Internal Affairs Plehve agreed with his director of the Foreign Agentura. New times meant new people. Plehve's desire to increase the quality and professionalism of his political police did not bode well for Rachkovskii. Plehve hated not only Rachkovskii but what he stood for. Rachkovskii, although a gifted provocateur whose strategy and tactics worked well against the émigrés who fled abroad in the 1870s and 1880s, represented the lack of professionalism within the Fontanka that Plehve so despised. The minister of internal affairs embarked upon a programme of professionalism and institutional expansion under the guidance of A. A. Lopukhin and S. V. Zubatov, his new director of the Department of Police and chief of the Special Section respectively. These men strove to construct a professional police system within the framework of modern bureaucratic institutions. Plehve believed that the police required a single systematic approach to political police work controlled by well-trained policemen and administrators. He wished every member of Fontanka from the lowliest clerk and detective to the men charged with directing the OOs throughout the Empire and the Special Section (which made its appearance in 1898) to be trained for their jobs and to have instilled in them an ethos of loyalty to Fontanka and dedication to the goals of forces of order.

There would be no place in these reformed police institutions for figures such as Rachkovskii, amateurs lacking in both training and dedication to the service. They must be removed and replaced by selfless men with modern policing skills. Proper record keeping, financial responsibility, agent reporting and obeying orders were not Rachkovskii's fortes. This wave of reform, despite the influence of his patrons, could sweep him away.

Rachkovskii, desperate to shore up his position, undertook an unprecedented action that caused him unknowingly to cross the one boundary which instantaneously ended the promising and even seemingly impregnable careers of those who transgressed it: the boundary of Imperial propriety.

In 1902 the tsar and tsaritsa made a state visit to France and during their tour they learned about a French hypnotist named Philippe who claimed that he could soothe the tsaritsa's perpetually raw nerves. Rachkovskii obeyed an Imperial order to bring this Philippe to Compiègne where the Royal couple were in residence. The very evening of his arrival Philippe conducted a seance which 'cured' the tsaritsa of her nervous condition. A grateful Nicholas II invited Philippe to accompany him and his wife to St Petersburg and to take up residence at Court. Phillipe took immediate advantage of the privileges and prerogatives that were bestowed on a member of the Imperial inner circle. The tsar, impressed with Philippe's succcessful ministration to his wife arranged for the election of this hypnotist to the St Petersburg Medical Academy and employed his Imperial Authority to have the magician appointed a doctor in the army.

The scandal and humiliation caused by the favours bestowed by the mesmerised Imperial couple on this intriguer angered the Dowager Empress Maria Fedorovna. The widow of Alexander III, through General Hesse, asked Rachkovskii to prepare a dossier on the present Court favourite and submit it to the Court Commandant's office. The Foreign Agentura complied with the request but to the vexation of both Hesse and Maria Fedorovna the dossier revealed nothing incriminating on the despised soothsayer. At this point Rachkovskii's involvement in the matter officially ceased. However, he made the fatal error of not letting the matter drop. The chief of the Paris Office wrote a personal letter to the Dowager Empress in which he accused Philippe of being a Freemason and despite Hesse's advice to the contrary Rachkovskii personally delivered the letter to Nicholas II's mother. The charge of Freemasonry, although without apparent factual basis, served the Dowager Empress's purposes. She presented the letter to her son and Philippe vanished from the Tsarist Court.

Nicholas II, however, did not let the matter rest here. Infuriated at Rachkovskii for interfering in his personal affairs he threw the letter on the floor and literally began to trample it underfoot.[81] The tsar summoned Plehve to his chambers and as the minister entered the room Nicholas II turned to him exclaiming, 'that scoundrel Rachkovskii'. Plehve needed no other words, with the tsar's approval he removed the director of the Foreign Agentura from his post and summarily ordered him to leave Paris at once and never to return to the city he so cherished. Rachkovskii's disgrace was so complete that not even Court Commandant Hesse who came to the police chief's defence could change Nicholas II's mind. The humiliated policeman and his friends were aware that for him to return to Russia at this time would mean a direct confrontation with Plehve or worse with the tsar himself possibly resulting in permanent exile from St Petersburg and Moscow. Rachkovskii's friends implored the tsar to give the disgraced official permission to travel in Europe, first to Brussels and then to Warsaw in the hope that by the time Rachkovskii returned home Nicholas' anger would have subsided sufficiently to allow the unemployed official to settle in St Petersburg without any further punishment. This is exactly what happened.[82]

Rachkovskii, the eternal optimist, believed all was not lost and almost immediately began to plot his return to influence. The tsar, a fickle man, swayed from one faction within the government to another almost at whim. Rachkovskii hoped that Plehve and his faction would fall victim to the tsar's arbitrariness and that his own friends would be restored to influence.

While events did not play themselves out exactly according to Rachkovskii's scenario, they did remove Plehve from power and carried Rachkovskii to the political heights for which he had so long craved.[83]

The picture of Rachkovskii's career abroad is marked by the lack of professionalism that plagued Russia's (and for that matter much of Europe's) political police institutions in the late nineteenth century. Yet looking through the amateurish haze that coloured Rachkovksii's eighteen-year tenure as director of the Foreign Agentura we can discern in Rachkovskii's approach to dealing with the emigration a valuable contribution to modern political policing which extends far beyond his tenure in office.

Certainly Rachkovskii's poor record keeping and inaccurate and sporadic reporting characterised by his cavalier attitude toward the facts were characteristics which plagued the entire Russian political police at that time.[84] On the other hand, he established reliable liaisons with the French, English, German and Belgian police forces[85] and during his tenure in office he placed agents in Britain, Switzerland, France, Germany and the United States.

Most important of all, Rachkovskii made a valuable contribution to political police theory itself. By example he instituted a pattern of active police methods against political dissenters. He harassed the emigration transforming their already difficult lives into a veritable nightmare of intrigue and suspicion. He manufactured propaganda campaigns and provocation, such as the Landezen Affair, which successfully turned public opinion against the emigration. He infiltrated the revolutionary movement with high quality *sotrudniki* with an intensity and sophistication that would soon become commonplace under men such as Sergei Zubatov, but of which Rachkovskii was a pioneer.

Rachkovskii intuitively knew that once the revolutionary emigration realised that they were no longer safe from the tentacles of the tsarist secret police, even within the borders of the most democratic nations in Europe, the great strain under which they already lived would overwhelm many of them and drive them into silence if not back into the tsarist camp itself. However, Rachkovskii had premised his strategy to isolate the émigrés on conditions which altered considerably after 1900.

In 1901 the Socialist-Revolutionary Party coalesced from various *Narodnaia Volia* factions, and terrorism became more systematic and more effective. Terrorists were no longer free agents abroad. This young Party formed its infamous *Boevaia Organizatsiia* (Battle Organisation) whose most famous terrorists resided abroad. Using democratic Europe as a safe haven they planned and launched their assaults against members of Tsardom's governing circles and returned there after the deed was done.[86] The heart of the young Social Democratic movement, too, emigrated westward in growing numbers and like the SRs did not worry much, as had publicists such as Stepniak-Kravchinskii and Feliks Volkhovskii, about blackening Tsardom's name abroad and participating in western socialist movements. It focused virtually all of their attention on fomenting revolution at home. These revolutionaries, as Rachkovksii recognised, were of a new generation not so easily toyed with and, although rather bumbling at first, strove to organise a counter offensive against the agents of the Foreign Agentura itself.[87]

Yet, while Rachkovskii noticed the ominous changes in the complexion of the emigration and the revolutionary movements as a whole and called for a new strategy to counteract these changing circumstances, he himself made no effort to alter his *modus operandi*. He continued to rely on his steadily less effective tactics.[88] Worse, at a time when the Special Section required accurate and sophisticated reporting – of which he was certainly capable – concerning the burgeoning revolutionary emigration Rachkovskii chose to focus upon his personal business interests and preferred to dally in areas of diplomacy which not only were beyond his brief as director of the Foreign Agentura but which were actually detrimental to its given purpose.[89] His approach to police work is marked by his refusal to follow orders and be tied down by the tedium of routine but important paper work. There is no doubt that his disgrace in 1902 saved him from a worse fate: to be stigmatised as an incompetent and traitor.

Plehve wanted to be sure that the Foreign Agentura would conform to his reforms and perform in a systematic manner and, in this, he at least partially succeeded. The Paris Office never flaunted such flagrant abuse of authority again. Never would another Rachkovskii serve as its director. Professionalism, standardisation, modern police methods became Plehve's goals for the Special Section's divisions.

In appointing L. A. Rataev, a long serving Fontanka *chinovnik* to the post vacated by Rachkovskii Plehve believed he had achieved this end. Unfortunately, it took more than sedentary bureaucratic skill to make a successful police official especially in the rapidly evolving political environment within the revolutionary emigration.

8
Alignments and Alliances: L. A. Rataev and A. M. Harting, 1902–1905

Leonid Aleksandrovich Rataev, Rachkovskii's successor in Paris, and Arkadii Mikhailovich Harting, the first chief of the Berlin Agentura, represented two dramatically different types of political police officials.

L. A. Rataev, the more senior of the two men, graduated from the prestigious Nicholas Cavalry School. He joined the Ministry of Internal Affairs in 1882 and after lengthy, loyal, but unremarkable service received a promotion to the position of *chinovnik osobykh poruchenii pri departamente politsii* (a civil servant for special commissions attached to the Department of Police) in 1897. In 1898 holding the exalted rank of *Deistvitel'nyi statskii sovetnik* he became the responsible and powerful first director of the Special Section. The appointment of Rataev to this post denotes the dearth of police talent within the MVD at that time.

A. M. Harting, Rataev's antagonist in Berlin, achieved his lesser but still valued post in the Department of Police through completely different means. Harting's social background placed him at the opposite end of Russian society's ladder. Born Abraham Hekel'man into a lower middle class Jewish family in the city of Pinsk, he had the good fortune to be allowed to attend the Mining Institute in St Petersburg. The study of mining technology supplied Harting with too little stimulation and perhaps prospects for a somewhat dull future. In any case, he was soon recruited as an undercover agent by the St Petersburg OO. When his fellow students became suspicious he moved to another polytechnic school in order to continue his police work. Finally, in 1884 the St Petersburg OO, probably believing Hekel'man's cover to be blown, allowed him to transfer to the Polytechnic Institute in Zürich. Once in Zürich, Hekel'man adopted the pseudonym of Landezen to cover his past. But again the dull life of an engineering student could not hold him for long. Landezen had enjoyed his undercover work with the political police with its sense of ever present danger titillating his emotions. Acting independently he began his slow and successful entrance into the world of the revolutionary Russian emigration, hoping that once entrenched in émigré circles he could again offer his service to the Department of Police. He did not have to wait long for his opportunity. As a matter of course, Fontanka had informed Rachkovskii that former *sotrudnik* Abraham Hekel'man now lived abroad, studying in Switzerland. Rachkovskii noted that Landezen had successfully ingratiated himself with members of the emigration and decided to offer the engineering student a job with the Foreign Agentura as an undercover agent. Landezen accepted the offer. He received the fabulous salary of 300 roubles per month. No one could say that Rachkovskii was not a generous employer. The size of the salary, of course, is also an indication that Rachkovskii saw Landezen as a diamond in the rough.

The Foreign Agentura encouraged Landezen to spend his time playing the role of student at an agricultural institute in Paris while he settled into the Populist milieu. Between 1885 and 1889 he reported to Rachkovskii on the lives of several prominent exiles including Lev Tikhomirov and Peter Lavrov. Many years later, after Tikhomirov discovered Landezen's undercover connection with the Foreign Agentura, he reminisced about the police *sotrudnik*. 'This was a Jew...rather goodlooking, with the personality of a boulevard idler. [He spoke] with a sharp Jewish accent, but was a dandy and a fop with the manners of a wealthy man.' Landezen hid behind the guise of a rich, diligent, innocent and openhearted student. He had claimed that he received his money from his wealthy father which he then gave away 'right and left' to his conspiratorial friends.[1]

Landezen played his role with aplomb, but despite his hard work he would have remained just another competent *sotrudnik* if it had not been for his starring role as the provocateur in Rachkovskii's plan for his own aggrandisement. We do not know what Rachkovskii told the MVD about Landezen's 'heroic' role in 'exposing the plot' to kill Alexander III (bearing his name). Surely the grateful Rachkovskii must have spun a wondrous tale before his superiors in St Petersburg, for this Jewish provocateur received the title and privileges of a Hereditary Honorary Citizen possessing the right to settle anywhere he chose within the Empire.[2] In addition he received a lifetime pension of 1,000 rubles per year.

From that moment on Rachkovskii considered Landezen the star amongst his undercover agents. In 1892 or 1893 Landezen converted to the Orthodox faith, unlocking the door to a successful career in the Russian bureaucracy. He again changed his name, this time officially to conform with his newly Russified soul. He would now be known as Arkadii Mikhailovich Harting, the Godson of friend M. N. Murav'ev, Tsarist Ambassador to Germany and a future minister of foreign affairs. Rachkovskii's high opinion of him combined with the influence of Murav'ev won Harting an important special duty. He became the personal bodyguard to several Royal Personages including Princess Alexandra of Coburg-Gotha upon her engagement to the Tsarevich

Nicholas Aleksandrovich. He then became a bodyguard for Alexander III and eventually for Nicholas II. Harting continued to climb up the social ladder by marrying into an old and much honoured Belgian family, settling in Europe where his duties invariably kept him. He was the perfect choice to direct the new Berlin Agentura in 1900.[3] Harting would, as we shall see, end his career with the same lofty rank held by Rataev, that of *Deistvitel'nyi statskii sovetnik*, and the universal respect of his fellow European policemen. His chest was covered with medals awarded to him by Denmark, Switzerland, Norway, Austria, France, Great Britain and Germany, including the French Legion of Honour and the British Victoria Cross.[4]

The differences in career patterns of the two men, one drab and ordinary but within the bureaucratic system, and the other colourful and stimulating but outside the bureaucracy, are further accentuated by the two men's personal temperaments and their intraministerial alliances. Harting was a close friend of Rachkovskii's and would remain close to his mentor until the former official's final departure from the service in 1906. But if Rachkovskii was his mentor, then Sergei Zubatov served at least indirectly as his tutor. A serious student of police methods and administration, he readily belonged to the 'Zubatov School' of modern police methods.[5] Despite his friendship for Rachkovskii, Harting remained dedicated to the police reformers Lopukhin, Zubatov, and to a lesser degree Plehve, a feat more easily accomplished after 1902 when Rachkovskii temporarily disappeared from the scene. These connections within the MVD and his friendships with Murav'ev and with Rachkovskii, especially after 1905 when the latter man returned to power (by this time Harting again did not have to worry about conflict of interest since Zubatov, Lopukhin and Plehve were now gone), presaged a bright future.

Rataev's story is quite the opposite; by 1902 his best days were behind him. He rightly considered his new posting as director of the Foreign Agentura, in November 1902, to be a demotion. It is significant that the bureaucratic generalist Rataev was replaced by the political police specialist Zubatov as director of the Special Section. The need for political police specialists, however, was not responsible for the displacement of the experienced Rataev. Although far from stupid Rataev had been an abject failure as director of the Special Section. Lazy, a Don Juan, more concerned with his position in society and the latest theatre performance than with political police work, Rataev carried out his assignments in an uninspired manner.

He had served in the Department of Police for more than 20 years and if he so desired he could hold his own even in difficult and complex administrative situations, but he rarely took the trouble and had only a cursory interest in the investigative side of his work. All this led the exasperated Plehve to openly state that Rataev was a 'blot' on the Department of Police. Still, men with so much experience could not be squandered. Plehve believed that Rataev could still be of service to the Department of Police, but where to send him? Perhaps he thought that a demotion might shake him from his lethargy and the Foreign Agentura appeared suited to a man who prided himself on being a 'European'. In addition, Plehve knew that a posting to Paris would do much to assuage Rataev's feelings. This tactic worked and despite Plehve's action against him and Rataev's low opinion of his new posting in Paris the police official remained in the minister's camp.[6]

The jolt of his sudden demotion seemed to be just the medicine Rataev needed and he worked at his new duties with unusual diligence. Nevertheless, hard work was new to him and he felt the strain imposed by his duties. On 22 December 1902, he wrote Director Lopukhin that he was still uncomfortable in his yet unfamiliar surroundings and could hardly get used to the constant flow of correspondence which seemed to come from every direction. To make matters worse, the Foreign Agentura was in complete disarray. Rataev told Lopukhin that better supervision of operations in London and Geneva was required and he noted that there were too few detectives in the Foreign Agentura's service to cope with the expanding emigration. He, therefore, had taken the liberty of adding three detectives to his organisation, one each in Munich and in Paris, and one to cover Brussels and Liège in Belgium. Rataev informed Lopukhin that these appointments were merely stopgap measures and that in order to carry out the Agentura's assignments he would have to do some of the detective work himself.[7] His report reveals the actual shabbiness behind the glitter of Rachkovskii's 18 years in office.

Rataev had turned over a new leaf and he expected to be rewarded for it. He certainly anticipated a reasonably large budget to implement the alterations in the Paris Office he thought necessary to make it an effective branch of the political police. He must have been surprised, therefore, when instead of complimenting him for his efforts and approving at least the same budget for him as Fontanka had issued to Rachkovskii in 1902, Lopukhin cut his budget to only 150,000 francs per year. This cutback continued the following year when Rataev received only 134,000 francs for the fiscal year.[8]

Lopukhin's action was only a small part of an overall plan to force fiscal responsibility upon the branches of the political police but Rataev, still smarting from his demotion, took the budget cut personally. In a fury he wrote Lopukhin that while he had spent money with proper caution he could not operate the Foreign Agentura on such a small sum of money. He realised that the Department of Police had every right to be wary of a *novichok* (new boy) in the directorship of the Paris Office, yet he argued that certain sums of money pro forma had to be paid. For example, co-operative British and French police officials expected their usual stipend. Rachkovskii may have been over generous, but a reduction in the stipend could not be explained to them in such terms and the Foreign Agentura would undoubtedly lose their co-operation. Such action would severely cripple the work of the Paris Office. Worse, he found Louis Lépine, the Prefect of

Police in Paris, to be in a recalcitrant mood and that only a large 'bonus' payment could assuage the Prefect's feelings and guarantee his continued co-operation.[9]

Director Lopukhin paid little attention to Rataev's pleas. Why? The political situation at home demanded much more of his attention and finances; it was a matter of priorities. Minister of Internal Affairs Sipiagin's murder in 1902, the *Zubatovshchina* in 1903,[10] and the Kishinev Pogrom in 1903 were only three infamous examples of the increasing level of popular unrest. In response to Tsardom's fragile state Fontanka expanded the political police's activities throughout the Empire, training competent personnel and modernising and standardising operative and investigative procedures. It strove to achieve these goals under the constraint of fiscal responsibility in an attempt to make good use of every *kopek* spent. Fontanka, however, did not bother to explain its policy decisions to the director of the Foreign Agentura. Rataev, isolated abroad and feeling aggrieved in any case, did not take note of these considerations on his own. It appeared to Rataev that a plot had been hatched to deprive the Foreign Agentura of sufficient funds in order to cause him further embarrassment by preventing him from properly carrying out his duties.

There is no doubt that Rataev believed himself to be under siege. In a revealing letter to Sergei Zubatov he complained bitterly about the illconsidered treatment he received at the hands of his superiors in St Petersburg:

> Here in a strange land a good word is especially valuable to a lonely man. You know I [want] no one to feel sorry, here [in Paris] there is enough work for me. Honestly speaking I have found no organised agentura here . . . but I did not write about it [of course he did write about it] in the first place because Rachkovskii found himself in a difficult situation . . . and in the second place I do not share the opinion of these persons who believe in placing [evidence] before their chief of the humiliating and negative service of one's predecessors. I am silent and work from morning to night. One cannot buy love or devotion.

Nevertheless, Rataev claimed his new-found devotion to duty did not save him from being continually undermined at home.

> At first, immediately after my departure from Russia, vague rumours reached me which were soon followed by even more definite rumours that some form of secret and persistent agitation is being carried on against me with the aim of depicting my earlier service and my personal life as well in an unpleasant light. [This is being done] in order to discredit me before the Director as they have already successfully done to me in the eyes of the Minister.[11]

Rataev also reminded Zubatov that he served Tsardom loyally and well and had always completed his assignments successfully. Yet these accomplishments did not prevent his name from being dragged through the mud (*smeshat' s griaz'iu*).[12] He sent St Petersburg glowing reports of his efforts. He told Fontanka that he had infiltrated all of the major revolutionary organisations. He praised his detectives' and undercover agents' diligence and the high quality of the information they supplied to him.[13] Indeed, Rataev did control some outstanding *sotrudniki* including Evno Azef, Lev Beitner and Iakov Zhitomoriskii (the latter two through Harting). Unfortunately, as we shall see further on, he knew nothing about proper agent management and made no serious effort to verify their reports. It is doubtful whether Zubatov was taken in by Rataev's parading his supposed accomplishments before him. The director of the Special Section thought very little of the man he had replaced.[14]

Unhappy and insecure, Rataev did not believe that he had a firm foothold as director of the Foreign Agentura, especially with such an able colleague as A. M. Harting only a few hundred miles away in Berlin. Rataev reckoned that survival demanded the subtle destruction of Harting's career. The chief of the Paris Office attacked the Berlin branch at its jugular – its pocketbook. The Paris chancery controlled Harting's finances. The Foreign Agentura maintained an account at the *Credit Lyonnais* and Rataev withdrew monthly the funds for the Berlin Agentura, but Rataev regularly began to withhold payment to Harting of his budgeted allotment.[15] The chief of the Berlin Agentura grew annoyed, then vexed and finally infuriated; he challenged his immediate superior with a not-so-veiled threat. Harting politely stated that the Berlin branch wished the director of the Foreign Agentura to comply with the request for its appropriate monthly budget so that it would not be necessary to bother St Petersburg.[16] The threat had no effect and the dispute between the two police chiefs rapidly blossomed into open warfare. Harting began to bombard the Department of Police with telegrams demanding redress against Rataev's arbitrary administration. He complained flatly that, 'running every month to you [Fontanka] for the maintenance of the people in the Berlin Agentura has been too much to demand of me'.[17]

Harting probably knew that he was whistling in the wind. Even though everyone admitted his excellence as a police official and even though he could boast of impeccable friendships, he still remained Rachkovskii's protegé and close friend. Plehve knew full well that if/or when the crunch came between him and Rachkovskii, Harting would side with the second man and his benefactor Sergei Witte. Another factor Plehve weighed in choosing between Rataev and Harting must have been the former's

St Petersburg, professional bureaucrat background. Rataev rose through the Table of Ranks just as his minister had done, an indispensable consideration for the man who cherished the bureaucracy above all else.

So, Harting faced Rataev's increasing barrage of criticism and harassing tactics alone. Accusations of slipshod work and reprimands for being too informal with his agents poured out of Paris plaguing the Berlin Agentura chief. Rataev refused to issue Harting's monthly pension guaranteed to him by the tsar for his service in the Landezen Affair and often refused to pay him his regular salary.[18] Not satisfied with this the chief of the Paris Office notified his subordinate that there could only be one director of the Foreign Agentura and only one centre for the collection and collation of information – Paris.[19] Since there is no evidence that Harting ever challenged Rataev's 'right to rule' or the predominance of Paris over Berlin one can only wonder about Rataev's mental stability. Perhaps the blow of losing the directorship of the Special Section went deeper than anyone suspected.

Rataev's tactics had some effect. The failure to adequately fund the Berlin Agentura forced it to function understaffed with only two detectives in Berlin. Harting wrote despondently that it 'is extremely harmful for our Berlin business. Not one of our surveillance [projects] can possibly turn out well.'[20] As can be imagined Rataev wished to keep his relationship with the Berlin Agentura a private matter by isolating Harting from St Petersburg to the greatest extent possible. In order to accomplish this end he diabolically ordered that Berlin Agentura correspondence destined for the Department of Police be mailed *via* the Paris Office.[21] This order permitted Rataev to delete any embarrassing comments from Harting's dispatches to Fontanka.

Under these truly adverse conditions Harting indeed proved his worth. In 1900 when he was placed in charge of the new Berlin Office three detectives and then soon three more were assigned to him. The Berlin Agentura primarily concerned itself with keeping track of Russian émigrés in Germany, an assignment that would tax the ability and endurance of the most experienced police official. Even though Russian émigrés had to have visas for their stay in Germany, the German police made little effort to check them. They also failed to keep up to date lists of Russians living in the *Reich*. Harting believed that a little extra inducement might result in a more conscientious approach to the problem on the part of the German police. The tactic never failed and a well-bribed German Police Commissioner did his best to keep track of Russians living under his authority. In conjunction with this action Harting 'encouraged' an aide of the Berlin Police President to help the Foreign Agentura gather 1,200 names for a list of Russian citizens living in Berlin.[22]

The Berlin Agentura chief's expertise extended beyond befriending and bribing German police officials. Harting wasted no time in establishing an effective agentura. He recruited several *sotrudniki* and rented three conspiratorial apartments for their use. In this last area he possessed real talent much in the same style as his superior Sergei Zubatov. Like Zubatov, a former undercover agent himself, he knew the type of person who possessed that rare combination of psychological quirks necessary for any long surviving undercover agent. In March 1902, he employed a young man who became one of the most valuable agents ever employed by the Russian political police. The *sotrudnik*, recruited when a medical student at Berlin University, came to be one of Lenin's closest associates. This man, Iakov Abramovich Zhitomirskii, became the most lustrous jewel amongst the undercover agents recruited by Harting in his role as chief of the Berlin Agentura. Zhitomirskii also had several illustrious companions within Harting's stable of *sotrudniki*. By the end of 1904 their number included two people whose reputations and deeds almost matched Zhitomirskii's: Lev Beitner and Zinaida Zhuchenko.[23]

While Rachkovskii remained in Paris Harting's work was well-funded,[24] and as a result the first two years of his administration in Berlin were his most effective. Still, Harting walked on a knife's edge. The German people endured intrusive and arrogant policing largely in silence but they did so, in part, because of what they witnessed across their Eastern borders. Socialists and conservative alike viewed the Russian police with horror as the embodiment of brutal and benighted repression. The Russian police forces made their German counterparts appear absolutely 'benign'.[25] It is not surprising, then, that the Russian government failed to convince the German populace that the Russian revolutionaries were 'anarchists' as dangerous to the stability of Germany as they supposedly were to Russia.[26]

In 1903 Harting slipped. The Socialist newspaper *Vörwarts* leaked a story to a *Reichstag* deputy that the rights of Russian émigrés living in Germany were being infringed upon by employees of the Russian police working out of a bureau of the *Okhrana* based in Berlin with the full knowledge of the Kaiser's government. The story threw the *Reichstag* into an uproar.

The German government represented by State Secretary for Foreign Affairs Baron Richtofen, admitted that a Russian police contingent operated in Berlin and its environs. During the ensuing heated debate in the *Reichstag* over this scandal, the German public learned, as we have seen in Chapter 2, that Russian émigrés were harassed constantly, their apartments searched with no cause, their personal papers seized, and that they were often charged with crimes that they did not commit. Indeed, it was discovered that Harting's agents interfered with German citizens as well (in one case stealing the mail of a *Reichstag* deputy!) and that the Berlin police often co-operated with its Russian colleagues. On 15 February 1902, for example, 15 German undercover agents invaded a meeting of Russian students whom they surmised were members of a secret society. Even though every arrested student possessed a valid student identification card the police detained them until morning, searched their lodgings, and composed a list of those arrested for the Russian authorities.[27] A socialist deputy in the *Reichstag* succinctly expressed the ignominious status of Russian émigrés and students living in the Second *Reich*:

> All of these cases which became known over the past year and have occupied our forces, have happened to people who have done nothing outside of our laws or who have undertaken anything against the safety of our state, but exclusively are persons whose ideas the Russian police spies thought were awkward for the Russian government.... Those who were unpleasant [citizens] for the Russian government now have become for our Government 'troublesome foreigners'.[28]

Although it never would have occurred to this *Reichstag* deputy, it is doubtful that anyone could have paid Arkadii Harting a greater compliment. As for the German government, it got off lightly too. Baron Richtofen was never forced to reveal that the orders to support the establishment of the Berlin Agentura came directly from Kaiser Wilhelm II himself.[29]

It seemed that neither Rataev nor the *Reichstag* could upset Harting's career. In fact, the Department of Police rewarded Harting for his achievements in Germany and reaffirmed its confidence in him by placing Harting in charge of the Russian counter-intelligence network in Northern Europe during the last year of the Russo-Japanese War (from mid-1904 to the beginning of peace negotiations).

In July 1904 Director of the Department of Police A. A. Lopukhin created a special unit within the Special Section under the direction of police functionary I. F. Manasevich-Manuilov which focused on Japanese activities in Scandinavia, western Europe and Great Britain as well as within the Empire itself.[30] It is Fontanka's military intelligence operations in Northern and Western Europe, however, which reveal Headquarter's opinion of the abilities of both Rataev and Harting. With the outbreak of the Russo-Japanese War on 27 January 1904 the Japanese Government placed Colonel Motojiro Akasi, a multi-lingual (he spoke Russian as well as several other European languages) and exceptionally intelligent officer familiar with European politics and military affairs, in charge of fomenting trouble in Russia. The Japanese General Staff ordered Akasi to undertake two assignments: to foment both protests and armed uprisings particularly by the subject nationalities such as the Finns, and to encourage inter-party conferences abroad of all revolutionary parties with the goal of establishing a single, united, opposition movement to the Romanov dynasty.[31] He endeavoured to achieve these assignments by organising through his Finnish and Georgian allies within the revolutionary movement, an inter-party conference in Geneva in the spring of 1904[32] on the one hand and for the purchase and shipment of arms to Russia on the other.[33] Nothing frightened Tsardom more than the nightmare of confronting a united, armed opposition and Rataev's sensational reports based on raw intelligence received from Azef only exacerbated these fears.[34]

At first the tsarist government underestimated the impact of Akasi's work and simply ordered Rataev to keep an eye on the Japanese Colonel. Rataev responded to Fontanka's orders by reporting on the arrival of Japanese agents in Sweden, on the one hand, and bribing higher Swedish police officials to keep an eye on the transportation through Stockholm of revolutionary publications to Russia on the other. Rataev reported steadily on the movements of Akasi, his Japanese agents and his allies amongst the Russian revolutionary movement as well. Nevertheless, the Special Section found Rataev's work unsatisfactory. Director of Fontanka Lopukhin believed the Foreign Agentura's reports concerning the ties between the Japanese and the Russian revolutionaries to be vague. The Department of Police concluded that the Foreign Agentura's detectives and undercover agents did not possess any experience in espionage and, as a result, that the Paris Office was not suited for counter-intelligence work.[35]

In the autumn of 1904 Lopukhin ordered Manuilov to establish counter-espionage operations throughout Europe. With the help of the French police and intelligence service Manuilov's agents successfully purloined Japanese correspondence from Japan's embassies and consuls in France, England, Germany, Belgium and Holland. Ten agents on loan from the French actually penetrated the Swedish, Serbian, Chinese and English diplomatic missions in Paris, the Roumanian and Chinese embassies in London, the Japanese and English diplomatic corps in Brussels, the German one in Madrid and the Japanese mission in the Hague! In addition, the French kept up a steady supply of intercepted telegrams dispatched by Japanese diplomats in France.[36]

Poor Rataev. The Foreign Agentura, not being told anything to the contrary, also kept up a steady flow of reports on the relationship between Akasi, the Russian revolutionaries and on arms purchases.[37] But although this information clarified Akasi's activities still further, it seems that Rataev, as we shall see, continued to be treated with disdain.

As for Harting, the Special Section seconded him from his post as chief of the Berlin Agentura and appointed him, along with an experienced gendarme officer, to run a spy network in order to short circuit any possible Japanese diversions in Northern Europe and the Dardenelles. Harting's domain covered the Baltic and North Sea coasts. Based in Copenhagen, he established surveillance points along the Baltic Sea littoral to keep an eye on shipping. He also established connections with Swedish steamship and insurance companies with the expectation that these relationships would help him to discover shipping schedules and destinations and, of course, the nature of cargoes. As the 1905 Revolution grew in intensity arms smuggling became an increasingly successful venture for the revolutionaries and port control seemed an insoluble problem for Tsardom;[38] so the government would, as we shall see in the subsequent chapter, turn to Harting for a solution.

The Special Section also expected him to protect Russian shipping travelling through the Baltic by detecting any Japanese attempts to use foreign vessels and crews to mine the shipping channels. In addition, Harting tracked Akasi and his agents when they moved through Northern and Central Europe using detectives he especially selected for counter-espionage work.[39]

His success in the delicate domain of counter-intelligence encouraged the tsarist government to give him the sensitive job of investigating the causes of the Dogger Bank Incident. The Baltic Fleet's firing upon British fishing boats in the North Sea was an embarrassing and potentially explosive issue which the Russian government wanted cleared up as quickly as possible. Harting reacted in an absolutely professional manner as his report placed the blame squarely where it belonged, on the irresponsible conduct of Admiral Rozhdestvenskii. The honesty of his reportage combined with the speed with which he concluded the investigation prevented the exacerbation of already strained Russo-British relations. Tsardom rewarded him well. The chief of the Berlin Office received a monetary reward and the Order of St Vladimir. Harting was rewarded with the greatest honour of all when the government raised him to the estate of *Potomstvennyi dvorianin* (Hereditary Noble).[40] His prestige continued to grow.

Harting's rise proved that the MVD could transcend social boundaries in search of talent. These two crucial and sensitive missions were assigned not to the director of the Foreign Agentura, a long-time bureaucrat with the appropriate social and professional background, but to a Jewish-born upstart of exceptional ability. It would be nice to conclude that talent had won out on its own merits. The evidence, however, does not permit for such a comforting conclusion. The internecine battles within the government had much to do with Harting's promotion to the Hereditary Nobility. Plehve was long dead by 1905, Witte and Rachkovskii were ascendant.[41] Again, within Fontanka, ability in itself was no guarantee of success without the helping hands of powerful friends.

While Harting continually impressed Fontanka with his hard work and levelheadedness, Rataev, too, eventually allowed his futile vendetta against his subordinate in Berlin to temporarily subside, thereby concentrating more on the purpose of his Agentura.[42] He informed the Department of Police that he had infiltrated the major revolutionary organisations: the Socialist-Revolutionary Party, the *Narodovoltsi* [*sic*!], the Anarchists, the *Iskra* group, the Finnish Separatists, and the Jewish Agitation Committees. He claimed that his agents were 'everywhere providing surveillance . . . knowing almost all the particulars concerning the chief people [in the revolutionary] movement'. Rataev boasted falsely that although he inherited not a single *sotrudnik* from Rachkovskii, he had placed agents in several revolutionary organisations. He neglected to tell Fontanka that Harting was responsible for the employment of many of these agents.[43]

Unfortunately, Rataev never mastered the skills nor the concern for detail that were such necessary parts of the political policeman's trade.[44] Worse, as noted above, Rataev understood absolutely nothing about agent procedures and made no effort to verify the reports of either his detectives or his *sotrudniki*. Boris Nikolaevskii succinctly exposed Rataev's *naiveté*, an unforgivable characteristic for a man who had been in the political police business for such a long time:

> It may be definitely stated that throughout the period of Azev's work under Rataev it was not Rataev who controlled Azev, but the latter who used him in his own interests, deftly employing him as a screen for his activities, learning from him the extent of the Department's knowledge [about his activities], and with his help getting rid of his party enemies.[45]

A twist of fate made Rataev pay for the lax handling of his *sotrudniki* for it resulted in the death of the one man, who even half-heartedly, supported his position: Minister of Internal Affairs Viacheslav Konstantinovich Plehve. One wonders if the irony escaped him. To make matters worse, Rataev had a long standing problem of not only exaggerating the revolutionary situation but of approaching it with a completely negative attitude. He saw the revolutionary movement spreading everywhere and he believed that the police were powerless to stop its development.[46] At best he could have offered solutions; at the least his superiors had the right to expect an accurate and detached description of the revolutionary 'situation'. Rataev communicated only a sense of panic.

Whatever little faith Fontanka might still have had in his ability disappeared altogether with the assassination of Plehve for which he was held to account. He attempted to defend his actions but could not do so to the satisfaction of Fontanka.[47] To be fair, the blame for Plehve's assassination could only in part be placed at Rataev's feet. In fact, the entire procedure of undercover agent control required overhauling.[48] The Department of Police, however, had no intention of accepting even partial blame for the murder of its own minister.

When the evidence is reviewed, then, it is amazing that Rataev survived in office for another 13 months. But even in retrospect one cannot fathom St Petersburg's sudden plan to increase Rataev's authority. Perhaps St Petersburg feared that his dismissal would publicise the brewing scandal over police incompetence. What better way to show 'confidence' in a colleague than not only to maintain him in his post but actually to increase his authority and responsibilities. On 17 January 1905, Director Lopukhin wrote Chief of the Special Section Makarov that:

> For the past year the heart of the Russian political emigration seems to be located in Switzerland and especially Geneva, where it is necessary to concentrate all the expanding surveillance of the Foreign Agentura. [This] might be accomplished by unifying the Parisian and Berlin Agenturas and transferring all the Berlin Agentura's surveillance and secret agents to... Rataev.[49]

This startling statement which must have come as an extremely pleasant surprise to Rataev undoubtedly took into account the fact that Harting was overwhelmed with counter-espionage work. Lopukhin correctly perceived that Germany had become less important as a place of residence for Russian émigrés – so much so that Harting could be seconded to the Special Section's counter-espionage department without a replacement being found for him in Berlin. Lopukhin's proposal that Harting be retired with severance pay in the amount of 6,500 roubles could only have been a ruse to hide the nature of his current assignment, which the Special Section went to some lengths to conceal.[50]

Nonetheless, why in effect strengthen the hand of L. A. Rataev, a man whom no one respected? There could only be one possible explanation for this decision. Lopukhin, a lame duck police chief who remained in his post as director of Fontanka only until the tsar appointed a replacement, exhausted and distraught over the mess of Bloody Sunday for which he bore a good deal of responsibility, was beyond caring who directed the Foreign Agentura.[51] In any case, it can be said in Lopukhin's defence that he may not have known that Azef was a police agent[52] until later and thus he could not have known the extent of Rataev's culpability in the Plehve murder. This most certainly made Lopukhin's decision easier.

The return of P. I. Rachkovskii to grace meant disaster for Rataev. When Rachkovskii's close friend D. F. Trepov became Governor-General of St Petersburg with dictatorial powers in January 1905, Rachkovskii found himself back not only within the political police but within the walls of Fontanka itself. Rataev was doomed. Rachkovskii began his campaign against the director of the Foreign Agentura on 11 June 1905 when he advised the minister of internal affairs, that, 'the Department of Police should...immediately re-establish the Berlin Agentura on its previous basis'. Rachkovskii reasoned that Russia's contiguous border with Germany provided Russian émigrés with either a quick escape from or a cautious return to their homeland. He claimed, therefore, 'that in the absence of our [Berlin] Agentura's organised surveillance [revolutionaries including terrorists] would be completely free to create their criminal inventions [in Germany]'.[53] Since the reoriented balance of power within Fontanka rested with Rachkovskii the Berlin Agentura reopened with Harting again at the helm (Japanese espionage ended with the initiation of peace negotiations between Russia and Japan[54]). This time, however, Fontanka ordered Rataev to supply Harting with sufficient funds to run the Berlin bureau properly. Leonid Aleksandrovich Rataev's days were numbered and his dismissal notice came on 6 August 1905, the day a Fontanka circular announced Rachkovskii's appointment as director of political police operations throughout the Empire.[55] The former chief of the Paris Office received 15,000 francs severance pay and retired in Paris under a pseudonym.

Rachkovskii certainly possessed strong, legitimate evidence for removing Rataev from his post in Paris because his record as director of the Foreign Agentura was one marked by squabbling, disorder, unnecessary expenditure and incompetent agent control. Rataev had devoted most of his energy to securing his own position. To be sure, he had increased the number of detectives and undercover agents in his service, but he did not use them well. Under his guidance the Paris chancery issued regular reports on revolutionary groups as prescribed by his orders and these were both more numerous than those of Rachkovskii and not intentionally inaccurate as were some of those produced by his predecessor. Nevertheless, it must be remembered that the information comprising Rataev's dispatches was supplied by agents mostly recruited by Harting and the increasing number of reports was to some extent a function of the steadily growing and more active revolutionary emigration. Indeed, there is considerable evidence that Rataev actually allowed the administrative machine of the Paris Office to operate without his participation. He left his files in a shambles, both the indispensable cross reference file for agentura documentation and the all-important alphabetical file were in a hopeless state.[56] Rataev was fiscally irresponsible as well. Despite his limited funds which should have encouraged him to conserve his money, Rataev took an over zealous interest in relatively unimportant tasks costing far too much for value returned. For example, he paid for the perlustration of émigré mail in Bulgaria of all places.[57] Rataev's accounts for his last months in office contain so much unusual and excessive expenditure that his successor implied that he had siphoned off the money for personal use.[58] Most damning of all, was the inadequate and unskilled attention that Rataev devoted to the work of his detectives[59] and undercover agents. As we have just seen his failure to keep Azef under tight rein cost the life of his minister.

Amazingly, none of these excellent grounds for Rataev's dismissal were employed by Rachkovskii. The enforced retirement of the Paris Office chief was an example of power politics plain and simple. It seems that Rataev paid the price for belonging to the wrong faction within the MVD and nothing more; and his was by no means an exceptional case. Rataev's career abroad reflected one of Fontanka's most serious problems: competence or incompetence too often played a small role in one's staying power. The selection of one police bureaucrat to replace another came to be based in part, if not entirely, on considerations that were deeply embedded in the tsarist bureaucracy's traditional and informal practices, and which were largely irrelevant to the professional criteria established for the job at hand. This is certainly the reason that Fontanka found it difficult to provide disgraced former officials such as Rataev with adequate explanations as to the causes for their removal from office.[60]

In sum, Leonid Aleksandrovich Rataev exactly fit the stereotype of a St Petersburg bureaucrat: unmotivated, unimaginative, somewhat dissolute, and very possibly corrupt. The posting of the mediocre Rataev to Paris at a critical time in the life of the revolutionary emigration and his forced retirement three years later points out the serious flaws in a system that, far too often, appointed or dismissed officials for reasons other than merit and the demands of the job at hand.

9

The 1905 Revolution and the Foreign Agentura: Harting's Campaign Against Munitions Contraband, 1905–1908

Arkadii Mikhailovich Harting replaced Rataev as director of the Foreign Agentura. Could there have been any other choice? Merit combined with political connections made Harting the inevitable selection. As director of the Foreign Agentura Harting proved to be a dynamic, innovative and ambitious leader. It is noteworthy that his tenure in office easily survived his mentor Rachkovskii's final swan-song in 1906. Ultimately a combination of factors including exhaustion and his exposure in the European press as none other than Landezen, the infamous, long escaped criminal from French justice, induced him to retire in 1908.

When Harting took command of the Paris Office, it was still small with almost no administrative staff. A single secretary and a typist did the paper work. The Foreign Agentura employed four detectives in Paris, only two of whom were still really useful. The third man, too old for field work, only compiled *spravki* and the fourth, Henri Bint, although still listed on the personnel role as a detective had of late served as Rataev's administrative assistant. In Geneva there were six people employed as detectives by the Foreign Agentura; one of them was no longer fit for service and the others also served in the Geneva police force.[1] Harting noted that such a skimpy number of detectives in Switzerland and France could not cope with increasing revolutionary activity abroad. The newly appointed chief of the Paris Office argued that detectives were needed in Great Britain and in the major ports of Europe in order to halt the flow of revolutionary contraband into Russia. To make matters worse, the calibre of the detectives employed by the Foreign Agentura reached a comically low level.[2] Harting attacked this problem at once, hiring several competent detectives whom he assigned as follows: two in Paris, one in rural France, one in Antwerp, two in London, one in Geneva, and three in Berlin. The Foreign Agentura also began to hire people in lesser investigative capacities to report overheard gossip or aid in the perlustration of the mails. Harting also bragged that after helping the Danish secret police in one of their investigations its chief gratefully reciprocated by creating a special bureau to work exclusively on requests received from the Foreign Agentura.[3]

Of course, the hard information required by Fontanka was provided largely by the undercover agents. Here, Harting applied his special talent for the recruitment of *sotrudniki*. The people he acquired were so effective and sufficiently numerous to allow the Foreign Agentura to attain a long-dreamt of goal: the thorough penetration of every segment of the Russian revolutionary emigration.[4]

Harting also knew how to use these forces effectively. Unlike his predecessors, this director took the initiative in developing a systematic campaign against the emigration. He told Fontanka that he hoped to carry out the following programme:

1. To maintain surveillance over those émigrés that remained abroad after the amnesty (issued by the tsarist government during the 1905 Revolution).
2. To maintain surveillance on persons who were travelling through Europe to Russia for revolutionary purposes.
3. To maintain surveillance on the centres of revolutionary activity of the various subversive organisations and to maintain surveillance on the leaders of the revolutionary movement.
4. To maintain surveillance on the editorial, printing offices, and typographies of the revolutionary movement that printed forged passport blanks and other documents necessary for revolutionary activity.
5. To maintain surveillance on persons who were occupied with the preparation of bombs and those who taught the craft of bomb-making to others.
6. To watch individuals who were undertaking the smuggling of munitions into Russia.
7. To place under surveillance all (Russian) persons travelling abroad or Russians living abroad who have connections with representatives of European socialism or the Anarchist Party.
8. To uncover the plans of Russian émigrés and anarchists during visits and stays abroad by the Imperial Family.[5]

The Foreign Agentura conscientiously tried to fulfil the tenets of Harting's programme, but the desperate situation in the homeland by mid-1905 drove the Foreign Agentura into emphasising one duty above others, number six: disrupting the smuggling of munitions into Russia. The director of the Foreign Agentura became obsessed with the endless 'cat-and-mouse' game with the revolutionary smugglers.

Harting's interest in the prevention of smuggling had begun a few years earlier when, as chief of the Berlin Agentura, he noted the ease with which Russian émigré contrabandists smuggled subversive literature, weapons, and explosives into the homeland. The smuggling, especially of literature and correspondence, was a regular part of émigré life. For instance, prior to 1905 the SDs routinely smuggled newspapers such as *Zvezda*, (*The Star*), *Mysl* (*Thought*) and, of course, *Iskra* (*The Spark*) into Russia.[6] The best route to illegally transport literature and correspondence into the Empire was through Stockholm into Finland, then from Finland into Russia. Once within Russia the courier delivered the contraband to predetermined contacts who stored or distributed it according to their instructions.[7]

Not every piece of revolutionary literature could be conveyed by this relatively safe route. Much of it travelled the more dangerous paths through the German and Austro-Hungarian borders contiguous with the Russian Empire. These trips involved considerable personal risk for the contrabandists and only the constant highly imaginative uses of prestidigitation offered a reasonable chance at success. Newsprint in large quantities is both heavy and bulky requiring as a means of conveyance the use of baggage, iceboxes or any other large case in which a false bottom could be placed. It did not take the Russian police long to uncover this method of smuggling propaganda and once they did it became incumbent on the revolutionaries to rapidly invent new tricks for passing their writings into Russia. The urgency was made necessary by the Special Section's practice of keeping the couriers of uncovered contraband under surveillance rather than arresting them at the border crossing, thereby permitting its detectives to discover the destination or 'drop points' for the contraband. Fontanka considered the discovery of these 'drop points' to be a significant victory over the local revolutionary organisations and indeed it was.[8] One of the most ingenious methods employed by smugglers to combat the growing sophistication of the political police was to print the issue of a particular newspaper on very thin paper so that 300 copies of *Iskra* (for example) could be hidden in trunks with the most inobtrusive false bottoms.[9] Also, the light weight of the paper allowed a courier to carry between 200 and 300 copies of a publication in the pockets of a specially designed waistcoat. When this trick became too risky the revolutionaries commissioned a Swiss bookbinder to invent a glue with which thin sheets of paper could be pasted together to form cardboard and be made into cases, cartons, book bindings and other innocuous items that would easily pass through Russian customs. The recipient of the material only needed to apply some warm water to unstick the construction, returning it to its original newsprint format. One wonders if the police ever guessed that the very trunks and suitcases they examined were actually manufactured of the contraband for which they were searching?[10]

Munitions, too, were smuggled into Russia by overland routes and these operations deeply concerned terrorist conscious Fontanka and its Foreign Agentura. In small quantities couriers carried munitions across Russia's borders attached to their person – a dangerous business if there ever was one. Dynamite, for example, was worn in belts or bandages tied closely to the body. Women smugglers masked the body heat induced stench of the dynamite by dousing themselves in cheap perfume or by standing on the open platform of the railway carriage transporting them even in the coldest weather. Rifles, less dangerous to carry but bulkier than dynamite, were broken down into barrels and stocks and the pieces suspended from a towel or cord tied around the transporter's neck. Some female students became amazingly expert in this particular art, carrying up to eight rifles each; a feat involving considerable strength and agility.[11]

In the years immediately preceding the 1905 Revolution Harting directed the Foreign Agentura's campaign from Berlin with commonsense countermeasures against these daring revolutionary contrabandists. He dispatched detectives from his Berlin bureau to the most frequently crossed check points on the German-Austro-Hungarian frontiers with Russia in order to watch for the entrance of contraband and revolutionaries onto Russian soil. These *filery* were especially chosen for their familiarity with the membership of the Russian revolutionary émigré colonies and therefore could identify couriers or illegal entrants to Russia on sight. In addition, Harting suggested to Fontanka that detectives who specialised in tracking down contraband and discovering its local depositories within Russia be assigned by the Special Section to border check points popularly crossed by smugglers. These *filery* who would be rotated monthly (so as to prevent contrabandists from discovering their identity), were to be drawn from the detective pools of Russia's OOs. Harting went so far as to offer small rewards (of between 20 and 50 roubles) to border guards who detained persons with false passports or uncovered a shipment of illegal literature.[12] The anti-contraband measures that Harting initiated from his Berlin office proved to be so effective that by 1905 smuggling by overland routes had become almost impossible.[13] Harting's frustration of the Bolshevik operation, for example, caused Krupskaia to comment that the police 'were on the track of everything' being smuggled into Russia.[14] Fontanka also recognised Harting's achievement and rewarded him accordingly.[15]

Harting did not have much time to savour his victory over the demoralised revolutionary contrabandists. The eruption of the 1905 Revolution soon dramatically altered the moods of both the revolutionary emigration and the Russian political police who were harassing them. The traumatic events made a deep impression in particular upon Harting, now the chief of the Foreign Agentura. Harting's world seemed suddenly to be turned upside down. After watching over a perpetually pensive and generally subdued emigration for so many years, how helpless the Foreign Agentura must have felt when the grey mood of émigré life turned overnight to glee upon the first rumblings of serious revolution within the Empire. It is amazing that the Foreign Agentura maintained its composure at all in this atmosphere, isolated from the homeland and disoriented by the reversal of psychological position with its adversaries.

Nothing illustrates the revitalisation of the revolutionary emigration better than the altered mood of the revolutionary contrabandists. Overjoyed by the outbreak of the 1905 Revolution they threw themselves into their smuggling operations with renewed energy, fresh imagination and, most important of all, substantially increased funds. The director of the Foreign Agentura himself exclaimed that not a week went by without the émigrés calling a general meeting to discuss 'the arming of the Russian people', and that thousands of francs and marks were being gathered for the purpose. Discussions concerning fund raising for the purchase of arms took place every day in Paris, Berlin and other German cities, wrote Harting. Huge contributions were being made to the revolutionary cause to be used specifically for the purchase of arms and munitions. Arms were being stored by Russian revolutionaries in cities such as Zürich, Berne, Liège and Hamburg and would soon be dispatched across the Finnish and Lettish borders by sea to Russia.[16] With feverish dedication the Foreign Agentura's operatives kept up a steady flow of reports concerning the smuggling of arms, and munitions into the Empire. Although some of these reports were undoubtedly false, their inaccuracy derived not so much from panic but from the inability to be absolutely sure about the contents of most of the cargoes being shipped to Russia by sea. The Foreign Agentura followed the dictum, 'it is better to be cautious than sorry'.

Harting, who desperately wanted to participate in the counter-revolutionary struggle, was convinced that he could best serve his nation's interests by repeating his successful campaign against revolutionary arms and munitions smuggling. During the 1905 Revolution the smuggling of arms and munitions into Russia took place by both overland and sea routes. Harting, having learned the tricks of the overland smuggling business during his tenure in Berlin, found preventing this form of transport a relatively easy task. He ordered his detectives to observe the warehouses where the contraband was stored and to confiscate the arms when the contrabandists tried to get them across the border. In response to Harting's action the revolutionaries resorted to professional local smugglers who helped them avoid the increasing attention of the Russian police. They also tried to bribe and if necessary threaten the officers of the Border Gendarmerie so that they placed their men with a view to leaving substantial gaps along the border which could easily be traversed. Revolutionary smugglers may have succeeded in bribing or cajoling some border gendarmerie into co-operating with them but overland smuggling of bulky, hard to conceal arms and munitions had little real chance of large scale success even under the best conditions. The loss of a shipment meant that a considerable sum of money and reliable couriers had been wasted. Thus, for the tsarist authorities, overland arms and munitions smuggling was at its most intensive level only a nuisance. The Foreign Agentura spoiled Fontanka's sense of relief, however, with the information that 'the movement of contraband in arms travelling overland ... is significantly less than by sea'.[17]

The job of bringing the complex sea-borne form of smuggling to an end, for the most part, became the responsibility of the Foreign Agentura. Weapons smuggled by ship were bought and stored abroad and then hidden amongst the hundreds of cargoes regularly delivered to Russia's Baltic and less frequently Black Sea ports. The tsarist authorities could only confiscate contraband of this sort if they received advance warning concerning its arrival and this alarm had to include the date of arrival, method of transport, and an accurate description of the munitions crates. The responsibility for gathering this data rested with the Foreign Agentura. Harting's plan for defeating this type of arms smuggling operation came in the wake of the *John Grafton* incident. The story of the gunrunning vessel, the *John Grafton*, is well known and an excellent account of the affair is readily available.[18] It is sufficient to note that the endeavour managed to get underway only to end in a shipwreck and frustration for the smugglers. Nevertheless, this highly publicised attempt to smuggle a shipload of munitions into Russia by gunrunner had an instantaneously unnerving effect on the Russian authorities.[19]

Fontanka's campaign to prevent gunrunning ventures by Russia's revolutionaries developed with a tremendous sense of urgency, the natural reaction to the *John Grafton* affair by a state undergoing a massive upheaval and a government reeling almost powerless in retreat before a spreading revolution. Harting told Fontanka that European armament firms dealt quite openly with the revolutionaries. The best method of preventing the sale of weapons to this riff-raff was through negotiations at the highest diplomatic level, a slow and inconclusive process. An alternative path suggested by Harting to ensure the discovery of munitions contraband involved intensive surveillance in the contrabands' ports of origin. The Foreign Agentura, Harting argued, should place agents in German, Belgian, Dutch, Danish, Norwegian and Swedish ports. He even made a case for placing Foreign Agentura operatives in custom houses or with shipping agents who were valuable sources of information. For the payment of a substantial sum they would notify the Foreign Agentura of the routes, cargo contents, and time of departure of suspected ships. Russian consulates established in small fishing villages as well as in large cities could serve as another source of data, passing on any tidbits of gossip on the movements of suspected ships. Harting hoped that this information would be communicated to Paris where he would read it to make sure that there was no duplication in the reports, synthesise the material and forward it to the Department of Police. A panic stricken MVD agreed to all these suggestions.[20]

Consulates, custom houses and shipping agents were not Harting's only sources of information. Thanks to what the Paris chief called his 'private connections' he organised with the connivance of the French *Sûreté Générale* and other European police departments a network of professional agents in the ports of Marseilles, Bordeaux, Nantes, Le Havre, St Nazaire, Dunkirk and

Antwerp. He boasted to Fontanka that his bureau through its network of agents and friends could supply St Petersburg with detailed, accurate information on every ship leaving for Russia from the above ports. Harting became so obsessed with what he saw as his mission to crush the smugglers that he decided to close down other sections of his Agentura in order to devote more funds to his port control measures. The less important functions to be curtailed included the surveillance of individual émigrés not connected with contraband operations since Harting honestly noted that the most important members of the emigration had already returned or were about to return home in response to the government's amnesty. He also suggested that unless additional funds were forthcoming he would be forced to retire several agents adding their former salaries to the money devoted to the port control system.[21] Fontanka made no response to Harting's comments, it had other more important things on its mind. Not receiving any reply one way or the other the director of the Foreign Agentura thought it best to take a middle path. He retired two over-age detectives, but made no other personnel or structural changes to the Foreign Agentura. He just continued his anti-smuggling campaign, emphasising it above other duties, a logical decision since the Special Section no longer needed the Paris bureau to tell it what the revolutionaries were up to. Everything was quite in the open now.

Harting must have felt himself to be the right man in the wrong place. The conflict he had tried to prevent was taking place beyond his reach. He could only persevere in that area of his work which helped to bolster his besieged government. By 1906 he achieved his goal of creating a broadly based anti-smuggling network stretching across Great Britain and Continental Europe.[22]

The picture is not as positive as it seems. In July 1906, Harting boasted 14 operatives in various European ports who were especially occupied with the control of the contraband in munitions.[23] These agents were abetted in their tasks by detectives and agents assigned by friendly German, Danish, Norwegian, and Swedish police chiefs. Even with this support the Foreign Agentura's failure to acquire additional funds from St Petersburg forced Harting to exclude the smaller ports from his control network. Small ports were avoided for other reasons as well. He had too few detectives. Even if he had had a larger force of operatives at his disposal, however, they still would have been ineffective in the small Scandinavian port towns where soon spotted they would not have received any help from the townspeople who had a distinct dislike of Russia. Furthermore, the Foreign Agentura could not cover the Italian Mediterranean ports except for Genoa. The director of the Paris Office just could not run two parallel organisations: one for the Baltic and another for the Mediterranean at the same time. The Foreign Agentura employed only two agents to cover the entire Italian Mediterranean coast and as might be expected they produced few results.[24] As early as January

1906, Harting became so desperate for operatives that he offered to hire agents at his own expense.[25]

The Foreign Agentura's problems went beyond personnel and geography. Some states, Britain and Holland in particular, did not support the Foreign Agentura's programme. This meant that Harting, though he placed operatives in Amsterdam, London, Manchester, Birmingham, Hull, and Liverpool and when the Belgians became recalcitrant in Antwerp as well, had to be rather circumspect. The revolutionaries, too, knew which countries did not co-operate with the Foreign Agentura and were therefore the most useful. Harting was no one's fool, and he sent specialist agents (probably former custom officials) to each of the above mentioned ports. These men were accompanied by one or two regular Foreign Agentura detectives who oversaw operations, 'so as to achieve the most productive results'.[26] In other words they made certain that the specialists did not succumb to the temptation of any financial considerations placed before them in exchange for looking the other way. Harting had great confidence in his regular detectives and believed they were above bribery.

Unfortunately, to his great exasperation, Harting was repeatedly made aware of the difficulty of his task not only from the reports of his agents[27] but also, humiliatingly, from articles extracted by Fontanka from revolutionary journals now legally published within the Empire. These articles bragged about the exploits of contrabandists and how easily they made fools of the political police. The final paragraph of one such piece must have vexed Harting no end:

> In general let me say that it is no longer difficult to play the game of blind man's bluff (*zhmurki*) as [it was] with Rachkovskii when [now] the whole of Europe serves as a playroom.[28]

No one knew better than Harting the accuracy of this boast, and he expressed his frustration in a dispatch to Fontanka.

> To my vexation it is not possible to prevent the Russian revolutionaries from buying arms and for us to organise surveillance of all factories. It is possible only to carry out limited controls in foreign ports which the agentura is occupied with at the present time.[29]

Harting did not find a sympathetic ear at Fontanka. The Department of Police ignored his operational problems and condemned the Paris Office for its failure to uncover *all* munitions shipments. Fontanka charged that Harting's operatives were supplying unreliable information. The director of the Foreign Agentura did not take such accusations quietly. He angrily replied to the criticism with the retort that the munitions were being transferred to barges at sea and therefore the suspected ships arrived at port without contraband amongst their cargo. The problem could not be solved by the Foreign Agentura.[30] In disgust he declared that the entire business of port control made him 'exceptionally wretched'.[31]

Harting suggested that his wretchedness could be relieved only if the Department of Police permitted him to establish a large bureau to act independently of the Foreign Agentura which would be solely devoted to the destruction of revolutionary smuggling operations.[32] Fontanka did not think the suggestion worthy of response. This did not deter Harting who kept pestering St Petersburg with requests that such an agency be established. Finally in May 1907, an exhausted and exasperated Department of Police could stand Harting's requests no longer. The chief of the Special Section accused Harting of 'wasting money' and complained about the uselessness of his undercover agents. The Foreign Agentura had wasted 'tens of thousands of roubles to no avail.[33]

The director of the Foreign Agentura must have sat in stunned silence as he read this St Petersburg dispatch. Certainly, his organisation endured failures but they were not the result of either his lack of enthusiasm or his prowess. On the contrary, the successes of the Foreign Agentura's anti-smuggling campaign were the product of his hard work and the co-operation of many of Europe's police forces encouraged by his close friendships with various European police chiefs. In fact, many of the failures to seize contraband can be attributed to the authorities within Russia. Even when the Foreign Agentura correctly identified shipments of arms and had informed the Department of Police well in advance of their arrival in Russian waters, the munitions often landed without being confiscated for there were not enough agents to seize the arms once they were deposited on the dock.[34]

It is therefore worth looking at other reasons for Fontanka's irritation with Harting. In 1907 the minister of internal affairs had to face the reality that the Department of Police, especially the political police, had not performed well during the 1905 Revolution. There was a move afoot to launch a police reform and Fontanka began some deep soul-searching into its problems. It was in this atmosphere that Fontanka replied to Harting's request. It undoubtedly viewed Harting's persistent attempts to establish a separate agency as a gambit to increase his own authority. The evidence of Harting's bloated budget could only have added fuel to that fire. The Foreign Agentura's financial allotment had increased by over 200,000 francs in the four years of his tenure in Paris. As the counter-revolution appeared victorious and heads cooled down within the police bureaucracy a feeling of wonder overcame Fontanka on how much money it had spent on the Foreign Agentura, primarily for anti-smuggling activities. Contraband in munitions probably seemed of much less significance in 1907 than it had in 1905 or early 1906.

Harting also faced the fact that the Department of Police had suffered heavy casualties during the Revolution caused by administrative turnover as well as revolutionary action. His friend Rachkovskii and Rachkovskii's benefactors Witte and Trepov no longer held any influence. But on a much broader scale the personnel at the highest levels of Fontanka had changed so completely that no one remained to fully appreciate Harting's hard work and accomplishments.[35] This man, once a bodyguard to Nicholas II and his wife, did not have to worry about the security of his position; yet his treatment by his superiors gave him no reason to hope for further advancement within the political police. Merit and patronage raised Harting to a prestigious rank but under these changed circumstances they could carry him no further and he knew it.

The success of the Foreign Agentura's anti-smuggling campaign should not be obscured by Fontanka's ingratitude. It forced the smugglers to use ever more devious and costly methods such as trans-shipping via the Norway–Finland border beyond the Arctic Circle. The Foreign Agentura made the expense of smuggling prohibitive and created an atmosphere of failure amongst the contrabandists.[36] To be sure, there were other reasons for the decline in the contraband in munitions such as fear of the escalated penalties for subversion in Russia and a general decline of revolutionary enthusiasm in the face of a victorious counter-revolution, but Harting's work especially during the height of the 1905 Revolution must be considered a success in its own right.

Although between 1905 and 1907 Harting devoted most of his personal attention to the problem of contraband, the other machinery of the Foreign Agentura continued to carry out its assigned functions although on a somewhat diminished scale. It continued to keep émigrés under surveillance and after 1906 the size of the emigration swelled anew as hundreds of revolutionaries were forced abroad by counter-revolutionary action. Harting, despite his preoccupation with his anti-smuggling activities, managed to increase the intensity of his bureau's investigations into the revolutionary movements.[37] The director of the Foreign Agentura worked diligently and with success. He reached a personal agreement with the Prefect of the Paris Police in which the prefect agreed to form a special detachment of agents who would maintain surveillance over Russian 'terrorists' and would inform the Foreign Agentura about the results of their observations. The plan had the co-operation of the French government which wished to ensure the tsar's safety during his proposed trip to France in 1910.[38]

This war of nerves, for that is what it became, was not all onesided and the victims were not only in the revolutionary camp. Many *sotrudniki* succumbed to the investigatory diligence of Vladimir Burtsev, the self-proclaimed policeman-guardian of the revolution. Burtsev's successful harassment of the tsarist political police, both at home and abroad, will be thoroughly discussed in Chapter 11, but he began his work of exposing agents during Harting's tour of duty in Paris, having in the chief of the Paris Office himself one of his biggest catches.

Burtsev's first exposé of note appeared in what became his typically sensational fashion.[39] Soon after his return to exile in 1907 Burtsev published between 50 and 60 names of suspected *sotrudniki* working within various revolutionary parties. From this point on Burtsev became an increasingly painful thorn in the side of the political police. His career reached its high point with the exposure of the infamous Evno Azef. Azef's exposure had a powerful impact on the Paris Office. The extent of the Agentura's perturbation over the Azef Affair can be discerned from the dispatches which it issued after the scandal broke. Harting's dispatches reflect his strain as they reported even the most ridiculous rumours back to Fontanka.[40] Fontanka did nothing to calm Harting's nerves when it blamed him for the Azef Affair. This was too much. Already disappointed and annoyed by his earlier rebuff in the matter of arms smuggling control, he decided to hand Fontanka a reprimand of his own. He replied to St Petersburg with the straightforward truth that Azef's downfall had nothing to do with the Foreign Agentura. He argued that Burtsev had lived in St Petersburg for the two years of the 1905 Revolution and during that time he gathered the information which was now demoralising the undercover agents' ranks.[41]

Exhausted, Harting escaped these pressures by taking a short leave in St Petersburg.[42] During this trip home he discussed his retirement from the service and, fed up, on his return to Paris he decided to retire. He received no peace. Upon his arrival back at his desk Harting discovered to his horror that Burtsev had now exposed him too. Fontanka's *bête noire* announced that Harting was none other than Landezen, a fugitive from French justice. The chief of the Foreign Agentura began to put his affairs in order, although he would not be rushed. He telegraphed Fontanka recommending that a captain of gendarmes, V. I. Andreev only just recently assigned to Paris as his assistant, be designated his successor. He also wanted to tell his staff and agents that his retirement was not caused by his sudden disgrace but was a voluntary decision. The Department of Police acquiesced in this request. Harting was tired, but he wanted it known that he had as much time as he needed to permit an orderly changeover in command.[43] Here stood a man of great pride both in himself and his accomplishments. Nothing would chase him out of office.

Harting directed the transfer of command with both patience and consideration to his staff. He introduced Andreev to the members of the Paris Embassy staff and other important members of Russian officialdom working in Paris. Andreev received practical training by managing the Foreign Agentura during his chief's absences from Paris and Harting noted with pleasure that Andreev carried out his duties 'rather correctly, normally, continuing to work in my spirit'.[44] In Harting's absences which became more frequent

Andreev began to develop ties with some of the Foreign Agentura's staff and Harting reasoned they would feel comfortable with him as their new chief since he was a somewhat known quantity. But familiarity with the Foreign Agentura's personnel and administrative procedures was not sufficient. Harting argued that the Department of Police had to confirm Andreev's appointment as soon as possible, permitting him to introduce Andreev to the director of the *Sûreté Générale* and the Prefect of Paris, thus giving his protegé easy access to the French police without first going through the regular channel of the Paris Embassy. Harting also wanted his successor to meet the directors of other European police establishments, a necessity if the excellent working relationships between the Foreign Agentura and Europe's police forces were to be maintained.[45]

To guarantee that the machinery of the Foreign Agentura ran smoothly after his departure Harting created a transitionary period, remaining as undercover director for a few months until the new manager became acquainted with the many facets of his office. Harting's sense of responsibility to his position denotes better than anything else his value to the Department of Police. He desired most of all that his retirement should not cause a break in the continuity of the Foreign Agentura's functions, something about which none of his predecessors cared. Whatever the origins of his career Harting viewed himself as a government official of some reputation with pride in his record and he repeatedly stressed in his correspondence with Fontanka that not only his own personnel but members of other branches of the Russian government serving abroad should be informed that his departure from office had not been instigated by any wrongdoing.[46]

Harting considered himself a selfless official. There is no doubt that he perceived the prevention of arms smuggling as an essential weapon in the arsenal of the political police in its struggle to preserve the Romanov dynasty in the face of the greatest threat the regime had confronted in its almost 300 year history. In fulfilling this task he placed obstinate demands on his superiors and rarely conceded to their point of view. Through his hard work and commitment he made the Foreign Agentura an indispensable weapon against the subversion of the tsarist regime.

A. M. Harting, the son of a Jewish merchant, had done well. He retired with the exalted rank of *Deistvitel'nyi statskii sovetnik* on a substantial pension of about 5,000 roubles per year. After a quarter of a century's residence in western Europe he felt himself more at home there than in Russia and like Rataev chose to live out his retirement in the West.[47]

10
A. A. Krasil'nikov and the Reshaping of the Foreign Agentura: Aspects of the Problems of Political Police Reform, 1909–1914

V. I. Andreev, Harting's young and inexperienced chosen successor as chief of the Foreign Agentura, faced several insecure and demanding months during his tenure as director of the Paris Office. Vladimir Burtsev's exposure of Harting as the provocateur Landezen combined with his publicising of Russian political police operations in France created a national scandal. The outcry reached its peak just as Harting left Andreev to his own devices as temporary director of the Foreign Agentura knowing only that Fontanka had reserved its judgement concerning his future abroad. Andreev's first report to the Department of Police described the turbulent state of affairs in Paris. The Chamber of Deputies ordered foreign police forces, citing the Russians in particular, to remove themselves from French soil. A somewhat placated Premier Clemenceau rescinded this order, however, when he learned that Harting was no longer director of the Foreign Agentura. The Premier immediately instructed the Paris Prefecture and the *Sûreté Générale* to renew its connections with the Foreign Agentura. Shortly thereafter Clemenceau's successor Aristide Briand told Russian Ambassador Nelidov that he also would not act against the Agentura and, as a guarantee, he confirmed Clemenceau's instructions to both the Prefecture and the *Sûreté*.[1] Briand, however, made one crucial stipulation: in order to avoid the possibility of scandal in the future the Foreign Agentura must reduce the number of French agents working for it and more narrowly define their duties.[2]

This presented Andreev with a very serious problem. His office had to cope with the increasing activities of the Socialist-Revolutionaries, Social Democrats and with Vladimir Burtsev's continuous stream of exposures. More operatives were needed, he told Fontanka, but an increase in the number of detectives could only be undertaken by drastically altering the External Agency's structure to make it conform with Briand's requirements and to calm the uproar in the Chamber of Deputies. He suggested that French detectives be officially discharged and then the best of them secretly rehired. Andreev believed that these measures could be carried out 'without special strain' and he requested that they be implemented at once.[3]

Andreev also began to worry about his insecure status at the helm of the Foreign Agentura. He thought that the summer months, when the revolutionaries were generally dormant, would be the perfect time to appoint a permanent director if, of course, Andreev wryly noted, he was not Fontanka's choice. In any case his present situation as temporary director could not be tolerated into the autumn, only a few weeks away, when serious work would begin again. Andreev courageously wrote that the Foreign Agentura required a director possessing the confidence supplied only by the security of his position.[4] The temporary director made these suggestions with reasonable expectation of becoming the permanent chief of the Paris Office. By August 1909 he felt comfortable with the operations of the Paris chancery and had become well acquainted with the members of the Russian ambassadorial mission who worked on the floor above his office. And, after all, Harting had taken the trouble to introduce him to both European police officials and useful politicians. Andreev was mistaken. The Department of Police had never even considered him for the post on a permanent basis. Only a captain in the gendarmes, he did not possess the necessary support from his superiors in St Petersburg. More importantly, Andreev could not escape the system of patronage within Fontanka which ultimately determined the length of his stay in Paris.

Captain Andreev gave way to Aleksandr Aleksandrovich Krasil'nikov. Krasil'nikov at least on the surface possessed few of the credentials needed to recommend him for an office requiring an experienced policeman as well as a clever diplomat. His entire professional life consisted of a career in the horse guards after being schooled at the prestigious Nicholas Cavalry School in the early 1880s at approximately the same time as L. A. Rataev, one of his predecessors as director of the Paris Office. In 1901 he retired from the army to the sedate life of a Russian gentleman living in Paris, never dreaming of further Imperial service of any type let alone succeeding the likes of Rachkovskii, Rataev and Harting. But Vice Director of Police General P. G. Kurlov had also spent his school days at the Nicholas Cavalry School and old school ties meant much to him. Of even greater significance, Krasil'nikov had served under Kurlov in the same horse guards regiment.[5] Then when Kurlov engaged in discussions over an appropriate successor to Harting who should come to mind but his old comrade Aleksandr Aleksandrovich Krasil'nikov. The appointment of such a man had its merits. As a gentleman by breeding and a long time resident in Europe Krasil'nikov swam easily through European society and felt comfortable in the milieu which out of necessity became part of a Foreign Agentura director's life. The appointment of Krasil'nikov also meant that someone completely unknown in revolutionary circles now directed the Foreign Agentura. This could only be to Fontanka's advantage and Kurlov desperately tried to keep Krasil'nikov's identity a secret. Even more important, Krasil'nikov was Kurlov's 'crony' (*stavlennik*) and could be relied upon to do whatever the assistant minister wished.[6] Yet the designation of a rank amateur to such a sensitive post, a man who had never even served in the bureaucracy, raised some very powerful eyebrows. Prime Minister Stolypin reacted with disbelief to Krasil'nikov's nomination, but he acquiesced assuming that Kurlov, immersed in police affairs, had sound reasons for suggesting such an outlandish appointment.[7]

Whatever Kurlov's motives for making the appointment he did not wish his old friend to appear a fool when he assumed his new post – such a performance would have done the General's career no good. Once Krasil'nikov accepted the job, Kurlov asked him to travel to St Petersburg to observe Fontanka in action and to study police methodology. During Krasil'nikov's training Andreev was left to linger in Paris in ignorance.

The manner of Krasil'nikov's appointment emphasised Fontanka's new sensitivity to the requirement for security. The fresh chief of the Paris Office came to his post under the guise of a liaison officer between the Ministry of Internal Affairs and the Ministry of Foreign Affairs. When asked, Krasil'nikov vigorously denied any connection with the Russian political police.[8] For a while Krasil'nikov's background helped make this subterfuge a success. The director of the Foreign Agentura had never been in public life and to make doubly sure of Krasil'nikov's anonymity Fontanka gave him eight or nine aliases.[9]

This security conscious approach to Krasil'nikov's appointment is a symptom of Fontanka's new found respect for the revolutionary emigration. The 1905 Revolution taught Russia's political policemen to no longer see their opponents merely as a discomforting rabble. Now even the dullest gendarme officer recognised these people to be dangerous subversives and a very real threat to the continued existence of the tsarist state. While the defeat of the 1905 Revolution had brought political tranquility to the Empire, Fontanka believed that the counter-revolution would not be completely successful until the activism of the emigration had been defused. Barring this ultimate victory, the Paris Office's diligent observation and infiltration of these groups would be Tsardom's best protection against revolutionary machinations. Also, the revolutionary emigration functioned as a barometer of revolutionary attitudes and morale in general, and, if nothing else, this made reliable gauging of these characteristics of the utmost importance to Tsardom's future.

The Foreign Agentura discovered that the post-1905 emigration was not so easily kept under surveillance as the naive émigrés of pre-revolutionary years. The number of revolutionaries living in Europe increased considerably, not only in the larger industrial cities but also in remote provincial towns where the Paris Office found surveillance quite difficult. This difficulty was compounded by the exposés of its activities through the investigations of Vladimir Burtsev. To make matters worse, the obvious need for the expansion of the Foreign Agentura's services conflicted with Briand's firm recommendation that the Russian police curtail the size of its operation by decreasing the number of French detectives it employed and the number of anti-émigré exercises undertaken.

The pressure to revamp the Foreign Agentura came from administrative considerations as well. A perusal of the Paris Office's fiscal record from 1902 to 1910 reflects the considerable expansion of the Foreign Agentura's size and workload over that eight year period.[10] Even after taking inflation into consideration the increase in these expenditures denotes the substantial growth of the Paris Office and the need for departmentalisation through the delegation of duties and responsibilities. No longer could one man possibly oversee the detectives, undercover agents and the administration of the Paris chancery by himself.[11]

Kurlov realised that he was placing Krasil'nikov in an extremely difficult position and, to the assistant minister's credit, he did not intend to abandon Krasil'nikov to his own devices. In late 1909 Kurlov sent Vice Director of Police S. E. Vissarionov to Paris to analyse the Foreign Agentura's ticklish and cumbersome position.[12] After studying Vissarionov's report Kurlov spoke to Krasil'nikov about the need to reorganise the Foreign Agentura. Its everyday political police business would become the province of gendarme officers to be assigned to Krasil'nikov's service. As a linguist and a man of natural intelligence the new director's only specific police functions would be to coherently transmit information furnished by his agents to St Petersburg and to maintain the long standing liaison with Europe's policemen and politicians.[13] In line with Kurlov's comments Fontanka placed all *sotrudniki* under the guidance of newly appointed case officers, the aforementioned Captain Dolgov and his assistant Captain Erghardt.[14] The Foreign Agentura's detectives worked under the supervision of the French detective Marcel Bittard-Monin[15] and the Paris chancery under State Councillor Sushkov.

Krasil'nikov took over the Foreign Agentura without incident and implemented these changes devised by his superiors. This reorganisation created a chain-of-command and division of authority; giving the Foreign Agentura at least a semblance of administrative specialisation which heretofore it really had not possessed. Its administration now resembled those of the standard OOs throughout the Empire. But this reorganisation did not solve the Paris Office's problems by any means since it failed to hide Russian police business from either the French government[16] or the prying eyes of Vladimir Burtsev. Nevertheless, following these initial alterations in its structure the Foreign Agentura waited until 1913 before it underwent further constructive change. Why? There were two reasons: the nature of Fontanka's concept and process of reform, and the method of appointment within the Department of Police itself.

Stolypin placed the enquiry into police operations and its reform under the guidance of A. A. Makarov, assistant minister of internal affairs, managing the police. General P. G. Kurlov soon joined Makarov in the MVD as vice director of the Department of Police, managing the Special Section, and he too participated in discussions of police reform as a member of the Makarov Commission. In 1909 Kurlov succeeded Makarov as assistant minister of the MVD, managing Fontanka.[17] Of course, Makarov and Kurlov can be categorised as reformers in only the narrowest construction of the word. As vice governor in Kursk Province, Kurlov acquired the well deserved reputation as a brutal reactionary.[18] Makarov is the same man who stood before the Duma in 1912 and defended the shooting of defenceless Lena goldfield workers.[19] These men, their immediate subordinates and successors (with the exception of V. F. Dzhunkovskii) considered reform simply as a process of gently applying oil to the creaking gears of Fontanka's machinery, nothing more.[20] As we will see later in the chapter the fiscal and administrative reforms of this type that Fontanka imposed on the Paris Office did not address the Foreign Agentura's operational requirements.

In any case, after Kurlov's initial burst of interest in the operations of the Paris Office, Fontanka was unable to come to grips with the Foreign Agentura's predicaments for quite some time. General Kurlov whole-heartedly believed in the practice customarily employed by newly appointed assistant ministers of internal affairs charged with supervising Fontanka of filling the most important police posts with candidates of their own choosing. Kurlov's wholesale changes within Fontanka's leadership caused confusion which led to stagnation as the new men took time to become acquainted with their tasks.[21] The assassination of Stolypin compounded the confusion.[22]

Krasil'nikov, however, could not afford to be inactive. Briand had forced the Foreign Agentura to restrict its operations, thereby reducing its effectiveness, and something had to be done to rectify this situation at once. The turmoil caused by the Harting exposé and Burtsev's investigations in general created an additional and possibly fatal problem for the Paris Office. While many detectives in this circumstance remained loyal, others were ready to exploit the Paris Office's situation for their own benefit. Burtsev and other journalists were ready to pay large sums of money to any employee of the Foreign Agentura who would divulge information about its workings. Some treacherous detectives, Krasil'nikov noted angrily, 'especially in cases of dismissal [from the F.A.] ... practice every form of blackmail or outright treason.'[23]

Krasil'nikov, for both the reasons of better administration over his growing Agentura and the need for greater security, was forced by Fontanka's inability to deal with the crisis caused by Briand and Burtsev to eventually devise a plan of his own to reorganise the Foreign Agentura. Krasil'nikov's reforms centred around the enhancement of agentura security. Political police security had become a serious business with the new found respect for the revolutionaries in the post-1905 era. They were a dangerous enemy who could no longer be treated in the cavalier fashion of previous administrations which allowed for Rachkovskii's antics or Rataev's incompetence. Krasil'nikov decided on a plan for the possible solution to the persistent breaches in security which (as we shall see in the following chapter) eroded the Foreign Agentura's confidence and its ability to fulfil its assignments. The director of the Foreign Agentura reasoned that surveillance operations would have to appear, 'essentially quite legal'.[24] To accomplish this embellishment of the Foreign Agentura's camouflage Krasil'nikov proposed the establishment of an absolutely 'legal' detective agency with no visible ties to the Foreign Agentura. He referred his superiors to a report he made in June 1910, which he again quoted for their benefit emphasising that detectives must 'not consider themselves in the service of the Imperial Russian Embassy and all measures must be taken to that end'.[25] Krasil'nikov might have seen Andreev's report on the same subject for his dispatch echoed the latter man's view. In any case, the chief of the Paris Office developed a clever and practical plan to alter the appearance of the External Agency.

At first, however, he attempted some less drastic measures on his own initiative. Early in 1911 he refused to admit his detectives to the Russian Embassy building housing the Foreign Agentura. He also commanded them not to send surveillance reports or any general conspiratorial correspondence to 79 Rue de Grenelle, the Embassy's address. Krasil'nikov informed his detectives that the Imperial Embassy is a diplomatic establishment, that it is not occupied with political or investigative affairs, and it does not employ agents of any sort. He went on to tell them that in reality they worked not for the Russian government but for Marcel Bittard-Monin 'a private person'. When this shallow ploy did not succeed, the director of the Foreign Agentura grasped his only remaining alternative. He decided to scrap the then present External Agency and begin again.

The plan called for the issuing of a statement proclaiming that because of 'repeated cases of treason the Foreign Agentura has finally ceased to exist' and that, 'this liquidation is to be concluded with all formality ...'.[26] Krasil'nikov's next step involved the creation of an ostensibly private detective bureau operating within French law. Such private agencies were both common and successful in France and one more would not be noticed. Indeed, this bureau should also appeal to Fontanka's pecuniary mentality since by handling private, legitimate clients as well it would be partially self-supporting. Krasil'nikov proposed his close associate Henri Bint, a long serving police detective with 32 years service with the Russian police abroad, for the directorship of the planned private detective bureau. In selecting his operatives Bint would choose only the best detectives of the defunct External Agency, all of whom would be registered as private detectives in agreement with French law.

He would also follow French regulations when hiring 'legitimate' operatives and in choosing the bureau's location. Like other detective agencies in Paris, this new agency would advertise in Parisian newspapers, noting the address of the bureau, its telephone number, and that it was under the direction of 'Henri Bint former Inspector of Criminal Police' who handled, 'Inquiries, Investigations, Private Surveillance'. The plan called for the bureau to fulfil the obligations of its advertising by hiring several operatives to handle only the completely legitimate cases of private persons. Krasil'nikov discussed the plan with Bint before he forwarded it to the Department of Police and Bint had his chief add a note to the dispatch confirming his agreement with the plan and that he was anxious to take charge of the proposed bureau. He also implored Fontanka to take his 32 years of experience into account when considering him for the position.[27] In addition, Krasil'nikov decided to give Bint a partner to help him with the expected demanding workload, assigning Albert Sambian, another capable detective employed by the Paris Office, as Bint's associate. One of the two partners was always to remain in their office in the other's absence 24 hours a day.[28] Krasil'nikov's proposal did not waste talent. He planned to transfer Bittard-Monin to special duty as a liaison with the lower echelon members of the Paris Prefecture and the *Sûreté Générale* – the inspectors and brigadiers – while Krasil'nikov would maintain a personal liaison only with the Prefect of Police and the director of the *Sûreté*. Besides this duty Bittard-Monin served as his chief's connection with the European press.[29]

The Foreign Agentura considered the formation of the Bint–Sambian detective agency as the best solution to the problems of exposure and scandal that plagued it. Krasil'nikov hoped that the new tranquility brought about by the covert nature of this operation would permit the detectives to work in a more secure atmosphere, keep them relatively honest, and ensure accurate reporting. Bint's detectives would not know for whom they worked, but only that they were being employed by an old friend in his new business venture. Even if by the nature of their assignments these people came to suspect who actually employed them, a likelihood, they would be unable to gather concrete evidence to support their suspicions. Krasil'nikov wished to pluck the operatives for the new bureau from the 28 French and Italian detectives who served under Bittard-Monin. To begin with he thought a dozen from this group, 11 French and one Italian, would be a reasonable number. He would enlarge the bureau as required, not a difficult task since the Paris Prefecture itself was undergoing a reorganisation and many older but still competent detectives were being retired. As a supplement to their pensions these operatives often worked for private detective agencies and could be readily recruited by the Bint–Sambian Agency.

The most crucial aspect of the plan, the denouement of the External Agency under Bittard-Monin and the dismissal of its detectives, needed to be accomplished with sufficient ballyhoo so as not to escape the attention of both the revolutionary emigration and the French Chamber of Deputies: a delicate business since the Paris Office could not be too open about it, after all it was a secret police. The Foreign Agentura faced the even more difficult task of convincing the released operatives as well. Krasil'nikov contrived to give his detectives severance pay in the sum of one month's salary. In return each detective would supply a signed declaration of his service to one Marcel Bittard-Monin, the director of a private detective bureau now liquidating its affairs. As Krasil'nikov suggested, each operative upon the termination of his employment would turn in those documents dealing with the cases he or she had been investigating for the Foreign Agentura. The chief of the Paris Office wanted to make certain that no evidence remained outstanding to connect French detectives with the Russian political police.[30]

Krasil'nikov forwarded his proposal to the Department of Police in September 1913. By this time Kurlov and Makarov had been replaced by other *chinovniki* and S. P. Beletskii now served as director of Fontanka. The appointment of Beletskii to the directorship of Fontanka in 1912 proved a case of the wrong man in a vital place at a critical time. General A. I. Spiridovich a most respected former police official, wrote of Beletskii, 'he was a man without principle and a rotter in every respect', and sorrowfully concluded, 'there was no hope of reform under Beletskii'.[31]

So, as might be expected, Beletskii took serious issue with several of Krasil'nikov's suggestions. The director of Fontanka argued that under this plan there would be fewer operatives, a factor increasing the pressure on detectives having to perform at maximum efficiency if they were going to make up for the decrease in their numbers. Beletskii reasoned that only well trained detectives aware of local revolutionary affairs and knowing the members of the Internal Agency on sight could function in the manner required by the reduction in the number of operatives. To his way of thinking even highly qualified operatives needed constant supervision to prevent them from becoming sloppy. He believed that only Russian detective supervisors could provide the quality of leadership required. Bint and Sambian, therefore, should be merely figureheads while the actual supervision should be undertaken by Russians imported for the purpose. Fontanka's director went further by flatly stating that at least half of the newly appointed detectives should be imported from Russia. Possibly, Beletskii thought that Russian detectives were superior in ability to their French colleagues and that they would be less likely to betray the Foreign Agentura to Vladimir Burtsev or anyone else. Nevertheless, it is hard to imagine a director of a powerful political police to be so naive that he could not envisage the ludicrous appearance of Russian detectives, who spoke little or no French (many could barely cope with their own language) and who would be totally unfamiliar with their foreign surroundings, working for the Foreign Agentura. Even dressing *filery* in the latest Parisian fashions still would not prevent them in these alien surroundings from sticking out like sore thumbs from the mass of Frenchmen and no doubt soon being discovered by Burtsev's sensitive eyes.[32]

The quality of Beletskii's character suggests a different motivation behind his counter-proposals to Krasil'nikov's plan. Russian detective supervisors could easily serve Fontanka's director as a fifth column within the Paris Office feeding the Department of Police a steady stream of information on the Foreign Agentura's activities. *Filery* assigned to duty in Paris remained under the supervision of St Petersburg not Paris. Krasil'nikov perceived the real intentions intrinsic in Beletskii's suggestions and fought continually against the posting of Russian detectives to his territory.[33] Beletskii's reply listed further suggestions, parroting those mentioned in Krasil'nikov's own plan, such as the necessity of choosing detectives carefully to prevent reoccurrences of blackmailing incidents. He also reiterated Krasil'nikov's suggestions for the founding of a private detective bureau. Beletskii seemed to be using the bureaucrat's trick of making a subordinate's suggestions appear to be his own, but with a new twist. He tried not only to impress his superiors within the MVD but also Krasil'nikov, the subordinate, who made the suggestion in the first place.

To be sure, Beletskii was willing to grant this new detective bureau a large sum of money, twice the sum supplied to Bittard-Monin. Still, if the operatives had to absorb and follow the procedures and regulations by the book as Beletskii required of them they would accomplish no useful work. Here we have the doctrine of a self-important martinet, without practical experience, who knew no better than to rely on traditional methods and whose response to Krasil'nikov's scheme, while wasting valuable time, served no useful purpose.[34]

Other high ranking police officials also read and commented upon Krasil'nikov's report. M. F. Broetskii, the chief of the Special Section argued like Beletskii that the Bint–Sambian Agency would not have a sufficient number of operatives to carry out each surveillance project and he claimed the removal of Bittard-Monin probably would create confusion amongst undercover agents who would no longer believe themselves to be protected from exposure. For these and even less justifiable reasons Broetskii suggested that Krasil'nikov's scheme be scrapped.[35]

The obstructionist and generally amateurish behaviour of these two highly placed police officials emphasises an important fact. In principle, these men were probably not against practical political police reform. In reality they just did not understand what that meant.[36]

Krasil'nikov's plan was saved, however, by Assistant Minister of Internal Affairs V. F. Dzhunkovskii who clearly saw the advantages of Krasil'nikov's project. Overriding the opinions of his subordinates he gave his approval to it. In fact, the final scheme receiving Dzhunkovskii's signature went beyond Krasil'nikov's original proposals by enhancing the role of the Paris chief in the establishment and management of the new detective agency.[37] In general, the liquidation of the External Agency of the Foreign Agentura went without a hitch. The only disquieting note came with the MVD's insistence that four Russian *filery* be attached to the Bint and Sambian Agency despite the potential for disaster intrinsic in this action.[38] Beletskii had decided to assert his authority with this petty and foolhardy action in order to make sure Krasil'nikov remembered to whom he would answer if his reform did not succeed.

What of Fontanka's own initiatives towards political police reform mentioned earlier in the chapter? The sterility of Fontanka's approach to this question is reflected in the critical period of the Foreign Agentura's life between 1909 and 1914. By 1910 a change of attitude seems to appear within the Department of Police. The Makarov Commission's inquiry into police failings undoubtedly had something to do with it, as did the appalling performance of the OOs between 1905 and 1907. The Makarov Commission's comments dealt almost exclusively with administrative inefficiency. Change to the Russian bureaucracy meant administrative reform. The mentality of Nicholas I, the Empire's most infamous *chinovnik*, had the lingering persistence of a fatal disease. But the special case of implementing even this type of alteration within the Special Section's agencies required circumspection. Making changes of any sort within a political police is at best an unwanted sign of disarray and at worst can directly contribute to a catastrophe similar to the one which befell Russia with the assassination of Alexander II in 1881 when the political police, undergoing the turmoil of a major transformation, proved unable to protect the tsar. If reforms are to be instituted, then they should be substantive, making the risk worthwhile.

What better place to try out some alterations than the Foreign Agentura? The Paris Office played an essential role in the Special Section's information gathering network and, of all the Special Section's branches, the Paris Office possessed certain attributes making it the safest testing ground for Fontanka's reforms. The Foreign Agentura's isolation from the Empire made it a good laboratory. Successful experiments in police reform conducted in Paris could be implemented elsewhere and unsuccessful ones could be discarded without fanfare. The Foreign Agentura confronted the elite of Russia's subversive movement and Vladimir Burtsev's organisation as well which meant, as Krasil'nikov repeatedly informed St Petersburg, it had an urgent need for improved procedures and methods to be quickly effected. Finally, the fact that Kurlov was Krasil'nikov's only friend within Fontanka reduced the potential for backbiting and politicking caused by any attempt to impose change from above of the sort that the branch office might not think beneficial.

What an excellent opportunity to be truly innovative. Unfortunately, Fontanka's senior administrators still, on the whole, considered reform in its narrowest context. Between 1910 and 1914 Fontanka's major drive towards reform within the Paris Office concentrated, of all things, on forcing the Foreign Agentura into financial accountability! In Fontanka's weak defence it can be said that its effort to make the Foreign Agentura fiscally responsible had been an ongoing and losing battle since the 1880s. A study of the Foreign Agentura's financial records reinforces this view, for there is hardly a semblance of accurate record keeping to be found in its archive prior to Krasil'nikov's administration.[39] The chiefs of the Foreign Agentura became quite hostile to any attempts to force them to divulge financial records. All of them knew that in making any such information available to Fontanka they would be opening their entire operation to the Special Section's scrutiny.[40] Fontanka found it difficult to discipline its bureau chiefs even for open refusal to obey orders, especially those dealing with administrative matters. Too many of Fontanka's 'reforms' just received lip service and nothing more.

This state of affairs sufficiently annoyed Fontanka so that it took advantage of the newly appointed Krasil'nikov's inexperience to impose financial accountability on the Foreign Agentura once and for all. When Krasil'nikov complied with the Department's orders to submit his accounts at the end of each month the Department of Police knew for certain that it had discovered a true gem.[41] The accounting system St Petersburg decreed for the Foreign Agentura demanded the time-consuming compilation of detailed supporting documents; nevertheless, it soon found even this system too haphazard.[42] As a result, Fontanka appeared to lose complete control of its senses as it sank Krasil'nikov and his chancery staff into an endless morass of paperwork caused by Fontanka's seemingly compulsive desire to possess a receipt and explanation for every transaction made by the Foreign Agentura no matter how trivial.[43]

Before Krasil'nikov had recovered from the shock of this incredibly enlarged workload, the Special Section struck again. This time it ordered the Paris Office to maintain detailed records of the performance of each of its *sotrudniki* on the standard forms issued by the Third Secretariat to the OOs within the Empire for this purpose. Fontanka commanded Krasil'nikov to follow the instructions printed thereon to the letter. On these forms *sotrudniki* were to be identified by their *klichki*, length of service and the subversive organisations to which they belonged. In addition to this information, the exact number of reports received from each *sotrudniki* had to be listed on each form. If an undercover agent did not receive a small extra consideration for the past month the Special Section wanted to know why. Had the agent been unproductive or just doing so-so work? Finally, every member of the Foreign Agentura received orders to present reports to the Special Section noting the purpose to which the money they had received would be used. Each report of this type listed the estimated time involved in the assignment and in rough figures how much the project would eventually cost the

Department of Police. The Special Section reminded Krasil'nikov to keep costs down through strict controls and also by coordinating the activities of the undercover agents and the detective service so as to prevent a duplication of costs.[44]

We should at least give Fontanka the courtesy of briefly evaluating this bookkeeper's reform on its own merits. When seen in this light there is nothing more apparent than the chaos it caused. This financial system involved a form of accounting which forced the Foreign Agentura to submit accounts and supporting documents for the month just completed in order to be granted funds for subsequent months. In the new month the Foreign Agentura received a portion of its annually allotted budget predicated on the expenses incurred the previous month. This procedure meant that large deficits or surpluses could be created depending on the accuracy of the estimation. Even worse than this, it resulted in a substantial increase in paperwork reducing the chancery's and Krasil'nikov's time for the important tasks of analysing and synthesising reports submitted to them by detectives and undercover agents in the field. In practice the new system of accounting operated like the Sorcerer's Apprentice and became an endless nightmare to the clerks of Fontanka's Third Secretariat. The Foreign Agentura's budget grew to huge proportions as the Department of Police stubbornly persisted with its new system. Substantial surpluses in cash accrued at the end of every month. In 1914, for instance, the Foreign Agentura's monthly cash on hand varied from approximately 58,000 francs for January up to a ridiculous maximum of 134,287 francs in December, a month in which the Foreign Agentura spent only 42,360 francs leaving itself with a surplus for the year of 91,927 francs. The director of the Foreign Agentura remarked that, when necessary, he would like to juggle his funds appropriately to ensure a rational distribution of excess funds to under budgeted categories of spending. This very reasonable suggestion infuriated Fontanka which directed Krasil'nikov to take no such independent action. Fontanka would consider each case separately on its own merits.[45] So stubbornly did Fontanka stick to the policy of overestimating the Foreign Agentura's requirements that by October 1915, it had about 281,400 francs of surplus cash on hand! Only in November 1916, did the Department of Police finally remove Krasil'nikov's surplus funds, so urgently needed elsewhere, from the Foreign Agentura's Paris bank account.

How could any of these measures contribute to the making of a more effective political police force? In counterpoint to Krasil'nikov's own practical proposals Fontanka's administrative changes in no way took the Foreign Agentura's brief into consideration. None of these changes made the Paris Office a more effective political police force or protected its operations and operatives against the machinations of a steadily more alert and ruthless revolutionary emigration. These alterations did not improve the Foreign Agentura's chances of infiltrating revolutionary groups or interpreting the information it collected. The subordination of every detail of the Foreign Agentura's operations to the scrutiny of the Department of Police seems to have been the sole purpose of the changes in record keeping demanded by Fontanka. In this respect the reform was a resounding success. The leadership of the Department of Police, bound by its own bureaucratic milieu, could not implement needed practical policies in tune with the changing complexion of the subversive movements. Despite the reports on the changing nature of both legal and illegal society Russian police leadership continued to persist in the view that all would be well if only the existing governmental administrative machine could be made to work more efficiently.

Far removed from the arena of battle, Fontanka's senior police officials just did not know what political policing was all about and, worse, they were unwilling to learn from their bureau chiefs. Clearly, they assumed that the fount of wisdom concerning political police operations was located solely in St Petersburg. They could not have been more mistaken. The highest positions within the Department of Police were mostly populated either by long serving unimaginative bureaucrats or by general officers, even the best of whose abilities seemed to lie in the cloistered routine of office work or the rigid and archaic 'gentlemen's code' of the regular army. This latter group is epitomised by the well-intentioned, reform-minded but naive General Dzhunkovskii who believed that *sotrudniki*, an immoral stain on Fontanka's reputation, were an unnecessary evil that the Special Section could do without! Indeed, Dzhunkovskii met with Krasil'nikov and listened while the director of the Foreign Agentura advised him that increased émigré activity combined with Burtsev's unmasking of undercover agents made it impossssible for the Foreign Agentura to carry out its duties without the addition of newly recruited undercover agents. Dzhunkovskii responded by informing Krasil'nikov that he wished to repudiate the use of undercover agents as political police weapons entirely. A flabbergasted Krasil'nikov just managed to express the opinion that effective surveillance could not be conducted without *sotrudniki*.[46]

If anything should have made this clear to Dzhunkovskii's military mind it was the significant role the Foreign Agentura played in Russian espionage and counter-spionage during the First World War. In Switzerland these activities came under the supervision of Henri Bint and Captain Boris Likhovskii the case officer assigned to manage undercover agents based in the Helvetic Republic. These men sent German-speaking Swiss agents into Germany and Austria from where, for example, they reported on prisoner-of-war camps near Hamburg where the Germans trained young Finns who would form the officer *cadres* for a possible German-inspired Finnish military uprising against Russia. Indeed, Bint went so far as to claim that his agents gave him thorough intelligence on the status of German military and transport affairs, the organisation of the German home front, the current mood of the German and Austrian peoples, the price of food-stuffs and so on. Sambian was charged with the Russian espionage network in Sweden and Denmark where his agents gathered information on German efforts to initiate a separatist revolt in Finland and reported on German espionage in Stockholm and on the Russo-Swedish border. Bint and Sambian even tried to suborn a German military attaché in Bonn! In England the Foreign Agenura's case officer there organised industrial espionage against Russia's own ally and maintained surveillance over the Russians working for the Russian Supply Commission as munitions inspectors in British factories. Finally, Krasil'nikov, while attempting to protect his undercover agents from being drafted into military service, assigned those who did serve in the French Army to spy on the conduct of fellow serving Russians.[47] St Petersburg rewarded Krasil'nikov for his war-time espionage work by promoting him to the distinguished *chin* of *Deistvitel'nyi statskii sovetnik*.[48]

Krasil'nikov deserved his promotion for more reasons than this. He showed himself capable of analysing the Special Section's problems in a multi-dimensional framework. Procedures and methods of operations had to be altered not just for the sake of administrative efficiency as Kurlov had done in duplicating the typical OO chancery in Paris, but also because the character of the opposition was changing and political police operational attitudes needed to progress accordingly.

The officials most sensitive to the operational requirements demanded by Russia's and Europe's changing political and societal circumstances were the bureau chiefs – those middle-ranking officials who through their every day experience ascertained the need for change, and if they were any good at their jobs, could propose useful innovations.[49] Bureau chiefs who exhibit these qualities and fight for the application of their ideas are indispensable members of any organisation. Krasil'nikov was such a man. He wished to alter the formal structure of his bureau and the behavioural patterns of his detectives not in accordance with his own interest, but in the interest of his organisation as a whole. Under his supervision the Paris chancery prepared comprehensive reports describing the lives of various revolutionary parties, not only abroad but within the Empire as well.[50] The quality and quantity of Krasil'nikov's work was the product of the excellent chancery staff and detective service he did so much to develop and the work of his undercover agents whose secret identities he worked so hard to preserve, as we shall see in the following chapter.

Krasil'nikov's accomplishments were achieved, as we have seen, without helpful suggestions or even the slightest encouragement from his superiors.

Instead, he encountered equivocation based upon *naiveté*, ignorance and jealousy combined with ponderous bureaucratic procedure. When his reform was at last approved, it came too late to give the Foreign Agentura any significant help. The political police had dallied with operational reform too long and now the commonplace expression 'chickens coming home to roost' began to have special meaning for the Department of Police. By 1913 the branches of the Special Section confronted a resurgent revolutionary movement capable of defending itself against the infiltration of its ranks by tsarist *sotrudniki*. Vladimir Burtsev's vexing success in exposing Tsardom's detectives and undercover agents brought home to St Petersburg the reality of an effective revolutionary police, tiny in size in comparison to the Special Section, but which nevertheless took maximum advantage of the weaknesses in Fontanka's armour, as we shall see in the next chapter.

Krasil'nikov, despite his talent as an administrator, became the victim of Fontanka's inability or perhaps refusal to take the real world into account. It refused to allow its political police bureaus the latitude to adjust to local conditions and the exigencies of political police work. The rigidity of Krasil'nikov's superiors over the bugbear of control buried the Paris Office in a mountain of paper work which did not have any relevance to the quality of police work Krasil'nikov's bureau produced. Formalism, that demon of Russian bureaucratic practice, drained the Foreign Agentura and other political police bureaus of both their independence and flexibility, thereby limiting their capacity to successfully react to their enemies' tactical innovations. As a result, neither the Paris Office nor the Special Section as a whole possessed any mechanism whatsoever for dealing with the newly encountered organised opposition directed specifically against them.

It is in this respect that we must consider the Foreign Agentura's struggle with Vladimir Burtsev as of such crucial significance. The Foreign Agentura under Krasil'nikov's leadership attained a high reputation within the Russian political police. Its administrative staff, detectives and undercover agents were far from infallible, to be sure, and some were outright scoundrels, but on the whole they were the most talented group of political policemen working on Tsardom's behalf. Operating in alien surroundings against the leadership of the revolutionary movement, they knew and felt both their value and sacrifice to the Empire. Why, then, despite these qualities did the work of Vladimir Burtsev and his small organisation bring the Foreign Agentura's operations to a virtual standstill and unnerve Russia's political police leadership, creating both panic and defection from its ranks? This story forms the last and in some ways the most important episode in the life of the Foreign Agentura.

11

A Revolutionary Strikes Back: Vladimir Burtsev Against the Tsarist Secret Police, 1907–1914

A fundamental yet little known episode from tsarist and soviet political police history is the conflict between the Russian political police and Vladimir L'vovich Burtsev, the self-proclaimed protector of the Russian revolutionary emigration and the creator-director of a detective bureau and propaganda network that became known as the 'revolutionary police'. This struggle helps to explain both the failings of the Russian political police and the development of new political police strategy and techniques. The subject of this chapter is the significance of this conflict, a conflict that, at best, contemporaries only vaguely understood. The confrontation between Burtsev and the tsarist political police in the years 1907 to 1914 actually served as the first major encounter between an organised policing service created to protect revolutionaries and a powerful counter-revolutionary autocratic police force.[1]

On the surface Burtsev's band of detectives and informers had little in common with a modern totalitarian political police organisation. His efforts, nevertheless, were an evolutionary step in the germination of those axioms which characterise modern totalitarian political police forces. Included in these axioms are: the subordination of the political police not to institutions of government, but to the highest echelons of the ruling party; the raw brutality with which the political police not only enforce but implement the ideology of the ruling party; an organisational structure and investigative methodology that permits the political police to carry out its duties effectively and which makes it seem all pervasive; the use of mass psychological techniques, particularly propaganda, to develop mistrust and fear amongst the opposition and even within the loyal cadres themselves which is then exploited to the party's benefit. These characteristics, to be sure, did not appear all at once. They were the product of ingenious minds developing the requisites to destroy the opposition and were often tell-tale after effects of a brutal competition for survival by the party in or on its way to power. Many of these ingredients were also acquired from observing and enduring earlier political police forces. Burtsev's activities belong in every one of these categories. He substantially added to the sum of political police techniques as well as to a hardening of attitudes toward party discipline. Burtsev also recognised the necessity of employing a brand of ruthlessness in the struggle with the counter-revolution which even the least naive revolutionary had not as yet contemplated.

What made this gadfly of the revolution, who belonged to no revolutionary party, create these new and effective political police methods which became an important link in the chronology of political police development and sophistication? Burtsev never intended to take up what would prove to be the thankless job of policing and protecting the revolutionary emigration. He was born into his uncle's household in the small city of Birsk in Ufa Province on 30 November 1862. His family life centred around the Russian Orthodox faith until his arrival at St Petersburg University in 1880, where his exposure to Russia's political and intellectual life began. In 1882 he experienced his first arrest, having been caught in a police dragnet after a student demonstration in which he had played little part. This episode initiated his disillusionment with the tsarist government. A subsequent arrest in 1884 for a minor offence resulted in his imprisonment for a year before being exiled to Siberia. On 3 July 1888, Burtsev fled Siberia and joined the Russian revolutionary emigration in Geneva. There he made the acquaintance of several terrorists whose courage and fanaticism he came to admire and would attempt to immortalise in writing for the remainder of his life.

Burtsev, however, viewed himself in the more passive role of journalist and historian. His first connection with political journalism saw him participate in the distribution of the Russian based journal *Samoupravlenie* (*Self-government*) in western Europe. This project came to an abrupt halt when a police raid brought publication to an end. Undaunted, he began a search for support within the Geneva émigré community for his own political journal. Burtsev wished to create a journal which would spread his belief that only acts of terrorism directed against the Imperial Family and Russia's *sanovniki* could induce the tsarist authorities to move towards establishing a constitutional government. He soon discovered that 'liberalism with terror' would find no supporters amongst the émigrés in Geneva. Burtsev wisely moderated his opinions, at least temporarily, and joined as a co-editor in a newly established non-revolutionary, liberal journal, *Svobodnaia Rossiia* (*Free Russia*). The first issue of the journal appeared in March 1889, but the editors soon disagreed over policy. Burtsev wanted to publish articles exhalting and encouraging terrorism for democratic ends but his fellow editors thought his themes illogical. They refused to allow Burtsev space in *Svobodnaia Rossiia* for the expression of these views. Thus thwarted, Burtsev withdrew from the publication; the organ, which was not popular with the emigration, ceased publication after the third number.

In 1894, after spending several years travelling in western and eastern Europe, Burtsev surfaced in London and worked extensively in the British Museum, where he wrote the still useful anthology of a century of Russian political life, *Za sto let [For a Hundred Years] (1800–1896)*. By 1897 he had gathered sufficient funds to undertake the publication of his own rabidly terrorist oriented *Narodovolets* (*The People's Will*). His preaching and glorifying of terrorism and regicide made him a primary target of the Russian political police abroad. In 1898, as we saw in Chapter 7, the Russian government pressured the British authorities into bringing him to trial for the inflammatory content of his articles and, as a result, Burtsev was sentenced to 18 months imprisonment. After his release from prison he suffered perpetual harassment at the hands of the Russian government and its representatives abroad.[2]

In 1902 he began to publish a journal devoted to the glorification of the revolutionary movement – *Byloe: Sbornik po istorii russkogo osvoboditel'nogo dvizheniia (The Past: A Collection on the History of the Russian Independence Movement)*. This and the five numbers which followed, all published in London, were true to Burtsev's original purpose to publish a journal which contained no more than memoirs of revolutionaries of the recent past.[3] Specifically, these volumes held short memoirs of well-known revolutionaries, reprints of articles originally seen in revolutionary publications, articles on the history of the revolutionary movement, some current events, a rare exposé of police activities, and at times procedural instructions for the revolutionary movement itself. Their tone, although obviously revolutionary was not sensational.[4]

Burtsev discontinued *Byloe* with the outbreak of the 1905 Revolution and returned to Russia where he contributed to a namesake journal with a more moderate political outlook.[5] His limited literary work in these days permitted him to meet and talk with several representatives of the government including police officials some of whom, perhaps wishing to appease the revolution, spoke freely about police affairs. He held long conversations with Sergei Zubatov and A. A. Lopukhin, and Mikhail Efimovich Bakai who was attached to the Warsaw OO. Burtsev claimed the latter two men, 'gave me extraordinarily important information and material...'.[6] Yet it is a reflection of Burtsev's *naiveté* – and that of revolutionaries in general – that at first he refused to believe that the tsarist political police had been so successful in its infiltration of the revolutionary movement. After listening to Bakai's story in amazement Burtsev replied by telling the police official that what he told him could not possibly be true. Burtsev claimed that there were only a few undercover agents within the revolutionary movement and that they were small fry. He continued to inform this knowledgeable police official how every search and arrest carried out by the police could be explained by the successful observation of individual revolutionaries by detectives. A disgusted Bakai exclaimed that, 'you [Burtsev], like all revolutionaries, turned out to be a virgin concerning the question of provocation . . .'.[7]

Burtsev remained unmoved and demanded that the police official document his charges. Bakai said he would. In accord with his promise the treasonous police official turned over to Burtsev information which incriminated several undercover agents. Nevertheless, Burtsev remained true to his revolutionary loyalties and despite his promise to Bakai he could not bring himself to expose erstwhile comrades. Undaunted, Bakai continued to supply the publicist with material, but Burtsev remained passive.[8]

As the evidence gathered by Bakai reached alarming proportions Burtsev slowly became convinced that there was some truth in the police official's allegations, but before he would take the repulsive step of charging a comrade with treason he needed further corroboration. He sought out and found at least one other member of the Department of Police who in those insecure times would be willing to aid the revolutionary cause as a hedge against a radical victory. 'For a modest reward', Burtsev boasted, 'he would supply me with complete secret documents from the [Department of Police] archive'.[9]

Bakai's charges were now at least partially corroborated, and Burtsev's disillusionment was compounded by the failure of the 1905 Revolution which dashed the dreams and illusions having arisen with it. He returned to exile a bitter, hardened, frustrated but still idealistic man carrying with him the shocking, almost unbelievable information he had gathered concerning police infiltration of the revolutionary movement. It seemed clear to him that if the Revolution was to be successful in the future the effectiveness of the political police had to be destroyed. He made this decision with the zealousness of a man who believed that this was the only course of action remaining to the defeated revolutionaries.

The Foreign Agentura became the central object of Burtsev's efforts and the subject of his policing techniques. This was only natural since the Paris Office was an indispensable branch of the Special Section. Indeed, by virtue of its location in western Europe where it was surrounded by relatively democratic institutions, the Foreign Agentura represented to the émigrés even more than did the Department of Police itself the arbitrary callousness of the autocracy. It became, therefore, the symbol of the counter-revolution on which the émigrés' hatred was focused.

Burtsev launched a two-pronged campaign against the Foreign Agentura. First he concentrated his efforts on the undercover agents whom he detested and who were the *bête noire* of the revolutionary movement. Without these 'provocateurs', as Burtsev called them, the Special Section would be both deaf and partially blind. He directed the second phase of his campaign against the detectives and the administrative personnel of the political police abroad. We will review both phases of his campaign and the new techniques he employed in the order of their importance to Burtsev.

His first efforts were passive in approach. A novice in police methodology but an expert publicist, he began his battle against the undercover agents by using his journalist's techniques. Burtsev knew the value of the printed word, innuendo and fact, in a campaign of subversion and disclosure. *Byloe*, renewed and revamped, was the first vehicle of his offensive. The journal now originated from Paris, his new home in exile and also the centre of the Foreign Agentura's activities. In the pages of *Byloe*, Burtsev used the information he had acquired in Russia to maintain a steady flow of sensational exposés. In addition, he requested that members of the revolutionary emigration submit publishable material concerning police activities so that *Byloe* might remain in the forefront of the revolutionary struggle. Burtsev went so far as to send letters to members of the Duma requesting that they dispatch to *Byloe* as much gossip as they could gather in Duma circles which might be of use to him in his desire to humiliate the political police and, as an inducement, he informed the deputies that any material they supplied would be published anonymously.[10]

In order to increase the impact of his work Burtsev required hard evidence from reliable sources within Fontanka and from the Foreign Agentura on a regular basis. At first this intelligence was supplied by the contact he had acquired in the Department of Police archives during his stay in Russia. Then in 1908, to Burtsev's good fortune, Mikhail Bakai retired from the political police and moved to Paris where he loudly declared to the shock of his former employer that he had come to Paris with the single purpose of uncovering the identity of every person in the employ of the Foreign Agentura, from the highest paid *sotrudnik* to the lowest paid clerk.[11] Bakai never undertook his grandiose plan; instead he wrote his police memoirs which were published by Burtsev to the great embarrassment of Fontanka and, more importantly, he supplied Burtsev with the names of dozens of suspected *sotrudniki*. Bakai was not sure of the guilt of most of these people, but Burtsev, having passed beyond scruple, published the names of about 50 persons supplied to him by Bakai despite his promise to the former police official not to do so before he had verified their guilt.[12] Bakai was furious, but this first example of Burtsev's hit-or-miss tactics began to attract the attention of his fellow revolutionaries and stunned the Foreign Agentura.[13] The director of the Foreign Agentura, A. M. Harting, reported to St Petersburg that:

> There is no doubt that the formation of a revolutionary political police in Paris is established with the aim of exposing the activities of the Foreign Agentura and its deep cover agents, not only to stir up the affairs of the [Russian] police abroad but also to deprive the agency of its most valuable agents and thus creating the possibility of its collapse.[14]

The Foreign Agentura had good reason to be concerned: Burtsev soon spread his press campaign to other journals more respected than his own.[15] Such reputable newspapers as *Le Temps*, *The Times*, *Le Matin* and *Il Lavoro* eventually published many of Burtsev's most sensational revelations.[16] Burtsev's articles covered an entire gamut of subjects exposing police agents, methods and plots.

Obtaining such information was costly and Burtsev continually claimed poverty. The political police in 1911 reported that he was without a single *kopek*.[17] His former associate Mikhail Bakai, on the other hand, claimed that Burtsev had collected thousands of francs for articles he had written exposing police agents and their activities or from donations made by sympathisers impressed with his work.[18] Such contrary views of Burtsev's financial condition, however, were not necessarily contradictory for he spent a fortune on the acquisition of information. In one instance Burtsev gave his closest operative, a former Foreign Agentura detective, 5,000 francs ostensibly as a reward for services rendered. Actually, the money was given in the hope that it would entice other Foreign Agentura detectives to desert to Burtsev bringing both their skills and information into the revolutionary camp.[19] As we shall see, these tactics worked. Such extravagance meant that Burtsev between 1907 and 1913 had to maintain a steady string of exposures in order to preserve a regular flow of money into his coffers. In 1913 his financial problems were suddenly and miraculously resolved when a well-disposed Russian banker, with a brother-in-law in the SRs, carried out a promise to place his entire fortune at Burtsev's disposal.[20]

But even when the bribe was paid and the often unsubstantiated intelligence collected, Burtsev still had several important obstacles to overcome. He discovered early that suspicions and flimsy evidence alone could not discredit a provocateur-revolutionary before his party comrades. Most of these agents had close friends within the emigration who would not be easily convinced of their fellow revolutionary's guilt. To Burtsev, this proved a frustrating experience for in most cases he had to rely upon nothing more than suspicions or the weakest of circumstantial evidence usually supplied by a former or present police official. Certainly revolutionaries would hardly take such a person's word by itself. Undercover agents, after all, were clever people with an uncanny instinct for survival and the ability to play the role of devoted revolutionaries without error.

In order to confirm his suspicions Burtsev established his own detective bureau. Who helped him to inaugurate this operation? Bakai denied that he did, although if police reports are to be believed he participated in its formation. Perhaps it was Francis Leroy, a detective formerly employed by the Foreign Agentura. Leroy joined Burtsev when the tsarist police refused to pay him the sum he demanded for his silence on matters relating to Russian political police affairs abroad.[21] Leroy and Burtsev managed to recruit several more Paris Office detectives for their organisation, most possessing as little character as Leroy, but all of whom were excellent policemen.[22]

Leroy and his colleagues gathered a web of evidence within which Burtsev could entangle a *sotrudnik*. Unfortunately, the process of exposure was usually not that simple. The revolutionary police had to use several techniques in its efforts to unmask suspected provocateurs. First, Burtsev made some sort of broad well publicised accusation in *Byloe* or another periodical, which if nothing else caused the accused some discomfort. Such accusations were made more frequently as Burtsev's record of successful exposures grew. He then paused to allow both the provocateurs and their comrades who were loyal to the Revolution time to mull over the accusation, waiting until he believed a situation of considerable curiosity and tenseness had been reached. At a point determined purely by intuition he announced that firm evidence had been received from an anonymous source. He then ceremoniously presented the incriminating data to the appropriate revolutionary authority.[23] If he had no evidence, but his policeman's intuition told him that an individual was an undercover agent, he risked the accusation of slander, and charged the person publicly by name anyway. Yet, when the revolutionary police labelled a revolutionary a provocateur, all was by no means lost for the accused. If the *sotrudnik* defended himself coolly and Burtsev did not have any firm evidence, the tribunal consisting of the accused's comrades (or in the case of the Bolsheviks, Lenin himself) was only too pleased to declare the person innocent. The level-headed *sotrudnik*, therefore, immediately demanded a revolutionary trial upon being charged by Burtsev, in the belief, often justified, that this was the last thing that he wanted.[24] Burtsev, of course, preferred that the suspect panic and run, thus sparing the need for a presentation before a hostile tribunal.

The revolutionary police succeeded best when it could substantiate its suspicions and circumstantial evidence by the use of its own surveillance agents. The case of agent Tatiana Tsetlin's undoing is an excellent example of Burtsev's police at work. Tsetlin had infiltrated the Socialist-Revolutionary Battle Organisation in time to participate in the planned assassination of General Gerasimov, the director of the St Petersburg OO and another police official, wrongly recorded as one Dobroshokov in the records (actually, this is probably Gerasimov's aide Ivan Vasil'evich Dobroskok). Tsetlin received an assignment as one of the executioners. She had to inform St Petersburg about the plot, but Dobroshokov was her lover and in her concern for him she permitted her emotions to take precedence over her judgement. She wrote Dobroshokov a personal letter requesting that he come to Paris immediately so that she could convey the terrorists' plan to him. The letter proved to be a serious mistake. It would have been much safer for her to notify Gerasimov of the plot directly – by suggesting that her lover come to Paris she invited trouble.

Dobroshokov arrived in Paris on Good Friday, 1909. Only three other people were supposed to know about his trip: Gerasimov, Gerasimov's assistant Colonel Komissarov, and an undercover agent named Kershner. Nevertheless, three of Burtsev's surveillance personnel were waiting for Dobroshokov at the railway station.[25] Dobroshokov remained at the station until he was joined by Kershner and then the two of them left for their hotel which was placed under constant surveillance by Burtsev's people. On the day after the police official's arrival Burtsev's operatives were surprised to see Tatiana Tsetlin enter the hotel where she remained until late that night.

On 13 April, Tsetlin was searched and arrested by members of her own Battle Organisation. Five hundred rubles were found on her person – an unusually large sum of money for a revolutionary to possess, let alone carry around. The SRs confiscated the cash. The next morning five judges appointed by the SR Party listened to Burtsev's affidavit. Faced with the overwhelming evidence of her crime and under the severe strain of cross examination Tsetlin broke down, admitted her guilt and was sentenced to death.

Burtsev's operatives did not take part in the arrest and Burtsev himself did not participate in Tsetlin's trial, attending only as an observer. He realised that his organisation had presented a strong case to the Socialist-Revolutionary leadership and believed it to be in the best interests of the revolutionary police's integrity to permit them to deal justice to their own traitor.[26]

Unfortunately, Burtsev's investigations rarely proceeded so smoothly to a satisfactory conclusion. For example, the revolutionary police learned from an informer that the prominent Bolshevik Iakov Zhitomirskii could possibly be an agent.[27] Burtsev, however, did not want to accuse with only hearsay evidence so highly placed and respected a revolutionary as Zhitomirskii. But in 1911 Burtsev learned that the Foreign Agentura had informed the Department of Police that one of its agents, Dr Zhitomirskii, had arrived on Russian soil. Such dispatches were part of normal operating procedure.[28] Burtsev, now convinced of Zhitomirskii's duplicity, quietly informed Lenin that his close associate was a provocateur. The altering of his usual approach in exposing undercover agents reflects Burtsev's desire not to alienate Lenin before he could speak privately to him. Lenin was very sensitive about such matters. It also indicated how badly Burtsev wanted to get Zhitomirskii. Despite Burtsev's best efforts at propriety Lenin ignored his warning even though the revolutionary policeman's evidence was indisputable.

Undaunted by Lenin's rebuff, Burtsev continued to keep Zhitomirskii under surveillance. He observed that the suspect met regularly with a known Foreign Agentura undercover agent in a café or in the latter agent's apartment. Burtsev assigned one of his people to keep watch outside of Zhitomirskii's apartment building.[29] By the end of 1913, the revolutionary police had gathered so much evidence against his quarry that Burtsev decided to take drastic steps; he sent Lenin an ultimatum, that he would create a public scandal if trust was not withdrawn from this man. Lenin responded by dispatching Roman Malinovskii to meet with Burtsev and feel him out in the hope of discovering the quality of the evidence he held against Zhitomirskii. This action guaranteed the undercover agent's safety. Malinovskii went to

Burtsev having been given two sets of instructions. Lenin had ordered him to discover Burtsev's source of information so that he might verify it on his own; but S. P. Beletskii, the director of the Department of Police, had assigned agent Malinovskii the tasks of uncovering who and how many *sotrudniki* Burtsev suspected of operating within the Bolshevik faction and which Department of Police officials supplied him with the intelligence.[30] Burtsev was too much the professional to tell Malinovskii anything concerning his sources of information or the directions of his suspicions. Malinovskii, however, must have convinced Lenin of Zhitomirskii's devotion, for the good doctor could be found as late as 1915 in Germany still close to Lenin and assigned by the Foreign Agentura to follow the activities of the revolutionaries engaged in the propaganda campaign among Russian prisoners of war.[31]

Although the revolutionary police had more success with other revolutionary leaders it never won their complete co-operation or friendship. Burtsev's motto, 'Neither Lenin nor Chernov nor reactionary'[32] prevented such friendships – his organisation, and himself were above party strife. This policeman disdained the machinations of the emigration – his sole concern being the destruction of the counter-revolution – that is how he saw himself. If he had to rout traitors from within the ranks of the revolution, he would do so no matter what the consequences. Often he accused innocent people of treason, ruining their reputations and perhaps their lives; but his only concern was the purification of the revolution, and individuals damaged by this process were of no importance to him. This approach to his work, although quite effective, won him few friends in the emigration. IA. Akimov an émigré falsely accused by Burtsev bitterly expressed the feelings of most émigrés when he blurted:

> What right does Mr. Burtsev have to carry out investigative experiments on his comrades? The right 'to verify' cannot belong to a separate person, no one likes Pinkerton tricks. It is for the collective [to police itself] for it can guarantee honesty and integrity in the investigation.... Mr. Burtsev, an imposter, is unfit to play the role of self-governing investigator and judge over his equals.[33]

The leaders of the revolutionary movement, unlike Akimov who was of little consequence, could not be so outspoken. Burtsev's successes forced them to recognise that he performed a despicable, but necessary task. Nevertheless, they did almost nothing to facilitate Burtsev's investigations. He never won Mark Natanson's confidence, for example, and as late as 1914 when Burtsev's value as the watchdog of the revolutionary movement had been well-established, the two men barely tolerated each other. Natanson, the acknowledged leader of the Socialist-Revolutionary Party, did as little as possible to help Burtsev in his investigations.[34]

Policemen, even when friendly, were seemingly not liked or appreciated for they uncovered things which their constituencies would rather have believed did not exist and which caused them considerable embarrassment. The people Burtsev protected scorned the very organisation attempting to shield them from their enemies.

Despite these obstacles, the revolutionary police proved quite successful. The exact number of *sotrudniki* unmasked by Burtsev is unknown, although one estimate is one-third of the undercover agents working abroad, including most of the important ones.[35] By 1914 the heart of the Foreign Agentura's undercover agency had been demolished. In this year alone, the last of Burtsev's activity, his detective bureau had accurately placed at least 24 *sotrudniki* under suspicion and surveillance.[36] In fact he never for a moment permitted any of the employees of the Russian police abroad to forget that they were always under the surveillance of his operatives. When, for instance, the detectives of the revolutionary police followed their opposite numbers employed by the Foreign Agentura, they did so quite openly and, making no pretence at secrecy, photographed their counterparts.[37]

Burtsev's detectives could be seen everywhere maintaining surveillance over the Russian Embassy, forcing the tsarist authorities to ask the French police to alleviate the harassment of Russian officials by these men and if possible to extradite Burtsev and Bakai to Russia.[38] But the French were helpless, for Burtsev's agents were not committing any crime and revolutionary surveillance over Russian diplomats, Foreign Agentura employees, and visiting Russian dignitaries continued. Burtsev's war of nerves affected even the most loyal of the Paris Office's operatives. The feeling of insecurity Burtsev stimulated amongst these people developed into paranoia. Several of the Agentura's detectives left the service claiming frayed nerves. One defector believed that Burtsev's police were everywhere, and that they knew most of the Agentura's detectives and administrative personnel. He, therefore, like many of his colleagues, switched sides and joined the revolutionary police, bringing with him information on the operations and personnel of the Paris chancery.[39]

Frightened Foreign Agentura detectives were joined by undercover agents who were unable to withstand the pressure of Burtsev's tactics. Knowing that he had no qualms about turning *sotrudniki* over to their erstwhile comrades for punishment and perhaps execution, they gave themselves up to Burtsev hoping to save their lives in exchange for intelligence on political police operations.[40] The more detectives and *sotrudniki* who deserted the more information fell into Burtsev's hands and the more insecure loyal police employees became. Thus desertions had a snowball effect which the political police never managed to control. Burtsev's use of fear as part of his psychological warfare strategy was a lesson which would not be forgotten by his successors in political police development.

To its horror, Fontanka watched as Burtsev's exposures spread beyond the lower echelon personnel of the Foreign Agentura to the chief of the Paris

Office itself. At the end of 1908 Director of the Foreign Agentura Harting endured the same fate as an ever increasing number of his undercover agents. Burtsev's sensational revelation that A. M. Harting was actually former *sotrudnik* Abraham Hekel'man-Landezen, a fugitive from French justice, humiliated the Russian government before French public opinion. Worse, Burtsev's exposure of Harting along with that of Evno Azef, the Special Section's most important undercover agent, had an increasingly detrimental effect on Fontanka's already tarnished image. The entire question of police provocation created a furor in the Duma, the press, and in Russian public opinion.

How did the political police react to the harassment of the revolutionary police? What effect did Burtsev's activities have on the administrative personnel of the Special Section and especially on those of the Foreign Agentura? Burtsev himself, who could not help but be completely aware of his position within the revolutionary community, must have been amused and impressed with his own tactics as he watched the Special Section and its Foreign Agentura misinterpret his position in the revolutionary emigration and exaggerate his successes. It was the overdrawn image of Burtsev's effectiveness to which a disgusted former assistant minister of internal affairs reacted when in retrospect he exclaimed:

> Secret police agents penetrated into revolutionary hiding places and in return revolutionaries penetrated into the sanctum of the secret police. It is almost impossible to determine where the secret police agents stopped and the revolutionaries began.[41]

The Special Section saw Burtsev as the incarnation of revolution and terror.[42] In contrast to these exaggerations and misjudgements no evidence exists that Burtsev ever planned the assassination of a single tsarist official although he glorified the assassins in *Byloe* and other publications. Despite this lack of evidence, the Foreign Agentura persistently accused Burtsev of planning terrorist acts.[43]

Burtsev's investigations seemed to reinforce the image of him as a bane to the Empire. At the end of 1908 the Paris Office nervously noted, 'it appears that in Paris Burtsev and Bakai have made up their minds to paralyse and uncover the activities of the Foreign Agentura . . .'.[44] Burtsev shrewdly exploited these fears until they caused a chain reaction of panic, depression, and paranoia reaching its peak in 1916.

The Department of Police, which was ultimately responsible for developing political police policy, did nothing to help calm or instruct the Foreign Agentura; it placed the entire blame for Burtsev's success on the Paris Office.

A. M. Harting, still the director of the Foreign Agentura, replied to his superiors' criticisms by noting that the downfall of Azef and other agents had nothing to do with the Foreign Agentura but rather was the work of Burtsev and Bakai. He argued that during the 1905 Revolution, the government had allowed Burtsev to live in St Petersburg unhindered while he gathered the information which was now so demoralising the ranks of undercover agents abroad.[45]

The following September the new, but temporary chief of the Paris Office, Captain Andreev, wrote despondently to St Petersburg that, 'Burtsev distinctly knew, knows, and will know *about every person who serves the Chief of the Agentura* [italics Andreev's]'.[46] What was the source of the information Burtsev received on the Foreign Agentura? Neither Andreev nor any other police official considered the thesis that his information could have come only from deserters or just plain keen observation by the revolutionary police. Andreev claimed that it had to have come from within the administration; the leak might be located in Petersburg, the Russian Embassy in Paris, or even in the French police administration with which the Foreign Agentura co-operated. The director of the Foreign Agentura offered Fontanka what he thought would be some consolation by informing Headquarters that Burtsev's ability to identify the personnel of the chancery did not affect the security of the Internal Agency. It was in this second area, Andreev believed, that the Foreign Agentura must go to any length in order to preserve the undercover positions of its *sotrudniki*. He took full responsibility for security measures;[47] yet he failed, for exposures of undercover agents continued at an increasing rate.

The Foreign Agentura's new director, A. A. Krasil'nikov, had lived in western Europe for many years. Suave and mature, Fontanka hoped that he would be able to cope with the situation. Krasil'nikov ordered Lev Beitner, one of his principal undercover agents, to infiltrate Burtsev's organisation which Beitner did by joining Burtsev in a publishing venture. Beitner's assignment was to somehow keep the names of the agents working for Fontanka out of print and to discover Burtsev's sources of information. He seems to have been unsuccessful in both endeavours and in 1912 Burtsev unmasked Beitner himself as a Foreign Agentura *sotrudnik*.[48] Undeterred, as we have seen, Krasil'nikov was not finished yet. As we saw in the previous chapter he restructured the detective agency in an attempt to thwart Burtsev's investigations, but the bureaucratic meddling of Fontanka delayed the implementation of this process and it had no practical effect. As a result, Krasil'nikov did not have any better luck than his predecessors. So in order to protect himself, he too attempted to place the blame for the crisis squarely on Fontanka:

> A high person...in an important position apparently a member of the Department of Police service or located in the Moscow Security Division has rendered very good enlightenment on the latest business [to Burtsev].[49]

The Department of Police never responded to this charge, but subsequently replied to Krasil'nikov by weakly admonishing the Paris Office, 'to be extremely careful in its activities'. Nothing was to be kept by Krasil'nikov in his apartment which related to police business, and he was not to absent himself from Paris without permission.[50] The refusal of Fontanka or its Special Section to offer concrete help or suggestions encouraged a feeling of isolation amongst the members of the Foreign Agentura's chancery which caused their insecurities to reach nightmarish proportions. The first serious indication of this transformation came with the Paris Office's request that Fontanka discharge its duty to protect Agentura personnel from harm, although no real threats had been made against their lives. The Department of Police actually looked into the possibility of purchasing bulletproof suits and shields on behalf of the Foreign Agentura, but nothing came of the idea.[51]

Krasil'nikov believed that his life was in constant danger so long as Burtsev remained in France.[52] Desperately, he searched for the solution to the problem of the revolutionary police. Like his predecessor, however, he carried out this task completely within the confines of his own organisation – hence contributing to the deteriorating morale. He notified Fontanka that he did not believe that Burtsev's success was the result of carelessness:

> In 1913 the life of the Foreign Agentura has been marked by the continuous downfall of undercover agents. Downfalls not resulting from the negligence of the undercover agents themselves or persons connected with them, but by treasonous persons. Persons who have access to their [the undercover agents] service status [personnel files], affairs, and documents related to persons who compose the Agentura . . . .[53]

Krasil'nikov had come to believe that the traitor lived within his own chancery. It is doubtful if Burtsev fully comprehended the serious effect his warfare was having on the Foreign Agentura, but by 1913 Krasil'nikov's suspicions had settled on his own small staff. The director's misgivings were seemingly confirmed by a lead given him by one of his operatives. The man accused of being an informer was none other than State Councillor Boris Sushkov. Ironically, Sushkov had been the most devoted and hardworking man in the chancery as its supervisor.[54] Krasil'nikov, a good friend of Sushkov, could hardly believe that a man of the State Councillor's integrity and history of loyal service would betray the Foreign Agentura; he, nevertheless, pursued the investigation. Although Sushkov had never met Burtsev, there was the nagging fact that the latter man had been receiving information by telegraph and telephone from the Russian Embassy building. Besides, Sushkov had been acting strangely of late.[55]

Sushkov's co-workers noticed that the State Councillor had undergone a personality change; he was becoming more and more irrational. However, a guilty conscience was not responsible for Sushkov's strange behaviour rather it was the result of acute depression caused by the harassment of the revolutionary police. During a conversation in which the problem caused by Burtsev were discussed Sushkov exclaimed, 'Well it is necessary to close the shutters . . . the chief undercover agents have fallen . . . Burtsev has won all.' He also babbled that he could no longer appear in public where he constantly heard the curses of Burtsev being directed against the Foreign Agentura and particularly against Krasil'nikov.[56] It seemed that long-time police official Sushkov could not tolerate Burtsev's successful campaign against his chancery. In his bitterness, Sushkov even spoke against Krasil'nikov and the regular embassy personnel for permitting such chaos to take place in his office. Sushkov's actions were not evidence of betrayal, on the contrary, they represented his excessive devotion to the bureau.[57]

On studying the affidavit dealing with the Sushkov case the Department of Police found him innocent of all charges and kindly transferred him to a post within Fontanka itself.[58] Sushkov's breakdown was a major victory for Burtsev. The State Councillor had directed the administrative machinery of the Foreign Agentura and sorted and synthesised field reports which were forwarded to St Petersburg. His replacement, Titular Councillor Iusefovich as noted earlier was not up to the job and despite subsequent efforts, the Foreign Agentura never discovered the spy in its midst.[59]

In 1912 a functionary of the Department of Police named Petrishchev arrived in Paris on special assignment for Fontanka. Petrishchev sought out Burtsev at once and offered him his services. He claimed that he had decided to join Burtsev's organisation after reading the publicist's articles exposing both the famous provocateur Evno Azef and the machinations of Fontanka.[60] Petrishchev proved the ideal informer, for he was above suspicion. Krasil'nikov seemingly never thought to question one of Fontanka's most trusted employees. Headquarters itself believed sufficiently in Petrishchev's fidelity to send him to Paris, the home of Vladimir Burtsev and the revolutionary emigration, on missions of the utmost importance.[61] Burtsev could hardly believe his good fortune. 'I saw unroll before me a widening horizon in the battle with provocation and reaction, which for me is personified in the activities of the Department of Police.'[62] Petrishchev lived up to Burtsev's expectations, for during the years 1912 to 1914 he regularly supplied the revolutionary police with important intelligence on tsarist political police operations. Burtsev gave him deserved credit. 'Petrishchev systematically supplied me . . . with very interesting and important information concerning political [police] investigations. Thanks to his reporting during that time, I exposed several serious provocateurs . . . '.[63]

The Special Section plagued for several years by Burtsev's disclosures succumbed to the same self-doubts, investigations and humiliations as had its Foreign Agentura. Petrishchev's betrayal merely accentuated its vulnerability, aggravating an already deteriorating condition. As early as 1910 the Special Section lamented that:

> Burtsev's 'Committee of Inquiry' is increasingly furnishing itself with information concerning the make-up of [those] investigatory agencies [which supervise] undercover agents.
>
> Reports concerning statements and discoveries of a similar type [as those mentioned above] are disorganising the business of political investigation and are placing the lives of many undercover agents in danger....[64]

The report ordered political police bureaus to undertake thorough investigations into their own operations to dig out the traitors and to be sure to preserve correspondence dealing with *sotrudniki* 'with special care and thoughtfulness'.[65]

Fontanka attempted to end the leakage of intelligence to Burtsev by conducting inquiries not only into their own shop, but amongst the general public as well! This assault, apparently instituted without any consideration of public opinion, relied heavily on gossip and only added to Fontanka's embarrassment. In one case, rumours were spread that the well-known police and Ministry of Internal Affairs functionary Manasevich-Manuilov possessed unauthorised copies of important police documents which he either had sold or was about to sell to Burtsev. Manuilov's quarters in St Petersburg were searched on the night of 10 January 1910. The police found dozens of reports relating to police matters he had participated in since 1900.[66] Despite the plethora of official documents found in Manuilov's apartment, the Special Section failed to connect him with Burtsev. Instead it discovered that Manuilov used the documents to blackmail people mentioned therein and the Ministry of Justice charged him with the civil crimes of blackmail and extortion.

Mass searches for Burtsev's informers within the Empire continued, instituted by the order of Assistant Minister of Internal Affairs Kurlov. Gendarmes entered the homes of many prominent citizens and created a public uproar even in right-wing circles. Upon being questioned by the Council of Ministers, Prime Minister Stolypin reluctantly admitted that the searches had been tactless.[67] The urgency of the problem increased drastically with the desertion to the Revolution and Burtsev of Leonid Men'shchikov. The defection of this high ranking and long time police official caused a serious break in Fontanka's morale and suspicious political police chiefs placed their *chinovniki* under surveillance.[68]

Isolated and without support from public opinion, the Department of Police resorted to purely administrative measures which it hoped would eliminate the surreptitious outflow of information. In 1910, in order to give its *sotrudniki* greater protection against exposures, Fontanka created a Highly

Secret Agents' Department (*Sverkhsekretnyi agenturnyi otdel*) within the Special Section. However this Department, about which little information is available, did not alleviate the problem.[69]

In 1914 the Department of Police enacted a much more daring measure by eliminating the regional offices of the political police. Fontanka thought that by simplifying and recentralising the administrative structure of the political police, it would be able to maintain a higher level of control and security.[70] These palliatives did not do any good. By 1914 it not only became difficult to place new *sotrudniki* within the revolutionary movement, it also became impossible to recruit new undercover agents. Even if the Special Section could have replaced them, however, it would have taken years for any of the new agents to attain the authority of an Azef. In the autumn of 1916, two years after Burtsev had ended the operations of the revolutionary police, Krasil'nikov advised the Special Section that:

> [In the past] we could properly acquire several undercover agents and [at least] one of them usually proved of great value ... but to my vexation offers of service abroad which are of value are rare and lately they do not join at all.
>
> All has completely changed and now all revolutionary groups have representatives who vigilantly watch every unnecessary change of linen or drink from a wine bottle. These acts call for suspicion and can lead on occasion to the charge of provocation. There is a Sword of Damocles high above the head of every revolutionary and there is spreading amongst them the opinion ... that the revolutionary police allegedly have informants nearly at the very heart of the Department of Police.
>
> Having in view all of the above one can only conclude that attempts to recruit for the Agentura ... in those conditions confronted abroad presents exceptionally little chance of success ....[71]

The situation was made worse when many undercover agents still operating within revolutionary organisations refused to inform, having been frightened into silence.[72]

In its own defence the Department of Police tried to discount Burtsev by arguing that he had done more damage to the revolutionary emigration than to the political police. As former Director of Police Vasil'ev comments in his memoirs:

> Burtsev's activities gave rise to the greatest confusion among the revolutionaries, who fell to suspecting each other, so that in the end one conspirator could not trust another. In consequence the activities of the rebels were seriously hampered for quite some time.[73]

Although Burtsev's operations did cause disillusionment, disappointment, suspicion, and cynicism within the revolutionary camp, these emotions are beneficial in a clandestine atmosphere. It is *naiveté* that is harmful. Burtsev's exposures forced the revolutionaries to be more cautious and realistic about the treasonous conduct of some of their comrades. The Department of Police noted the change:

> There is developing in the last years amongst party activities a reciprocal lack of faith. Revolutionaries [now] strictly observe the law of conspiracy, so that frequently members of one such organisation know the members of others only by their *klichki*.[74]

The revolutionary police thus made a significant contribution to the security of revolutionary groups. Burtsev's discoveries hardened them and taught these émigrés the value of a ruthless, unrelenting political police force.

Despite his success, Burtsev did not come near to unmasking all the undercover agents the tsarist police placed amongst the revolutionaries abroad, and his activities only affected a few *sotrudniki* operating within Russia. Yet, acquiring his intelligence mostly from political police defectors and a small staff of detectives, and working with a precarious source of income Burtsev managed to maintain an effective hold over the attention of the tsarist political police at home and abroad.

Why, on the other hand, was the Special Section so helpless against Burtsev? Why did the Foreign Agentura fail to assassinate him when attempts at extradition failed? The answer to these questions lies within the contradictory attitudes of the Department of Police itself and the very times and circumstances in which it operated. It is exceptionally important to note that the two former police officials, Mikhail Bakai and Leonid Men'shchikov, were so repulsed by Burtsev's tactics they abandoned working with him and publicly condemned his methods.[75] Bakai charged that Burtsev's activities:

> Were not sanctioned by revolutionary organisations. And it seems to me that for pure and ethical reasons you [Burtsev] did not have the right to place your comrades under surveillance by Leroy and his associates. In addition to the immorality, these actions were undesirable, and in my opinion even harmful.[76]

Bakai berated Burtsev for his use of innuendo and circumstantial evidence which the former police official considered despicable. 'You will not disorganise the political police' with such tactics Bakai tells Burtsev,[77] and he issues the maximum insult, 'You and Sherlock Holmes represent to me two opposite poles in social position and in moral posture'.[78]

In essence what we observe in this struggle between Burtsev and the Foreign Agentura is the evolution of that segment of Russian political culture concerned with societal control. The methods employed by Burtsev were startlingly unique. The inability of Bakai and Men'shchikov to appreciate the value of Burtsev's tactics is a signal telling us that here was something different, something new, an innovation in political police methodology that the Special Section did not understand and, therefore, with which it could not deal. The Special Section's revolutionary stereotypes, their entire framework of references and reactions to revolutionaries and their operations were not applicable to Burtsev or his activities. Vladimir Burtsev's motto, 'Neither Lenin nor Chernov nor reactionary' was more than rhetoric. Because he held himself responsible, at least nominally, only to the leaders of the various revolutionary factions, the tsarist police could not entangle him with any one faction and thus discredit him with the others. The Special Section so accustomed to classifying its enemies by the subversive movements to which they belonged, ignored the facts and announced to its branches that Burtsev was a dangerous SR terrorist and propagandist. Therefore, although the Special Section was well aware that Burtsev directed an agency bent on sabotaging the Russian political police system, it always treated him as a terrorist and vicious journalist rather than as a fellow policeman, an opposite and equal enemy to be destroyed. After all, the Special Section could cope with a straightforward terrorist, but the techniques employed by Burtsev were of a totally different sort and these flourished in the evolving revolutionary atmosphere spawned by the 1905 Revolution and the bitterness bred by its defeat. In this somber environment the revolutionary emigration began to lose its remaining innocence and became increasingly resistant to the machinations of the Foreign Agentura whose agents Burtsev began to hunt and through the offices of revolutionary tribunals to eliminate.

Tsardom's political policemen did not possess the systematic brutality bred by zealous attachment to a cause. They undoubtedly believed that the ends were more important than the means. However, unlike Burtsev whose unconscionable ruthlessness was directed toward the attainment of a specific goal benefiting the revolutionary community, Fontanka's political policemen were burdened with diffuse goals, causing them to strive for the ends that were the most self-serving. They were often at their most ruthless and venal when engaged in furthering their own careers or giving vent to their prejudices against minorities. To take an admittedly extreme example of the difference in approach to their enemies, the Special Section never implemented a policy of premeditated murder:[79] Burtsev did. He knew and seemed untroubled that his indictments against erstwhile comrades often served as their death sentences.

The crisis (caused by Burtsev) confronting the Foreign Agentura demanded action by the Department of Police, but as we have just seen, the remedies required were beyond its understanding. Tsardom's political policemen and their superiors at Fontanka found themselves in a paradoxical situation.

The social and political environment from which the political police officials themselves sprang restricted their ability to contend with the hardening of the subversive environment (as represented by Burtsev's activities). The Special Section's leadership as well as that of the entire Department of Police proved insufficiently flexible and lacked the daring, imagination and the aggressiveness to devise new tactics in their battle with Burtsev, the revolutionary emigration and with the revolutionary movement as a whole. Dominated by a world view that was rapidly becoming obsolete, they could not react to what they clearly did not understand. Instead they resorted to the standard administrative palliatives they traditionally relied upon and ultimately turned their suspicions inward, undermining their own bureaus, as we have seen in the case of the Foreign Agentura.

Burtsev on the other hand led an active organisation which in fulfilling its mission of destruction demonstrated for the revolutionary movement the weaknesses of the tsarist political policing system and how these flaws could be exploited through the use of propaganda, innuendo, rumour, and the psychologies of fear and constant pursuit. Burtsev's zealous callousness, induced by a seemingly compulsive desire to purify the revolution, facilitated the organisation's goals. The Bolshevik successor to the Special Section applied these same methods too well.

Conclusion and Epilogue

September 11, 2001, the first significant attack on American soil by international terrorists, unleashed a tidal wave of fear that has since affected everyday life around the world. Few other events during the past century have so challenged the egocentric sense of superiority that permeates western society. Indeed only two other catastrophes of this magnitude and with this impact come to mind: the Japanese attack on Pearl Harbor on 7 December 1941 and the fall of Singapore to the Japanese Army in February 1942. Both these prior successful challenges by an 'Outsider' to the pre-eminent place of 'western civilisation' in the world rocked western society's perceptions of the non-western world and demonstrated its own vulnerability.

The Twin Tower catastrophe, an act of terror on a scale which heretofore had never been envisioned by even the most pessimistic commentators on international terrorism, is a stark reminder of that forgotten message. The tidal wave of hysteria that immediately engulfed the world as it witnessed the attack on the World Trade Center has subsided but its ripple effect continues. At least one of these ripples is now undulating through the historical profession forcing western scholars to at least re-evaluate the world from a different perspective, that of cultures which live on the periphery of their own. If nothing else, one outcome of that tragic day should be that even the best intentioned Eurocentric historians are encouraged to shed their remaining hubris and ethnocentrism which unduly colour, even if ever so slightly, their view of the 'Other'.

A tiny eddy emanating from this ripple has washed over this book. This 'psychological eddy' has tinted and strengthened a major theme of this work. At the same time, however, it risks focusing the author's and the reader's attention, much more than intended, on the dilemma that international terrorism presented (and still presents) to governments: that varied legal and political cultures combined with the vagaries of diplomacy hamper a co-ordinated campaign against the blight of international terrorism.

As a result the shifting of the reader's attention to this issue may have unintentionally obscured a major theme of this work. This theme was drawn from the life of the Foreign Agentura of the Russian secret police and the milieux in which it operated. The study of the Foreign Agentura is quite suggestive in shedding light upon the persistent Russian dilemma which forms the core of the preceding chapters: the place of Russia in Europe.

Both themes – the place and role of the Russian secret police in Europe and the related sub-theme of the European-wide struggle against terrrorism – need to be addressed below since they both reinforce the importance of History in understanding the present and coping with challenges to humankind in the future.

To repeat what I wrote in the Preface to this volume, the dynamics of Russian historical development did not take place in isolation from Europe and Russia's separation from European life as a political cultural entity is often overplayed. The Russian European land mass is not beyond the borders of western civilisation. Nevertheless, the geopolitical divisions of Europe into 'western', 'central' and 'eastern' Europe and then 'Russia' have for too long prevented most scholars from conceiving of European development through a variant refraction on the historical prism.[1] This book has been influenced by such an alternate point of view. As I wrote at the outset, the history of the struggle for modernity on the European continent and the role the forces of order played in this struggle between 1880 and the First World War intimately involved Russia.

By the late 1870s the tsarist government believed that in the revolutionary emigration it confronted a group of radicals capable of disrupting Russian society through the commission of acts of terror. Tsardom reacted to this perceived threat, as we have seen, by pursuing both diplomatic and political police remedies.

In this case study of the Foreign Agentura, Russia and the other Great Powers were not a comfortable match. The remainder of industrial Europe preferred to believe that the dynamics of Russian political culture and the problems it confronted were 'un-European'. To believe otherwise, to any degree whatsoever, said things about western political and social life that made it uncomfortable.

Between 1880 and 1914 tsarist Russia fought increasingly ineffective actions against the forces of political and social modernity. What is clear from this work and others cited throughout the text is that industrial Europe was fighting – with somewhat different tools and to different extents – the same battles. By the late nineteenth century the traditional order throughout Europe had become increasingly recalcitrant in the face of newly arising social and political agents. Terrorism was one of the manifestations of these agents bubbling to society's surface. Politically inspired terror spread panic across Europe increasing the desire of the establishment to recapture the imagined social and political tranquillity (at least for them) of a bygone age. Governments turned to their forces of order especially to their police for security.

Some states, such as France, relied on long-standing traditions of intrusive police behaviour as the basis for increasing the power of the Prefect of Paris and eventually the *Sûreté Generale*. Sadly, despite the French awareness of the nastiness involved in political policing amongst its own population, the Third Republic became wedded to it more than ever before.[2] Others such as Great Britain slowly slipped into the dark and unfamiliar waters of modern political policing.

Generally, the final decades of the nineteenth century saw the beginnings of the spread of bureaucratically rationalised and professional police institutions across the industrialising world.[3] By the outbreak of the war all the states in which the Foreign Agentura operated possessed police systems at least as professional as their own.[4] The view of some scholars 'that a government is recognized as being authoritarian if its police are repressive, democratic if its police are restrained' [5] reads well but serves only to obfuscate the charged European atmosphere which gave birth to and encouraged the growth of modern, often covert, often arbitrary political policing on the one hand and that created an operational and professional bond amongst Europe's policemen on the other.[6] Remember, that in the 1890s, for instance, Republican France possessed a political police which in its venality, arbitrary behaviour and lack of concern for the law almost matched the *Okhrana*. And by the outbreak of the First World War the British Home Office could boast, although it would never have done so, of supporting perhaps the most professional political police of all; one that was growing by leaps and bounds. In the years prior to the First World War only two states possessed highly specialised institutions devoted solely to political policing; these were Imperial Russia and Great Britain. As one would expect in Europe's most democratic state, the activities of the Special Branch were far more secretive than those of Russia's Special Section and its associated agencies.

In fact this work has shown that the Foreign Agentura of the Russian political police, although demonised by the Russian emigration and by the left-wing and liberal European press was, even in its most venal aspects, accepted by its fellow policemen and somewhat more grudgingly by their superiors in government as part and parcel of the European internal security network. The operational methodology, the professional bonds and informal co-operation united them against a common enemy – the outsiders – the dissenters who wished to modify (at least) the political structure of society by means beyond those the political culture deemed as acceptable.

In four out the five states discussed within these pages – France, Germany, Great Britain and Italy – a tension arose between the law and order bureaucracy's brief to protect society and especially the state from its enemies and the limitations set upon achieving these goals by the requirements of constitutional representative government and the law. This dichotomy between practice and inhibiting parliamentary and legal institutions forced senior police officials and their ministers to adopt a delicate strategy. They worked hard to convince their populations of the benevolent role of the police while, at the same time, carrying out deeply secret and perhaps more often than not illegal activities in the defence of the state which infringed upon the very civil rights they were sworn to protect.

Europe's politicians responsible for internal affairs knew that a branch of the tsarist secret police operated amongst them. Despite their displays of public outrage when the Paris Office's operations were periodically unmasked they allowed the Russian police to stay put and play a role in their struggle with the ever widening world of political dissent with which they had to deal.

Between 1905 and the war the traditional order in Europe tightened its hold over power. Conservatives adopted an ever more rigid posture as they strove to contain, if not crush, the likes of radical labour, peasant and suffragette movements while endeavouring to derail moderate reformism.[7] As part of this process, as we have seen, the established order devoted itself to the development of policing systems.

The Foreign Agentura should have felt right at home and it did until 1909. For a quarter of a century, especially during the Rachkovskii and Harting eras, the Foreign Agentura swam comfortably in European waters. Rachkovskii for most of his tenure abroad successfully harrassed the Russian revolutionary emigration as did Harting in Berlin driving the émigrés to distraction. Harting's anti-smuggling campaign succeeeded admirably during the 1905 Revolution. By 1909, however, changes taking place at home were beginning to have a serious impact on the life of the Foreign Agentura.

In the world of post-1905 Russia the political police faced growing criticism both within and outside of the Ministry of Internal Affairs. The Department of Police as a whole came under the scrutiny of men who wished to strengthen the police system by reforming its administration. These *sanovniki* possessed professional backgrounds far closer to that of the mediocre L. A. Rataev, than to those of the swashbuckling pair of Rachkovskii and Harting. The reforms the MVD's officials proposed were designed to gain more reliable control over the Foreign Agentura's finances and to more closely supervise its activities and to increase its professionalism – laudable tasks all. Unfortunately the reforms carried with them the traditional odour of tsarist bureaucratic formalism.[8]

The impact of these partially implemented reforms on the Foreign Agentura did not resolve the Paris Office's administrative or financial problems. They did, however, manage to reduce the Paris Office's effectiveness at a time when the Foreign Agentura confronted a ruthless enemy of its own. Vladimir Burtsev launched an assault on the Paris Bureau with which A. A. Krasil'nikov could not cope. Burtsev turned the tables on the Foreign Agentura by employing psychological warfare against the Paris Office and it worked. Krasil'nikov sought help from his superiors in St Petersburg but Headquarters offered only useless bureaucratic remedies and carping criticism. The Foreign Agentura's days as a useful tool of the Special Section and a surreptitious ally of the forces of order in western Europe were coming to an end. Only the outbreak of the First World War saved the Foreign Agentura from collapse.[9]

Russia was part of Europe and yet it was not. The Foreign Agentura, as it fell under the suffocating bureaucratic culture and mind set that so inhibited Tsardom's ability to cope with change, found dealing with the cynical and battle-hardened world of the post-1905 revolutionary emigration to be an increasingly frustrating and frightening task.

The war against terrorism in the past, present and future: an epilogue

When I conceived the framework of this book I thought of the role of international terrorism as a mechanism to introduce the reader to the principal reasons for Tsardom's decision to create the Foreign Agentura. This device would establish the common thread that joined the Russian police operations with their colleagues particularly but not solely in France, Germany, Italy and Great Britain. Then came the attack on the World Trade Center. The magnitude of the attack, the sophisticated planning that went into its remarkable execution, the horrific number of casualties and, finally, the 'war on terror' that embodies the American and European reaction to it placed my discussion more towards centre stage than I had originally intended warranting an Epilogue of its own.

The international campaign to squelch terrorism in the late nineteenth and early twentieth centuries divided itself – not to belabour the point – into both informal and formal international co-operation. On one level there came into existence a masked joint effort of policemen working together with a common goal facilitated by an increasingly homogenous professional police culture. On a higher although less effective plane, governments struggled to co-operate with each other through a set of formal treaties and lower level agreements such as the protocols emanating from the Rome and St Petersburg Conferences. Both of these Conferences receive far too little attention (if any at all) from today's criminologists who are still struggling with the establishment of an effective international system of police co-operation. While international police co-operation today is concerned with additional crimes such as drug trafficking and financial fraud, terrorism, smuggling and white slavery remain at the centre of its concerns. By briefly discussing the linkage between the past and the present I intend to emphasise the role both directly and indirectly Russia has played in the evolution of international policing and how the problems faced by the tsar's government as it strove to acquire the support of Europe had less to do with its reputation abroad than with the difficulties the process confronted in the intricacies of European legal and political culture. These problems persist to this day.

Before we embark on the discussion a few important points must be made. First, from the analyst's perspective the number of people killed by terrorists and the style in which they have been murdered are not necessarily important issues. Why? Because they are not a critical criteria of success for the terrorists themselves. Killing royalty, officials – elected or otherwise – innocent people sipping apéritifs in a café, or crashing planes in the Twin Towers all produce the desired effect. They traumatise official and public opinion and make the population at large doubt the ability of its government to protect society. This was and remains the immediate aim of terrorists; to instil doubt and to psychologically destabilise the targeted society.

A second critical point is that terrorism occurs in waves. Terrorists suffer from the vigorous responses of their victims and then lick their wounds and rebuild their organisations to strike again. During the time frame of this book terrorism in western and southern Europe and the United States faded in the early years of the twentieth century just at the very time it began to grow exponentially in Russia where by 1910 it too subsided.[10] Nevertheless, the fear of terror remained unabated throughout industrial Europe up until the outbreak of the First World War when other events even more inimical to the survival of governments distracted both officials and people alike.

As a result, up until 1914 there existed a diminished but still common ground for international police co-operation. As we have seen this was more easily discussed by contemporaries than accomplished. What is important is that this work has proven that to a considerable degree it was tsarist Russia that laid the foundation upon which both informal and formal international police co-operation has been intermittently constructed ever since.[11]

By 1910 the French were pushing for an international conference in the hope that Europe would be able to co-operate in a campaign to destroy the white slavery trade. Prince Albert I of Monaco supported the idea and convened another conference in Monte Carlo in 1914. The conference (*Premier Congres de Police Judiciare Internationale*) accomplished nothing. Only three Great Powers attended the meeting – France, Italy and Russia. The parlous state of European diplomacy combined with the division between those who wished to establish an organisation based on administrative and criminal police collaboration and those who wished to concentrate on the political goals of the suppression of Anarchism and Socialism condemned the conference to failure. The delegates did agree that a joint international effort was needed to combat international crime and they pledged to propagate this opinion upon their return home. But the outbreak of war swept the Monaco meeting into the backwater of international concerns. As this study of the Foreign Agentura shows, during the first decades of the twentieth century international police co-operation for the most part remained based upon the personal and professional connections amongst Europe's senior police officials.

Underlying the failure of the three pre-war conferences, especially this final one, was a fear that the establishment of an international police organisation not responsible to a national government would come to resemble the *Okhrana*, a policing body known for its independence from government authority and its unsavoury practices including provocation.[12]

It would be difficult to find a better example of the schizophrenic attitude toward Russia in Europe that both united and separated Russia from its fellow Great Powers than this unjustified fear of creating a super-*Okhrana* with the establishment of international police co-operation. It is more than noteworthy that the tsarist government initiated and pursued the establishment of international police co-operation, helping to lay the foundations for what became Interpol. At the same, time, it found itself an outcast amongst those nations who were themselves striving to construct political police institutions that would hold often surreptitious power over their own populations.

I repeat again what I have stated less pointedly above: the established order believed that mass democracy required surveillance and, at times, containment. The more broadly based the democracy the more venal and alien the dissenter. For in a democracy, the argument went, an attack on the government was no less than an assault on the people itself.

Then came the Bolshevik Revolution. The new Bolshevik State gave revolutionary Marxism a platform from which it could launch its promised assault on industrial Europe. Bolshevism's war on industrial Europe combined with the socio-political dislocation generated by the outcomes of the First World War served as wonderful growth food for political policing systems. The prime minister of Italy, for instance, wrote that in Italy 'no government, from the most conservative to the most extreme, can maintain itself without a [political] police force which is reliable and efficient'.[13]

During this era political policing focused most closely on the 'Red Menace'. As the dust from the Russian Civil War settled only the dark side of Russia remained in the western mind. Russia's image in the non-Soviet European world became identified with the despotism which Lenin and his minions wished insidiously to spread across Europe. The greatest boost then to the remarkably rapid growth of political policing in the short twentieth century was the October Revolution and its aftermath between 1917 and 1989.[14] Both in theory and practice the definition of political crime 'had expanded unimaginably since 1917'.[15] One scholar argues that the creation of Interpol in 1923 resulted from the desire of the participating nations' principally to maintain order and safety in western Europe in the face of the Soviet sponsored Communist threat.[16]

This is not the place to review the unfortunate history of Interpol to the outbreak of the Second World War or its re-establishment after the war concluded. Suffice it to say that Interpol proved itself to be an ineffective weapon against the war on terrorism.[17]

At the end of June 1978 the ministers of internal affairs of the European Council, meeting in Luxembourg, adopted a resolution to establish study groups to review the various obstacles confronting the creation of a uniform front against the terrorist violence spreading across Europe like wildfire in 1976 and 1977. These study groups were attached to a new organisation called TREVI named after the famous Roman fountain. One author claims that the combined effort of the West's forces of order under TREVI's auspices had 'borne fruit particularly in connection with terrorism and other forms of extremism'.[18] The European Community took a further step in tackling terrorism by signing the European Convention for Terrorist Control in 1977. This agreement dealt with the problem of cross border surveillance, a perpetual bugbear that touched on the sensitive issue of national sovereignty.[19]

The comments of experts over succeeding years show clearly that international police co-operation remained at best partially successful. In 1987 the Dutch hosted an International Symposium on surveillance; the purpose of the symposium, said one of the hosts, was to upgrade the standards of surveillance operations and to reinforce, nationally and internationally, the contacts in the field.[20] Several days later he concluded the meeting with a statement that leaves the historian both frustrated and disappointed. He claimed that the symposium was 'unique' offering the following reasons:

1. The subject is a sensitive one within Europe, especially in this day and age, where the police in almost every European country have to fight terrorism.
2. The participation in the Symposium of such a large number of countries.
3. The free and frank manner in which subjects were discussed, without any reservations, without being 'covert', to use one of the key words of the symposium.
4. The subjects that were dealt with: international aspects of counter terrorism 'in the first place', the legal pitfalls of international police co-operation, the joint application of applied technology and the practice of surveillance.[21]

The content of this symposium was hardly 'unique'. It was reminiscent of both the Rome and St Petersburg conferences more than 80 years before.

And what did this symposium achieve? Since much that goes in the world of counter-terrorism remains out of public sight it is difficult to know. Comments by specialists made in the 1990s, however, are not encouraging. The original wrangling concerning the basis upon which police co-operation should proceed persists. Most telling of all as one expert wrote:

> [I]f for pressing reasons of security it is considered necessary to co-operate internationally, the co-operation will be organised in secret or through informal channels.
>
> The major political governmental and legal differences between the EC countries will neither be overcome easily nor within . . . a short span of time. Not only are these differences too large in themselves, but also both the active and passive opposition to their elimination is too substantial to be ignored.[22]

In January of this year the United States Institute of Peace issued a Special Report entitled 'The Diplomacy of Counterterrorism: Lessons Learned, Ignored, and Disputed'. The Report is based upon a meeting of the International Research Group on Political Violence (IRGPV) held at the home of the Institute of Peace in Washington DC. The Report, although originally drafted before 11 September, was subsequently revised to reflect the events of that day.

Several points strike the reader familiar with the early history of modern international terrorism: firstly, the surprisingly inadequate historical context of the Report which treats international terrorism as a post-Second World War phenomenon; secondly, the Report reveals – as did the International Symposium on Surveillance 14 years earlier – how little has been achieved since Russia started pushing for the development of an international anti-terrorist campaign in the late 1870s.

Terrorism had appeared to threaten the survival of the Romanov Dynasty far more than it did the regimes of Europe. But what is important is that the *perception* of the threat was as great within Italy, Germany and France during different periods within the framework of this book as it was in Russia, especially prior to the 1905 Revolution. The Special Report recommends that states under attack avoid 'a crisis mentality that is ultimately satisfying to terrorists'.[23] So far this has proved impossible. It is indeed that mentality that unites Europe and the United States now as it did at the turn of the twentieth century.

The Special Report also firmly distinguishes between the criminal act and the cause in whose name it was committed. The crucial passage in the Report proclaims:

> Law enforcement, with its focus on the illegal act itself, removes the temptation to try to judge between just and unjust motivations, legitimate

> and illegitimate concessions, worthy and unworthy political causes: there can be no progress toward social justice by *any* [italics in the original] definition in an atmosphere of violence or insecurity.[24]

Of all the European states Tsardom fought against the forces of modernity with the greatest energy. 'Social justice' was anathema to those few tsarist officials who understood the meaning of the phrase. Yet, in the end, the outlook that tsarist officials strove to impress upon the remainder of Europe *vis-à-vis* terrorism is virtually identical to that of the Special Report: terrorism is a criminal act which should be punished without reference to 'just and unjust motivations'.

While the Russians' motivations for an 'anti-anarchist pact' could hardly have been more self-serving and, as we have seen, were coloured in part by nefarious aims in relation to the revolutionary emigration as a whole, Tsardom was right to seek an international alliance against terrorism and it eventually received a serious hearing within the European community.

According to the evidence supplied through its 'Special Report' by the United States Institute of Peace the strategies for combating terrorism today are virtually unchanged – although enhanced by modern technology – from those proposed at the Rome Conference, the St Petersburg Conference and by the Russians, again, in bilateral negotiations, for example, with the Germans in 1907. These are:

> To enhance international and bilateral co-operation with other states, particularly in areas such as intelligence, public diplomacy, and anti-terrorism measures; control of borders; and developing law enforcement techniques and counter terrorist training.[25]

Clearly, 11 September was the tragic result of a sporadically implemented and poorly co-ordinated international counter terrorist campaign that works best (when it works at all) in response to acts of terrorism. It still operates, as it has for more than a century, through informal *ad hoc* and fragile arrangements. As a result, prevention of acts of terrorism through the methods of international policing remains an ambitious and probably distant goal.

The demise of the Eastern Bloc and the collapse of the USSR has reunited Europe. Russia today, as never before, is an integral part of Europe, a new far more mature and sophisticated Europe. Its role in international policing as in so many other areas of European life should again be welcomed.

Unfortunately western attitudes toward Russia have remained remarkably consistent with those of the pre-Bolshevik era. It appears that European (and of course American) statesmen remain leery of dealing with the present-day Russia. Although Russia should undoubtedly be integrated into the new campaign to establish international police co-operation, along the lines suggested most recently in the Special Report of the United States Institute of Peace, Russia remained until recently – except perhaps for covert activities – on the periphery of Europe. Its inclusion as a non-voting 'observer' at NATO, however, may be the start of a truly united Europe. But this will only occur if the 'western world' ceases to consider the new Russia, as it did the old, something different, something unknowable, something suspicious.

Appendix A.1: The Foreign Agentura's Undercover Agents – Personal Data

Name	Age upon entering the F.A.	Former occupation	Military		Service unknown	Single	Married	Children
			Yes	No				
J. Aebersold	36 (1911)	Valet		X			X	
C. Aubert	23 (1903)	Civil Servant	X				X	X (2)
A. Barthes	33 (1911)	Employee of Tramways	X				X	X (2)
A. Berthold	33 (1911)	Hotelier	X				X	X (2)
H. Bint	28 (1880)	Inspector of Police			X		X	
M. Bittard-Monin	35 (1908)	Prefect of Police	X				X	X (1)
L. Capusso	37 (1912)	Student of Medicine		X			X	
R. Cazayus	26 (1913)	Inspector of Police	X			X		
C. Charlet	23 (1913)	Foreign Language Student	X			X		
E. David	28 (1911)	Agent of the Sûreté Générale	X			X		
C. Delangle	28 (1912)	Wood Engraver	X				X	
J. Decluseaux	29 (1910)	—	X				X	
B. Drouchet	34 (1911)	—		X (woman)		—	—	
J. H. Durin	40 (1907)	Chief of Sûreté – Versailles	X				X	X (2)
G. Dusseaussois	42 (1912)	Director of Police – Reims	X				X	
L. Feuger	32 (1912)	—	X				X	X (2)
L. Fontana	32 (1911)	Journalist	X				X	X (1)
A. Frumento	37 (1912)	Commerce			X	—	—	
G. Godard	29 (1912)	Grocer	X				X	

Appendix A.1 *(Continued)*

Name	Age upon entering the F.A.	Former occupation	Military		Service unknown	Single	Married	Children
			Yes	No				
R. Gottlieb	33 (1912)	Representative (?)	X				X	
P. Hamard ('Fontaine')	26 (1909)	Bookkeeper	X				X	X (1)
M. Halpen	—	Prefect of Police	X			—	—	
E. Hennequin	23 (1910)	Cashier-Bookkeeper	X			X		
C. Henry	45 (1912)	Landscape Gardener	X				X	X (2)
E. Invernizzi	32 (1907) Nov. 1899–July 1905 was in the service of Manuilov	Without Profession	X				X	
G. Jollivet	39 (1911)	Inspector of Investigation of the Sûreté	X				X	
A. Kerr	50 (1912)	—		X			X	X (2)
B. Laurent	27 (1912)	Commerce	X			X		
E. Lecointe	41 (1909)	Inspector of the Sûreté	X				X	X (2)
F. Leone	—	Journalist		X		X		
E. Leveque	50 (1902)	Inspector of Police	X				X	
A. Lodie	—	—			X	—	—	
Leon Otte	58 (1910)	Detective	X				X	X (1)
H. Neuhaus	34 (1901)	Agent of the Berlin Police	X				X	X (2)
F. Pavesi	33 (1912)	Maitre d'hotel		X		—	—	
A. Pouchet	29 (1910)	Inspector of Police	X				X	X (1)
F. Powell	51 (1912)	Inspector of Police – Scotland Yard		X			X	X (6)
E. Riant	32 (1881)	Inspector of Police	X			—	—	
G. Richard	35 (1911)	None		X (woman)			X	X (1)

Appendix A.1 (*Continued*)

Name	Age upon entering the F.A.	Former occupation	Military		Service unknown	Single	Married	Children
			Yes	No				
G. Rime	24 (1911)	Artist	X				X	X (1)
L. Riot	32 (1912)	Schoolmaster	X				X	
J. Robail	23 (1909)	Commerce	X				X	X (1)
A. Roselli	23 (1912)	Train Conductor	X			—	—	
F. Rougeaux	45 (1912)	—	X				X	X (1)
A. Sambian	38 (1901)	Warrant Officer	X			X		
A. Sauvard	27 (1910)	—	X				X	
E. Schmidelin	34 (1909)	Military	X			X		
E. Tarisson	32 (1908)	Warrant Officer	X				X	X (1)
R. Thomas	25 (1908)	Bookkeeper	X			X		
M. Thorpe	49 (1901)	—		X			X	X (1)
M. Tiercelin	37 (1911)	—		X (woman)		—	—	
V. Vizardelli	31 (1912)	Agent of the Monaco Sûreté			X	—	—	
M. Vogt	39 (1908)	Commerce	X				X	X (1)
C. Woltz	26 (1901)	Agent of Berlin Sûreté	X				X	X (2)

Appendix A.2: The Foreign Agentura's Undercover Agents – Professional Information

Name	Recommended for service by	Languages known (in addition to French)	Salary per month (in francs)
Jean Aebersold	H. Bint	English, German	250
Henri Bint	*ancien agent**	None	800
M. Bittard-Monin	—	None	1000
Aime Barthes	Prefect of Police	None	250
Marius Bonoil	*Sûreté Générale*	None	250
Armand Berthold	Prefect of Police	None	250
R. Cazayus	*Sûreté Générale*	Spanish	250
C. Charlet	*Sûreté Générale*	German	250
G. Cousonnet (G. Rime)	Prefect of Police	—	250
Etienne David	Maurice Vogt	Italian	250
C. Delangle	H. Bint	None	250
B. Drouchet	*Sûreté Générale*	None	250
H. Durin	Prefect of Police	None	300
G. Dusseaussois	*Sûreté Générale*	Spanish	250
L. Feuger	*Sûreté Générale*	None	250
P. Fontaine (Hamard)	Prefect of Police	None	300
Louis Fontana	*Sûreté Générale*	Italian	250
A. Frumento	Questure de Genes	Spanish, Italian	250
Georges Godard	H. Bint	None	250
Rene Gottlieb	H. Bint	None	250
E. Hennequin	Prefect of Police	German	250
C. Henry	Gravier, Moire de Vitry	Turkish, Armenian Arabic	250
E. Invernizzi	*ancien agent**	Italian	300
G. Jollivet	Prefect of Police	Italian	250
A. Kerr	Scotland Yard	English	300
B. Laurent	Bittard-Monin	None	250
G. Leon	Bittard-Monin	None	250
E. Leveque	*ancien agent**	None	250
A. Lodie	H. Bint	None	250
H. Neuhaus	*ancien agent**	German	300
L. Otte	Bittard-Monon	None	150
F. Pavesi	Questure de Genes	Spanish, Italian	250
A. Pouchet	*Sûreté Générale*	None	250
F. Powell	Scotland Yard	English	410
G. Richard	*Sûreté Générale*	None	200

Name	Recommended for service by	Languages known (in addition to French)	Salary per month (in francs)
L. Riot	Bittard-Monin	None	250
J. Robail	Prefect of Police	None	300
G. Rougaux	Bittard-Monin	English	250
A. Roselli	Delegato Genes	English, Italian	250
A. Sambian	H. Bint	None	400
A. Sauvard	Prefect of Police	None	250
M. Thorpe	*ancien agent**	English	300
J. Tuppinger	Service (Police?)	German	265
M. Tiercelin	Chief of the Bureau of Agriculture	None	200
V. Vizardelli	Delegato de Genes	German, English	250
M. Vogt	—	None	300
K. Wotz	—	German, English	—

* *Ancien agent* – A detective hired before or during the tenure of P. I. Rachkovsky. No other information exists concerning the circumstances of their employment by the Foreign Agentura.

Notes

Preface

1. F. S. Zuckerman, *The Tsarist Secret Police in Russian Society, 1880–1917* (Basingstoke: Macmillan – now Palgrave Macmillan, 1996), 229–33.
2. Two important and otherwise thoroughly researched books will suffice as recent examples of this scholarship: C. Emsley, *Gendarme and the State in Nineteenth-Century Europe* (Oxford: Oxford University Press, 1999); and H. Liang, *The Rise of Modern Police and the European State System from Metternich to the Second World War* (Cambridge: Cambridge University Press, 1992).
3. L. Wolff, *Inventing Eastern Europe: The Map of Civilization on the Mind of the Enlightenment* (Stanford: Stanford University Press, 1994), 11–12, 13.
4. Ibid., 7.
5. N. Davies, *Europe: A History* (London: Random House, 1996 (reprinted with corrections 1997), 35–6.
6. The exception to this posture comes from scholars of Russian studies. The political scientist R. Johnson in his thesis 'The Okhrana Abroad, 1885–1917: A Study of International Police Co-operation' (PhD diss., Columbia University, 1971), aspects of which he later presented in an article that appeared in the *Journal of Contemporary History*. The thesis focused largely on issues of professionalisation, and methods and motives of liaison within an administrative and social theory framework which remove the Foreign Agentura from its historical and chronological context. My own thesis 'The Russian Political Police at Home and Abroad (1880–1917): Its Structure Functions, and Methods and Its Struggle with the Organized Opposition' (PhD diss., New York University, 1973) studies the Foreign Agentura , its evolution, personnel and its operations but within the Russian context of the tsarist political police as a whole.

1 Europe in Turmoil: Protest, Violence and Maintaining Order in a Changing World

1. Both of these quotations are cited in: D. E. Emerson, *Metternich and the Political Police: Security and Subversion in the Hapsburg Monarchy (1815–1830)* (The Hague: Martinus Nijhoff, 1968), 137, 182.
2. For thorough and fascinating discussions offering different perspectives on the evolution of European society from the second half of the nineteenth century to the outbreak of the First World War see: A. J. Mayer, *The Persistence of the Old Regime: Europe to the Great War* (New York: Pantheon Books, 1981) and N. Stone, *Europe Transformed 1878–1919* (Cambridge, Mass.: Harvard University Press, 1984).
3. C. Tilly, *et al., The Rebellious Century, 1830–1930* (London: Dent, 1975), 55. Tilley's time frames are slightly different from mine, because he has not included the waves of Russian strikes which struck periodically beginning in the mid-1890s.
4. M. B. Millard, 'Russian Revolutionary Emigration, Terrorism and the "Political Struggle" ' (PhD diss., University of Rochester, 1973), 57–9.

5. F. S. Zuckerman, *The Tsarist Secret Police in Russian Society, 1880–1917* (Basingstoke: Macmillan – now Palgrave Macmillan, 1996), 84–5, 120, 190–1.
6. M. A. Miller, *Kropotkin* (Chicago: University of Chicago Press, 1976), 173–4; R. B. Jensen, 'The International Anti-Anarchist Conference of 1898 and the Origins of Interpol', *JCH*, **16**, 2, (April 1981): 324–5.
7. B. L. Ingraham, *Political Crime in Europe: A Comparative Study of France, Germany and England* (Berkeley: University of California Press, 1979), 168; H. Liang, *The Rise of Modern Police and the European State System from Metternich to the Second World War* (Cambridge: Cambridge University Press, 1992), 157–8, 168; R. W. Lougee, 'The Anti-Revolution Bill of 1894 in Wilhelmine Germany', *CEH*, **15**, 3, (September 1982); 225; Jensen, 'The International Anti-Anarchist Conference', 324–5.
8. Tilley *et al., The Rebellious Century*, 5, 243.
9. Jensen, 'The International Anti-Anarchist Conference', 174.
10. Ingraham, *Political Crime in Europe*, 13.
11. Ibid., 3, 5, 9.
12. R. Pipes, *Russia Under the Old Regime* (London: Weidenfeld & Nicolson, 1974; Penguin Books, 1977), 293–5.
13. R. Fosdick, *European Police Systems* (New York: The Century Co., 1915), 167; D. Bayley, *Patterns of Policing: A Comparative International Analysis* (New Brunswick, NJ: Rutgers University Press, 1985), 211.
14. Ingraham, *Political Crime in Europe*, 29.
15. Liang, *The Rise of Modern Police*, 36–7.
16. R. B. Jensen, *Liberty and Order: The Theory and Practice of Italian Public Security Policy, 1848 to the Crisis of the 1890s* (New York: Garland Publishing, Inc., 1991), 165–6.
17. Ingraham, *Political Crime in Europe*, 83–4.
18. A. F. Calhoun, 'The Politics of Internal Order: French Government and Revolutionary Labor, 1898–1914' (PhD diss., Princeton University, 1973), 24.
19. Ingraham, *Political Crime in Europe*, 139.
20. J. Galtier-Boissière, *Mysteries of the French Secret Police*, trans. Ronald Leslie-Melville (London: Stanley Paul & Co. Ltd., 1938), 216–17, 228–9.
21. H. C. Payne, *The Police State of Napoleon Bonaparte 1851–1860* (Seattle: University of Washington Press, 1966), 64–5.
22. Ibid., 282; H. C. Payne and Henry Grosshaus, 'The Exiled Revolutionaries and the French Political Police in the 1850s', *AHR*, **68** (1963): 956–7.
23. J. Berlière, 'A Republican Political Police? Policing under the Third Republic', in *The Policing of Politics in the Twentieth Century: Historical Perspectives*, ed. Mark Mazower (Oxford: Berghahn Books, 1997), 2.
24. J. Mayeur and Madeleine Reberioux, *The Third Republic from its Origins to the Great War*, trans. J. R. Foster (Cambridge: Cambridge University Press, 1984), 21, 37–40, 46, 50, 54, 71, 74. Much of the discussion about French society that follows is derived from this work.
25. P. Kropotkin, *Memoirs of a Revolutionist* (London, 1899), 2: 258.
26. Quoted in: Mayeur, *The Third Republic*, 144.
27. Ibid., 144–5.
28. Ibid., 249–50.
29. Calhoun, 'The Politics of Internal Order', 213; Mayeur, *The Third Republic*, 223, 246, 255.
30. Mayeur, *The Third Republic*, 264–5.
31. Ibid., 268, 320, 327.
32. Calhoun, 'The Politics of Internal Order', 33–4.

33. J. Berlière, *Le Préfet Lépine: Vers La Naissance de la Police Moderne,* (Paris: Editions de Noël, 1993) 8, 108.
34. Ibid., 21.
35. J. Berliére, *Le Monde de polices en France XIXe–XXe siècles* (Paris, 1996), 149.
36. Ibid., 158; Calhoun, 'The Politics of Internal Order', 68–9; Galtier-Boissière, *Mysteries of the French Secret Police,* 245–6.
37. The methods pursued by Puibaraud are discussed in Berlière, *Le Monde des Polices,* 145–59: and more briefly in Berlière, 'A Republican Political Police?', 40–2.
38. Ibid., 21; Brian Chapman, *Police State* (London: Pall Mall Ltd., 1970), 87–8; Richard Bach Jensen, *Liberty and Order: The Theory and Practice of Italian Public Security Policy,* 215–16, citation 17.
39. Calhoun, 'The Politics of Internal Order', 69.
40. Ibid., 68–9.
41. Ibid., 114–16, 158; Berlière, 'The Professionalisation of the Police Under the Third Republic, 1875–1914', in *Policing Western Europe: Politics, Professionalism and Public Order, 1850–1940,* eds C. Emsely and B. Weinberger (Westport Conn.: Greenwood Press, 1991), 36, 42–5, P. J. Stead, *The Police of France* (New York: Macmillan Inc., 1983), 60.
42. Calhoun, 'The Politics of Internal Order', 55.
43. Fosdick, *European Police Systems,* 4.
44. Berlière, *Le Préfet Lépine,* 191; Berlière, 'A Republican Political Police', 123–4; Calhoun, 'The Politics of Internal Order', 45, 46, 145–6.
45. Well into the first decade of the twentieth century the *Sûreté* remained understaffed, poorly organised and little more than a vehicle for communicating the government's orders to the countryside. Only in 1907 with the appointment of Claude Hennion, a professional policemen who came up through the ranks as chief of the *Sûreté* did serious reform begin to take place. Even so, the *Sûreté* remained poorly funded and understaffed. As a result, the best of reforms fell far short of Hennion's goals. Berlière, *Le Monde des polices,* 143–5, 150; Berlière, *Le Préfet Lépine,* 24–5; Berlière, 'A Republican Police?' 36–7; C. Emsley, 'Introduction: Political Police and the Nation-State', in *The Policing of Politics in the Twentieth Century,* 17–18; Mayeur, *The Third Republic,* 338. For a succinct description of the structure of the French police system in the Third Republic in English see: J. Berlière, 'The Professionalisation of the Police Under the Third Republic, 1875–1914', in *Policing Western Europe, Professionalism, and Public Order, 1850–1940,* 33–4, 36–9.
46. For example, see the works by Berlière, Calhoun, Ingraham, and Stead cited in this chapter. Of course one should not become too sanguine about this point. Calhoun, 'The Politics of Internal Order', 141–4.
47. Ingraham, *Political Crime In Europe,* 184.
48. J. A. Davis, *Conflict and Control: Law and Order in Nineteenth Century Italy* (Basingstoke: Macmillan – now Palgrave Macmillan, 1988), 314–16, 336.
49. Tilly *et al., The Rebellious Century,* 96–7, 116–17, 143–6.
50. Davis, *Conflict and Control,* 223; Jensen, *Liberty and Order,* 23.
51. Ibid., 214.
52. Ibid., 4–5.
53. Jensen, *Liberty and Order,* 125.
54. Ibid., 86.
55. Ibid., 2–4, 86–7, 90, 157–8,177, 182; Davis, *Conflict and Control,* 343; R. O. Collin, 'The Italian Police and Internal Security from Giolitti to Mussolini', (D. Phil., Oriel College, Trinity, 1983), 29–30.

56. Davis, *Conflict and Control*, 350–1.
57. For a succinct discussion of the Carbonari see: C. Emsley, *Gendarmes and the State in Nineteenth Century Europe* (Oxford University Press, 1999), Chapter 13.
58. Unfortunately, General Pelloux, Rudini's successor, dismantled a portion of these reforms. Jensen, *Liberty and Order*, 5–6, 94, 146–8; Davis, *Conflict and Control*, 350–1.
59. Ibid., 344–5; 356–7; Tilly, *Rebellious Century*, 104–05.
60. R. B. Jensen, 'Police Reform and Social Reform: Italy from the Crisis of the 1890s to the Giolittian Era', *CJH*, **10** (1989): 194–5; D. Snyder and W. Kelly, 'Industrial Violence in Italy, 1878–1903', *AJS*, **82** (July 1976): 139.
61. Jensen, *Liberty and Order*, 177; Jensen, 'Police Reform and Social Reform', 183, 193.
62. Jensen, *Liberty and Order*, 176.
63. Collin, 'The Italian Police', 24, 31, 52–3, 60.
64. For a through and elegant discussion of this subject see: M. Raeff, *The Well-Ordered Police State: Social and Institutional Change through Law in the Germanies and Russia 1600–1800* (New Haven: Yale University Press, 1983).
65. A. Lüdtke, *Police and State in Prussia, 1815–1850*, trans. Peter Burgess (Cambridge: Cambridge University Press, 1989), 70.
66. If the police to population ratio was bad in Prussia in most other German states it can only be described as appalling. Tilly *et al.*, *The Rebellious Century*, 218–20.
67. Lüdtke, *Police and State in Prussia*, 100, 192.
68. E. G. Spencer, *Police and the Social Order in German Cities: The Düsseldorf District, 1848–1914* (DeKalb Illinois: Northern Illinois University Press, 1992), 38–9.
69. Lüdtke, *Police and State in Prussia*, 130–1.
70. Ibid., 125.
71. Chapman, *Police State*, 48; Fosdick, *European Police Systems*, 78–9.
72. Spencer, *Police and the Social Order*, 76.
73. Tilley *et al.*, *The Rebellious Century*, 204; Spencer, *Police and the Social Order*, 53, 66, 80; K. S. Pinson, *Modern Germany: Its History and Civilization*, 2nd edn (London: Collier-Macmillan, 1966), 210–11.
74. R. W. Lougee, 'The Anti-Revolution Bill of 1894 in Wilhelmine Germany', 226–8, 239–40; Spencer, *Police and the Social Order*, 87–8, 127–8.
75. Quoted in: Lüdtke, *Police and State in Prussia*, 102.
76. Spencer, *Police and the Social Order*, 127–8, 146, 161.
77. Tilly *et al.*, *A Century of Rebellion*, 198–9, 204.
78. Ingraham, *Political Crime in Europe*, 120, 199.
79. Quoted in: P. T. Smith, *Policing Victorian London: Political Policing Public Order and the London Metropolitan Police* (Westport Conn.: Greenwood Press, 1985), 55.
80. Fosdick, *European Police Systems*, 308.
81. C. Andrew, *Her Majesty's Secret Service: the Making of the British Intelligence Community* (New York: Viking, 1986), 15.
82. B. Porter, *The Origins of the Vigilant State: The London Metropolitan Police Special Branch before the First World War* (London: Weidenfeld & Nicolson, 1987), 13.
83. B. Porter, *Plots and Paranoia: A History of Political Espionage in Britain, 1790–1988*, (London: Unwin Hyman, 1989), 99; Andrew, *Her Majesty's Secret Service*, 16–17.
84. Ingraham, *Political Crime in Europe*, 115–16, 209.
85. Porter, *The Origins of the Vigilant State*, 34, 51; Smith, *Policing Victorian London*, 77.
86. Porter, *The Origins of the Vigilant State*, 110–11, 151–2.
87. Bernard Porter, 'The British Government and Political Refugees, *c.* 1880–1914', in *From the Other Shore: Political Emigrants in Britain*, ed. John Slatter (London: Frank Cass, 1984), 24.

88. Andrew, *Her Majesty's Secret Service*, 19; Porter, *The Origins of the Vigilant State*, 135: Porter, 'The British Government and Political Refugees', 33; H. Brust, *I Guarded Kings: The Memoirs of a Political Police Officer* (London: Stanley Paul & Co, n.d), 35, 64.
89. A. Lansdowne, *A Life's Reminiscences of Scotland Yard* (London: Leadenhall Press, 1890) (reprinted, Garland Publishing, New York, 1984, *passim*); Smith, *Policing Victorian London*, 77; Fosdick, *European Police Systems*, 227.
90. Brust, *I Guarded Kings*, 66.
91. G. Dilnot, *The Story of Scotland Yard* (London: n.d.), 123; Porter, *The Origins of the Vigilant State*, 133, 176
92. Porter, *Plots and Paranoia*, 135.
93. Berlière, *Les mondes des polices*, 132.
94. Berlière, 'A Republican Poltical Police?', 29.
95. Lüdtke, *Police and State in Prussia*, xvii; Ingraham, *Political Crime in Europe*, 164–5, 169; Kirchheimer, *Political Justice: The Use of Legal Procedures for Political Ends* (Princeton: Princeton University Press, 1961), 36.

2 Émigré Lives: the Russian Revolutionary Abroad

1. Quoted in: J. M. Meijer, *Knowledge and Revolution: the Russian Colony in Zuerich* (Assen: Van Gorcum & Co., 1965), 112.
2. H. Speier, 'The Social Conditions of the Intellectual Exile', in *Social Order and the Risk of War: papers in political sociology* (Cambridge Mass.: MIT Press, 1952), 87.
3. Aron Liberman's story can be found in: W. Fishman, *East End Jewish Radicals 1875–1914* (London: Duckworth, 1975), 97–8, 102–3, 121, 126–30; P. Pomper, *Peter Lavrov and the Russian Revolutionary Movement* (Chicago: University of Chicago Press, 1972), 174–5.
4. The Association and its conflict with Plekhanov and the *Iskra* group is discussed in: F. Ortmann, *Revolutionäre im Exil: Der 'Auslandund Russischer Sozialdemokraten' Zwiachen Autoritärem Führungsanspruck und Politischer Ohnmacht (1888–1903)* (Stuttgart: Franz Steiner Verlag 1994), 68–70, 83, 119, 127–9, 138, 141–60, 213, 217–19; J. L. H. Keep, *The Rise of Russian Social Democracy in Russia* (Oxford: Clarendon Press, 1963), 54–66; Robert C. Williams, *Culture in Exile: Russian Emigrés in Germany, 1881–1941* (Ithaca: Cornell University Press, 1972), 28–9.
5. R. H Johnson, *New Mecca, New Babylon: Paris and the Russian Exiles 1920–1945* (Kingston Montreal: McGill-Queen's University Press, 1988), 7–8; R. Johnson, 'The Okhrana Abroad: A Study of International Police Cooperation' (Phd diss., Columbia University, 1971), 4–5; Martin A. Miller, *The Russian Revolutionary Emigrés, 1825–1870* (Baltimore: The Johns Hopkins Press, 1986), 7–9, 224.
6. Dispatch no. 660 , Paris, 12/25 May 1911, FAAr, 194, XVIb (7), 2; Dispatch no. 419, Paris, 13/26 March 1913, FAAr, 194, XVIb (7), 4; Ortmann, *Revolutionäre im Exile*, 51.
7. J. W. Daly, *Autocracy under Siege: Security Police and Opposition in Russia 1860–1905* (DeKalb Illinois: Northern Illinois University Press, 1998), 45; Ortmann, *Revolutionäre im Exil*, 47; Miller, *The Russian Revolutionary Emigrés*, 207, 211; V. K. Agafonov, *Zagranichnaia okhranka* (St Petersburg: 1918), 45: A. P. Koznov, 'Zagranichnaia politicheskii sysk (1900-fevral' 1917 gg.)', *Kentavr*, 1992, nos. 1–2: 96.
8. V. V. Obolenskii, *Mezhdunarodnye i mezhkontinental'nye migratsii v dovoennoi Rossii i SSSR* (Moscow: 1928), 5; M. B. Millard, 'Russian Revolutionary Emigration, Terrorism and the "Political Struggle"' (PhD diss., University of Rochester, 1973), 10.

9. Ibid., 86–7.
10. A. Tamborra, *Esuli Russi in Italia Dal 1905 al 1917* (Rome: 1977), 35–6.
11. E. A. Taratuta, *S. M. Stepniak-Kravchinskii revoliutsioner i pisatel'* (Moscow 1973), 200.
12. Ortmann, *Revolutionäre im Exile*, 90.
13. Ibid., 47.
14. Meijer, *Knowledge and Revolution: The Russian Colony in Zuerich*, 60, 132.
15. Quoted in: Ibid., 142.
16. Ibid., 1–2, 47, 60–1, 142, 145, 147, 163; A. Senn, *The Russian Revolution in Switzerland, 1914–1917* (Madison: University of Wisconsin Press, 1971), 8.
17. Ibid., 3–4.
18. H. Liang, *The Rise of the Modern Police and the European State System from Metternich to the Second World War* (Cambridge: Cambridge University Press, 1992), 132.
19. Taratuta, *S. M. Stepniak-Kravchinskii revoliutsioner*, 203.
20. The terrorist-oriented populist movement was responsible for the assassination.
21. *Pis'ma Azefa, 1893–1917*, comp. D. B. Pavlov and Z. I. Peregudova (Moscow: 1994), 85; B. Savinkov, *Memoirs of a Terrorist*, trans. J. Shaplen (New York: Albert & Charles Boni, 1931), 10–11; Senn, *The Russian Revolutionary Movement in Switzerland*, 3.
22. Liang, *The Rise of the Modern Police*, 131, 177; Senn, *The Russian Revolutionary Emigration in Switzerland*, 4–6.
23. Savinkov, *Memoirs*, 10–11; 'Pis'ma Azefa', 85.
24. Ibid., 5.
25. Report of Rachkovskii to the Department of Police 20/July/2August 1901, in L. Menshchikov, *Russkii politicheskii sysk za granitsei* (Paris: 1914), 129–30, 141.
26. Harting to the Department of Police, January 1906, FAAr, 34, Va, 1.
27. Krasil'nikov to the Department of Police, Report on the Zürich émigré colony, 1910, FAAr, 191, XVIb (3), 4.
28. Williams, *Culture in Exile*, 9, 25.
29. Miller, *The Russian Revolutionary Emigration*, 113; Williams, *Culture in Exile*, 16–17.
30. Ibid., 24–5.
31. B. Brachmann, *Russische Sozialdemokraten In Berlin 1895–1914* (Berlin: Akademie Verlag, 1962), 7.
32. Rachkovskii to the Department of Police 14/27 September 1900 in: Menshchikov, *Russkii politicheskii sysk*, 72.
33. Brachmann, *Russische Sozialdemokraten In Berlin*, 40–8, 53.
34. Ibid., 40–8, 56–9.
35. Dispatch no. 47, Paris, 1912, FAAr, 191, XVIb(3), 5c.
36. Dispatch no. 637, Paris, 1912, FAAr, 194, XVIb(7), 4.
37. Williams, *Culture in Exile*, 29.
38. Report on Socialist-Revolutionary Activities and Leaders in Munich, 1909 (?), FAAr, 191, XVIb(3), 5e.
39. Dispatch no. 39, Paris, 12/25 January 1910, Paris, FAAr, 191, XVIb(3), 5e.
40. Dispatch no. 164, Paris, 31 January/13 February 1911, FAAr, 194, XVIb(7), 4; Dispatch no. 154, Paris, 194, XVIb(7), 4.
41. Brachmann, *Russische Sozialdemokraten In Berlin*, 79.
42. Ibid., 40, 134.
43. Ibid., 171; R. B. Spence, *Boris Savinkov: Renegade on the Left* (Boulder, Colorado: East European Monographs, 1991), 17.
44. Obolenskii, *Mezhdunarodnye i mezhkontinental'nye migratsii*, 17.
45. Williams, *Culture in Exile*, 33–4, 45, 49.
46. Brachmann, *Russische Sozialdemokraten In Berlin*, 81, 148.

47. Dispatch no. 381, Paris, 1907, FAAr, 194, XVIb (4).
48. Dispatch no. 27, 19 August 1907, FAAr, 194, XVIb(4).
49. Ibid.
50. Brachmann, *Russische Sozialdemokratren In Berlin*, 72–9; Williams, *Culture in Exile*, 50–1.
51. Ibid., 88–9; Williams, *Culture in Exile*, 51.
52. The Swiss, now becoming inundated with foreigners, suffered from a sense of being overwhelmed by outsiders and this fear made them less welcoming and somewhat xenophobic. See: Senn, *Revolutionaries in Exile*, 4.
53. Dispatch no. 422, Paris, 6/19 November 1908, FAAr, 196, XVId, 1.
54. Savinkov, *Memoirs*, 76; 'Les refugiés revolutionnaire russes a Paris', *Cahiers du monde russe et sovietique*, 6 (July–September 1965): 433–4.
55. I. Maisky, *Journey into the Past*, trans. F. Holt (London: Hutcheson & Co., 1962), 45.
56. B. L. Ingraham, *Political Crime in Europe: A Comparative Study of France, Germany and England* (Berkeley: University of California Press, 1979), 204–5.
57. I. V. Orzhekhovskii, *Samoderzhavie protiv Revoliutsionnoi Rossii* (Moscow: 1982), 116; Kropotkin, *Memoirs*, 183.
58. P. T. Smith, *Policing Victorian London: Political Policing, Public Order and the London Metropolitan Police* (Westport Conn.: Greenwood Press, 1985), 81.
59. Fishman, *East End Jewish Radicals*, 31, 135.
60. The terrible living conditions in Whitechapel are described in: J. White, *Rothschild Buildings: Life in an East End Tenement Block, 1887–1920* (London: Routledge & Kegan Paul, 1980), 16, 63.
61. Other prominent SDs such as Vera Zasulich and Maxim Litvinov also resided in England for periods of time without leaving an impression. Keep, *The Rise of Social Democracy*, 69; Maisky, *Journey into the Past*, 57.
62. Taratuta, *S. M. Stepniak-Kravchinskii revoliutsioner*, 326–7, 332, 335, 340, 420.
63. Kropotkin, *Memoirs*, 310–11.
64. Miller, *Kropotkin*, 166.
65. Taratuta, *S. M. Stepniank-Kravchinskii revoliutsioner*, 428. For a discussion of Rachkovskii's activities in England see Chapter 7 herein.
66. We mostly have available to us only glimpses of the relationship between the English police institutions and their Russian colleagues. The only reliable record of this relationship comes from Russian police archives as we will see later on in this book.
67. The attitude of CID and Special Branch officers toward political émigrés varied from officer to officer. See: E. T. Woodhall, *Detective and Secret Service Days* (London: nd), 56; B. Porter, 'The British Government and Political Refugees, *c.* 1880–1914', in *From the Other Shore: Russian Political Emigrants in Britain*, ed. John Slatter (London: Frank Cass, 1984), 37; H. Brust, *I Guarded Kings, The Memoirs of a Political Police Officer* (London, n.d.), 66–7; Johnson, 'The Okhrana Abroad', 71.
68. Maisky, *Journey into the Past*, 16.
69. Brust, *I Guarded Kings*, 35.
70. Porter, 'The British Government and Political Refugees', 34, 36.
71. Ibid., 25–7.
72. To understand just how short a step this is see: F. S. Zuckerman, *The Tsarist Secret Police in Russian Society, 1880–1917* (Basingstoke: Macmillan – now Palgrave Macmillan, 1996), Chapter 4.
73. Porter, 'The British Government and Political Refugees', 36–7.

74. For a sample of some of the material on Burtsev's life in England, including his imprisonment, see: A. Kimball, 'The Harassment of Russian Revolutionaries Abroad: The London Trial of Vladimir Burtsev in 1898', in *Oxford Slavonic Papers*, ns, Vol. 6, eds R. Auty and J. L. Fennell (New York: Oxford University Press, 1973), 48–9; D. Senese, *S. M. Stepniak-Kravchinskii: The London Years*, Russian Biography Series 33 (Newtonville, Mass.: Oriental Research Partners, 1987), 101–3; V. Burtsev, *Bor'ba za svobodnuiu Rossiiu: Moi vospominaniia (1882–1912 gg.)* (Berlin: 1923).
75. Senese, *S. M. Stepniak-Kravchinskii*, 64–5.
76. Miller, Kropotkin, 206, 230.
77. Fishman, *East End Jewish Radicals*, 262–4, 268–9. It seems that Russian émigrés and their immigrant disciples made their most lasting contribution to British, not Russian, Socialism.
78. Quoted in: Miller, *Kropotkin*, 169.
79. Maisky, *Journey into the Past*, 48.
80. Ibid.
81. Quoted in Miller, *Kropotkin*, 169.
82. 'Les refugiés revolutionnaire russes', *passim*.
83. Johnson, *New Mecca, New Babylon*, 18.
84. 'Les refugiés revolutionnaires russes', 429.
85. Liang, *The Rise of the Modern Police*, 121. At the level of policeman to policeman the connection between the Russian Third Section and Prefect of Police in Paris in the early 1880s was quite strong. As we shall see in Chapters 3 and 4, however, this co-operation was far more limited at the ministerial level. Orzhekovskii, *Samoderzhavie protiv Revoliutsionnoi Rossii* (Moscow: 1982), 178–9.
86. Liang, *The Rise of the Modern Police*, 181.
87. Ibid., 420.
88. Johnson, 'The Okhrana Abroad', 116; M. A. Miller, *Kropotkin* (Chicago: University of Chicago Press, 1978), 306.
89. For example see: Report on the Socialist Revolutionary Movement (in French) prepared by the *Sûreté*, 6 December 1912, FAAr, 191, XVIb(3), 4; and 'Les refugiés revolutionnaire russes', 434–5.
90. For example: MVD, Department of Police, Circular no. 104193, issued by the Special Section, 17 September 1913, FAAr, 196, XVId, 1; 'Les refugiérs revolutionnaires russes', 423, 427; Maisky, *Journey into the Past*, 46–7.
91. Obolenskii, *Mezhdunarodnye i Mezhkontinental'nye*, 17.
92. Arthur Fryar Calhoun, 'The Politics of Internal Order: French Government and Revolutionary Labor, 1898–1914', (PhD diss., Princeton University, 1973), 68.
93. Allison Blakely, 'The Socialist Revolutionary Party 1901–1907: the Populist Response to the Industrialization of Russia', (PhD diss., University of California, Berkeley, 1971), 238.
94. 'Les refugiés revoluionnaire russes', 429; Johnson, *New Mecca, New Babylon*, 27.
95. MVD, Department of Police Circular no. 104193, issued by the Special Section, 17 September 1913, FAAr, 196, XVId, 1.
96. Tamborra, *Esuli Russi in Italia Dal 1905*, 3–5, 8–10, 59, 123–8.
97. Ibid., 3–4.
98. E. Koliari, 'Russkaia tainaia politsiia v Italii', *Byloe*, ns, 1924, no. 25: 131–2.
99. Tamborra, *Esuli Russi in Italia*, 49.
100. E. Koliari 'Russkaia tainaia politsiia', 56–60.
101. Tamborra, *Esuli Russi in Italia*, 6, 10, 29, 180–99.

102. Memo from the field (in French) to the Foreign Agentura's Chief of Detectives Marcel Bittard-Monin, 8 August 1911, FAAr, 14, IIIe, 8; Copy of a circular issued by the Chief of the St Petersburg OO in the name of the Director of the Department of Police no. 224, from 24 June 1912, FAAr, 191, 1, XVIb(3); Johnson, 'Okhrana Abroad', 49–50; Koliari, 'Russkaia tainaia politsiia', 150.
103. Report (in French) from Detective Daguerre to Bittard-Monin, 16 August 1911, FAAr, 14, IIIe, 8. For evidence of the intense level of this surveillance see FAAr, IIIe, 8 generally.
104. Tamborra, *Esuli Russi in Italia*, 50–1.
105. Invernizzi's story is derived from: Koliari, 'Russkaia tainaia politsiia', 131–45; Note à Service Genoa, 23 June 1913, FAAr, 14, IIIe, 10.
106. Tamborra, *Esuli Russi in Italia*, 56.
107. Ibid., 36, Chapter 14 *passim*.
108. Ibid., 85.
109. Ibid., 12–14, 30.
110. MVD, Department of Police Circular no. 133289, issued by the Special Section, FAAr, 158, XIIId(1), 10.
111. See: Chapter 4 and 8 herein; Koznov, 'Zagranichnaia politicheskii sysk', 100, note 21; Miller, *The Revolutionary Emigrés*, 207; Tamborra, *Esuli Russi in Italia*, 12–14, 35–6, 140–51; MVD, Department of the Police, Circular no. 133289, issued by the Special Section, 12 July 1909, FAAr, XIIId(1), 10.
112. Tamborra, *Esuli Russi in Italia*, 140–51.
113. Dispatch no. 258, Paris, 21 February/6 March 1911, FAAr, 191, XVIb(3), 1; Tamborra, *Esuli Russi in Italia*, 151.
114. Ibid., 22, 29; MVD, Department of Police, Circulart no. 133289, issued by the Special Section, 12 July 1909, FAAr, 158, XIIId(1), 10; A. T. Vasilyev, *The Ochrana: The Russian Secret Police*, trans. René Fülop-Miller (Philadelphia: J. P. Lipincott, 1930), 182.
115. S. H. Baron, *Plekhanov: The Father of Russian Marxism* (Stanford: Stanford University Press, 1963), 321.
116. Quoted in: Tamborra, *Esuli Russi in Italia*, 221.

3 Brothers in Arms? The Beginnings of International Police Co-operation and the Russian Revolutionary Emigration

1. J. Berlière, *Le Préfet Lépine: Vers La Naissance de la Police Moderne* (Paris: Editions Denoël, 1993), 59.
2. A contemporary discussion of the nature of extradition practice in Europe is to be found in: J. Westlake, *International Law, Part One: Peace* (Cambridge: Cambridge University Press, 1904), 210.
3. M. B. Millard, 'Russian Revolutionary Emigration, Terrorism and the "Political Struggle"' (PhD diss., University of Rochester, 1973), 87–9.
4. R. M. Kantor, 'Frantsuzskaia okhranka o russikh emigrantakh (neisdannye materialy)', *KaS*, 1927, no. 21: 81–2; R. Johnson, 'The Okhrana Abroad: A Study in International Police Cooperation' (PhD diss., Columbia University, 1971), 47–8.
5. M. Lemke, 'Nash zagranichnyi sysk 1881–1883', *KL*, 1922, no. 5: 71–2, 79, 80–1, 84.
6. A. P. Koznov, 'Zagranichnaia politicheskii sysk (1900-fevral' 1917gg.)', *Kentavr*, 1992, nos. 1–2: 98.

7. Kantor, 'Frantsuzskaia okhranka', 82, 88; Millard, 'Russian Revolutionary Emigration', 100–2.
8. E. A. Taratuta, *S. M. Stepniak-Kravchinskii revoliutsioner i pisatel'* (Moscow: 1973), 292–3.
9. Ibid., 202–3.
10. H. Liang, *The Rise of the Modern Police and the European State System from Metternich to the Second World War* (Cambridge: Cambridge University Press, 1992), 130, 133–4; Millard, 'Russian Revolutionary Emigration', 154.
11. Westlake, *International Law*, 243–4; 246–7.
12. D. E. Emerson, *Metternich and the Political Police: Security and Subversion in the Hapsburg Monarchy (1815–1830)* (The Hague: Martinus Nijhoff, 1968), 51–4, 127–8.
13. For brief descriptions of the history of the evolution of record keeping of this sort and the rivalry between the different systems see: M. Fooner, *Interpol: The Inside Story of the International Crime Fighting Organization* (Chicago: Henry Regnery Company, 1973), 6–11; R. Fosdick, *European Police Systems* (New York: The Century Co., 1915), 323–4, 334.
14. R. B. Jensen, 'The International Anti-Anarchist Conference of 1898 and the Origins of Interpol', *JCH*, **16** (April 1981): 327; Liang, *The Rise of the Modern Police*, 158–9, 163–4.
15. Jensen, 'The International Anti-Anarchist Conference', 327.
16. Liang, *The Rise of Modern Police*, 164.
17. Ibid., 164, 166; B. Porter, 'The British Government and Political Refugees, *c*.1880–1914', in *From the Other Shore: Russian Political Emigrants in Britain*, ed. J. Slatter (London: Frank Cass, 1984), 29.
18. Jensen, 'The International Anti-Anarchist Conference', 334–5.
19. Ibid., 336.
20. MVD, Department of Police, Lopukhin to Manuilov, 15 February 1904, FAAr, 66, IXb, 2A; MVD, Department of Police, Lopukhin to Manuilov, 7 March 1904, FAAr, 66, IXb, 2A.
21. Liang claims Portugal and Spain as signatories to the Protocol. Liang, *The Rise of the Modern Police*, 173.
22. See for example, the view of Count Mensdorff the Austro-Hungarian ambassador towards Great Britian in: Ibid., 173.
23. C. Fijnaut, 'Police Co-operation within western Europe', in *Crime in Europe*, ed. F. Heidensohn and M. Farrell (London: Routledge, 1991), 104–5; Liang, *The Rise of the Modern Police*, 173; Jensen, 'The International Anti-Anarchist Conference', 337.
24. MVD, From the Director of the Department of Police, Memorandum no. 3731, 17 March 1904, FAAr, 34, Va, 3; MVD, From the Director of the Department of Police, Memorandum no. 6528, 22 May 1904, FAAr, XIVc, 1.
25. Johnson, 'The Okhrana Abroad', 45.
26. Letter from Jornot to Harting, 26 December 1905, FAAr, 36, Vf, 2.
27. Letter from Harting to Jornot, 29 December 1905, FAAr, 34, Va, 1a.
28. Johnson, 'The Okhrana Abroad', 54.
29. MVD, from Minister of Internal Affairs Stolypin, Memorandum no. 124130, 19 February 1909, FAAr, 34, Va, 4.
30. Johnson, 'The Okhrana Abroad', 66.
31. MVD, from Minister of Internal Affairs Stolypin, Memorandum no. 122907, 30 January 1909, FAAr, 34, Va, 3.
32. Izvolskii to Kurlov, Memorandum no. 10290, 17 April 1909, FAAr, 34, Va, 1.

33. The Russians were quite disappointed by the Germans lack of commitment to the Russo-German joint effort to search out and arrest the participants in the Tiflis robbery. Dispatch no. 41, Munich, 27 January/9 February 1908, FAAr, 34, Va, 4.
34. Dispatch no. 4, Paris, 17/4 January 1907, FAAr, 34, Va, 1.
35. *Zagranichnaia Agentura Departamenta Politsii (Zapiski S. Svatikov i dokumenty zagranichnoi agentury)*, Glavnoe Arkhivnoe UPRAVLENIE NKVD SSSR (Moscow: 1941), 108–16; MVD, Report of the Director of the Department of Police Trusevich to the Minister of Internal Affairs, 31 July 1907. It should be noted that police co-operation with the Austrians deteriorated apace. See: Johnson, 'The Okhrana Abroad', 98.
36. Michael Levi, 'Developments in business crime control in Europe', in *Crime in Europe*, 175.
37. The idea of rewarding European policemen for exceptional service on behalf of the Russian government belonged to V. K. Plehve in the early 1880s when he served as the Director of the Department of Police. See: Lemke, 'Nash zagranichnyi sysk', 77.
38. Dispatch no. 349, Paris, 27/14 December 1906, FAAr, 34, Va, 1.
39. Dispatch no. 510, Paris, 2 December/19 November 1907, FAAr, 34, Va, 4; B. Porter, *The Origins of the Vigilant State* (London: Weidenfeld & Nicolson, 1987), 159.
40. Dispatch no. 141, Paris, 26 April/9 May 1908, FAAr, 34, Va, 4.
41. Dispatch no. 1627, Paris, 7/20 December 1911, FAAr, 26, IVa, 3; Dispatch no. 248, Paris, 21 February/5 March 1912, FAAr, 26, IVa, 4a; Letter from Superintendent Quinn to A. A. Krasil'nikov, 11 September 1913, FAAr, 35, Vc, 2.
42. Dispatch no. 552, Paris, 24 April/7 May 1912, FAAr, 35, Vc, 1; Programme and Menu of the Annual Dinner for Chief Officers and Inspectors of the Criminal Investigation Department of the Metropolitan Police, 3 June 1914, FAAr, 35, Vc, 2.
43. B. Chapman, *Police State* (Basingstoke: Macmillan – now Palgrave Macmillan, 1970), *passim*.

4 The Russian Secret Police Abroad: the Early Years

1. F. S. Zuckerman, *The Tsarist Secret Police in Russian Society, 1880–1917* (Basingstoke: Macmillan – now Palgrave Macmillan, 1996), 19. For studies of the Russian political police prior to 1880 see: J. Daly, *Autocracy Under Siege: Security Police and Opposition in Russia 1860–1905* (DeKalb Illinois: Northern Illinois University Press, 1998); M. K. Lemke, *Nikolaevskye Zhandarmy i literatura, 1826–1855 gg.* (St Petersburg, 1909); S. Monas, *The Third Section: Police and Society under Nicholas I* (Cambridge: Harvard University Press, 1961); I. V. Orzhekhovskii, 'Trete otdelenie', *VI*, 1972, no. 2: 102–9; I. V. Orzhekhovskii, *Samoderzhavie protiv revoliutsionnoi Rossii* (Moscow, 1982); P. S. Squire, *The Third Department: The Political Police in the Russia of Nicholas I* (Cambridge: Cambridge University Press, 1968).
2. The Separate Corps of Gendarmes was officially attached to the Third Section in 1839 when the post of the chief of staff of the Corps of Gendarmnes was combined with the post of the director of the Third Section. Orzhekhovskii, *Samoderzhavie protiv revoliutsionnoi Rossii*, 40, 45–6.
3. V. V. Komin and M. M. Cherviakova, *Istoriia Rossiiskoi Revoliutsionnoi Emigratsii* (Kalinin, 1988), 85.
4. M. A. Miller, *The Russian Revolutionary Emigrés 1825–1870* (Baltimore: The Johns Hopkins University Press, 1986), 52, 58, 84–5; Orzhekhovskii, *Samoderzhavie protiv revoliutsionnoi Rossii*, 52–3, 67.

5. E. A. Taratuta, *S. M. Stepniak-Kravchinskii revoliutsioner i pisatel'* (Moscow, 1973), 196.
6. A. Kimbal, 'The Harassment of Russian Revolutionaries Abroad: The London Trial of Vladimir Burtsev in 1898', *Oxford Slavonic Papers*, n.s., Vol. 6, eds R. Auty and J. L. Fennel (New York: Oxford University Press, 1973), 50. For a concise history of the Holy Brotherhood and, in particular, the Brotherhood's campaign of disinformation in western Europe see: A. Lukashevich, 'The Holy Brotherhood: 1881–1883', *SR*, 1959, 18: 498–502, 505.
7. 'Graf Bismark-organizatsii russkoi politicheskoi agentury zagranitsei', *Byloe*, June (1907): 300.
8. M. K. Lemke, 'Nash zagranichnyi ssysk 1881–1883 gg., *KL*, 1922, no. 5: 68.
9. A. P. Koznov, 'Zagranichnaia politicheskii sysk (1900-fevral' 1917gg.)', *Kentavr*, 1992, no. 102: 96; Orzhekhovskii, *Samoderzhzhavie protiv revoliutsionnoi Rossii*, 113.
10. A discussion of 'administrative authority' and the forms of punishment this could entail is to be found in Zuckerman, *The Tsarist Secret Police*, Chapter 1.
11. Orzhekhovskii, *Samoderzhavie protiv revoliutsionnoi Rossii*, 130–1.
12. For example see: G. F. Kennan, *Siberia and the Exile System*, 2 Vols (1891: reprint New York: Russell & Russell, 1970); N. A. Troitskii, *Bezumstvo khrabrykh: Russkie revoliutsionery i karatel'naia politika tsarizma, 1866–1882gg.* (Moscow: 1978); A. V. Bogdanovich, *Tri poslednikh samoderztsa: Dnevnik A. V. Bogdanovich[a]* (Moscow: 1924), 33.
13. R. Pipes, *Russia Under the Old Regime* (London: Weidenfeld & Nicolson, 1974: Penguin Books, 1977), 290, 296–7; Orzhekovskii, *Samoderzhavie protiv revoliutsionnoi Rossii*, 123–4, 168, 172–3.
14. Ibid., 117.
15. Lemke, *Nash zagranichnyi*, 68.
16. Orzhekovskii, *Samoderzhavie protiv revoliutsionnoi Rossii*, 178.
17. Ibid., 179.
18. Ibid., 179; Liang, *The Rise of the Modern Police*, 149.
19. Orzhekovsky, *Samoderzhavie protiv revoliutsionnoi*, 180.
20. The following summary of Russian police reform and the creation of the Department of State Police (renamed the Department of Police in 1883) is taken from my book, *The Tsarist Secret Police*, 21–5.
21. See: J. Berlière, *Le Monde des polices en France XIXe – XXe Siècles* (Paris, 1996).
22. Zuckerman, *The Tsarist Secret Police*, especially Chapter 6.
23. V. K. Agafonov, *Zagranichnaia okhranka* (Moscow, 1918), 70.
24. Ibid., 70.
25. Lemke, 'Nash zagranichnyi', 77–9.
26. Kimball, 'The Harassment of Russian Revolutionaries', 50–1.
27. Agafonov, *Zagranichnaia okhranka*, 15–17, 20–2.
28. For example see: G. Dilnot, *The Story of Scotland Yard* (London, n.d.), 273; B. Weinberger, 'Are the Police Professionals? An Historical Account of the British Police Institutions', in *Policing Western Europe: Political Professionalism and Public Order, 1850–1940*, eds C. Emsley and B. Weinberger (Westport, Conn.: Greenwood Press, 1991), 79–80, 82–3.
29. The phrases 'state crime' and 'state criminal' in the Russian context refer to so-called political crimes described most thoroughly in Articles 1030 and 1031 of the Code of Criminal Procedure (*Ustav Ugolovnogo Sudoproizvodstva*). For an elaboration on these statutes see: Zuckerman, *The Tsarist Secret Police*, 254–5, note 1.
30. Agafonov, *Zagranichnaia okhranka*, 20–2.
31. Ibid., 21.

32. R. Johnson, 'The Okhrana Abroad, 1885–1917: A Study of International Police Cooperation' (PhD diss.: Columbia University, 1970), 32; E. Koliari, 'Russkaia tainaia politsiia v Italii', *Byloe*, n.s., 1925, no. 25: 137.
33. L. Tikhomirov, *Vospominaniia Leva Tikhomirova* (Moscow: 1927), 169.
34. Quoted in: Johnson, 'The Okhrana Abroad', 31.
35. Agafonov, *Zagranichnaia okhranka*, 62.
36. Richard Johnson, 'The Okhrana Abroad', 46; Agafonov, *Zagranichnaia okhranka*, 45–50; 'Departament politsii v 1892–1908 (Is vospominanii chinovnika)', *Byloe*, n.s. no. 5/6 (27/28) (November/December 1917): 21.
37. Agafonov, *Zagranichnaia okhranka*, 4.

5 Bureaucrats and Case Officers: the Sinews of the Paris Office

1. P. M. Blau, *The Dynamics of Bureaucracy: A Study of Interpersonal Relationships in Two Government Agencies*, rev. edn (Chicago: Chicago University Press, 1963), 228, 259–60.
2. V. K. Agafonov, *Zagranichnaia okhranka* (Petrograd: 1918), 6–8.
3. Dispatch no. 1, Paris, 1/14 September 1905, FAAr, 5, IIa, 1.
4. *Spravka* 15 March 1915, FAAr, 12, IIIc, 1.
5. Dispatch no. 84, Paris, 6/19 March 1908, FAAr, 12, IIIc, 6.
6. Dispatch no. 1541, Paris, 22 November/5 December 1911, FAAr, 12, IIIe, 1.
7. Ibid.
8. Dispatch no. 1738, Paris, 31 December 1913/13 January 1914, FAAr, 12, IIIc, 2; Dispatch no. 852, Paris, 4/17 July 1915, FAAr, 13, IIIc, 13; Dispatch no. 1055, Paris, 17/30 August 1913, 12, IIIc, 5.
9. Dispatch no. 1376, Bordeaux, 20 August/12 September 1914, FAAr, 12, IIIc, 7.
10. Dispatch no. 473, Paris, 13/26 May 1910, FAAr, 12, IIIc, 9; Dispatch no. 1051, Paris, 17/30 August 1912, FAAr, IIIc, 5.
11. The following information has been extracted from the personnel files of; Mikhail Bobrov, Maria Fedorova, Aleksandr Il'in, Ivan Mol'chanov, and Nikolai Volkovskii. None of these people held higher rank than the *X chin*.
12. List of salaries for chancery personnel of the Foreign Agentura, FAAr, 10, IIc, 10.
13. MVD, Department of Police Circular issued by the Ninth Secretariat, April 1914, FAAr, 13, IIIc, 18.
14. Dispatch no. 852, Paris, 4/17 July 1915, FAAr, 13, IIIc, 13.
15. MVD, Department of Police Circular no. 190329, issued by the Sixth Secretariat, 24 July 1915, FAAr, 13, IIIc, 18.
16. Letter from Harting to the Minister of Internal Affairs, 27 January/9 February 1907, FAAr, 13, IIIc, 13.
17. Dispatch no. 192, Paris, 1/14 April 1909, FAAr, 13, IIIc, 13.
18. MVD, Department of Police Circular no. 134786, issued by the Special Section, 20 August 1909, FAAr, 13, IIIc, 13; Letter from Mol'chanov to Vice Director of Police Vissarionov, 6/19 November 1909, attached to Dispatch no. 567, FAAr,13, IIIc, 13.
19. Dispatch no. 430, Paris, 27 August/9 September 1909, FAAr, 13, IIIc, 13.
20. Ibid.
21. MVD, Department of Police Circular no. 111241, issued by the Special Section, 29 May 1910, FAAr, 13, IIIc, 13.
22. MVD, Department of Police Circular no. 112903, issued by the Special Section, 21 June 1910, FAAr, 13, IIIc, 13.

23. MVD, Department of Police Circular no. 190414, 9 April 1914, FAAr, 12, IIIc, 9.
24. Dispatch no. 1534, Paris, 21 November/4 December 1912, FAAr, 12, IIIc, 1.
25. Dispatch no. 1541, Paris, 22 November/5 December 1911, FAAr, 12, IIIc, 1.
26. Dispatch no. 1534, Paris, 21 November/5 December, FAAr, 12, IIIc, 1.
27. Dispatch no. 1325, Paris, 10/23 October 1911, FAAr, 12, IIIc, 1.
28. *Spisok sluzhashchikh v Zagranichnoi Agenture Departamenta Politsii udostoennikh v 1909 gody nagrazhdeniiu Vysochaishimi podarkami i ordenami za uchastie v okhrane Gosudaria Imperatora vo vremia prebivania Ego Velichestva v Shvetsii, Germanii, Frantsii, Anglii, Italii*, FAAr, 12, IIIc, 1.
29. Dispatch no. 1728, Paris, 31 December 1911/13 January 1912, FAAr, 12, IIIc, 1. Sushkov received 150 rubles, while Mel'nikov and Bobrov were given 100 rubles each.
30. Dispatch no. 1300, Paris, 13/26 October 1912, FAAr, IIIc, 1.
31. MVD, Department of Police Circular no. 190036 issued by the Special Section, 13 January 1914, 12, IIIc, 1.
32. MVD, Department of Police Circular no. 166546, February 1914, FAAr, 12, IIIc, 5.
33. Dispatch no. 682, Paris, 3/16 April 1914, FAAr, 12, IIIc, 5; MVD, Department of Police Circular no. 14024, issued by the Ninth Secretariat, 24 February 1914, FAAr, 12, IIIc, 5; MVD, Department of Police Circular no. 50484, issued by the Ninth Secretariat, 8 March 1914, FAAr, 12, IIIc, 5.
34. See: FAAr, 184, XIVb, 2.
35. MVD, Department of Police Circular no. 140792, issued by the Special Section 31 October 1908, FAAr, 34, IVe, 1.
36. For example see Dispatch no?, Paris, 9/22 December 1909, FAAr, 65, IXa, 1b in particular and folder 1b generally.
37. Dispatch no. 1446, St Petersburg (Incoming), 13 September 1912, FAAr, 42, VIh, 1.
38. Nurit Schleifmann, 'The Internal Agency: Linchpin of the political police in Russia', *Cahiers du monde Russe et Sovietique*, no. 24 (1983): 159.
39. Ibid., 158–9.
40. Some of Fontanka's complaints were ludicrous. For example, the condemning of Krasil'nikov for excessive verbosity by citing a cable of thirty-five words which it had received from him, claiming that thirteen words of the words making up its contents were superfluous! Ibid., 159.
41. 'Dopros gen. E. K. Klimovicha', *PTsR*, 1: 85.
42. MVD, Department of Police Circular no. 171317, issued by the Sixth Secretariat, 5 July 1916, FAAr, 34, IVc, 2.
43. MVD, Department of Police Circular no. 105332, issued by the Sixth Secretariat, 5 July 1916, FAAr 34, IVe, 2.
44. Not every communication between St Petersburg and Paris took the form of a dispatch, both telegrams and regularly posted letters were also used. But the disadvantages of these forms of communication far outweighed their benefits and they were not normally employed. Dispatch no. 272, Paris, 28 August/10 September 1906, FAAr, 184, XIVc, 1; Dispatch no. 112 (?), Paris, 11/24 April 1906, FAAr, XIVc, 1; Dispatch no. 342, Paris, 9/22 December 1906, FAAr, 184, XIVc, 1; Dispatch no.?, Paris, 11/24 March 1909, FAAr, 184, XIVb, 2.
45. MVD, Department of Police Circular no. 176386, issued by the Ninth Secretariat, 30 September 1914, FAAr, 34, IVe, 1.
46. MVD, Department of Police Circular nos. 1372 and 1934, issued by the Sixth Secretariat, 11 December 1915, FAAr, 34, IVe 2; MVD, Department of Police Circular no. 165816 issued by the Ninth Secretariat, 31 January 1915, FAAr, 34, IVe, 1.

47. MVD, Department of Police Circular no. 103749, issued by the Special Section, FAAr, 34, IVe, 1.
48. F. S. Zuckerman, *The Tsarist Secret Police in Russian Society, 1880–1917* (Basingstoke: Macmillan – now Palgrave Macmillan, 1996), 46–7.
49. V. N. Russiian, 'Rabota okhrannykh otdelenii v Rossii', MS Moravsky Collection, Hoover Institution, n.p.
50. For the classic telling of this story see: Boris Nikolaejewsky, *Aseff the Spy: The Russian Terrorist and Police Stool* (New York: Doubleday, Doran & Co., 1934).
51. R. Johnson, 'The Okhrana Abroad, 1885–1917: A Study of International Police Cooperation' (PhD diss., Columbia University, 1970), 24.
52. *Spravka* (Summary of the appointment of Captain Rek to the Foreign Agentura and his return home), 16 May 1915, FAAr, 42, VIh, 4.
53. MVD, Department of Police Circular no. 125647, issued by the Special Section, 22 June 1910, FAAr, 12, IIIb, 28.
54. MVD, From the Director of the Department of Police, Circular no. 125425, 3 May 1910, FAAr, 12, IIIb, 28.
55. MVD, Department of Police Circular no. 24873, 24 February 1911, FAAr, 12, IIIb, 28; MVD, From the Director of the Department of Police, Circular no. 125425, 3 May 1910, 12, IIIb, 28.
56. In February 1912 Rek rejoined the Railway Gendarmerie. *Spravka*, 16 May 1915, FAAr, 42, VIh, 4.
57. Dispatch no?, Paris, 17/30 April 1915, FAAr, IIIb, 13; Dispatch no. 779, Petersburg (Incoming), 13 May 1915, FAAr, II, IIIb, 14.
58. From the chief of the St Petersburg Provincial Gendarme Directorate, Memorandum no. 1331, 22 April 1915; FAAr, 12, IIIb, 28; MVD, Department of Police Circular no. 190158, issued by the Sixth Secretariat, FAAr, 12, IIIb, 28.
59. Agafonov, *Zagranichnaia okhranka*, 123, 137.
60. See Erghardt's and Lustig's accounts, FAAr, 11, IIIb, 18 and 12, IIIb, 25.
61. Dispatch no. 1213, Paris, 19 September/2 October 1911, FAAr, IIIb, 1.
62. Protocol nos. 1 and 9, Testimony of Captain Lustig, FAAr, IIf, 10.
63. Dispatch no. 1369, Bordeaux, 28 August/11 September 1914, FAAr, 185, XVa, 5.
64. MVD, Department of Police Circular no. 134857, issued by the Special Section, 24 December 1916, FAAr, 12, IIIb, 27.
65. Herbert A. Simon and James G. March, *Organizations* (New York: Wiley & Sons, 1958), 98.

6 Europeans and Russians in the Service of the Tsarist Secret Police: the Detectives and Undercover Agents in Exile

1. For a discussion of the lives of undercover agents and detectives within the Empire see: F. S. Zuckerman, *The Tsarist Secret Police in Russian Society, 1880–1917* (Basingstoke: Macmillan – now Palgrave Macmillan, 1996), Chapters 3 and 4.
2. V. K. Agafonov, *Zagranichnaia okhranka* (Petrograd: 1918), 31–3. In this chapter I am concerned only with the long-term, regular employees of the Foreign Agentura's surveillance service. See Appendices A.1 and A.2 for the names and personal data of most of the detectives on whose dossiers this chapter is partially based.
3. The data for the personnel information discussed in this chapter is derived from the detective's service records located in FAAr, Boxes 14–19, IIIe.

4. Although there are 123 detectives' dossiers in the FAAr, the Paris Office only appointed about 54 detectives on a regular basis. These are the dossiers of the most important and longest serving detectives and contain fairly complete service records.
5. Dispatch no. 1, Paris, 1/17 September 1905, FAAr, 4, IIa, 1; Report dated 1/14 September 1905, FAAr, 14, IIIe, 1.
6. *Spisok sluzhashchikh v Zagranichnoi Agenture Departamenta Politsii udostoennikh v 1909 gody nagrazhdeniiu Vysochaishimi podarkami i ordenami za uchastie v okhrane Gosudaria Imperatora vo vremia prebivania Ego Velichestva v Shvetsii, Germanii Frantsii, Anglii, Italii,* FAAr 12, IIIc, 1; Bittard-Monin's agent list for 1910, FAAr, 98, Xe, 57d; Appendix A. 1 of this work.
7. Dispatch no. 1755, Paris, 6/19 November 1913, FAAr, 12, IIIc, 1; E. Koliari, 'Russkaia tainaia politsiia v Italii', *Byloe*, n.s., 1924, no. 25: 146.
8. Bittard-Monin's file, FAAr, 98, Xe, 57d.
9. Personnel dossier of Bittard-Monin, FAAr, 14, IIIe.
10. Letter from Ed Lowdell to the Director of the Department of Police, FAAr, 38, VIb, 1a.
11. Letter attached to MVD, Department of Police Circular no. 10527, issued by the Special Section, 28 January 1910, FAAr, 38, VIb, 2.
12. FAAr Boxes 37–38 (on foreign nationals) and in particular FAAr, 38, VIb, 1–4.
13. Dispatch no. 559, Paris, 6/19 April 1913, FAAr, VIb, 2.
14. MVD, Department of Police Circular no. 1479, issued by the Special Section 7/20 March 1902, FAAr, 34, IVb, 2; Dispatch no. 356, Paris, 20 June/3 July 1909, FAAr, XVb, 2c.
15. *Service État de Surveillances à la date du 18 juin 1912 – Répartition des agents,* FAAr, IIIe, 1e.
16. Dispatch no. 1017a, Dieppe, 3/16 November 1910, FAAr, 192, XVIb (4), 1.
17. Summary of the career of detective Genevieve Gabrielle Richard in her own words, FAAr, 18, IIIc, 3.
18. Dispatch no. 191, Paris, 26 April/8 May 1909, FAAr, 98, Xe, 55f; Nurit Schleifmann, 'The Internal Agency: Linchpin of the political police in Russia', *Cahiers du monde Russe et Sovietique*, 1983, no. 24: 160.
19. Dispatch no. 916, Berlin, 13/26 July 1911, FAAr, 98, Xe, 57c.
20. Dispatch 1676a, Paris, November 1911, FAAr, 26, Va, 3; Année 1913 mois d'Octobre Règlement Général, FAAr, 14, IIIe, 2.
21. *Spisok sluzashchikh.*
22. Personnel dossiers of Foreign agents in alphabetical order FAAr, 15–19, IIIe, 3.
23. Dispatch no. 66, Paris, 21 February/6March 1907, FAAr, 18, IIIe, 3; Dispatch no. 105, Paris, 13/26 March 1908, FAAr, 18, IIIe, 3; Dispatch no. 400, Paris, 5/18 August 1909, FAAr, 18, IIIe, 3.
24. Dispatch no. 191, Paris, 26 March/8 April 1909, FAAr, 98, Xe, 55f; Dispatch no. 916, Berlin, 13/26 July 1911, FAAr, 98, Xe, 57c.
25. Dispatch no. 581, Paris, 28 April/11 May 1912, FAAr, 98, Xe, 59g.
26. Dispatch no. 413, Paris, 5/18 November 1908, FAAr, 98, Xe, 59g.
27. Draft of dispatch written by Krasil'nikov to Fontanka, FAAr, 41, VIf, 2. A thorough search by the author did not uncover a final copy; it is more than likely that one did not exist.
28. Dispatch no.?, Paris, 3/16 January 1911, FAAr, 41, VIf, 3; FAAr, 41, VIf, 1b generally; and Agafonov, *Zagranichnaia okhranka*, 102–03.
29. Dispatch no. 651, Paris, 31 March/13 April 1914, FAAr, 41, IIIf, 2.

30. S. G. Svatikov, 'Sozdanie "Sionskikh protokolov" po dannim ofitsial'nogo sledstviia 1917 goda', MS Nikolaevsky Collection, Hoover Institution, 24.
31. Agafonov, *Zagranichnaia okhranka*, 9.
32. Dispatch no. 1, Paris, 1/14 September 1905, FAAr, 4, IIa, 1.
33. Dispatch no. 618, Paris, 4/17 May 1911, FAAr, 37, IIIa, 3.
34. Dispatch no. 1374, Paris, 6/19 August 1913, FAAr, 212, XXIVc, 1.
35. Agafonov, *Zagranichnaia okhranka*, 167.
36. MVD, Department of Police Circular no.?, issued by the Special Section, 28 April 1910, FAAr, 26, IVa, 1.
37. Agafonov, *Zagranichnaia okhranka*, 9.
38. Dispatch no. 478, Paris, 14/27 May 1910, FAAr, 26, IVa, 3a.
39. MVD, Department of Police Circular no. 190055, and the attached *spravka* issued by the Ninth Secretariat, 5 February 1915, FAAr, 42, VIb, 5.
40. Dispatch no. 401, Paris, 13/26 April 1910, FAAr, 26, IVa, 1; Dispatch no. 1298, Paris, 5/18 October 1911, FAAr, 34, IVe.
41. Agafonov, *Zagranichnaia okhranka*, 135–6.
42. Dispatch no. 188, Paris, 15/28 May 1908, FAAr, 216, XXVIId.
43. Dispatch no. 169, Paris, 5/18 May 1908, FAAr, 212, XXIV, 2–0.
44. Service record of Aleksandr Mass, FAAr, 21, IIIf, 1b.
45. Service record of Lev Dimitriev Beitner, FAAr, 21, IIIf, 1a.
46. Service record of Fedor Dorozhko, FAAr, 21, IIIf, 1a.
47. Dispatch no. 606, Paris, 6/19 May 1912, FAAr, 98, Xe, 59g, 1; Agafonov, *Zagranichnaia okhranka*, 137–138.
48. Dispatch no. 170, Paris 6/19 May 1908, FAAr, 210, XXIVa, 1.
49. Agafonov, *Zagranichnaia okhranka*, 139, 157–8.
50. Service Record of Il'ia Chiryev, FAAr, 21, IIIf, 1a.
51. Ibid.
52. Dispatch no. 359, Paris, 10/29 December 1906, FAAr, 37, VIa, 1b.
53. MVD, From the Vice Director of the Department of Police, Memorandum no. 194, 26 February/10 March 1916, FAAr, 37, VIa, 3.
54. MVD, From the Director of the Department of Police, Memorandum no. 7095, 4 June 1905, FAAr, 41, VIe, 1.
55. Dispatch no. 512, Paris, 20 November/3December 1907, FAAr, 42, VIh, 4.
56. Dispatch no. 384, Paris, 6/19 July 1909, FAAr, 42, VIh, 1.
57. Dispatch no. 430, Paris, 19 April/3 May 1916, FAAr, 42, VIh, 5.
58. Dispatch no. 73, Paris, 19 October/1 November 1905, FAAr, 185, XVb, 2a.
59. Dispatch no. 473, Paris, 7/20 April 1912, FAAr, 42, VIh, 1.
60. Dispatch no. 1358, Paris, 24 August/6 September 1913, FAAr, 42, VIh, 5.
61. Dispatch no. 399, Paris, 19 March/1 April 1913, FAAr, 42, VIh, 5.
62. Dispatch no. 30, Paris, 20 January/2 February 1907, FAAr, 103, XIc (4), 1.

7 P. I. Rachkovskii: Adventure, Intrigue and the Foreign Agentura, 1884–1902

1. Fredric S. Zuckerman, *The Tsarist Secret Police in Russian Society, 1880–1917* (Basingstoke: Macmillan – now Palgrave Macmillan, 1996), 156–7, 159, 162–4, 167–70.
2. Ibid., Chapters 6 and 7.
3. There exists some confusion concerning the pattern of Rachkovskii's civil service career to 1878. See: 'Kar'era P. I. Rachkovskago. Dokumenty', *Byloe*, n.s., 30

(February 1918): 79; S. G. Svatikov 'Sozdanie "Sionskikh protokolov" po dannym ofitsial'nago sledstviia 1917', MS, Nikolaevsky Collection, Hoover Institution, 13; *PTsR* 7: 405.

4. 'Kar'era P. I. Rachkovskago', 79.
5. Svatikov, 'Sozdanie "Sionskikh protokolov" ', 13–14.
6. Ibid., 15–17; E. K. Semenoff, *The Russian Government and the Massacres* (London: 1907), 146.
7. Svatikov, 'Sozdanie "Sionskikh protokolov" ', 22, 42.
8. V. K. Agafonov, *Zagranichnaia okhranka* (Petrograd: 1917), 18.
9. *Vechernee Vremia*, no. 149, 21 May, 1912.
10. Ibid., no. 150, 22 May, 1912. Rachkovskii spoke French, but not well at first.
11. Ibid.
12. MVD, Department of Police to Rachkovskii Memorandum no. 472, 4 August 1886. FAAr, 98, Xe, 59g.
13. *Zagranichnaia Agentura Departamenta Politsii (Zapiski S. Svatikov i dokumenty zagranichnoi agentury)* GLAVNOE ARKHIVNOE UPRAVLENIE NKVD SSSR (Moscow: 1941), 6–8.
14. Jean Galtier-Boissière, *Mysteries of the French Secret Police*, Donald Leslie-Melville trans. (London: Stanley Paul & Co. Ltd., 1938), 237 and Chapter 5 herein.
15. Ibid., 7; E. A. Taratuta, *Etel' Lilian Voinich: Sud'ba pisatelia i sud'ba knigi*, 2nd edn, (Moscow: 1964), 101; E. A. Taratuta, *S. M. Stepniak-Kravchinskii revoliutsioner i pisatel'* (Moscow: 1973), 475.
16. M. B. Millard, 'Russian Revolutionary Emigration, Terrorism and the "Political Struggle" ' (PhD thesis, University of Rochester, 1973), 110–17.
17. Quoted in Ibid., 111.
18. Ibid., 117.
19. Svatikov, 'Sozdanie "Sionskikh protokolov" ', 21–2.
20. Ibid., 25.
21. Zuckerman, *The Tsarist Secret Police*, 49–51, 186.
22. Rachkovskii to Fragnan, 1887, FAAr, 4, IIa, 3.
23. Ibid.
24. Svatikov, 'Sozdanie "Sionskikh protokolov" ', 54.
25. Ibid., 54–5.
26. N. Cohn, *Warrant for Genocide: The Myth of Jewish World Conspiracy and the Protocols of the Elders of Zion* (London: Eyre and Spotteswood, 1967), 88. Rachkovskii actually established such a league (*La ligue pour le salut de la patrie russe*) in 1902 without the prior approval of the MVD. See: Rachkovskii, The Nikolaevsky Collection, no. 132, Box 1.
27. Agafonov, *Zagranichnaia okhranka*, 30.
28. 'Nalet P. I. Rachkovskago na narodovol'cheskuiu tipografiiu', *Byloe*, n.s., 23 (July 1917): 277.
29. 'Nalet P. I. Rachkovskago', 277–80.
30. Agafonov, *Zagranichnaia okhranka*, 34.
31. Leonid Menshchikov, *Russkii politicheskii sysk za granitsei* (Paris: 1914), 151.
32. Taratuta, *S. M. Stepniak-Kravchinskii revoliutsioner*, 383.
33. 'G. V. Plekhanov i shpionskie zabavy: Soobshchil S. N. Valk', *KA*, 1924, 5: 264–5.
34. Dispatch no. 24 from St Petersburg to Rachkovskii, 7 May 1885, FAAr, 26, IVa, 1; Dispatch no. 61 from St Petersburg to Rachkovskii, October 1886, FAAr, 26, IVa; 'Nalet P. I. Rachkovkago', 281.

35. Rachkovskii also interested himself in the improvement of Anglo-Russian relations. See: *Vechernee Vremia*, no. 153, 31 May 1912.
36. L. B., 'Franko-russkoe shpionstvo i franko-russkii soiuz', *Byloe*, Paris, 1908, no. 8: 58.
37. Ibid., 58, 60–2. Also for an excellent example of French coverage of the affair can be found in *L'Eclair* 5 July 1890.
38. L. B., 'Franko-russkoe shpionstvo', 59.
39. Ibid., 64.
40. Quoted in: Millard, 'Russian Revolutionary Emigration', 143.
41. Ibid., 144.
42. Ibid., 145.
43. Ibid., 144.
44. Ibid., 149.
45. Volkhovskii arrived in London in 1890 and began to work with Kravchinskii on *Free Russia*. During the remainder of Kravchinskii's lifetime Volkhovskii was regarded as his alter ego. They were amazingly similar in habits and personality and although they differed in degree on several tactical and ideological points they became fast friends. Donald Senese, *S. M. Stepniak-Kravchinskii: The London Years*, Russian Biography Series, 33, (Newtonville Mass.: Oriental Research Partners, 1987), 50–1.
46. Ibid., 49–51; Taratuta, *S. M. Stepniak-Kravchinskii revoliutsioner*, 424–5, 474–5; Senese, *S. M. Stepniak tepniak-Kravchinskii*, 95–6.
47. Taratuta, *Etel' Lilian Voinich*, 102; Taratuta, *S. M. Stepniak-Kravchinskii revoliutsioner*, 426.
48. Ibid., 426.
49. B. Porter, *The Origins of the Vigilant State: The London Metropolitan Police Special Branch Before the First World War* (London: Weidenfeld & Nicolson, 1987), 143; H. Brust, *I Guarded Kings: The Memoirs of a Political Police Officer* (London: Stanley Paul & Co., n.d.), 64.
50. B. Porter, 'The British Government and Political Refugees, *c.*1880–1914', in *From the Other Shore: Russian Political Emigrants in Britain*, ed. J. Slatter (London: Frank Cass, 1984), 37.
51. Porter, *The Origins of the Vigilant State*, 143–4.
52. Taratuta, *S. M. Stepniak-Kravchinskii revoliutsioner*, 427.
53. Taratuta, *Etel' Lilian Voinich*, 103.
54. Ibid., 428, Senese, *S. M. Stepniak-Kravchinskii*, 98.
55. Ibid., 98–9; Taratuta, *Etel' Lilian Voinich*, 104; Taratuta, *S. M. Stepniak-Kravchinskii revoliutsioner*, 471–2, 477.
56. Taratuta, *Etel' Lilian Voinich*, 104.
57. V. Burtsev, *Bor'ba za svobodnuiu Rossiiu: Moi vospominaniia (1882–1912 g.)* (Berlin: 1912), 1: 127–8.
58. Porter, *The Origins of the Vigilant State*, 144.
59. Burtsev, *Bor'ba za svobodnuiu Rossiiu*, 128–31.
60. Ibid., 117, 141, 143.
61. MVD, Department of Police Circular no. 2282, 6 April 1894, FAAr, 26, IVa, 2.
62. Agafonov, *Zagranichnaia okhranka*, 36.
63. 'Kar'era P. I. Rachkovskago', 80–2, 86–7; Boris Nikolaejewsky, *Aseff the Spy and Police Stool* (New York: 1934), 118.
64. 'Kar'era P. I. Rachkovskago', 82–4.
65. Taratuta, *S. M. Stepniak-Kravchinskii revoliutsioner*, 519.
66. Rachkovskii to the Department of Police, Dispatch no. 7515, 24 October 1894, Spiridovich Collection, Sterling Memorial Library, Yale University.

67. A. V. Bogdanovich, *Tri poslednikh samoderzhtsa. Dnevnik A.V. Bogdanovich[a]* (Moscow-Leningrad: 1924), 247.
68. Ibid., 209.
69. M. La Porte, *Histoire de l'Okhrana la police secrète des tsars, 1880–1917* (Paris: 1935), 27, 187.
70. 'Kar'era P. I. Rachkovskago', 80.
71. 'Prikliucheniia I. F. Manuilova. Po arkhivnym materialam', *Byloe*, n.s., nos. 5/6 [27/28] (December 1917): 236–88.
72. La Porte, *Histoire de l'Okhrana*, 187; 'Kar'era P. I. Rachkovskago', 78.
73. Sergei IU. Witte, *Vospominaniia: Tsarstvovanie Nikolaia II*, (Berlin: 1922), 1: 150–1; *Vechernee Vremia*, no. 155, 28 May 1912.
74. 'Razoblachennyi Azef', *Byloe*, n.s., 1917, no. 2 [30]: 211; *Vechernee Vremia*, no. 153, 25 May 1912.
75. 'Kar'era P. I. Rachkovkago', 83.
76. Svatikov, 'Sozdanie "Sionskikh protokolov" ', 39.
77. La Porte, *Histoire de l'Okhrana*, 187.
78. Menshchikov, *Russkii politicheskii sysk*, 70, 111–12, 124–5.
79. See the sample of Azef's dispatches in: *Pis'ma Azefa, 1893–1917*, comp. D. B. Pavlov and Z. I. Peregudova (Moscow: TERRA, 1994), 71, 74, 77 and Rachkovskii's Dispatch to St Petersburg, Dispatch no. 634 from the Paris Office to the Special Section, 4 February 1901, FAAr, 190.
80. Menshchikov, *Russkii politicheskii sysk*, 123–4.
81. A. A. Polovtsov, 'Dnevnik A. A. Polovtsova', *KA*, 1923, no. 3: 153.
82. Witte, *Vospominaniia*, 246; Agafonov, *Zagranichnaia okhranka*, 53.
83. Zuckerman, *The Tsarist Secret Police*, 165–81.
84. Even when Rachkovskii's reports to Fontanka were prepared without intentional falsifications, their accuracy was far from certain. See: *Doklad Rachkovskago* 20 July/2 August 1901, FAAr, 189, XVIa, 2: Bogdanovich, *Tri poslednikh samoderzhtsa*, 247.
85. The extent of these successful liaisons with Europe's police forces could be seen on his bemedalled chest. He received awards from eight countries including the French Legion of Honour. See: Rachkovskii to the Director of the Belgian *Sûreté*, 26 September 1896, FAAr, 36, Vf, 1.
86. Intelligence Summary, no. 17, 24 January 1903, FAAr, 152, XIIIc(2), 2 There was nothing new in this of course, terrorists had been seeking sanctuary abroad for more than a generation. The difference is in the systematic, structured way in which their operations were conducted and the fact that when they returned to Europe they ensconced themselves in an established political organisation: the SR Party.
87. Menshchikov, *Russkii politicheskii sysk*, 111–12 and Chapter 11 herein.
88. Throughout the latter years of Rachkovskii's tenure abroad London's literary emigration remained the principal concern of the Foreign Agentura. Agafonov, *Zagranachnaia okhranka*, 53–4: Senese, *S. M. Stepniak-Kravchinskii*, 91; Menshchikov, *Russkii politicheskii sysk*, 79.
89. Agafonov, *Zagranichnaia okhranka*, 51–2.

8 Alignments and Alliances: L. A. Rataev and A. M. Harting, 1902–1905

1. L. Tikhomirov, *Vospominaniia L'va Tikhomirova* (Moscow: 1927), 312–14.
2. Under the law, except in extraordinary conditions Jews could only reside in a designated area within the Empire known as the Pale of Settlement.

3. The data on Rataev's and Harting's careers is derived from: V. K. Agafonov, *Zagranichnaia okhranka* (Petrograd: 1918), 25–6, 46–9, 55–6, 102; V. Burtsev, *Borba za svobodnuiu Rossiiu: Moi vospominaniia* (1882–1923) (Berlin: 1923), 90, 102; *PTsR*, 'Ukazatel' Imen', 7: 322, 403.
4. Agafonov, *Zagranichnaia okhranka*, 46–7.
5. For discussions of Zubatov's career see: J. Schneiderman, *Sergei Zubatov and Revolutionary Marxism: The Struggle for the Working Class in Tsarist Russia* (Ithaca: Cornell University Press, 1976) and F. S. Zuckerman, *The Tsarist Secret Police in Russian Society, 1880–1917* (Basingstoke: Macmillan – now Palgrave Macmillan, 1996), Chapter 7.
6. B. Nikolaejewsky, *Aseff the Spy: Russian Terrorist and Police Stool* (New York: Doubleday, Doran & Co., 1934), 73.
7. Agafonov, *Zagranichnaia okhranka*, 55–6.
8. Ibid., 57–8.
9. Ibid., 55–6, 59.
10. The *Zubatovshchina* refers to the failure of Zubatov's police trade union movement, and the resulting wave of strikes and peasant *jacqueries* in South Russia. Minister of Internal Affairs Plehve reacted to the strikes and their political consequences by firing Zubatov and banishing him to the provinces. He never returned to police work.
11. 'Pis'ma L. A. Rataeva – S. V. Zubatovu 1900–1903: Soobshchil S. P. Mel'gunov', *GM*, 1922, no. 1: 59.
12. Ibid., 59.
13. Dispatch no. 4, Paris, 5 January 1904/23 December 1903, FAAr, 26, IVa, 1.
14. B. P. Koz'min, *S. V. Zubatov i ego korrespondenty* (Leningrad: 1928), 28–9.
15. Dispatch no. 1568, Rataev to Harting, 5 May 1903, FAAr, 26, IVa, 2.
16. Dispatch no. 118, Harting to Rataev, 13 December 1902, FAAr, 26, IVa, 2.
17. Dispatch from Berlin, 9 February 1903, FAAr, 26, IVa, 1.
18. Letter from Harting to Rataev, registry no. 286, 18 February/3 March 1903, FAAr, 26, IVa, 2
19. Dispatch no. 60a, Rataev to Harting, 4/17 March 1903, FAAr, 4, IIa, 1.
20. Harting to Rataev, 26 April/9 May 1903, FAAr, 26, IVa, 2.
21. Letter from Harting to Rataev 7/20 May 1903, registry no. 459, FAAr, 26, IVa, 1.
22. Agafonov, *Zagranichnaia okhranka*, 48–9.
23. Ibid., 49, 66.
24. Ibid., 50.
25. E. G. Spencer, *Police and the Social Order in German Cities: The Düsseldorf District, 1848–1914* (DeKalb Ill.: Northern Illinois University Press, 1992), 159–60.
26. K. D., 'Russkie shpiony pered sudom Germanskogo parlamenta', *Osvobozhdenie*, no. 15/16 (39/40), January 16, 1904, p. 274.
27. Aziat, *Russkie shpioni v Germanii* (Berlin: 1904), 13–16, 30, 32.
28. Ibid., 23–4.
29. B. Brachmann, *Russische Sozialdemokraten In Berlin 1895–1914* (Berlin: Akademie Verlag, 1962), 27.
30. D. B. Pavlov, 'Rossiiskaia kontrrazvedka v gody Russko-Iaponskoi voiny', *OI*, no. 1 (January/February 1996): 16–17.
31. Antti Kujala, 'March Separately – Strike Together: The Paris and Geneva Conferences Held by the Russian and Minority Nationalities' Revolutionary Opposition Parties, 1904–1905', in Motojiro Akashi, *'Rakka Ryusui'. Colonel Akashi's Report on His Secret Cooperation with the Russian Revolutionary Parties during the Russo-Japanese*

War, Selected chapters trans. I. Chiharu and ed. O. K. Fält and A. Kujala (Helsinki: Finnish Historical Society, 1988), 103; I. Chiharu, 'The Politics of Subversion: Japanese Aid to Opposition Groups in Russia during the Russo-Japanese War', in Ibid., 75–6; D. B. Pavlov and S. A. Petrov, 'Polkovnik Akasi i osvoboditel'noe dvizhenie v Rossii (1904–1905 gg.)', *Istoriia SSSR*, no. 6 (November/December 1990): 65.

32. Ibid., 55, 59. The first of two. The second conference was held in Paris in 1905. See the article by Antti Kujala cited above.
33. Pavlov, 'Polkovnik Akasi', 59, 60–3; Pavlov, 'Rossiiskaia kontrrazvedka', 24.
34. Pavlov, 'Polkovnik Akasi', 61.
35. Ibid., 59–60; Pavlov, 'Rossiiskaia kontrrazvedka', 23–4.
36. Ibid., 18, 23–4; Pavlov, 'Polkovnik Akasi', 59.
37. Ibid., 60; Pavlov, 'Rossiiskaia kontrrazvedka', 24.
38. Akashi, *Rakka ryusui*, 53; Pavlov, 'Polkovnk Akasi', 63.
39. Dispatch no. 1, Paris, 1/14 September 1905, FAAr, 4, IIa, 1; Pavlov, 'Rossiiskaia kontrrazvedka', 19–20.
40. Agafonov, *Zagranichnaia okhranka*, 67.
41. Sergei Witte, Russia's great industrialising Minister of Finance between 1892 and 1903 was again ascendent as the negotiator of the Portsmouth Peace Treaty and author of the October Manifesto. His friend P. I. Rachkovskii had risen on the coattails of D. F. Trepov to become the most powerful political police official in Russia during the first period of the 1905 Revolution. See: Zuckerman, *The Tsarist Secret Police*, Chapter 10.
42. Letter from Harting to Rataev, 7/20 May 1903, registry no. 459, FAAr, 26, IVa, 1.
43. Dispatch no. 4, Paris, 23 December 1903/5 January 1904, FAAr, 26, IVa, 1.
44. Dispatch no. 135, Paris, 29 December 1905/11 January 1906, FAAr, 98, Xe, 55D.
45. Nikolaejewsky, *Aseff the Spy*, 73.
46. Rataev, 'Pis'ma L. A. Rataeva', 53. As this correspondence reveals, Rataev's hopelessly negative attitude permeated his reports as early as 1900 when he was still chief of the Special Section.
47. Nikolaejewsky, *Aseff the Spy*, 78.
48. *Zagranichnaia Agentura Departamenta Politsii*, 12.
49. Agafonov, *Zagranichnaia okhranka*, 68–9.
50. Pavlov, 'Rossiiskaia kontrrazvedka', 19.
51. Zuckerman, *The Tsarist Secret Police*, Chapter 9.
52. The story of the Azeff Affair has been repeated many times, but never better than in Nikolaejewsky, *Aseff the Spy*.
53. Agafonov, *Zagranichnaia okhranka*, 69.
54. Pavlov, 'Polkovnik Akasi', 65.
55. MVD, Department of Police Circular no. 9965, 6 August 1905, issued by the Special Section, FAAr, 158, XIIId (1), 9. Also it should be noted that the Treaty of Portsmouth was signed on 10/23 August 1905.
56. Dispatch no. 135, Paris, 29 December 1905/11 January 1906, FAAr, 98, Xe, 55D.
57. Dispatch no. 19, Paris, 17/30 September 1905, FAAr, 26, IVa, 1.
58. Harting, however, only managed to supply circumstantial evidence in support of his allegation and Fontanka chose not to pursue the matter. Ibid.; Dispatch no. 1, Paris, 1/14 September 1905, FAAr, 4, IIa, 1.
59. Dispatch no. 135, Paris, 29 December 1905/11 January 1906, FAAr, 98, Xe, 55D.
60. Agafonov, *Zagranichnaia okhranka*, 70.

9 The 1905 Revolution and the Foreign Agentura: Harting's Campaign Against Munitions Contraband, 1905–1908

1. Dispatch no. 1, Paris 1/14 September 1905, FAAr, 4, IIa, 1.
2. Dispatch no. 135, Paris, 29 December 1905/11 January 1906, FAAr, 98, Xe, 55D.
3. Dispatch no. 76, Paris, 10/23 March 1906, FAAr, 4, IIa, 1.
4. Ibid.
5. Ibid.
6. N. K. Krupskaya, *Memoirs of Lenin*, trans. E. Vernoy (New York: International Press, 1930), 1: 63; B. I. Gorev, 'Leonid Men'shchikov: Iz istorii politicheskoi politsii provokatorii (po lichnym vospominiiam)', *KaS*, 1924, no. 3: 133; M. Futrell, *Northern Underground: Episodes of Russian Revolutionary Transport and Communications through Scandinavia and Finland, 1863–1917* (London: Faber and Faber, 1963), 45.
7. Gorev, 'Leonid Men'shchikov', 133.
8. Futrell, *Northern Underground*, 60–1; MVD, Department of Police Circular no. 118859, issued by the Special Section, 2 December 1910, FAAr, 158, XIIId (1), 10; Report no. 281 from Rataev, 5/18 October, 1904, FAAr, 213, XXIVh, 2.
9. MVD, Department of Police Circular no. 5787, 15 June 1903, FAAr, 158, XIIId (2), 8.
10. Futrell, *Northern Underground*, 39–40.
11. Ibid., 60–1.
12. Dispatch no. 224, Paris, 18/31 October 1902, FAAr, 213, XXIVh, 4a.
13. Ibid.
14. Krupskaya, *Memoirs of Lenin*, 1: 63.
15. V. K. Agafonov, *Zagranichnaia okhranka* (Petrograd: 1918), 50.
16. Dispatch no. 121, Paris, 13/26 December 1905, FAAr, 213, XXIV, 4.
17. Dispatch no. 34, Paris, 4/17 February 1906, FAAr, 213, XXIVh, 1.
18. See: Futrell, *Northern Underground*.
19. Ibid., 82–3.
20. Dispatch no. 121, Paris, 13/26 December 1905, FAAr, 213, XXIV, 4.
21. Ibid.
22. The ports covered by Harting's agents included: Amsterdam, Rotterdam, London, Liverpool, Hull, Manchester, Hamburg, Copenhagen, Antwerp, Genoa, Lübeck, Stockholm, Norrkoping, Gavle, Marseilles, Memel, Königsberg, Danzig, Stettin, Bremen and Ghent. R. Johnson, 'The Okhrana Abroad, 1885–1917: A Study of International Police Cooperation' (PhD diss., Columbia University, 1970), 132–3.
23. Dispatch no. 242, Paris, 13/26 July 1906, FAAr, 213, XXIVh, 1.
24. Johnson, 'The Okhrana Abroad', 54.
25. Dispatch no. 9, Paris, 18/31 January 1906, FAAr, 213, XXIVh, 4c.
26. Dispatch no. 76, Paris, 10/23 March 1906, 4, IIa, 1.
27. Harting's detectives were trained to track people not cargo and the chief of the Foreign Agentura wrote of their absolute unpreparedness for this work. Harting to the Department of Police, 17 November 1906, FAAr, 106, XIIe, 2a; Johnson, 'The Okhrana Abroad', 134.
28. From the Director of the Department of Police, attached to Circular no. 24497, 13 December 1906, FAAr, 213, XXIVh, 1.
29. Dispatch no. 132, Paris, 24 December 1905/6 January 1906, FAAr, 213, XXIVh, 1.
30. Dispatch no. 226, Paris, 24 June/7 July 1906, FAAr, 42, VIg, 1.
31. Dispatch no. 88, Paris, 6/19 March 1907, FAAr, 213, XXIVh, 5f.
32. Dispatch no. 9, Paris, 18/31 January 1906, 213, XXIVh, 4c.

33. MVD, Department of Police Circular no. 12411, issued by the Special Section, 8 May 1907, FAAr, 213, XXIVh, 5g.
34. Dispatch no. 330, Paris, 30 November/13 December 1906, FAAr, 213, XXIVh, 1.
35. During Harting's tenure in office he had to contend with: three ministers of internal affairs (A. G. Bulygin, P. N. Durnovo and P. A. Stolypin); five directors of Fontanka (S. G. Kovalenskii, N. P. Garin, E. I. Vuich, P. I. Rachkovskii, M. I. Trusevich); and three chiefs of the Special Section (N. A. Makarov, L. A. Timofeev, A. T. Vasil'ev).
36. Johnson, 'The Okhrana Abroad', 155.
37. Agafonov, *Zagranichnaia okhranka*, 78.
38. Ibid., 98–9.
39. Burtsev's sources of information, his methods, effect on the Department of Police and Fontanka's reaction to him are discussed in Chapter 11.
40. Dispatch no. 56, 20 January/2 February 1909, FAAr, 212, XXVc, 1.
41. Dispatch no. 211, Paris, 11/24 April 1909, 4, IIa, 1.
42. Agafonov, *Zagranichnaia okhranka*, 98–9.
43. Dispatch no. 140, Paris, 4/17 March 1909, FAAr, 4, IIa, 1.
44. Ibid.
45. Ibid.
46. Ibid.
47. Dispatch no. 188, Paris, 25 March/7 April 1909, FAAr, 11, IIIb, 5.

10 A. A. Krasil'nikov and the Reshaping of the Foreign Agentura: Aspects of the Problems of Political Police Reform, 1909–1914

1. The relationship between the Prefecture of Police and the Foreign Agentura was probably much closer than either Clemenceau or Briand suspected. In exceptional cases, when the Foreign Agentura found itself short staffed it would request that an appropriate number of detectives be seconded to it by the Prefect of Paris in order to complete the task at hand. The Prefect complied. Krasil'nikov to the Department of Police 11/24 June 1910, cited in: *Zagranichnaia Agentura Departamenta Politsii (Zapiski S. Svatikov i dokumenty Zagranichnaia Agentury)* GLAVNOE ARKHIVNOE UPRAVLENIE NKVD SSSR (Moscow: 1941), 119.
2. Dispatch no. 404, Paris, 6/19 August 1909, 4, IIa, 1.
3. Ibid.
4. Ibid.
5. 'Ukazatel' Imen', *PTsR*, 7: 359.
6. 'Pokazaniia V. L. Burtseva', *PTsR*, 1: 327.
7. A. I. Spiridovich, *Les dernières années de la Cour du Tsarskoe-Selo*, trans. M. Jeanson (Paris: Payot, 1928), 1: 313.
8. M. La Porte, *Histoire de l'Okhrana, la police secrete des tsars, 1880–1917* (Paris: Payot, 1935), 187.
9. V. K. Agafonov, *Zagranichnaia okhranka* (Petrograd: 1918), 11.
10. Ibid., 53–4, 57–8; MVD, Department of Police Circular issued by the Third Secretariat, 22 December 1909, FAAr, 26, IVa, 1.
11. Agafonov, *Zagranichnaia okhranka*, 53–4.
12. MVD, Department of Police Circular issued by the Third Secretariat, 22 December 1909, 26, IVa, 1.

13. Krasil'nikov was the third chief of the Foreign Agentura to hold respected rank upon his appointment. He served as a *statskii sovetnik* (V *chin*) with the designation of *chinovnik osobykh poruchenii*, Spiridovich, *Les dernières années*, 1: 313; Extraordinary Commission, Protocol no. 3, 'Pokazaniia Krasil'nikova', FAAr, 9, IIf, 10.
14. MVD, Department of Police Circular, issued by the Third Secretariat, 22 December 1909, 26, IVa, 1.
15. Marcel Bittard-Monin, a former employee of the Prefecture of Police in Paris joined the Foreign Agentura in 1908 when he was 35 years old. He soon became one of its finest detectives and Krasil'nikov's close associate.
16. French counter-intelligence intercepted all communications between the the Russian Embassy and St Petersburg at any rate. So the French Ministry of Interior was fully aware of Krasil'nikov's activities. *Zagaranichanai Agentura Departamenta Politsii*, 100.
17. P. G. Kurlov, *Gibel' imperatorskoi Rossii* (Berlin: 1923), 103–4.
18. For Kurlov's own description of his administration in these provinces see Ibid., Chapters 5–6.
19. 'Ukazatel' Imen', *PTsR*, 7: 392.
20. F. S. Zuckerman, *The Tsarist Secret Police in Russian Society, 1880–1917* (Basingstoke: Macmillan – now Palgrave Macmillan, 1996), Chapter 12.
21. Kurlov replaced Fontanka's director, the chief of the Special Section and the chief of the St Petersburg OO (over the Azef Affair) with his own men. See: Ibid., Chapter 12
22. A. A. Makarov, the new minister of internal affairs, was so ignorant of the Foreign Agentura's operations that he requested a detailed explanation of its duties. He claimed that the Foreign Agentura's functions were not clear in his mind. Dispatch no. 1213, Paris, 19 September/2 October 1911, FAAr, 11, IIIb, 7.
23. Dispatch no. 1360 (Krasil'nikov to Beletskii), Paris, 23 August/5 September 1913, 8, IId, 15.
24. Ibid.
25. Ibid.
26. Ibid.
27. Ibid.
28. Ibid.
29. Agafonov, *Zagranichnaia okhranka*, 116.
30. Dispatch no. 1360, (Krasil'nikov to Beletskii), Paris, 23 August/5 September 1913, FAAr, 8, IId, 5.
31. A. Spiridovich, 'Poslednie gody Tsarskosel'skogo Dvora', MS Spiridovich Collection, Sterling Memorial Library, Yale University, 2: 597–601, 668–9.
32. MVD, Department of Police Memorandum no. 112180 (Beletskii to Krasil'nikov), September 1913, FAAr, 8, IId, 2.
33. Ibid.
34. Ibid.
35. *Spravka*, a review of Krasil'nikov's proposals for the reorganisation of the Foreign Agentura by M. E. Broetskii, chief of the Special Section attached to Memorandum no. 41469, 9 September 1913, FAAr, 8, IId, 4.
36. For their career biographies see: 'Ukazatel' Imen', *PTsR*, 7: 307, 311. Zuckerman, *The Tsarist Secret Police*, Chapter 12.
37. For a copy of the reform itself see, MVD, Department of Police Circular no. 112382, 23 November 1913, FAAr, 8, IId, 6.

38. Dispatch no. 1840, Paris, 20 November/3 December 1913, FAAr, IId, 6.
39. See: FAAr, 26–27, IVa.
40. For an unpleasant exchange between Fontanka and Harting over this issue see MVD, Department of Police Circular no. 130189, issued by the Special Section, 10 July 1907, FAAr, 26, IVa, 2; Dispatch no. 320, Paris, 17/30 July 1907, FAAr, 26, IVa, 2.
41. See, FAAr, 26, IVa, 1 for the year 1910; MVD, Department of Police Circular no. 13053, 16 September 1912, FAAr, 26, IVa, 1.
42. The type of supporting information required by Fontanka can be gleaned from any of Krasil'nikov's accounts maintained in FAAR such as the financial report for November 1912. Dispatch no. 74, Paris, 18/31 January 1913, FAAr, 26, IVa, 4a.
43. MVD Department of Police Circular no. 1115508, 19 April 1913, FAAr, 26, IVa, 1.
44. MVD Department of Police Circular no. 111698, issued by the Special Section, 28 May 1913, FAAr, 26, IVa, 1.
45. Ibid.
46. A. I. Spiridovich, 'Poslednie gody Tsarskosel'skogo Dvora', 2: 743.
47. *Zagranichnaia Agentura Departamenta Politsii*, 18–19, 63, 86.
48. Agafonov, *Zagranichnaia okhranka*, 182–5. For a sample of the reports that Bint and Sambian received from their spies see, FAAr, IIe.

    Bint was not so fortunate. He had made 14 trips to Switzerland during the war, each lasting between four and two weeks. His luck ran out during his fifteenth trip, on 2 February 1917 when the Lausanne police arrested him for suspected surveillance of Russian émigrés within Switzerland.The 65 year old Bint sat in a Swiss prison while the regime he had so loyally defended collapsed. With no one left to defend him, Bint was released from prison on a bond of 3,000 francs at the end of April. When his case came to trial in May, he did not appear. A. E. Senn, *The Russian Revolution in Switzerland, 1914–1917* (Madison: the University of Wisconsin Press, 1971), 220–1.
49. H. A. Simon and J. G. March, *Organizations* (New York: Wiley & Sons, 1958), 197.
50. Agafonov, *Zagranichnaia okhranka*, 129.

11 A Revolutionary Strikes Back: Vladimir Burtsev Against the Tsarist Secret Police, 1907–1914

1. The concept of a revolutionary police bureau to protect subversive groups was first developed not by Burtsev but by a French revolutionary during the Second Empire. The experiment survived to the end of the Empire in 1870; it never attained the level of sophistication and effectiveness which would be exhibited by Burtsev's organisation over thirty years later. See: E. K. Bramstedt, *Dictatorship and Political Police: The Technique of Control by Fear* (New York: Oxford University Press, 1945), 48–9.
2. For material on Burtsev's career see A. Kimball, 'The Harassment of Russian Revolutionaries Abroad: The London Trial of Vladimir Burtsev in 1898', in *Oxford Slavonic Papers*, n.s., vol. 6, ed. R. Auty and J. L. Fennell (New York: Oxford University Press, 1973), 48–9; V. Burtsev, *Bor'ba za svobodnuiu Rossiiu: Moi vospominaniia (1882–1912 gg.)* (Berlin: 1923).
3. Burtsev, *Bor'ba za svobodnuiu Rossiiu*, 144.
4. *Byloe: sbornik po istorii russkogo osvoboditel'nogo dvizheniia*, 1–6 (1902–1904).
5. *Byloe: zhurnal posviashchenyi istorii osvoboditel'nogo dvizheniia*, was scholarly in tone and therefore Burtsev found his role reduced to occasional contributor.

Intercepted letter from 'Vladimir' postmarked St Petersburg, 30 November 1905 FAAr, 197, XVIId, 1A.

6. Burtsev, *Bor'ba za svobodnuiu Rossiiu*, 177–8.
7. M. Bakai, *O razoblachiteliakh i razoblachitel'stve (pis'mo k V. Burtsevu)* (New York 1912), 24.
8. Ibid., 27–8.
9. Burtsev, *Bor'ba za svobodnuiu Rossiiu*, 297–8.
10. Intercepted letter from Burtsev addressed to Duma Deputy Shingarev, 21 November 1910, FAAr, 1917, XVIIb.
11. Dispatch no. 347, Paris, 18 September/1 October 1908, 185, XVIIa, 1.
12. Although Burtsev considered Bakai a junior partner in his organisation, Bakai thought differently. By early 1909, however, Bakai became disgusted with Burtsev's tactics and disillusioned with police work, moved to Belgium where he undertook a new profession. Burtsev, *Bor'ba za svobodnuiu Rossiiu*, 213; Bakai *O razoblachiteliakh*, 10.
13. Report on *Byloe* 12/25 May 1908, FAAr, 192, XVIb (4). For the two articles cited in the report see *Byloe*, Paris, no. 7; Burtsev, *Bor'ba za svobodnuiu Rossiiu*, 217.
14. Dispatch no.?, Paris, 30 October/12 November 1908, 210, XXVIa, 1.
15. Burtsev established two subsequent journals. The first of these, *Obshchee Delo (Common Cause)* appeared in only four numbers in 1910. The second *Budushchee (The Future)* established in 1911, was bilingual. It appeared in Russian with the French translation on the opposite page and issues appeared into 1914.
16. F. S. Zuckerman, 'The Russian Political Police at Home and Abroad (1880–1917) Its Structure, Functions, and Methods, and its Struggle with the Organized Opposition' (PhD diss., New York University, 1973), 528–87.
17. Dispatch no. 1563, Paris, 26 November/9 December 1911, FAAr, 197, XVIId, 3b.
18. Bakai, *O razoblachiteliakh*, 49, 60–1.
19. Ibid., 50; Dispatch no. 812, Paris, 28 May/10 June 1913, FAAr, 197, XVIId, 3b, Dispatch no. 907, Paris, 6/19 October 1910, FAAr, 197, XVIId, 36; Dispatch no 1574, Paris, 12/25 October 1913, FAAr, 211, XXIVb, 1.
20. MVD, Department of Police Circular no. 163074, issued by the Special Section, FAAr, 211, XXIV, 1b; Dispatch no.1563, Paris, 26 November/9 December 1911, FAAr, 197, XVIId, 3b.
21. Bakai, *O razoblachiteliakh*, 44.
22. Dispatch no. 1360, Paris, 23 August/5 September 1913, FAAr, 8, IId, 5.
23. Dispatch no. 1391, Paris, 31 August/15 September 1913, FAAr, 197, XVIId, 18; Dispatch no. 137, Paris, 25 January/7 February 1913, FAAr, 210, XXIV, 1.
24. Dispatch no. 634, Paris, 9/22 May 1911, FAAr, 210, XXIVa, 1; Dispatch no. 152, Paris, 1/14 February 1912, FAAr, 197, XVIId, 1b.
25. V. K. Agafonov, *Zagranichnaia okhranka* (Petrograd: 1918), 39–40.
26. Record of Tatiana Tsetlin, FAAr, 21, IIIe, 1b.
27. B. I. Gorev, 'Leonid Men'shchikov: Iz istorii politicheskoi politsii i provokatsii (po lichnym vospominanaiam)', *KaS*, no. 3 (1924): 135–6.
28. C. Bobrovskaya, *Provocateurs I Have Known* (London: [1931]), 16.
29. Dispatch no. 1892, Paris, 28 November/11 December 1913, FAAr, 212, XXIVc, 2h.
30. B. D. Wolfe, *Three Who Made a Revolution*, 4th rev. edn (1948; reprint, New York: Dell, 1964), 536–7.
31. Record of Iakov Zhitomirskii, FAAr, IIIf, 1b.
32. Burtsev, *Bor'ba svobodnuiu Rossiiu*, 216.
33. IA. Akimov, *Ne mogu molchat'* (New York: 1912), 43.

34. Dispatch no. 37, Paris, 7/20 January 1914, 211, XXIVa, 1b. Burtsev himself wrote with bitterness about the ingratitude and obstructionism of the revolutionaries, especially the Socialist-Revolutionaries. See: V. Burtsev, 'Moia bor'ba s provokatorami 1912–1914', MS Nikolaevsky Collection, Hoover Institution.
35. Burtsev exposed at least 33 important agents. Agafonov, *Zagranichnaia okhranka*, 167.
36. See: FAAr, 210, XXIVa, 2.
37. Dispatch no. 253, Paris, 1909, FAAr, 212, XXIVc, 2q, 1.
38. Dispatch no. 321, Paris, 29 May/11 June 1909, 195, XVIIf, 1; Dispatch no. 1694, Paris, 23 December/5 January 1912, FAAr, 197, XVIId, 1b.
39. Dispatch no. 754, Paris, 26 December 1909/8 January 1910, FAAr, 211, XXIVb, 7; Dispatch no. 1360, Paris, 23 August/5 September 1913, FAAr, 8, IId, 5.
40. When undercover agent Batushanskii was exposed and interrogated by a revolutionary tribunal, he supplied it with information which in turn led to the downfall of five other *sotrudniki*. Dispatch no. 129, Paris, 16 February/1 March 1910, 210, XXIVa, 1.
41. V. Gurko, *Features and Figures of the Past: Government and Opinion in the Reign of Nicholas II*, trans. Laura Matveev, the Hoover Library on War, Revolution, and Peace Publication no. 14 (Stanford: Stanford University Press, 1939), 119–20,
42. MVD, Department of Police Circular no. 144422, 31 December 1908, FAAr, 198, XVIId, 4.
43. Dispatch no. 356, Paris, 20 June/3 July 1909, FAAr, 185, XVb, 2a.
44. Dispatch no. 139, Paris, 23 April/5 May 1908, FAAr, 102, XIb, 1.
45. Dispatch no. 211, Paris, 11/24 April 1909, FAAr, IIa, 1.
46. Dispatch no. 449, Paris, 9/22 September 1909, 185, XVb, 1.
47. Ibid.
48. Personnel File of Lev Dimitriev Beitner, FAAr, IIIf, 1a.
49. Dispatch no. 579, Paris, 5/18 June 1910, FAAr, 210, XXVa, 1.
50. MVD, Department of Police Circular no. 118082, issued by the Special Section, 20 July 1911, FAAr, 185, XVa, 1.
51. MVD, From the Office of the Vice Director of Police, Circular no. 8539, 18 January, 1911, FAAr, 185, XVj, 1.
52. Dispatch no. 1256, Paris, 9/22 July 1914, FAAr, 216, XXVIId, 7.
53. Agafonov, *Zagranichnaia okhranka*, 164.
54. Dispatch no. 1541, Paris, 22 November/5 December 1911, FAAr, 12, IIIe, 1.
55. Dispatch no. 20, Paris, 1/14 January 1914, FAAr, 212, XXIVc, 2k.
56. Dispatch no. 22, Paris, 2/15 January 1914, FAAr, 211, XXIVb, 1.
57. Ibid.
58. MVD, Department of Police Circular no. 190018, 8 January 1914, FAAr, 12, IIe, 1. As an extra precaution the Department of Police placed him under surveillance. Agafonov, *Zagranichnaia okhranka*, 172.
59. Dispatch no. 6, Paris, 3/16 January 1915, FAAr, 211, XXVa, 5p.
60. Although Burtsev dealt with Petrishchev for two years, the actual length of the informer's stay in Paris is not known. Burtsev, 'Moia bor'ba', 4, 14–15.
61. Krasil'nikov continued to believe that Sushkov was the culprit. In 1920 Burtsev happened to meet Krasil'nikov in Paris. Ibid., 12.
62. Ibid., 15.
63. Ibid., 5.
64. 'Tsirkuliar o V. L. Burtseva', *Byloe*, n.s., 1917, nos. 5/6 (27/28): 125; I. V. Alekseev, *Provokator Anna Serebriakova* (Moscow: 1932), 60.

65. Ibid., 60.
66. 'Prikliucheniia I. F. Manuilova: Po arkhivnym materialam', *Byloe*, n.s., 1917, nos. 5/6 (27/28) 237–8.
67. Ibid., 276–7.
68. A. P., 'Departament politsii v 1892–1908: Iz vospominanii chinovnika', *Byloe*, n.s., 1917, nos. 5/6 (27/28): 22.
69. N. P. Eroshkin, *Istoriia gosudarstvennykh uchrezhdenii dorevoliutsionnoi Rossii*, 2nd edn (Moscow: 1968), 283; 'Dopros S. P. Beletskogo', *PTsR*, 3: 264.
70. Eroshkin, *Istoriia gosudarstvennykh uchrezhdenii*, 288–9.
71. Dispatch no. 924, Paris, 19 September/2 October 1916, FAAr, 37, VIa, 5.
72. Agafonov, *Zagranichnaia okhranka*, 167.
73. A. T. Vassilyev, *The Okhrana: The Russian Secret Police*, trans. René Fülop-Miller (Philadelphia: J. P. Lippencott, 1930), 96.
74. MVD, Department of Police Circular no. 104760, 7 July 1911, FAAr, 185, XVb, 2a.
75. Bakai, *O razoblachiteliakh*, 44–5; Akimov, *Ne mogu molchat'*, 9.
76. Bakai, *O razoblachiteliakh*, 45.
77. Ibid., 56–7, 63.
78. Ibid., 54.
79. For example, the Russian political police never contemplated murdering Burtsev (although he encouraged public opinion to believe that it did), an action that would have saved Fontanka considerable discomfort. Dispatch no. 396, Paris, 30 July/12 August 1910, FAAr, 197, XVIId, 1a.

Conclusion and Epilogue

1. For a stimulating discussion of alternate perspectives from which to view European History see; N. Davies, *A History of Europe*, especially his introductory chapter, and L. Wolff's *Inventing Europe: The Map of Civilization on the Mind of the Enlightenment*, especially his Introduction and Conclusion.
2. J. Berlière, 'A Republican Political Police? Political Policing in France under the Third Republic', *in The Policing of Politics in the Twentieth Century, ed. Mark Mazower Historical Perspectives* (Oxford: Berghahn Books, 1997), 46–7, 49.
3. C. Emsley and B. Weinberger, 'Introduction', in *Policing Western Europe: Politics, Professionalism and Public Order, 1850–1940*, ed. C. Emsley and B. Weinberger (Westport Conn.: Greenwood Press, 1991), xi.
4. D. Bayley, *Patterns of Policing: A Comparative International Analysis* (New Brunswick, NJ: Rutgers University Press, 1985), 49–52.
5. Quoted in: J. Daly, *Autocracy under Siege: Security Police and Opposition in Russia 1860–1905* (DeKalb Illinois, Northern Illinois University Press, 1998), 1.
6. R. Johnson, 'The Okhrana Abroad: A Study in International Police Cooperation' (Ph. D diss., Columbia University, 1971), 81.
7. Arno J. Mayer, *The Persistence of the Old Regime: Europe to the Great War* (New York: Pantheon Books, 1918),15, 301.
8. F. S. Zuckerman, *The Tsarist Secret Police in Russian Society, 1880–1917* (Basingstoke: Macmillan – now Palgrave Macmillan, 1996), 197–9 and Chapter 12.
9. *Zagranichnaia Agentura Departamenta Politsii (Zapiski S. Svatikov i dokumenty zagranichnoi agentury)*, Glavnoe Arkhivnoe UPRAVLENIE NKVD SSSR (Moscow: 1941), 57.

10. The assassination of Prime Minister Peter A. Stolypin in 1911 by a lone terrorist is the exception that proves the rule. By this time terrorism in Russia had been discredited as means of political action. For a discussion of Russian terrorism between 1900 and 1911 see Zuckerman, *The Tsarist Secret Police, passim.*
11. R. B. Jensen, 'The International Anti-Anarchist Conference of 1898 and the Origins of Interpol', *JCH*, 16, 2 (April 1981): 339.
12. *Police Cooperation in Europe: Lectures at the International Symposium on Surveillance*, ed. C. J. E. F. Fijnaut and R. H. Hermann (Lochen: Van den Brink, 1987), 34.
13. R. O. Collin, 'The Italian Police and Internal Security from Giolitti to Mussolini' (D.Phil. Thesis, Oriel College, Trinity, 1983), 114.
14. B. L. Ingraham, *Political Crime in Europe: A Comparative Study of France, Germany and England* (Berkeley: University of California Press, 1979), 220; Mark Mazower, 'Conclusion: The Policing of Politics in Historical Perspective', in *The Policing of Politics in the Twentieth Century*, 244–5.
15. Ibid., 246.
16. *Police Cooperation in Europe*, 35: For a thumbnail sketch dealing with the creation of the Internal Criminal Police Commission see: C. Fijnaut, 'The International Criminal Police Commission and the Fight Against Communism, 1923–1945', in *The Policing of Politics in the Twentieth Century*, 111–13.
17. J. van Dijk, 'More than a matter of security: trends in crime prevention in Europe', in *Crime in Europe*, ed. F. Heidensohn and M. Farrell (London: Routledge, 1991), 110–11; *Police Cooperation in Europe*, 36.
18. C. Fijnaut, 'Police co-operation within western Europe', in *Crime in Europe*, 109.
19. *Police Cooperation in Europe*, 69.
20. Ibid., 17–18, 87.
21. Ibid., 87–8.
22. *Crime in Europe*, 119.
23. United States Institute of Peace, 'Special Report: The Diplomacy of Counterterrorism, Lesson Learned, Ignored and Disputed', January 2002.
24. Ibid., 5–6.
25. Ibid., 8.

Select Bibliography

I Unpublished sources

Archives

The Hoover Institution, Stanford, California:
The Records of the Foreign Agentura of the Russian Political Police.
The Boris Nikolaevsky Collection.
The Moravsky Collection.
The Papers of General V. N. Russiian.
Yale University, Sterling Memorial Library:
The Spiridovich Collection.
Columbia University, New York:
The Boris Bakhmeteff Archive.

Manuscripts, reports and depositions

'Attachment [*sic*!] to Bulletin No. 7 of the Executive Committee of the Paris Council of Representative Political Organizations (received for publication from the Special Commission engaged in investigating the Archives of the Paris Okhrana).' [English translation], 10 October 1917. The Records of the Foreign Agentura . . . (FAAr), (Folder) IIa, (Box) 4.

Deposition of A. A. Lopukhin before the Extraordinary Investigating Commission investigating the illegal activities of former ministers and others, 6 November 1917 (in Russian). Untitled MS, Nikolaevsky Collection.

Director of the Department of Police Lopukhin to the Committee of Ministers, 6 December 1904 (in Russian). Untitled MS, Nikolaevsky Collection.

'Dopros D.S.S. A. A. Krasil'nikova. Protokoly: No. 3 7/20 Iiunia; No. 5 9/22 Iiunia 1917; No. 7 27 Iiunia/10 Iiulia 1917', FAAr 9, IIf, 10.

Hollis, Ernest V. Jr. 'Police Systems of Imperial and Soviet Russia'. Boris Bakhmeteff Archive, Columbia University.

Procurator's pre-trial statements, the Lopukhin treason case (in Russian). Untitled MS, Nikolaevsky Collection.

Russia, MVD, Departament politsii. Po 2 deloproizvodstvu. *O preobrazovanii politsii v Imperii*, 1 Sentiabria 1913g. No. 20. 083, Sterling Memorial Library, Yale University.

Russia, MVD, Departament politsii, *Sbornik sekretnykh Tsirkuliarov obrashchennykh k Nachal'nikam gubernskikh zhandarmskikh upravlenii, Gubernatoram i pr. v techenie 1902–1907*. New York Public Library. These circulars were apparently a file of the Nizhnii Novgorod Gendarme Directorate.

Russiian, V. N. 'Rabota okhrannykh otdelenii v Rossii'. Moravsky Collection.

Schneiderman, Jeremiah. 'Sergei Zubatov and Revolutionary Marxism: The Struggle for the Working Class in Tsarist Russia'. MS loaned by the author.

Spiridovich, A. I. 'Peter Ivanovich Rachkovskii'. Spiridovich Collection, Sterling Memorial Library, Yale University.

Spiridovich, A. I. 'Poslednie gody Tsarskosel'skogo Dvora'. 2 Vols. Spiridovich Collection, Sterling Memorial Library, Yale University.

Svatikov, S. G. 'Sozdanie "Sionskikh protokolov" po dannym ofitsial'nago sledstviia 1917 goda'. Nikolaevsky Collection.
Tennant Ellis [Edward Ellis Smith]. 'The Department of Police 1911–1912: From the Recollections of Nikolai Vladimirovich Veselago'. Hoover Institution.
United States Institute Of Peace. 'Special Report: The Diplomacy of Counterterrorism, Lessons Learned, Ignored and Disputed'. January 2002.

Doctoral dissertations

Blakely, Allison. 'The Socialist Revolutionary Party, 1901–1907: The Populist Response to the Industrialization of Russia'. PhD diss., University of California, Berkeley, 1971.
Calhoun, Arthur Fryer. 'The Politics of Internal Order: French Government and Revolutionary Labor, 1898–1914'. PhD diss., Princeton University, 1973.
Collin, Richard Oliver. 'The Italian Police and Internal Security from Giolitti to Mussolini'. DPhil diss., Oriel College, Trinity, 1983.
Johnson, Richard J. 'The Okhrana Abroad, 1885–1917: A Study of International Police Cooperation'. PhD diss., Columbia University, 1971.
Judge, Edward H. 'The Russia of Plehve: Programs and Policies of the Ministry of Internal Affairs, 1902–1904'. PhD diss., University of Michigan, 1975.
McDaniel, Frank James. 'Political Assassination and Mass Execution: Terrorism in Revolutionary Russia, 1878–1938'. PhD diss., University of Michigan, 1976.
Millard, Michael B. 'Russian Revolutionary Emigration, Terrorism and the "Political Struggle" '. PhD diss. University of Rochester, 1973.
Schneiderman, Jeremiah. 'The Tsarist Government and the Labor Movement 1898–1903: The Zubatovshchina'. PhD diss., University of California, Berkeley, 1966.
Zuckerman, Fredric S. 'The Russian Political Police at Home and Abroad (1880–1917): Its Structure, Functions, and Methods and Its Struggle with the Organized Opposition'. PhD diss., New York University, 1973.

II Selected published sources

Books and pamphlets and government documents

Agafonov, V. K. *Zagranichnaia okhranka.* Petrograd: 1918.
Akashi, Motojiro. *Rakka ryusui. Colonel Akashi's Report on his Secret Cooperation with the Russian Revolutionary Parties during the Russo-Japanese War.* Selected chapters. Edited by Olavi K Fält and Antti Kujala. Studia Historica 31. Helsinki: Finnish Historical Society, 1988.
Alekseev, I. V. *Istoriia odnogo provokatora: Obvinitel'noe zakliuchenie i materialy k protsessu A. E. Serebriakova.* Moscow: 1925.
——*Provokator Anna Serebriakova.* Moscow: 1932.
Andrew, Christopher. *Theophile Delcassé and the Making of the Entente Cordiale: A Reappraisal of French Foreign Policy 1898–1905.* New York: Macmillan, 1968.
——*Her Majesty's Secret Service: The Making of the British Intelligence Community.* New York: Viking Press, 1986.
Aziât (pseud.). *Russkie shpiony v Germanii.* Berlin: 1904.
Bakai, M. *O razoblachitel'iakh i razoblachitel'stve, pis'mo k V. Burtsevu.* New York: 1912.

Baron, Samuel H. *Plekhanov: The Father of Russian Marxism*. Stanford: Stanford University Press, 1963.
Bayley, David. *Patterns of Policing: A Comparative International Analysis*. New Brunswick: Rutgers University Press, 1985.
Berlière, Jean Marc. *Le Préfet Lépine: Vers La Naissance de la Police Moderne*. Paris: Editions de Noël, 1993.
——*Le Monde des polices en France XIXe–XXe siècles*. Paris: 1996.
Betskii, K., and P. Pavlov. *Russkii rokambol': Prikliucheniia I. F. Manasevich – Manuilova*. Leningrad: 1925.
Blau, Peter M. *Bureaucracy in Modern Society*. New York: Random House, 1956.
——*The Dynamics of Bureaucracy: A Study of Interpersonal Relationships in Two Government Agencies*. Rev. edn. Chicago: Chicago University Press, 1963.
Bobrovskaya, C. *Provocateurs I Have Known*. London, [1931].
Boevye predpriiatiia sotsialistov-revoliutsionerov v osveshchenii okhranki. [1918].
Bogdanovich, A. V. *Tri poslednikh samoderzhtsa: Dnevnik A. V. Bogdanovich[a]*. Moscow: 1924.
Brachmann, Bothe. *Russische Sozialdemokraten In Berlin 1895–1914*. Berlin: 1962.
Bramstedt, E. K. *Dictatorship and Political Police: The Technique of Control by Fear*. New York: Oxford University Press, 1945.
Brust, Harold. *I Guarded Kings: The Memoirs of a Political Police Officer*. London: n.d.
Bukhbinder, N. A. *Zubatovshchina i rabochee dvizhenie v Rossii*. Moscow: 1926.
Burtsev, Vladimir. *Tsarskii listok*. Paris: 1909.
——*Bor'ba za svobodnuiu Rossiiu: Moi vospominaniia (1882–1912g.)*. Vol. 1. Berlin: 1912.
——*Protokoly sionskikh mudretsov: Dokazannyi podlog*. Paris: 1938.
Chapman, Brian. *Police State*. London: Macmillan, – now Palgrave Macmillan, 1970.
Cohn, Norman. *Warrant for Genocide: The Myth of the Jewish World – Conspiracy and the Protocols of Zion*. London: Eyre and Spotteswoode, 1967.
Crime in Europe. Edited by Frances Heidensohn and Martin Farrell. London: Routledge, 1991.
Daly, Jonathan W. *Autocracy under Siege: Security Police and Opposition in Russia 1860–1905*. DeKalb Illinois: Northern Illinois University Press, 1998.
Davies, Norman. *Europe: A History*. London: Random House, 1996. Reprinted with corrections, 1997.
Davis, John A. *Conflict and Control: Law and Order in Nineteenth Century Italy*. Basingstoke: Macmillan – now Palgrave Macmillan, 1988.
Delevskii, IU. *Protokoly sionskikh mudretsov Istoriia odnogo podloga*. Berlin: 1923.
Delo A. A. Lopukhina v osobom prisutsvii pravitel'stuiushchago senata: Stenograficheskii otchet. St Petersburg: 1910.
Emerson, Donald E. *Metternich and the Political Police: Security and Subversion in the Hapsburg Monarchy (1815–1830)*. The Hague: Martinus Nijhoff, 1968.
Emsley, Clive. *The English Police: A Political and Social History*, 2nd edn. London: Longmans, 1996.
——*Gendarmes and the State in Nineteenth Century Europe*. Oxford: Oxford University Press, 1999.
Erenfel'd, B. *Tiazhelyi front: Iz istorii bor'by bol'shevikov s tsarskoi tainoi politsiei*. Moscow: 1983.
Eroshkin, N. P. *Istoriia gosudarstvennykh uchrezhdenii dorevoliutsionnoi Rossii*. 2nd edn. Moscow: 1968.
Fishman, Willam J. *East End Jewish Radicals 1875–1914*. London: Duckworth, 1975.

Fooner, Michael. *Interpol: The Inside Story of the International Crime-Fighting Organization.* Chicago: Henry Regnery Co., 1973.

Fosdick, Raymond. *European Police Systems.* New York: The Century Co., 1915.

From the Other Shore: Russian Political Emigrants in Britain. Edited by John Slatter. London: Frank Cass: 1984.

Futrell, Michael. *Northern-Underground: Episodes of Russian Revolutionary Transport and Communications through Scandanavia and Finland 1863–1917.* London: Faber & Faber, 1963.

Galtier-Boissière, Jean. *Mysteries of the French Secret Police.* Translated by Ronald Leslie-Melville. London: 1938.

Gartner Lloyd P. *The Jewish Immigrant in England, 1870–1914.* Studies in Society no. 6. London: George Allen & Unwin Ltd., 1960.

Gerasimov, A. V. *Na lezvii s terroristami.* Paris: YMCA Press, 1985.

Gessen, V. M. *Iskliuchitel'noe polozhenie.* St Petersburg: 1908.

Glavnoe Arkhivnoe Upravlenie NKVD SSSR. *Zagranichnaia Agentura Departamenta Politsii (Zapiski S. Svatikov i dokumenty zagranichnoi agentury).* Moscow: 1941.

Guerassimov, Aleksandr Vasil'evich. *Tsarisme et Terrorisme, souvenirs du général Guerissimov.* Paris: Plon, 1934.

Gurko, Vladimir I. *Features and Figures of the Past: Government and Opinion in the Reign of Nicholas II.* Translated by Laura Matveev. The Hoover Library on War, Revolution, and Peace Publication no. 14. Stanford: Stanford University Press, 1939.

Hingley, Ronald. *The Russian Secret Police: Muscovite, Imperial Russian and Soviet Political Security Operations.* New York: Simon and Schuster, 1970.

Ingraham, Barton L. *Political Crime in Europe: A Comparative Study of France, Germany and England.* Berkeley and Los Angeles: University of California Press, 1979.

Isvolsky, Alexander. *Recollections of a Foreign Minister (Memoirs of Alexander Isvolsky).* Trans. Louis Seeger. New York: Doubleday, Page and Co., 1921.

Izoblichennye provokatory. Petrograd, [1917].

Jensen, Richard B. *Liberty and Order: The Theory and Practice of Italian Public Security Policy, 1848 to the Crisis of the 1890s.* New York: Garland Publishing, Inc., 1991.

Johnson, Robert H. *New Mecca, New Babylon: Paris and the Russian Exiles 1920–1945.* Montreal: McGill-Queen's University Press, 1988.

Judge, Edward H. *Plehve: Repression and Reform in Imperial Russia 1902–1904.* Syracuse: Syracuse University Press, 1983.

Keep, J. L. H. *The Rise of Social Democracy in Russia.* Oxford: Oxford University Press, 1963.

Kennan, George Frost. *Siberia and the Exile System.* 2 vols 1891. Reprint. New York: Russell and Russell, 1970.

Kirchheimer, Otto. *Political Justice: The Use of Legal Procedure for Political Ends.* Princeton: Princeton University Press, 1961.

Knight, Amy W. *The KGB: Police and Politics in the Soviet Union.* Rev. edn. Boston: Unwin Hyman, 1990.

Kokovtsov, Vladimir Nikolaevich. *Out of My Past: The Memoirs of Count Kokovtsov.* Ed. H. H. Fisher, trans. Laura Matveev. The Hoover Library on War, Revolution, and Peace Publication no. 6. Stanford: Stanford University Press, 1935.

Komin V. V. and M. M. Cherniakova. *Istoriia Rossiskii Reoliutsionnoi Emigratsii.* Kalinin: 1988.

Koz'min, B. P. *S. V. Zubatov i ego korrespondenty.* Moscow: 1928.

Kropotkin P. *Memoirs of a Revolutionary.* Preface by George Brandes. Volume 2. London: 1899.

Krupskaya, Nadezhda K. *Memoirs of Lenin*. Trans. E. Vernay. New York: International Publishers, 1930.
Kurlov, P. G. *Gibel' imperatorskoi Rossii*. Berlin: 1923.
Lansdowne, Andrew. *A Life's Reminiscences of Scotland Yard* (London: Leadenhall Press, 1890? [reprint New York: Garland Publishing, New York, 1984].
La Porte, Maurice. *Histoire de l'Okhrana la police secrete des tsars, 1880–1917*. Paris: Payot, 1935.
Leggett, George. *The Cheka: Lenin's Political Police*. Oxford: Clarendon Press, 1981.
Liang, Hsi-Huey. *The Rise of Modern Police and the European State System from Metternich to the Second World War*. Cambridge: Cambridge University Press, 1992.
Longuet, Jean and George Silber. *Terroristy i Okhranka*. Moscow: 1924.
Lowenthal, Max. *The Federal Bureau of Investigation*. New York: Harcourt Brace Jovanovich, 1950.
Lüdtke, Alf. *Police and State in Prussia, 1815–1850*. Trans. Pete Burgess. Cambridge: Cambridge University Press, 1989.
Maisky, Ivan. *Journey into the Past*. Trans. Frederick Holt. London: Hutchinson & Co., 1962.
Mannheim, Karl. *Ideology and Utopia: An Introduction to the Sociology of Knowledge*. London: Routledge and Kegan Paul, 1960.
Manning, Roberta Thompson. *The Crisis of the Old Order in Russia: Gentry and Government*. Princeton: Princeton University Press, 1982.
Martov IU., P. Maslov and A Potresov, eds. *Obshchestvennoe dvizhenie v Rossii v nachale xx-go veka*. 4 vols St Petersburg: 1909–1914.
Martynov, A. P. *Moia sluzhba v Otdel'nom korpuse zhandarmov: Vospominaniia*. Stanford: Hoover Institution Press, 1972.
Mayer, Arno I. *The Persistence of the Old Regime: Europe to the Great War*. New York: Pantheon Books, 1981.
Mayeur, Jean-Marie and Madeleine Reberioux. *The Third Republic from its Origins to the Great War, 1871–1914*. Trans. J. R. Foster. Cambridge: Cambridge University Press, 1984.
Meijer, J. M. *Knowledge and Revolution: The Russian Colony in Zuerich*. Assen: Van Gorcum & Co., 1965.
Men'shchikov, L. P. *Okhrana i revoliutsiia. K istorii tainykh politicheskikh organizatsii sushchestvovavshikh vo vremena samoderzhaviia*. 3 vols in 2. Moscow: 1925–1932.
——ed. *Russkii politicheskii sysk za granitsei*. Pt 1. Paris: 1914.
Miller, Martin A. *Kropotkin*. Chicago: University of Chicago Press, 1976.
——*The Russian Revolutionary Émigrés 1825–1870*. Baltimore: The Johns Hopkins University Press, 1986.
Mommsen Wolfgang, and Gerhard Herschfeld, eds. *Social Protest, Violence and Terror in Nineteenth- and Twentieth-Century Europe*. New York: St. Martin's Press – now Palgrave Macmillan, 1982.
Monas, Sidney. *The Third Section: Police and Society under Nicholas I*. Cambridge: Harvard University Press, 1961.
Moskovskoe okhrannoe otdelenie. [1917].
Mosse, George L., ed. *Police Forces in History*. London: Sage Publications, 1975.
Naimark, Norman M. *Terrorists and Social Democrats: The Russian Revolutionary Movement under Alexander III*. Cambridge: Harvard University Press, 1983.
Nikolaejewsky, Boris. *Aseff the Spy: The Russian Terrorist and Police Stool*. New York: Doubleday, Doran and Co., 1934.
——*Aseff the Spy: Russian Terrorist and Police Stool*. 1934. Reprint. The Russian series, vol. 14. Hattiesburg Miss.: Academic International, 1969.

Novitskii, V. D. *Iz vospominanii zhandarma*. Leningrad: 1929.

Obolenskii, V. V. *Mezhdunarodnye i mezhkontinental'nye migratsii v dovoennoi Rossii i SSSR*. Moscow: 1928.

Orlovsky, Daniel T. *The Limits of Reform: The Ministry of Internal Affairs in Imperial Russia 1802–1881*. Cambridge: Harvard University Press, 1981.

Ortmann, Frank. *Revolutionäre im Exil. Der 'Auslandsbund Russischer Sozialdemokraten' Zwischen Autoritärem Führungsangspruch und Politischer Ohnmacht (1888–1903)*. Stuttgart: Franz Steiner Verlag, 1994.

Orzhekhovskii, I. V. *Iz istorii vnutrennei politiki samoderzhaviia v 60–70-x godakh XIX veka*. Gorkii: 1974.

——*Samoderzhavie protiv Revoliutsionnoi Rossii*. Moscow: 1982.

Pamiati Viacheslava Konstantinovicha Pleve (Sbornik). St Petersburg: 1904.

Pavlov, P. *Agenty, zhandarmy, palachi: Po dokumentam*. Petrograd: 1922.

Payne, Howard C. *The Police State of Napoleon Bonaparte 1851–1860*. Seattle: University of Washington Press, 1966.

Pipes, Richard, *Russia Under the Old Regime*. London: Weidenfeld & Nicolson, 1974; Penguin Books, 1977.

Pis'ma Azefa, 1893–1917. Composed by D. B. Pavlov and Z. I. Peregudova. Moscow: 1994.

Police Cooperation in Europe: Lectures at the International Symposium on Surveillance. Edited by C. J. C. F. Fijnaut and R. H. Hermann. Lochen: Van der Brink, 1987.

Policing Western Europe: Politics, Professionalism and Public Order, 1850–1940. Edited by Clive Emsley and Barbara Weinberger: Westport Conn.: Greenwood Press, 1991.

Pomper, Philip. *Peter Lavrov and the Russian Revolutionary Movement*. Chicago: University of Chicago Press, 1972.

Porter, Bernard. *The Origins of the Vigilant State: The London Metropolitan Police Special Branch Before the First World War*. London: Weidenfeld & Nicolson, 1987.

——*Plots and Paranoia: A History of Political Espionage in Britain, 1790–1988*. London: Unwin Hyman, 1989.

Raeff, Marc. *The Well-Ordered Police State: Social and Institutional Change through Law in the Germanies and Russia 1600–1800*. New Haven: Yale University Press, 1983.

——*Understanding Imperial Russia: State and Society in the Old Regime*. New York: Columbia University Press, 1984.

Rogger, Hans. *Russia in the Age of Modernization and Revolution 1881–1917*. London: Longman, 1983.

Russia. Chrezychainaia Sledstvennaia Komissiia. *Padenie Tsarskogo Rezhima: Stenograficheskie otchety doprosov i pokazanii dannykh v 1917g. v Chrezvychainoi Sledstvennoi Komissii Vremennogo Pravitel'stva*. Moscow-Leningrad: 1924–1927.

Russia. Gosudarstvennaia Duma 3d 1909. *Zapros ob Azefe v Gosudarstvennoi dume (zasedaniia 50 i 51 oe): Po stenograficheskomu otchetu*. St Petersburg: 1909.

Russia. Gosudarstvennyi Sovet. Pervyi departament. *Zhurnaly i departamenta Gosudarstvennago soveta*, no. 5 (20 March 1912); no. 13 (11 May 1912).

Savinkov, Boris. *Memoirs of a Terrorist*. Trans. Joseph Shaplen. New York: Albert and Charles Boni, 1931.

Schleifman, Nurit. *Undercover Agents in the Russian Revolutionary Movement: The SR Party 1902–1914*. Basingstoke: Macmillan – now Palgrave Macmillan, 1988.

Schneiderman, Jeremiah. *Sergei Zubatov and Revolutionary Marxism: The Struggle for the Working Class in Tsarist Russia*. Ithaca: Cornell University Press, 1976.

Senese, Donald. *S. M. Stepniak-Kravchinskii. The London Years*. Russian Biography Series 33. Newtonville Mass.: Oriental Research Partners, 1987.

Senn, Alfred Erich. *The Russian Revolution in Switzerland 1914–1917*. Madison: University of Wisconsin Press, 1971.

Serge, Victor. *Memoirs of a Revolutionary, 1901–1941*. Trans. Peter Sedgwick. New York: Oxford University Press, 1963.

Shchegolev, P. E., ed. *Provokator: Vospominaniia i dokumenty o razoblachenii Azefa*. Leningrad: 1929.

Shepelev, L. E. *Otmenennye istoriei chiny, zvaniia i tituly v rossiiskoi imperii*. Leningrad: 1977.

Simon, Herbert A. *Administrative Behaviour: A Study in Decision-Making Processes in Administrative Organizations*. 2nd. edn. New York: The Free Press, 1957.

——and James G. March. *Organizations*. New York: John Wiley & Sons, 1958.

Smith, Phillip Thurmond. *Policing Victorian London: Political Policing, Public Order and the London Metropolitan Police*. Contributions in Criminology and Penology Number 7. Westport Conn.: Greenwood Press, 1985.

Spence, Richard B. *Boris Savinkov: Renegade on the Left*. Boulder Colo.: East European Monographs, 1991.

Spencer, Elaine G. *Police and the Social Order in German Cities: The Düsseldorf District, 1848–1914*. DeKalb Ill.: Northern Illinois University Press, 1992.

Spiridovich, A. I. *Revoliutsionnoe dvizhenie v Rossii: Rossiiskaia Sotsial-Demokraticheskaia Rabochaia Partiia*. Pt. 1. St Petersburg: 1914.

——*Revoliutsionnoe dvizhenie v Rossii: Partiia Sotsialistov-Revoliutsionerov i eia predshestvenniki*. Pt. 2. Petrograd: 1916.

——*Istoriia bol'shevizma v Rossii: Ot vozniknoveniia do zakhvata vlasti 1883–1903–1917*. Paris: 1922.

——*Les derniéres années de la cour de Tsarskoe-Sélo*. Trans. M. Jeanson. 2 vols. Paris: 1928–1929.

Squire, P. S. *The Third Department: The Political Police in the Russia of Nicholas I*. Cambridge: Cambridge University Press, 1968.

Stepniak [Kravchinskii, Sergei M.]. *Underground Russia*. New York: n.d.

Stone, Norman. *Europe Transformed 1878–1919*. Cambridge Mass.: Harvard University Press, 1984.

Svod zakonov rossiiskoi imperii. 16 vols. St Petersburg: 1892.

Tamborra, Angelo. *Esuli Russi in Italia Dal 1905 al 1917*. Rome: 1977.

Taratuta, E. A. *Etel' Lilian Voinich: Sud'ba pisatelia i sud'ba knigi*. 2nd edn. Moscow: 1964.

——*S. M. Stepniak-Kravchinskii revoliutsioner i pisatel'*. Moscow: 1973.

Tekhnika bol'shevistskogo podpol'ia: Sbornik statei i vospominanii. 2nd edn. Moscow: 1925.

The Policing of Politics in the Twentieth Century: Historical Perspectives. Edited by Mark Mazower. Oxford: Berghahn Books, 1997.

Tikhomirov, Lev. *Vospominaniia L'va Tikhomirova*. Moscow: 1927.

Tilly Charles, Louise Tilly and Richard Tilly. *The Rebellious Century, 1830–1930*. London: Dent, 1975.

Troitskii, N. A. *Bezumstvo khrabrykh: Russkie revoliutsionery i karatel'naia politika tsarizma, 1866–1882 gg*. Moscow: 1978.

——*Tsarizm pod sudom progressivnoi obshchestvennosti, 1866–1895 gg*. Moscow: 1979.

Vasilyev, A. T. *The Ochrana: The Russian Secret Police*. Trans. René Fülop-Miller. Philadelphia: J. P. Lipincott, 1930.

——*The Okhrana: The Russian Secret Police*. Trans. René Fülop-Miller. London: George G. Harrap, 1930.

Volkov, A. *Petrogradskoe okhrannoe otdelenie*. Petrograd: 1917.

Westlake, John. *International Law, Part I: Peace*. Cambridge: Cambridge University Press, 1904.
White Jerry. *Rothschild Buildings: Life in an East End Tenement Block, 1887–1920*. London: Routledge & Kegan Paul, 1980.
Williams, Robert C. *Culture in Exile: Russian Émigrés in Germany 1881–1941*. Ithaca, NY: Cornell University Press, 1972.
Witte, Sergei IU. *Vospominaniia: Tsarstvovanie Nikolaia II*. 2 vols. Berlin: 1922.
Wolff, Larry. *Inventing Eastern Europe: The Map of Civilization on the Mind of the Enlightenment*. Stanford: Stanford University Press, 1994.
Woodhall, Edwin T. *Detective & Secret Service Days*. London: n.d.
Wortman, Richard S. *The Development of a Russian Legal Consciousness*. Chicago: University of Chicago Press, 1976.
Za kulisami okhrannago otdeleniia: S dnevnikom provokatora pis'mami okhrannikov, tainymi instruktsiiami. Berlin: 1910.
Zaionchkovskii, P. A. *Krizis samoderzhaviia na rubezhe 1870–1880 godov*. Moscow: 1964.
——*Rossiiskoe samoderzhavie v kontse XIX stoletiia, (politicheskaia reaktsiia 80-X-nachala 90-X godov)*. Moscow: 1970.
——*Pravitel'stvennyi apparat samoderzhavnoi Rossii v XIXv*. Moscow: 1978.
Zavarzin, P. P. *Rabota tainoi politsii*. Paris: 1924.
——*Zhandarmy i revoliutsionery: Vospominaniia*. Paris: 1930.

Articles

A. P. 'Departament politsii v 1892–1908 (Iz vospominanii chinovnika)'. *Byloe*, n.s. nos 5/6 [27/28] (November/December 1917): 17–24.
Bakai, M. E. 'Iz vospominanii M. E. Bakaia: O chernykh kabinetakh v Rossii'. *Byloe*, Paris, no. 7 (1908): 119–33.
——'Iz vospominanii M. E. Bakaia'. *Byloe*, Paris, nos. 11/12 (1909): 162–7.
——'Iz vospominanii M. E. Bakaia: Provokatory i provokatsiia'. *Byloe*, Paris, no. 8 (1909): 99–136.
——'Iz zapisok M. E. Bakaia'. *Byloe*, Paris, nos 9/10 (1909): 191–211.
Bennet, Helju A. 'Evolution of the Meanings of *Chin*: An Introduction to the Russian Institution of Rank Ordering and Niche Assignment from the Time of Peter the Great's Table of Ranks to the Bolshevik Revolution'. *California Slavic Studies* 10 (1977): 1–43.
Bobrovskaia, Tsetlina, and Osip Piatnitskii. 'Zagranichnyi sysk vokrug Lenina'. *Krasnaia Letopis'*, no. 13 (1925): 156–64.
Brovtsnova, E. P. 'Karatel'noe zakonodatel'stvo tsarizma v bor'ba s Revoliutsiei 1905–1907 godov'. *Istoriia SSSR*, 1975, no. 5: 110–17.
Burtsev, V. 'Lenine and Malinovsky'. *Struggling Russia* 1 (May 1919): 138–40.
——'Kak Departament Politsii otpustil Lenina zagranitsu dlia bolshevitskoi [*sic*!] propagandy.' *Byloe*, Paris, n.s. no. 2 (1933): 85–92.
Cherkunov, A. N. 'Provokator Vladislav Feliksovich Gabel': (Iz vospominanii smolenskogo katorzhanina)'. *Katorga i Ssylka*, no. 22 (1926): 195–206.
'D. F. Trepov v bor'be s obshchestvennost'iu'. *Russkoe Proshloe*, 1923, no. 4: 42–54.
Daly, Jonathan W. 'On the Significance of Emergency Legislation in Late Imperial Russia.' *Slavic Review*, 54 (Fall 1995): 602–29.
'Doklad P. Rachkovskago Zavedyiushchego zagranichnoi agentury'. *Istoriko-Revoliutsionnyi Sbornik* 2 (1924): 191, 247–53.

'Doneseniia Evno Azefa (Perepiska Azefa s Rataevym v 1903–1905 gg.)'. *Byloe*, n.s. no. 1 [23] (July 1917): 196–228.

'Doneseniia iz Berlina S. S. Tatishcheva V. K. Pleve v 1904: Soobshchil E. V. Tarle'. *Krasnyi Arkhiv* 17 (1926): 186–92.

'Donosy tsariu o russkoi emigratsii'. *Byloe*, Paris, nos 11/12 (July/August 1909): 138–61.

'Dva dokumenta iz istorii zubatovshchiny'. *Krasnyi Arkhiv* 19 (1926): 210–11.

Falaev, N. I. 'Rossiia pod okhranoi'. *Byloe*, St Petersburg, no. 10 [22] (October 1907): 1–43.

'G. V. Plekhanov i shpionskie zabavy: Soobshchil S. N. Valk'. *Krasnyi Arkhiv* 5 (1924): 263–6.

'G. V. Plekhanov: Materialy sobrannye departamentom politsii'. *Byloe*, n.s. 3 [31] (March 1918): 229–36.

Geertz, Clifford. 'Thick Description: Toward an Interpretive Theory of Culture'. In *The Interpretation of Cultures. Selected Essays by Clifford Geertz*, 1–30. New York: Basic Books, 1973.

'Iz pisem L. A. Rataeva: L. A. Rataev – N. P. Zuevu'. *Byloe*, n.s. no. 1 [23] (July 1917): 144–8.

'Iz proshlago russkoi politicheskoi politsii zagranitsei'. *Na Chuzhoi Storone* 10 (1925): 181–5.

Jensen, Richard Bach. 'The International Anti-anarchist Conference of 1898 and the Origins of Interpol'. *Journal of Contemprary History* 16 (April 1981): 323–47.

——'Internal Police Exile'. In *Essays in European History: Selected from the Annual Meeting of the Southern Historical Association, 1986–1987*. Lanham: University Press of America, 1988.

——'Police Reform and Social Reform: Italy from the Crisis of the 1890s to the Giolitti Era'. *Criminal Justice History* 10(1989): 179–200.

K. D. 'Russkie shpiony pered sudom germanskago parlamenta'. *Osvobozhdenie*, nos. 39/40 (January 1904): 274–75.

'K istorii zubatovshchiny v Moskve: (Po neizdannym protokolam zubatovskikh soveshchanii)'. *Istoriia Proletariata SSSR*, Collection 2 (1930): 169–232.

Kantor R. M. 'Frantsuzkaia okhranka o russkikh emigrantakh' *Katorga i Ssylka*, no. 31 (1927): 81–7.

'Kar'era P. I. Rachkovskago. Dokumenty'. *Byloe*, n.s. no. 2 [30] (February 1918): 78–87.

Kimbal, Alan. 'The Harassment of Russian Revolutionaries Abroad: The London Trial of Vladimir Burtsev in 1898'. *Oxford Slavonic Papers*, n.s.. Vol. 6. Edited by Robert Auty and J. L. I. Fennell (New York: Oxford University Press, 1973), 48–64.

Koliari, Edoardo. 'Russkaia tainaia politsiia v Italii'. *Byloe*, n.s. no. 25 (1924): 130–54.

Korelin, A. P. 'Russkii "politseiskii sotsializm": (Zubatovshchina)'. *Voprosy Istorii*, 1968, no. 10: 41–58.

——'Krakh Ideologii 'Politseiskogo sotsializma v Tsarskoi Rossii'. *Istoricheskie Zapiski* 92 (1973): 109–52.

Koznov, A. P. 'Bor'ba bol'shevikov s podryvnoi agenturoi tsarizma v period reaktsii (1907–1910 g.g.)'. *Voprosy Istorii KPSS*, 1986, no. 12: 59–74.

——'Zagranichnaia politicheskii sysk (1900-fevral' 1917 gg.'. *Kentavr*, 1992, nos. 1–2: 96–108.

L. B. 'Franko-russkoe shpionstvo i franko-russkii soiuz'. *Byloe*, Paris, no. 8 (1908): 58–64.

Lemke, Mikhail, 'Nash zagranichnyi sysk 1881–1883'. *Krasnaia Letopis'*, no. 5 (1922): 67–84.

'Les refugiés revolutionnaires russes à Paris'. Edited by Michel Lesure. *Cahiers du monde russe et sovietique* 6 (July–September 1965): 419–36.

Long, James William. 'Russian Manipulation of the French Press 1904–1906'. *Slavic Review* 31 (June 1972): 343–54.
Lougee, Robert W. 'The Anti-Revolution Bill of 1894 in Wilhemine Germany'. *Central European History* 15 (September 1982): 224–40.
Lukashevich A. 'The Holy Brotherhood: 1881–1883'. *Slavic Review* 18 (1959): 491–509.
Miroliubov, A. A. 'Dokumenty po istorii Departamenta politsii perioda pervoi mirovoi voiny'. *Sovetskie Arkhivy*, 1988, no. 3: 80–4.
'Nalet P. I. Rachkovskago na narodovol'cheskuiu tipografiiu'. *Byloe*, n.s. no. 1 [23] (July 1917): 277–83.
Novikov, V. I. 'Leninskaia 'Iskra' v bor'be s Zubatovshchinoi'. *Voprosy Istorii*, 1974, no. 8: 24–35.
'Novoe o zubatovshchine: Soobshchil S. Piontkovskii'. *Krasnyi Arkhiv* 1 (1922): 289–314.
'Obvinitel'nyi akt: Ob otstavnom deistvitel'nom statskom sovetnike Aleksee Aleksandroviche Lopukhine, obviniaemom v gosudarstvennom prestuplenii'. *Byloe*, Paris, nos 9/10 (1909): 218–36.
'Orlovsky, Daniel T. 'Political Clientelism in Russia: The Historical Perspective'. In *Leadership Selection and Patron–Client Relations in the USSR and Yugoslavia*. Edited by T. H. Rigby and Bohdan Harasymiri, 174–199. London: George Allen and Unwin, 1983.
Or-vskii, V. 'Iz zapisok politseiskago ofitsera'. *Na Chuzhoi Storone*, no. 14 (1925): 143–52.
Orzhekhovskii, I. V. 'Tret'e otdelenie'. *Voprosy Istorii* no. 2 (1972): 109–20.
Shch. 'K delu 1 marta 1881 goda : Neizdannye doklady grafa Loris-Melikova, V. K. Pleve, A. V. Komarova'. *Byloe*, n.s. nos 4/5 [32/33] (April/May 1918): 12–69.
Pavlov D. B. and S. A. Petrov. 'Polkovnik Akasi i osvoboditel'noe dvizhenie v Rossii (1904–1905 gg.)'. *Istoriia SSSR* 6 (November/December 1990): 50–71.
—— 'Rossiiskaia kontrrazvedka v gody Russko-Iaponskoi voiny'. *Otechestvennaia Istoriia*, 1996, no 1: 14–28.
Payne, Howard C. and Henry Grosshaus. 'The Exiled Revolutionaries and the French Police in the 1850s'. *American Historical Review* 68(1963): 954–73.
Peregudova, Z. I. 'Istochnik izucheniia sotsial-demokraticheskogo dvizheniia v Rossii (materialy fonda departamenta politsii)'. *Voprosy Istorii KPSS*, 1988, no. 9: 88–100.
'Pis'ma Mednikova Spiridovichy'. *Krasnyi Arkhiv* 17 (1926): 192–219.
'Pis'ma N. K. Krupskoi E. D. Stasovoi'. *Istoricheskii Arkhiv*, 1957, no. 1: 2–27.
'Pis'mo Gartinga k provokatoru'. *Byloe*, Paris, no. 8 (1908): 153–4.
'Pis'mo L. A. Rataeva–S. V. Zubatovu 1900–1903: Soobshchil S. P. Mel'gunov'. *Golos Minuvshago*, no. 1 (June 1922): 51–9.
'Pis'mo S. V. Zubatova [ot 7 avgusta 1916 g.]: A. I. Spiridovichu po povodu vykhoda v svet ego knigi "Partiia s.r. i ee predshestvenniki"'. *Krasnyi Arkhiv* 2 (1922): 280–3.
'Pis'mo V. K. Pleve k A. A. Kireevu: Soobshchil E. V. Tarle'. *Krasnyi Arkhiv* 18 (1926): 201–03.
Pogozhev, A. 'Iz vospominanii o V. K. von-Pleve'. *Vestnik Evropy* 7 (July 1911): 259–80.
'Posle pervogo marta 1881 g.: Soobshchil S. Valk'. *Krasnyi Arkhiv* 45 (1931): 147–64.
Polovtsov, A. A. 'Dnevnik A. A. Polovtsova'. Parts 1, 2. *Krasnyi Arkhiv* 3 (1923): 75–172; 4 (1923): 63–128.
—— 'Iz dnevnika A. A. Polovtsova (1895–1900 gg.)'. *Krasnyi Arkhiv* 46 (1931): 110–32.
'Prikliucheniia I. F. Manuilova: Po arkhivnym materialam'. *Byloe*, n.s. nos 5/6 [27/28] (December 1917): 236–88.
'Psikhologia predatel'stva: (Iz vospominani "sotrudnika")'. *Byloe*, n.s. nos 27/28 (December 1924): 225–37.

'Rataev, L. 'Evno Azef. Istoriia ego predatel'stva'. *Byloe*, n.s. no. 2 [24] (August 1917): 187–210.
'Razoblachennyi Azef'. *Byloe*, n.s. no. 2 [24] (August, 1917): 211–15.
'Rossiia pod nadzorom politsii'. *Osvobozhdenie*. Parts 1–5. nos. 20/21 (19 April 1903): 357–8; no. 29 (19 August 1903): 86–7; no. 30 (2 September 1903): 110–11; no. 33 (19 October 1903): 165; no. 35 (12 November 1903): 185–7.
'Russkii sysk v Shvetsii'. *Osvobozhdenie*, no. 57. (7 September 1904): 101–03.
Schleifmann, Nurit. 'The Internal Agency: Linchpin of the Political Police in Russia'. *Cahiers du monde Russe et Sovietique* 24 (1983): 151–77.
Schneiderman, Jeremiah, 'From the Files of the Moscow Gendarme Corps: A Lecture on Combatting Revolution'. *Canadian Slavic Studies* 2 (Spring 1968): 86–99.
'Sekretnye sotrudniki v avtobiografiiakh'. *Byloe*, n.s. no. 2 [24] (August 1917): 232–61.
Senn, Alfred E., 'The Bolshevik Conference in Berne'. *Slavic Review* 25 (December, 1966): 676–8.
—— ed. 'Russian Emigré Funds in Switzerland 1916; An Okhrana Report'. *International Review of Social History* 13, Pt. 1 (1968): 76–84.
'Shkola filerov'. *Byloe*, n.s. no. 3 [25] (September, 1917): 40–67.
Slukhotskii, L. 'Ocherk deiatel'nosti ministerstva iustitsii po bor'be s politicheskimi prestupleniiami'. *Istoriko-Revoliutsionnyi Sbornik* 3 (1926): 247–86.
Snyder, David and William Kelly. 'Industrial Violence in Italy, 1878–1903'. *American Journal of Sociology* 82 (July 1976): 131–62.
Speier, Hans. 'The Social Conditions of the Intellectual Exilte'. In *Social Order and the Rise of War: Papers in Political Sociology*. Edited by Hans Speier. Cambridge Mass.: MIT Press, 1952.
Spiridovich, A. I. 'Pri tsarskom rezhime'. *Arkhiv Russkoi Revoliutsii* 15 (1924): 85–209.
Stefanovich, IA. V. 'Russkaia revoliutsionnaia emigratsiia: Zapiska IA. V. Stefanovicha'. *Byloe*, n.s. no. 16 (1921): 75–85.
'Svod pravil vyrabotannykh v razvitie utverzhdennago Gospodinom Ministrom Vnutrennikh Del 12 avgusta tekushchago goda [1902]: Polozheniia o Nachal'nikakh Rozysknykh Otdelenii'. *Byloe*, Paris, no. 8 (1908): 54–67.
Szeftel, Marc. 'Personal Inviolability in the Legislation of the Russian Absolute Monarchy'. *The American Slavic and East European Review* 17 (February 1958): 1–24.
'Tainyi doklad: I.d. Moskovskogo Ober-Politsmeistera (po okhrannomy otdeleniiu) 8 Aprelia 1898 g.'. *Rabochee Delo*, 1899, no. 1: 24–34.
Tikhomirov, Lev. '25 let nazad: Iz dnevnika L. Tikhomirova'. Parts 1, 2. *Krasnyi Arkhiv* 38 (1930): 20–69; 61 (1933): 82–128.
Tiutiunik, L. I. 'Istochniki po istorii Departamenta politsii (1880–1904 gg.)'. *Sovetskie Arkhivy*, 1984, no. 3: 50–4.
'Tsarizm v bor'be s revoliutsionnoi pechat'iu 1905 g.: Vvodnaia stat'ia I. Kovaleva'. *Krasnyi Arkhiv* 105 (1941): 140–55.
Weissman, Neil. 'Regular Police in Tsarist Russia, 1900–1914'. *The Russian Review* 44 (January 1985): 45–68.
Yaney, George. 'Law, Society, and the Domestic Regime in Russia in Historical Perspective'. *American Political Science Review* 59 (1965): 379–90.
'Zapiska A. A. Lopukhina: O razvitii revoliutsionnago dvizheniia v Rossii (1904g.)'. *Byloe*, Paris, nos 9/10 (1909): 74–8.
'Zapiska direktora depart. pol. Lopukhina o stachkakh v iiule 1903 g. v Odesse, Kieve, Nikolaeve'. *Krasnaia Letopis'*, no. 4 (1922): 382–95.
Zhilinskii, V. 'Organizatsiia i zhizn' okhrannago otdeleniia vo vremena tsarskoi vlasti'. *Golos Minuvshago*, nos 9/10 (September/October 1917): 246–306.

Zubatov, S. V. 'Iz nedavniago proshlago: g. Zubatov o Zubatovshchine'. *Vestnik Evropy* 3 (March, 1906): 432–6.
——'Zubatovshchina '. *Byloe*, n.s. no. 4 [26] (October, 1917): 157–78.
Zuckerman, Fredric S. 'Vladimir Burtsev and the Tsarist Political Police in Conflict, 1907–14'. *Journal of Contemporary History* 12 (1977): 193–219.
—— 'Self-Imagery and the Art of Propaganda: V. K. von Plehve as Propagandist'. *The Australian Journal of Politics and History* 28 (1982): 68–82.
—— 'Political Police and Revolution: The Impact of the 1905 Revolution on the Tsarist Secret Police'. *Journal of Contemporary History* 27 (1992): 279–300.

Other newspapers and journals consulted

Budushchee
Il'Lavoro
L'Eclair
Le Matin
Le Temps
Obshchee Delo
The Times (London)
Vechernee Vremia

Index

Entries in this index in bold type indicate the location of a table.